En marge du classicisme

En marge du classicisme

ESSAYS ON THE FRENCH THEATRE
FROM THE RENAISSANCE
TO THE ENLIGHTENMENT

edited by
ALAN HOWE & RICHARD WALLER

LIVERPOOL UNIVERSITY PRESS

First published in 1987 by
Liverpool University Press
PO Box 147
Liverpool
L69 3BX

Distributed in the United States of America by
Humanities Press International Inc
Atlantic Highlands
New Jersey 07716

British Library Cataloguing in Publication Data
En marge du classicisme : essays on the French
 theatre from the Renaissance to the
 Enlightenment.
 1. French drama—History and criticism
 I. Howe, Alan II. Waller, Richard
 842'.009 PQ521

 ISBN 0-85323-105-2

Printed and bound by
The Alden Press in the City of Oxford

CONTENTS

Acknowledgements

The Editors wish to thank the Advisory Committee of the Liverpool University Press for encouraging and supporting the publication of this volume, and the staff of the Press, particularly Rosalind Campbell and Robin Bloxsidge, for their expert and cheerful assistance in guiding the work through to completion. Our thanks go also to Jeanette Christian, Alice Kershaw, and especially Pat Brooksbank and Sandra Burns, for their sterling efforts in word-processing the typescript and in helping the Editors with their daunting task of producing camera-ready copy. Finally, we are grateful to Editions A.-G. Nizet for permission to reproduce the illustration which appears as Figure 1 in Chapter Three.

Introduction

In a recent comment on the Royal Shakespeare Company's new theatre in Stratford-upon-Avon, Trevor Nunn remarked that: 'What we should aim to be presenting in the Swan Theatre at the widest range is plays from 1570 to 1750 because we think that it is a mightily neglected area. There is a terrific published outlet that most theatre audiences have never come across'.[1] His comment on the neglect of a huge corpus of texts is equally valid for a similar (and even longer) period in the French theatre - though in France, alas, there does not as yet appear to be any concerted policy of introducing the theatre public to a wide range of plays composed between the Renaissance and the Revolution.

Like that of Shakespeare, the enduring reputation of Corneille, Molière and Racine has caused most of their predecessors and successors as well as their contemporaries to be overshadowed and, in many cases, undervalued. And this has occurred not only in the professional theatre but also, until relatively recently, in scholarship and criticism. Although the work of retrieving and illuminating some of these talents had been gathering pace since the end of the nineteenth century, Daniel Mornet still felt the need in 1940 to protest at the deleterious effect of too exclusive a concentration on the masterpieces of the Trois Grands, warning that 'en s'enfermant en eux, ou en ne faisant en dehors d'eux que de trop rapides et de trop courtes excursions, il est impossible de savoir exactement ce qu'a été, au XVIIe siècle, la vie générale du théâtre'.[2] The difficulty of making less rapid excursions into the margins of Classicism was highlighted two decades later by F.C. Green, when he wrote: 'It is no longer possible, owing to the lack of texts, to offer a course on the evolution of eighteenth-century comedy except with a very small discussion group using library copies'.[3] His complaint would have applied equally to most dramatic genres in the sixteenth to eighteenth centuries, as also did his next statement: 'This is a great pity for there is much to be learned [...] from some of the lesser playwrights'.

Happily, this situation has improved in the last two or three decades. Critical editions of many previously inaccessible texts have appeared in such valuable series as Textes Littéraires Français (Geneva, Droz) and Textes Littéraires (University of

Exeter). The Bibliothèque de la Pléiade, too, has issued extensive anthologies of lesser-known dramatic works from the seventeenth and eighteenth centuries and, perhaps more importantly from the point of view of students' purses, the 10/18 series has produced an excellent selection of plays from the **théâtre de la foire**. Meanwhile, as a perusal of **The Year's Work in Modern Language Studies** or other annual bibliographies of French literature will show, the volume of critical studies has steadily increased. Of course, Corneille, Molière and Racine still hold the centre of the stage, but it is often to the less well-explored areas of their œuvre - for example, to the early comedies of Corneille - that attention is increasingly directed. Major studies have also recently appeared on secondary authors from the seventeenth century (e.g. Rotrou, Mairet) as well as on Mornet's 'vie générale du théâtre', the actors and questions of staging. The sixteenth and eighteenth centuries have shared in this upsurge of interest and activity, with the initiative coming often from outside France: from the English-speaking world have come several major reassessments of humanist drama, from Italy archival research into the Italian troupes in France, and from the United States the first detailed studies of the theatre of the Boulevards and the Revolution. It is also significant that the Que sais-je? series has recently included a title devoted to eighteenth-century theatre (by P. Larthomas) and that J. Truchet's 1976 study, **La Tragédie classique en France,** pays an unwonted amount of attention to the sixteenth and eighteenth centuries.

The present volume both reflects and seeks to contribute to this increasing interest in the pre-Revolutionary theatre in its multifarious aspects. The century of the Renaissance is represented by two essays. While recent drama criticism has concentrated on mainstream works from the second half of that century, it is in the college theatre of the 1540s that Carol Chapman finds an interesting example of dramatic experimentation involving a mixture of medieval and Renaissance ideas and techniques. The years between 1550 and 1610 are covered by Alan Howe, who studies the evolution, at the hands of numerous writers of tragedy (several of whom are little known), of a type of speech which would have important dramatic and psychological functions in major works of the seventeenth century. The latter period is represented by four essays, three of which focus on 'secondary' dramatists. The modern interest in seventeenth-century stagecraft is reflected by Philip Tomlinson, whose detailed analysis of a comedy by Mairet uses the play as a key to an understanding of contemporary theatre practice. It is dramatic structure that concerns Guy Snaith, whose study of four tragedies by La Calprenède highlights the importance for this neglected dramatist of another major ingredient of Cornelian drama, the arousal of suspense. And a theme recurrent in many French and Spanish seventeeth-century plays, that of honour, is discussed by John Trethewey in his study of its **romanesque** and burlesque treatment in the nine comedies and tragicomedies of Paul Scarron. Corneille and Racine are also given a place. But the Corneille considered by Stephen Scott is the author of one of the least discussed of his relatively neglected (hence 'marginalized') later plays which reveals the sad destiny of the heroic ethos celebrated in his more renowned masterpieces; while Racine appears here in only a supporting role, to Diderot. The five essays on the eighteenth century similarly reflect major aspects of the theatrical experience. Richard Waller and L.A. Zaina use varied approaches to demonstrate the problem of making bedfellows of Italian and French theatrical worlds at both the beginning and end of the century. Derek Connon and Ahmad Gunny illustrate the techniques used by Diderot and Voltaire to introduce fresh emphases in the spheres of morality and the emotions in their attempts to renew serious drama. Richard Parish questions a **locus classicus** of flawed dramatic structure, arguing for a reappraisal of the comic vision of Lesage in **Turcaret.**

The volume treats a variety of genres, from nativity plays and satyr-plays to improvised drama and **drame bourgeois,** including of course tragedy, tragicomedy and comedy. The playwrights considered range from the familiar (e.g. Lesage, Voltaire) to the more obscure (e.g. Barthélemy Aneau, Charles Bauter, Jacques Autreau). Underlying this richness and diversity, however, are certain unifying strands. Several of the essays treat, for example, aspects of dramatic structure or recurrent themes. In particular, many of the plays studied are related by their authors to a wider background of literary, theatrical, social and cultural issues; and the **interférences** explored include not only those of the French theatre with the literature of Antiquity, but also with phenomena as diverse as the Spanish **pundonor,** Italian comedy, and Moslem fanaticism. Moreover, French dramatists from the Renaissance to the Enlightenment are shown in these essays to be engaged in the pursuit of experimentation and novelty. Such a process, of course, was common to the creative genius of Corneille, Molière, Racine, Marivaux and Beaumarchais. What we hope this volume demonstrates is that many other writers grappled with the same problems, adopting similar strategies in the quest for dramatic excellence, and that their endeavour and accomplishment deserve not to be ignored.

Finally, this book derives from a realization that a considerable amount of research in the 'margins' of the French classical theatre has been conducted by scholars currently or formerly based in the Department of French at the University of Liverpool. Of the eleven authors whose work is represented here, six are members of staff of that University - five (Carol Chapman, Ahmad Gunny, Guy Snaith, and the Editors) in the Department of French, while L.A. Zaina, a former member of that department, is Senior Lecturer in Italian within the School of Modern Languages. John Trethewey and Richard Parish were also Lecturers in the Department of French before moving to their present posts at the University College of Wales, Aberystwyth, and St Catherine's College, Oxford.   Philip Tomlinson, now Senior Lecturer at the University of Salford, and Derek Connon, formerly Lecturer in French at the Queen's University, Belfast, both prepared their doctoral theses within the Liverpool French Department, as too currently does Stephen Scott.   This is not to lay claim to a 'Liverpool school' or even a 'Liverpool approach'.   The volume is characterized by a diversity of approaches which reflects the variety of the material under consideration. What the 'Liverpool connection' does underline, however, is the extraordinary vitality of the subject, the wide fascination exercised by the practice and practitioners of a theatre which refuses to be eclipsed by the towering reputations of Corneille, Molière and Racine.

NOTES

1.   Judith Cook, **At the Sign of the Swan: An Introduction to Shakespeare's Contemporaries,** with a Foreword by Trevor Nunn (London, 1986), p.9.

2.   **Histoire de la littérature française classique, 1660-1700: ses caractères véritables, ses aspects inconnus,** third edition (Paris, 1947), p.208.

3.   'Some Marginal Notes on Eighteenth-Century French Comedy', in **Studies in Modern French Literature Presented to P. Mansell Jones,** edited by L.J. Austin, Garnet Rees and Eugène Vinaver (Manchester, 1961), pp.133-43 (p.133).

ONE

French Renaissance Dram. Soc.:
The Plays of Barthélemy Aneau
Carol Chapman

The humanist Barthélemy Aneau[1] may well have been exposed to the delights of the theatre from an early age for he was born and educated in Bourges,[2] a town with a thriving theatrical tradition, where it would have been possible for him to witness annually in the Cathedral the dramatic accompaniment to the feasts of the Holy Innocents and the Epiphany, and occasionally larger-scale productions of a mystery play including perhaps the lavish **Mystère des Actes des Apôtres** in 1536.[3] On arriving in Lyons sometime towards the end of the 1530s[4] to take up a post at the recently established Collège de la Trinité,[5] he would have found that theatrical productions in the town, which earlier in the century had been infrequent and beset with problems,[6] were, for a brief period, being held regularly, and that, moreover, in one of France's first permanent theatres.[7] In 1538, the merchant Jean Neyron had had constructed in the rue des Bouchers a theatre where, according to the historian Claude de Rubys, writing at the beginning of the following century, 'par l'espace de trois ou quatre ans, les jours de Dimanches et les festes apres disner, furent representées la plus part des histoires du viel et nouveau Testament, avec la farce au bout, pour recreer les assistants'.[8] Regrettably, the repertory of the Jean Neyron theatre was either never published or is lost, but in any case it was probably not original.[9] Petit de Julleville suggests that the mystery plays would have been selected from the fifteenth-century cycles,[10] and that some of the farces might well have been those which the Lyons printing house of **feu** Barnabé Chaussard edited and printed between 1542 and 1548, and which later found their way into the famous British Library collection known as **Le Recueil de Londres**.[11]

An enlightened teacher, whose innovatory educational ideas rapidly led to his promotion in 1540 from **premier régent** to Principal of the Collège de la Trinité,[12] Aneau was no doubt aware that in colleges throughout France the pedagogical value of acting was being recognized.[13] A clause in the terms of employment which were drawn up for all twenty-one teachers appointed at the foundation of the Collège de Guyenne in 1533 states that each of them is required to 'composer et prononcer oraisons, arangues, dialogues, comedies et lire publiquement'.[14] A document dated ten years later indicates that the composition of **comédies** formed part of the regular duties of the **premier grammairien** of the Collège de la Marche in Paris.[15] The **régent** Jean Calmus, who taught in various Paris colleges from the 1530s to the 1550s and who wrote French and Latin comedies for his pupils,[16] considers school plays to be useful training in the following respects:

> Juvenilem vocem formant, memoriam
> Exercent, gestum componunt.[17]

The first and last of these beneficial effects seem to be in Montaigne's mind when, recalling almost forty years later his experiences as a schoolboy actor in the early 1540s, he writes:

> Mettray-je en compte cette faculté de mon enfance: une asseurance de visage, et soupplesse de voix et de geste, à m'appliquer aux rolles que j'entreprenois? Car, avant l'aage,
>
> > Alter ab undecimo tum me vix ceperat annus,
>
> j'ai soustenu les premiers personnages és tragedies latines de Bucanan, de Guerente et de Muret, qui se representerent en nostre college de Guienne avec dignité.[18]

Motivated perhaps by one or by all of these influences - early experience of liturgical drama in Bourges, the current popularity of abridged mystery plays and of farces in Lyons, the approval accorded to drama by many humanist teachers - Aneau lost no time after his arrival at the Collège de la Trinité before composing plays for his own pupils to perform. In 1539 Sebastien Gryphe published the **Chant Natal, Contenant Sept Noelz, ung chant Pastoural, et ung chant Royal, avec ung Mystere de la Nativité, par personnages. Composez en imitation verbale et musicale de diverses chansons. Recueilliz sur l'escripture saincte, et d'icelle illustrez.**[19] A dedicatory **dizain** gives the name of the author and indicates that the work was indeed performed.[20] Two years later Aneau's pupils trod the boards again, this time in the **Lyon marchant, Satyre Francoise. Sur la comparaison de Paris, Rohan, Lyon, Orleans, et sur les choses memorables depuys Lan mil cinq cens vingtquatre. Soubz Allegories, et Enigmes.   Par personnages mysticques iouée au College de la Trinité à Lyon, 1541.**[21] It is possible that around this time Aneau's translation of one of Erasmus's **Colloquia,** the **Uxor Mempsigamos,**[22] was also performed, either publicly or as a class exercise. In many establishments the college play was an annual event,[23] and one might have expected to find Aneau writing more such plays, but if there were any further efforts in this direction they have not survived. That Aneau composed other plays is, moreover, doubtful, since his duties during his first period as principal of the Collège de la Trinité[24] would seem to have left him little time for writing; after the publication of the **Lyon marchant** his literary output declines noticeably and does not revive until towards the end of the decade.[25]   Notices on the **Chant Natal** and the **Lyon marchant** are to be found in several histories of the French theatre, and at the beginning of this century J.L. Gerig briefly paraphrased the two plays, but the only detailed analyses are those of C.A. Mayer and V.-L. Saulnier.[26]

The purpose of this essay is to define the position occupied by Aneau's plays, and in particular by the **Lyon marchant**, the more interesting of the two, in the spectrum of the college theatre of the period.   In the 1530s and 1540s this spectrum was extremely wide.   At one end, the national tradition was well represented by schoolchildren in, for example, Béthune and Abbeville, who regularly performed farces, and biblical and historical morality plays.[27]   Such plays were not, as one might have expected, borrowed from the national repertory, but were usually the work of a teacher;   thus we find, in 1544, Eloi du Mont, **régent** of the Collège du Mont in Caen, admitting to the authorship of a farce which his pupils had acted in the streets.[28]   At the other end of the spectrum, there was experimentation as humanist **régents** imitated the dramatic genres of Antiquity.   The Latin comedies which Calmus wrote in Paris for his pupils at the Collège de Sainte-Barbe, and subsequently for those at the Collège de Lisieux, were in imitation of Terence.[29]   At the Collège de Guyenne in Bordeaux a deliberate attempt was made by a group of teachers to encourage their pupils, among whom was the young Montaigne, to abandon the national passion for allegorical moralities in favour of Latin tragedies, which the **régents** had either composed or translated from the Greek.[30]   Hence the performances, in the early 1540s, of George Buchanan's Latin translation of the **Medea** and the **Alcestis** of Euripides, and of his two biblical tragedies, **Baptistes** and **Jephthes**.[31]   The tragedy, or tragedies of Buchanan's colleague, Guillaume Guérente, which, according to Montaigne, were also performed by himself and his schoolmates, have unfortunately not survived.   A similar experiment was made elsewhere in Guyenne, at the Collège d'Auch, where, in 1544, the **régent** Marc-Antoine Muret wrote a Latin tragedy with a classical subject, **Julius Caesar**, for his pupils;[32]   this tragedy, again if one is to believe Montaigne, was given a further performance at the Collège de Guyenne after Muret had arrived to teach there in 1547.[33]   Between these two extremes of tradition and experimentation were various intermediate stages.   Some of the Latin comedies written at this time managed to combine the two extremes, one example being the comedy performed in 1532 at the Collège du Mans in Paris, **Advocatus**, which is in fact a mixture of farce and the Roman comedy of Terence and Plautus.[34]   In other cases, traditional French genres acquired a new look by being written in Latin and given a Latin name;   the **régent** Ravisius Textor wrote and had performed at the Collège de Navarre in Paris **dialogi** which are in essence moralities.[35]

That Aneau should choose to write in French for the college theatre is entirely in keeping with his pedagogical thinking. In the **Formulaire** which he presented to the **Consulat** on his appointment as principal of the Collège de la Trinité in 1540, he declares that he would prefer his young pupils to speak good Lyonnais rather than corrupt Latin, until such time as they should be fluent in the classical languages:

> Item, tant en jeu que hors jeu, sera commis, non pas du chef mais de la diverse, parler autre langue que grecque ou latine, sinon es bien petitz enfantz, lesquelz vault mieulx qu'ilz parlent bon lionnois que de s'accoustumer à mauvays et barbare latin, qui jamais ne se amenderoit et est une tres mauvaise chose en toutes escolles, jusques à ce qu'ilz ayent aprins en escoutant les bien parlans, et mieulx vauldroit que par aucun temps ilz fissent la silence pitagoric que s'acoustumer à parler latin corrompu.[36]

The first of the plays, the **Chant Natal**,[37] clearly belongs to the traditional end of the spectrum, containing, as it does, all the elements of a nativity mystery: we find the dramas of the Nativity and of the Kings (the **Chant Royal**), the pastoral scenes,[38] the holy songs which formed musical interludes in the mysteries,[39] and the epilogue-cum-sermon which often terminated them.[40]   The anachronisms and local allusions,which constituted such a striking feature of the mysteries,[41] are also much in evidence here: Aneau's shepherds use French coins, such as the **patard**, dance French dances, the **tirelire** and the **branle**, and the third Shepherd of the **Mystere** bought his set of pipes at the All Saints' Fair on the Pont de Saône in Lyons (**Chant Pastoural**, ll.8 and 46; **Mystere**, ll.187-89). At times these shepherds indulge in the crudity commonly found in the mysteries:[42] when the shepherdess of the **Chant Pastoural**, Rachel, slips on the ice and, being without knickers, reveals all, she invites one of the two shepherds, Raguel, to come and cover her, since if she has tipped up, she says, it is for want of a good horse between the shafts (**Chant Pastoural**, ll.47-54).

In all likelihood the entire **Chant Natal** was performed,[43] and not just the **Mystere** as the majority of critics claim or at least imply.[44] There is no reason to assume that Aneau did not intend his exhortation in the dedicatory **dizain** to apply to the whole work.[45] It is true that it is only the **Mystere** which contains any stage directions, but both the **Chant Pastoural** and the **Chant Royal** are in dialogue form, and there is ample evidence in the text of these episodes to suggest that actions are taking place. The **Chant Pastoural** is crammed with first- and second-person imperatives as the shepherds set off for Bethlehem, run to keep warm, play their pipes and dance, slip on the ice, arrive at the stable, and present their gifts (ll.8-80). In the **Chant Royal**, we witness Herod ordering the departure of the Magi; Baltasar comments on their journey as they follow the star; and each in turn describes his actions on arriving at the stable (ll.15-40). It would seem therefore that the **Chant Pastoural**, the **Mystere** and the

Chant Royal were acted out, interspersed with the **Sept Noelz** sung by a choir.[46] This would have led to some incoherence since all the elements of the **Chant Pastoural** - the angel's message to the shepherds, their journey to the stable, and the presentation of their gifts - are duplicated in the **Mystere.** Such a repetition, however, would not necessarily have constituted a defect in the eyes of a sixteenth-century audience, for so well loved were pastoral episodes in the fifteenth and sixteenth centuries that authors inserted them at inappropriate points in the nativity mysteries, and even included them in mysteries which do not belong to the nativity cycle.[47]

Only 618 lines long, the **Chant Natal** is, of course, an abridged mystery of the kind that was being performed regularly in Lyons when Aneau arrived there. These short mysteries seem to have been popular throughout France in the first half of the sixteenth century, but very few found their way into print, and if we know of their existence it is principally due to the journals and records left by local dignitaries.[48] They would have made ideal school productions, and probably did, although, not surprisingly, we have little evidence that this was the case, a notable exception being the four mysteries which the schoolmaster François Briand composed for his pupils at the Ecole St. Benoît in Le Mans, to be acted on each of the four Sundays of Advent in 1512. **Noëls** were sung at the beginning and end of each of these mysteries, and the third mystery contains a farce. The entire work was printed,[49] but the volume had become extremely rare by the time Henri Chardon, towards the end of the last century, discovered and subsequently edited it.[50] It is probably those features which are common to Briand's and Aneau's plays which justified their being printed and ensured their survival. Both teachers peppered the margins of their works with biblical references, so that it would have been possible to use them for didactic purposes; and more importantly, both works contain **noëls,** for which there was a great vogue in France throughout the sixteenth century.[51] It is worth noting in this context that the **noël** element features first in both titles.

It was, in fact, Aneau's enthusiasm for the **noël** which led to the one innovation in the otherwise totally traditional **Chant Natal,** for not only the **noëls** but the entire spectacle was sung, and, like the majority of sixteenth-century **noëls,** was set to the popular tunes of the day.[52] Aneau indicates the relevant tune before each **noël** or episode, and the majority of them are to be found in the songbooks of Pierre Attaingnant and Jacques Moderne.[53] This innovation caused critics to hail the **Chant Natal** as 'la première idée de nos opéras',[54] or as 'l'origine de nos opéras-comiques',[55] but such comments exaggerate the originality of Aneau's experiment. Aneau has merely carried Briand's mixture of mysteries and **noëls** one stage further, and achieved a total fusion of these two genres which already shared several features.

Not only do they have the same subject, but the mysteries, as we have seen, frequently contained musical interludes and the **noëls** were often in dialogue form.[56]

That Aneau liked mixtures is even more evident from his next play, the **Lyon marchant,** which is an amalgam of much more disparate elements. It will be necessary to give some description of this little-known play, but I shall endeavour not merely to reproduce the analyses of Saulnier and Mayer. The cast, in order of appearance as each character presents himself or herself in the opening **Cry,** is as follows: Lyon, Arion, Vulcan, Paris 'monté sur un cheval roan', Aurelian, Androdus, Europe, Ganymedes, Verité. The majority of these characters are allegorical and many of them have more than one allegorical identity, personification being combined, in an often confusing way, with animal, mythological or analogical allegory. Thus Lyon is frequently at one and the same time the king of the beasts and the personification of the town which owes its prosperity to the silk trade (sig. A2r). Arion, who as the play opens is sitting astride a dolphin playing his lyre, tells his story straight from the pages of Herodotus,[57] and then it is revealed by Verité that he is a somewhat clumsy allegory for Francis I, betrayed by his 'shipmates' and thrown into the sea of captivity at Pavia; during the difficult period which followed his release from captivity his musical talents somehow passed to his mother and sister, Louise de Savoie and Marguerite de Navarre, who sang to obtain the Peace of Cambrai. If Arion/Francis I has found his voice once more, it is, sadly, in order to lament the recent death of the Dolphin hostage who had rescued him after Pavia (sigs Blr-Blv). Vulcan is quite simply the mythological fire god, but Paris combines his mythological identity with the personification of the capital, and in the same speech identifies himself as Priam's son and then boasts of his University (sig. B8r). The roan horse he rides in the **Cry** is intended to be a personification of the town of Rouen, although this only becomes clear in a marginal note. Aurelian goes one better than Paris, possessing no less than three identities: in the **Cry** he is both the Roman Emperor, Aurelian, and the personification of Aurelianum, the Latin name for the town of Orleans (sigs A2r-A2v), but elsewhere (sigs Blv-B2r) he is Charles, duc d'Orléans, complaining about an attempt on his life. We are indebted to Gerig for spotting in the character of Androdus, an accepted spelling in the sixteenth century of the classical name, Androcles, an analogical allegory for the then Sénéchal of Lyons, Jean d'Albon, seigneur de St André, who was, in fact, shortly to become Governor of the city.[58] Androdus-St André is an evident pun, and Aneau will exploit it again in the 'ystoires et dictons' which he provided on the occasion of the solemn entry into the city of Jacques d'Albon, maréchal de St André, who succeeded his father to the governorship on the death of the latter in 1550.[59] Europe is both the mythological Europa, who tells the story of her rape (sigs B4r-B4v), and the personification of the continent, a personification which is highlighted in this case when the map of Europe is described as having the human form of a queen, with Spain as her head, Italy and Sicily her right arm, Germany her left, and her heart being, inevitably, France (sig. B6v). Saulnier is tempted to see in Ganymedes, who represents, Aneau tells us, 'Joye en conseil divin' (sigs A2v and B5v), an allegory for the dedicatee of the work Guillaume du Bellay, Seigneur de Langey.[60] He bases his argument on the fact that the Seigneur de Langey is twice alluded to in the play by means of the obvious pun, 'l'ange' (sigs B2r and B5r). The link is at best a tenuous one, and, moreover, a close reading of the text reveals that 'l'ange' and Ganymedes cannot possibly be one and the same person. Shortly after Europe has regaled the audience with an account of the noble deeds of this angel, who is clearly well known to her,[61] she is approached by Ganymedes, of whom she asks: 'Mais qui es tu?' (sig. B5v). If Ganymedes does have a second identity, therefore, it has yet to be discovered. The final character, Verité, is quite simply a personification of that abstract quality.

The action is extremely slight. After the **Cry,** the opening monologue is given to Arion/Francis I. Vulcan then appears from underground and fires a couple of shots, the second of which causes all the other characters, with the exception of Ganymedes and Verité, to come onto the stage 'esbahiz et espoventez'. Thereafter, when not telling their personal stories, the characters discuss the 'choses memorables' from 1524 (and even slightly earlier) to 1541 as announced in the title, not, unfortunately, in any chronological or even logical order. The memorable events range from local to international affairs. Writing his play at a time when a precarious **entente** between Francis I and Charles V had just broken down, and when yet another war seemed inevitable,[62] Aneau proceeds to review the past conduct of the potential enemies and allies of France. Accounts of previous struggles against the Emperor, usually referred to as 'l'Aigle', figure prominently: the never-ending quarrel over the possession of the Duchy of Milan (sigs A6r and B5r); the defection of the Duc de Bourbon to the Emperor in 1523 (sig. B4v); the disaster of Pavia and subsequent departure of the Dauphin as a hostage to Spain, later released as a result of the Peace of Cambrai in 1529 (sig. B1r); the French triumphs of 1536, when simultaneous attacks by the Emperor in Provence and by Henry of Nassau in northern France were repelled (sigs A6r and B3r); the Ghent revolt of 1538, and the Emperor's journey through France during the period of **entente** on his way to the Netherlands (sig. A6r). Aneau's tone is almost always one of attack; only once does he grudgingly praise the Emperor, called on this occasion 'l'Austriche', for his victories against the Turks in 1532 and against Barbarossa in the re-capture of Tunis in 1535 (sig. B6v). The English, identifiable in 'les trois leopards', an allusion to their coat-of-arms, seem, if anything, to be given even harsher treatment, Aneau's criticisms being concentrated in one long diatribe (sigs B2r-B2v). After an initial derisory comment on the panic-stricken measures the English had taken in 1539 to defend their realm in the face of rumours of an imminent Franco-imperial offensive against them, Aneau lists the major misdemeanours of Henry VIII since the early 1530s: his divorce from Catherine of Aragon and marriage to Anne Boleyn; the abolition of the monasteries and execution of Sir Thomas More; the burning of the Pope's effigy and death of Cardinal Wolsey; the executions of Anne Boleyn and her brother, Lord Rochford; and, finally, the desecration of St Thomas Becket's shrine in 1538.[63] The Turks, with whom Francis I was on good terms in 1541, are nevertheless criticized by Aneau, who deplores the actions of the 'grand Saigneur' [sic] in the early 1520s; he is said to have bled Europe by the capture of Belgrade and of Rhodes (sigs B3v and B5r). Two Popes are given contrasting treatment: Clement VII, whose death in 1534 destroyed the recently established Franco-papal **entente**, is lamented (sig. A7r), whereas his successor, Paul III, is ridiculed for his struggle against the Colonna family (sig. B3r). There are scornful comments too on Charles III, Duke of Savoy, who lost his duchy to his nephew, Francis I, in 1536 (sigs B4v-B5r). The discussion of home affairs is dominated by the death of the Dauphin in the same year (sigs A3r-A3v, B1v, B4v). Clearly, Aneau subscribed to the widespread contemporary opinion which held that Antonio de Leyva, Charles V's principal Lieutenant, was implicated in this death, and Lyon boasts proudly that he housed the cruel execution of Sebastiano de Montecuculli, one of the Dauphin's squires, who was accused of his murder (sig. A6v). There are brief allusions to two very recent events, namely the disgrace and subsequent reinstatement of Admiral Chabot and the fall of the Constable Anne de Montmorency (sig. B1v); and two items of local interest are included for the Lyons audience: the passage through the city in 1524 of Swiss troops on their way from Francis I's camp in Avignon to northern Italy (sig. B8v), and the establishment of the **Aumône générale** in Lyons in 1531 (sig. B7v).[64] Ganymedes terminates this discussion by declaring that France need not fear any new threat of war since she has strong cities to defend her. There then follows a debate between Lyon, Paris and Aurelian as to which of the three is the most capable of defending France, and Verité has the final word judging Lyon to be the winner of this competition: 'Mais devant tous est le Lyon marchant' (sig. C2v).

On three occasions Aneau makes a particular political point by means of pictorial riddles which are glossed by one of the characters. Thus, when the attack on the English is over, the move to the next topic is indicated by the following stage direction: 'Icy soit mise une Tente, ou Pavillon en un coing du chauffault qui sera de

Taffetas pers, vert, et changeant, ou n'y aura point de couleurs blanches, et dessus le pommel y aura un Aigle noir, et dedans sera un homme sans teste habillé à la mode d'un Allemant' (sig. B2v). This stage effect, together with its subsequent commentary, is most probably an allusion to the political scene of 1532. The eagle, whose tent is of a bluish-green shot fabric, representing no doubt both inconstancy and unpleasantness ('pervers'), and where there must be no white since, we are told, 'la blancheur de verité luy fault' (sig. B3r), is evidently the Emperor. The headless man in German dress is the German people, lacking any true leadership since the Reformation, and putting their trust (mistakenly, in Aneau's view) in the Emperor to press Pope Clement VII for a general council of the church. Two short speeches later, a new stage effect leads into the mocking passage on Clement VII's successor: 'Icy doibt estre une sorte [de] colonne dressée et un personnage qui avec un pal de bois vieil, et vermolu bat icelle colomne a grandz coups mettant peine a l'abbatre' (sig. B3r).   Pal/Paul, colomne/Colonna: the puns are obvious, and the gloss provided by Vulcan and Aurelian scarcely necessary. Immediately after this gloss (the swift succession of these effects must have required some snappy staging), we are given the third pictorial riddle: 'Soit assez loing un grand personnage armé et aorné en figure d'empereur en habitz Turquois: tenant en une main une lancete de Phlebotomie et en l'aultre une poillete a saigner, regardant furieusement contre Europe' (sig. B3v). Europe's terror at the sight of this Emperor in Turkish costume carrying the instruments of bloodletting is increased as Vulcan reminds her of the bloodthirsty attacks made on her in the past by the Turks, and threatens further such attacks.

The majority of the other political comments are couched in verbal riddles, chiefly **rhétoriqueur**-type puns on proper names,[65] of which just two examples will suffice.[66] Towards the end of the play Ganymedes reassures Europe with these words:

> N'ayes doncq paour que ce saigneur te saigne
> Car tous ses fers de la forge Payenne
> Furent froissez par l'Austriche a Vienne.
> L'Austriche fer mengeant, et fer disnant
> Par qui aussi la Barbe rousse sienne
> Fut arrachée a Thunis indignant.   (sig.B6v).

A marginal note identifies all those referred to in the puns except Barbarossa: 'Le turc chassé de Vienne par Charles d'Austriche empereur: Ferdinand son frere Roy d'Hongrie. Thunis pris par ledict'. The Ferdinand pun is an indication of Renaissance interest in the iron-eating ostrich.[67]   Chatting of home affairs, Androdus uses the same type of pun together with allegory:

> Si l'element de l'eau a fait oultrage,
> Mesme au Daulphin voire oultrage de mort

Et la gecté tout a plat roide mort,
Merveille n'est si le Chabot aussi
Hors de la mer est iecté jusque a bort,
Puys replongé, le mont demourant si
Quoy, que rien plus.   (sig. B1v)

Here again, a marginal note helps the reader: 'Messire Philippe Chabot Admiral, mis hors la court puis redintegré par le Roy. Montmorancy connestable'. The verbal riddles are, in fact, always accompanied by explanatory marginal notes in the printed edition, no doubt because such riddles would have been much clearer to the live audience than they are to the reader. Saulnier misses the point completely when he states the contrary.[68]   Spoken aloud, the **Lyon marchant** riddles surrender their secrets; it is a similar technique to the one we find today in those two delightful volumes, **Mots d'Heures: Gousses, Rames** and **N'heures, Souris, Rames,**[69] where the French words, looked at on the page, convey nothing whatever; but when they are read out, an English nursery rhyme ('N'heures, souris, rames'), albeit recited in a strong French accent, is heard, for 'Un petit d'un petit' becomes Humpty Dumpty, 'Chacun Gille', Jack and Jill, 'Oh, les mots d'heureux bardes', Old Mother Hubbard, and so on.

The versification of the **Lyon marchant** is extremely varied, passages of decasyllabic couplets being interspersed with stanzas and fixed verse forms, such as a ballad (sigs C2r-C2v) or a virelay (sigs A5r-A6r).[70]

Taken separately, these features of the **Lyon marchant** would not have appeared in any way innovatory to an audience accustomed to traditional spectacles.[71] Allegorical characters, although never as complex as those of Aneau, abound in the **sotties** and the moralities, and both the earlier **sotties** and some of the moralities lack any appreciable dramatic action.[72] Political comment and satire is much in evidence in these two genres,[73] and the college theatre of the time performed both pro- and anti-Establishment plays.   Thus the Collège de Navarre, for instance, gave performances in the early 1520s of Textor's **Dialogi,** which frequently commented favourably on the actions of Louis XII and Francis I,[74] and in 1533 created an uproar by composing a violently satirical **comédie** attacking Marguerite de Navarre.[75] Verbal fantasy was at its height in French medieval theatre, although it must be reiterated that Aneau's riddles owe more to the **rhétoriqueur** poets than to previous dramatists,[76] and several moralities show considerable metrical variety.[77] The pictorial riddles in the **Lyon marchant** are reminiscent more of the type of spectacle one would have witnessed at a Royal Entry than of the theatre proper, and indeed Aneau will twice be called upon subsequently to organize such spectacles in Lyons, once, as has already been mentioned, for the Solemn Entry into the city óf Jacques d'Albon, maréchal de St André, governor of Lyons,[78] and again in 1559 for the 'grands triomphes' held to celebrate the Peace of Cateau-Cambrésis. On the latter occasion Aneau organized a remarkable pageant on the Rhône featuring our old friends, the dolphin and the lion, in the company this time of a hippopotamus and several actors, who all disported themselves amidst a huge fire and fireworks.[79] It is no doubt the crowding of all these elements - complex allegory, political comment, verbal and pictorial riddles, metrical variety - into one short play which has driven critics to condemn the **Lyon marchant** as an 'absurde moralité', a 'mélange bizarre de mythes et de jeux de mots des plus inintelligibles', and to call its author 'un maniaque inoffensif',[80] but I shall shortly offer an explanation of this strange mixture.

In all that we have seen so far there is little, apart from some praise in passing of the Renaissance (sigs B6r-B6v) and a Protestant passage on the emergence of 'verité ensevelie' (sig. C1r),[81] which would indicate that this play is the work of a humanist teacher with progressive ideas. Indeed, the very title, **Lyon marchant**, being no doubt a conscious echo of a well-known **rhétoriqueur** poem, **Le Lyon rampant** of Georges Chastellain,[82] immediately suggests that Aneau's second play will, like his first, belong to the traditional end of the spectrum of college theatre. The second element of this title, however, **Satyre Francoise**, should give us pause for thought. Critics have paid scant attention to the question of the genre of the **Lyon marchant**; the majority avoid this aspect altogether,[83] but Lebègue considers it to be a morality play, and Saulnier thinks that Aneau intended us to see in **Satyre** the Latin 'satura', with its connotations of a mixture.[84] To C.A. Mayer must go the credit of realizing that Aneau's **Satyre Francoise** is a humanist experiment, an attempt to import into French literature a Greek dramatic genre, the satyr-play.[85] While convinced that Mayer's conclusion is correct, I do not feel that his supporting arguments do, in fact, prove the case. Mayer claims that Aneau was basing his innovation on the definition of the satyr-play given by the fourth-century Roman grammarian, Donatus, in his **De tragoedia et comoedia**, a work which had considerable influence in the Renaissance.[86] Unfortunately, however, the **Lyon marchant** does not correspond to Donatus's definition, which runs as follows: 'Haec quae Satyra dicitur eiusmodi fuit, ut in ea quamuis duro et ueluti agresti modo de uitiis ciuium, tamen sine ullo proprii nominis titulo carmen esset'.[87] Aneau makes no attempt to satirize the general failings of citizens, and he does name names. His punning style is certainly clumsy, but there is no discernible rusticity, and indeed there are moments of eloquence.[88] It is interesting to note, as Mayer does, that a contemporary of Aneau, Charles Estienne, writing in 1542, included in his definition of the satyr-play, which is expanded from that of Donatus, the following statement: 'En icelle [la Satyre] ne se declaroit riens que par enigmes et circonlocutions, principalement touchant les haultes et ardues matieres'.[89]   Matters of import discussed in riddles - this would indeed describe two major aspects of the **Lyon marchant**, but the play had already been performed when Charles Estienne published his definition, so there can be no question of the latter influencing Aneau.

Since it is clear, then, that Aneau was not basing his experiment on the definitions of the satyr-play given by Donatus and his imitators, definitions which we now know in any case to have been ill-founded,[90] we have to ask to what other sources of information about the Greek satyric drama did he have access. He would certainly have known the passage on the satyr-play in Horace's **Ars Poetica**,[91] since he claims to have translated this work in the late 1520s,[92] and indeed, the idea for Aneau's and Charles Estienne's 'enigmes' may well stem from the following two lines of Horace:

> non ego inornata et dominantia nomina solum
> verbaque, Pisones, Satyrorum scriptor amabo.   (ll.234-35)

A desire to avoid 'the plain nouns and verbs of established use' could easily be taken to mean a wish to write in riddles. Aneau might also have encountered the description of the appropriate setting for a satyr-play given by Vitruvius in his **De architectura**: 'genera autem sunt scaenarum tria: unum quod dicitur tragicum, alterum comicum, tertium satyricum. [...] Satyricae vero ornantur arboribus speluncis montibus reliquisque agrestibus rebus in topiarii speciem deformati'.[93]   Certainly, the setting for the **Lyon marchant** conforms remarkably well to these requirements: there is a cave, from which Vulcan emerges (sig. A3v), a mountain, Mount Ida, at the foot of which Paris lies sleeping when the play opens, and a cluster of rocks, Lyon's lair (sig. A4r). What is even more important is that Aneau appears to have known one of the only two satyr-plays to have survived from Antiquity, namely the **Cyclops** of Euripides.[94]   The **Cyclops** had been published, together with all of Euripides's tragedies except the **Electra**, by the Aldine press in 1503, and again in Basle in 1537, and either of these editions would have been accessible to the competent Hellenist we know Aneau to have been.[95]   I hope to show that Aneau's **Satyre Francoise** represents a deliberate attempt to produce a French equivalent to the **Cyclops**.

Aneau signals his intentions clearly at the beginning of the **Lyon marchant**. Three of the characters we meet in the **Cry**, Lyon, Roan and Aurelian, whom Lyon describes in heraldic terms as 'un fort chien couchant' (sig. A2v), are part animal, part human, and might well have been costumed as modern satyrs, men with animals' ears and tails.[96]   Just as the **Cyclops** opens with a lament, Silenus bewailing the kidnapping of Bacchus by pirates (ll.1-24),[97] so does the **Lyon marchant**, where Arion, having dismounted from a dolphin and set aside his lyre, tells in his opening speech of his grief at the death of the best of dolphins (sigs A3r-A3v). Aneau would have known from

Herodotus, whom he uses subsequently when Arion tells his story,[98] that the latter, being the author of a dithyramb, was closely associated with the origins of satyric drama. The next speech brings a lengthy allusion to the Cyclops and to Sicily, as Vulcan describes the type of war he will bring. It is a war

> Forgée a mort (si le coup, et ton, n'erre)
> Dessus l'enclume a feu, esclair, tonnerre
> Au mont Bolcar, et ses ardentes Eroppes
>   Pour esmovoir les parties Europes
> Par Pyracmon, par Brontes, et Steropes
> Tresgrandz ouvriers de tous tourments belliques
> Car ces trois sont mes forgerons Cyclopes
> N'ayants qu'un oeil.   (sigs A3v-A4r)

A marginal note explains 'mont Bolcar': 'Bolcar montaigne ardente en Sicile jadis dicte Aethna'. Here we have, then, the villains and the setting of Euripides's **Cyclops,** although Aneau takes the proper names from Virgil.[99]

After these strong initial hints, Aneau presents us with a play containing most of those features of the **Cyclops** which scholars have singled out as being characteristic of the satyr-play.[100] Satyric drama involved the burlesque treatment of a well-known myth; the **Cyclops** is a comic adaptation of an episode of the **Odyssey,** whereas the **Lyon marchant** takes a contemporary hero, Francis I, and tells, in puns and riddles, of the notable events, the 'choses memorables', of his reign. Scholars agree that a major motif of the satyr-play is the enslavement and subsequent liberation of the satyrs. Silenus's opening speeches in the **Cyclops** are, true enough, peppered with allusions to slavery (ll.24, 78, 79), and it is the declared aim of Odysseus to set these slaves free (1.442), an aim which is eventually achieved. This motif is equally evident in the **Lyon marchant:** in the **Cry** no fewer than three of the characters, Aurelian, Androdus and Europe, express fears or hopes with regard to slavery (sig. A2v), and the opening scenes of the play show Vulcan totally dominating the other characters, terrifying them with cannon shots and threats of war (sigs A3v-A5v). Their fright is not alleviated until towards the end of the play, when Ganymedes advises Europe as to how she may avoid being subjugated by her enemies (sigs B6r-B6v). A counterpart to this motif is that of the overthrow of a bully, Polyphemus in the case of the **Cyclops,** and Vulcan in the **Lyon marchant.** To bring about this discomfiture Euripides extends his characteristic use of the **deus ex machina** device from his tragedies to his satyr-play, the god in this case being, in fact, that exceptional hero, Odysseus. In Aneau's play we have a pair of characters with superhuman powers who appear at the denouement to provide a solution. Firstly Ganymedes, Jove's emissary, enters in the nick of time to prevent Europe committing suicide (sig. B5v), and then, when his proposals lead to the competition between the three towns, Verité is obliged to intervene, and rises up out of the earth to do so (sig. C1v). Linked to all these motifs of the satyr-play is the recurrent theme of cruelty, and here the parallel between the **Cyclops** and the **Lyon marchant** is particularly striking, since Aneau appears to imitate the cannibalistic language of Euripides's man-eating giants.   One may compare, for example, the following two passages:

CYCLOPS

Just you look sharp, then, and set
A fine edge on my carving-knives, and get
A good big faggot on the hearth, and start
The fire; and these shall promptly do their part
Of filling up my crop. Hot from the embers
I'll eat them. I'm the carver who dismembers
My game, and I'm the cook who does the boiling
And stewing here! My appetite's been spoiling
For something of a change from one long run
Of mountain-game: my stomach's overdone
With lion-steaks and venison. Now for a taste
Of man! - I don't know when I ate one last. (ll.241-49)

VULCAN (addressing Europe)

C'est le saigneur, et le barbier tresaigre,
Qui t'a couppé un membre a grand destresse,
Qui te rendit paovre, chetive, et maigre
Quand il tira hors de ton corps ta Gresse,
Et maintenant de rechief il t'aggresse
Pour attirer tout le sang du corps tien,
Car puys qu'il a gousté le sang Chrestien,
Comme un Lyon, ou Tygre, qui parit
Est escharné. Et c'est enragé chien
Apres le sang tirera l'esperit.   (sigs B3v-B4r)

Finally, although we noted earlier the metrical variety to be found in the **Lyon marchant,** and the fact that this was a feature Aneau's play shared with the national tradition, it must be pointed out that such variety was equally a characteristic of the satyr-play, where choruses frequently interrupt the action with the lyrical metre of a song.[101] The only element of the **Cyclops** which Aneau does not exploit is that of slapstick and ribaldry, and this omission may well be due to the influence of Horace, who maintained that the satyrs should avoid market-place behaviour, and bawdy jokes, lest they give offence:

silvis deducti caveant, me iudice, Fauni
ne velut innati triviis ac paene forenses
aut nimium teneris iuvenentur versibus umquam,
aut immunda crepent ignominiosaque dicta:
offenduntur enim quibus est equus et pater et res. (ll.244-48)

At a time when, in France, interest in Euripides was in its infancy, when Buchanan had translated into Latin the **Medea** but not yet the **Alcestis,** when

Guillaume Morel had only just published, in 1540, a Latin translation of Ecuba, and when no translations into French at all had appeared, although Guillaume Bochetel was perhaps working on his Hécube, which would be published in 1544,[102] this conscious attempt to create a French Cyclops constitutes a major new departure.[103] Aneau is already practising what Du Bellay, towards the end of the decade, in his Deffence et illustration de la langue francoyse, will preach as a new necessity. Du Bellay urges French authors not merely to translate the works of Antiquity, but to use them in the same manner as the Romans did Greek literature: 'Immitant les meilleurs aucteurs Grecz, se transformant en eux, les devorant, et apres les avoir bien digerez, les convertissant en sang et nouriture'.[104] The fact that Aneau's attempt to do just this was not recognized by Du Bellay may well explain the vitriolic tone of the Quintil Horatian, Aneau's anonymously published reply to the Deffence. Indeed, he reproaches Du Bellay at one point for advocating that the term 'coq à l'asne' be replaced by 'satyre', declaring that 'Satyre est autre chose'; he evidently wished to reserve the term for his new dramatic genre.[105] Through his experiment Aneau is, of course, linked with humanist-pedagogue dramatists such as Buchanan, and if today the Lyon marchant strikes us as bizarre it is because it endeavours to combine tradition with innovation, both ends of the spectrum of college theatre as it existed in Aneau's day.

NOTES

1. On Barthélemy Aneau,   see especially Cochard's article in C. Bréghot du Lut, **Nouveaux Mélanges biographiques et littéraires pour servir à l'histoire de la ville de Lyon** (Lyons, 1829-31), pp.189-213; John L. Gerig, 'Barthélemy Aneau: A Study in Humanism', **Romanic Review**, 1 (1910), 181-207, 279-89, 395-410; 2 (1911), 163-85; 3 (1912), 27-57; and Georgette Brasart-de Groër, 'Le Collège, agent d'infiltration de la Réforme', in **Aspects de la propagande religieuse**, edited by Henri Meylan (Geneva, 1957), pp.167-75.

2. Aneau twice names Bourges as his birthplace; see the dedication of his translation of Alciati's emblems, **Emblemes d'Alciat de nouveau Translatez en François** (Lyons, Roville, 1549), p.18, and the dedicatory epistle of his novel **Alector** (Lyons, Pierre Fradin, 1560), fol. iv. It is in the preface to his own volume of emblematic poetry that he tells us that he attended school in the Hôtel Jacques Cœur in Bourges, **Picta Poesis** (Lyons, Macé Bonhomme, 1552), p.4. The exact date of Aneau's birth is not known, but we can deduce that it was between 1500 and 1510.

3. It is not known at what point in the 1530s Aneau left Bourges; it is possible that he spent some time in Paris before going to Lyons (see note 4, and **Alector**, fol. v). On the theatre in Bourges, see Louis Raynal, **Histoire du Berry**, 4 vols (Bourges, 1844-47), III, 191-97 and 312; and Jean Mellot, 'A propos du théâtre liturgique à Bourges, au Moyen-Age et au XVIe siècle', in **Mélanges offerts à Gustave Cohen** (Paris, 1950), pp.193-98. The **Mystère de la Passion** was acted in

Bourges in 1515 and the **Mystère de Saint Jacques-le-Majeur** in 1530.

4.   The exact date of Aneau's arrival in Lyons is not known. Cochard, p.189, places it in 1529, Gerig, 'Barthélemy Aneau', 1910, p.185, in 1533, whereas Brasart-de Groër, p.168, hesitates between 1533 and 1538; none of these critics offers any proof. I would suggest, however, that Aneau did not come to Lyons until 1538 or just a little earlier. The first of the numerous references to him in the municipal archives is found in an entry dated 21 December 1538 (Archives municipales de Lyon, CC 915, fol. 95r. Aneau is designated in this document as 'principal Regent du colliege de la trinité'). Moreover, it is in this same year that Aneau, by an exchange of Latin epigrams with his colleague at the Collège de la Trinité, Gilbert Ducher (see **Gilberti Ducherii Vultonis Aquapersani Epigrammaton Libri Duo** (Lyons, Sebastien Gryphe, 1538), pp.133 and 159), begins his long list of publications with the Lyons printers (there are thirty-seven publications in all over a period of twenty-four years if one includes the translations, prefaces, and incidental poems), and it seems somewhat improbable that he should have spent several years in Lyons before embarking upon his literary career.

5.   The private school founded in 1519 by the Confrérie de la Trinité was assigned to the Consulat of Lyons for use as a municipal college on 27 July 1527. See John L. Gerig, 'Le Collège de la Trinité à Lyon avant 1540', **Revue de la Renaissance,** 9 (1908), 73-94 (p.77); 10 (1909), 137-56.

6.   These difficulties were chiefly due to the censorship exercised by the Consulat. See Claudius Brouchoud, **Les Origines du théâtre de Lyon** (Lyons, 1865), pp.16-20.

7.   The Confrérie de la Passion had had a permanent theatre in the Hôpital de la Trinité in Paris since 1402, but this was exceptional, and elsewhere in Aneau's day the custom was still to erect a temporary theatre for the duration of the performance either in the open or indoors. See Grace Frank, **The Medieval French Drama** (Oxford, 1954), pp.166-67.

8.   **Histoire veritable de la ville de Lyon** (Lyons, 1604), p.370. Rubys implies that the theatre was opened in 1540, but Brouchoud, p.11, corrects this to 1538 and explains, pp.23-24, that the short-lived nature of this enterprising venture was due to the death of Jean Neyron and the subsequent sale of the property in 1541.

9.   The Père de Colonia, **Histoire littéraire de la ville de Lyon** (Lyons, 1728-30), II, 430, claims that the Jean Neyron repertory was published in 1542 and that it was the work of Loys Choquet, but this is an error. See L. Petit de Julleville, **Les Mystères,** 2 vols (Paris, 1880), I, 333.

10.   **Les Mystères,** II, 135-36.

11.   L. Petit de Julleville, **Répertoire du théâtre comique en France au Moyen Age** (Paris, 1886), pp.4-5. **Le Recueil de Londres** (British Library, C.20.e.13) is reprinted in a facsimile edition by Slatkine (Geneva, 1970).

12.   The document which Aneau presented to the Consuls of Lyons in 1540 in response to their request for his advice, and as a result of which he was appointed principal, contains several progressive ideas, notably the teaching of Greek and Latin by means of games and an insistence upon less passive methods of learning. See 'Formulaire et Institution du colliege de la Trinité de Lion', Arch. munic. de Lyon, BB 58, fols 61v-63v.

13.   On college theatre in sixteenth-century France, see especially Raymond Lebègue, **La Tragédie religieuse en France: les débuts (1514-1573)** (Paris, 1929). See also L. Petit de Julleville, **Les Comédiens en France au Moyen Age** (Paris, 1885), pp.291-323, and L.-V. Gofflot, **Le Théâtre au collège du Moyen Age à nos jours** (Paris, 1907).

14. See Ernest Gaullieur, **Histoire du Collège de Guyenne** (Paris, 1874), pp.57-58.

15. See Lebègue, p.146.

16. Lebègue, pp.145-46.

17. From the prologue to a Latin comedy which Calmus published in 1555, quoted by Lebègue, p.143, note 2.

18. **Essais**, edited by Albert Thibaudet and Maurice Rat, Bibliothèque de la Pléiade (Paris, 1962), p.176. The Latin tragedies performed at the Collège de Guyenne are discussed below.

19. The only copy of the **Chant Natal** in existence today is in the Bibliothèque Nationale, Réserve Ye 782. It is possible that this work was reprinted in Lyons in 1559 by Godefroy Beringen as part of a volume, now lost, entitled **Genethliac Musical et historial de la conception et nativité de Iesus-Christ par vers et chants divers, entresemez et illustrez des noms royaux, et de princes, Anagrammatisez en diverses sentences, soubs mystique allusion aux personnes divines et humaines. Avec un chant Royal pour chanter à l'acclamation des Rois. Ensemble la 4. Eclogue de Virgile intitulee Pollion, ou Auguste, extraicte des vers de la Sibylle Cumee prophetisant la nativité de Iesus Christ advenue bien tost apres, et au mesme temps et empire d'Auguste**: see J.C. Brunet, **Manuel du libraire et de l'amateur de livres**, 6 vols (Paris, 1860), I, col. 284, and J. Baudrier, **Bibliographie lyonnaise**, 12 vols (Lyons, 1895-1921), III, 54. In the nineteenth century Henri Lemeignen reprinted the **Chant Natal**, excluding the seven **noëls**, in his **Vieux Noëls composés en l'honneur de la Naissance de Notre Seigneur Jésus-Christ**, 2 vols (Nantes, 1876), II, 62-84; the spelling and punctuation have been modernized. There is no bibliographical evidence whatsoever to support the erroneous claim first made by Cochard, in Bréghot du Lut, p.191, and subsequently repeated by many other critics, that the **Mystere** element of the **Chant Natal** had been published two years earlier, in 1537.

20. **Chant Natal**, verso of the title-page. The **dizain**, headed 'B. Aneau, a ses Disciples', begins:

> Louez Enfans, le seigneur, et son nom:
> Les chants qu'a vous je dedie, chantants
> Chants, mais quelz chants, de Poesie? Non,
> Mais chants Natalz, que requis ha le temps.

21. Lyons, Pierre de Tours, 1542. The dedicatory epistle, addressed to Monseigneur de Langey, is signed 'Barptolemy Aneau'. Copies of the original edition are to be found in the Bibliothèque Nationale, Réserve Ye 1656, and in the Bibliothèque de la Ville de Lyon, 805248 (Fonds Coste 11734). A facsimile reproduction of the original edition (forty-two copies only) was printed by G. Veinant (Paris, 1831).

22. **Comedie ou dialogue matrimonial, Exemplaire de Paix en Mariage, extraict du devis d'Erasme, translaté de Latin en Francoys: duquel est le tiltre, Uxor Memphigamos, C'est à dire: La femme mary plaignant** (Paris, Denis Janot, 1541). There is a copy of this dialogue in the Bibliothèque Nationale, Réserve Yf 4354. The identity of the translator is revealed in the dedicatory **dizain**, sig. A2r.

23. Buchanan tells us in his autobiography that this was the case at the Collège de Guyenne: see **Poemata** (Lyons, 1628), sig. A4r. In Paris the students at the Collège de Navarre performed literary exercises and plays annually on the feast-day of St Louis: see Lebègue, p.146.

24. From 1540 until Aneau's resignation in 1551. Approached by the Consulat in 1558, Aneau accepted the post of principal a second time and held it until his

death in 1561.   See Arch. munic. de Lyon, BB 72, fols 176-77, and BB 81, fol. 72r.

25.   Between the publication of the **Lyon marchant** in 1542 and that of his next work of any importance, the **Decades de la description, forme, et vertu naturelle des animaulx,** in 1549, Aneau published only a couple of translations and some incidental verse.

26.   See François and Claude Parfaict, **Histoire du theatre françois, depuis son origine jusqu'à present,** 15 vols   (Paris, 1745-48), III, 43-46; La Vallière, **Bibliotheque du théatre françois, depuis son origine,** 3 vols (Dresden, 1768), I, 111-13; A.F. Delandine, **Bibliothèque de Lyon. Catalogue des livres qu'elle renferme dans la section du théâtre** (Paris, n.d.), pp.11-13; Petit de Julleville, **Les Mystères,** II, 613-14, and **Répertoire du théâtre comique,** pp.78-79; Lebègue, pp.41 and 151; G.D. Jonker, **Le Protestantisme et le théâtre de langue française au XVIe siècle** (Groningen, 1939), pp.73-74; and J.L. Gerig, 'Barthélemy Aneau', 1910, pp.186-91, 195-201, 281-86. C.A. Mayer treats the **Lyon marchant** at some length in his unpublished Ph.D. dissertation, 'Satire in French Literature from 1525 to 1560 with Particular Reference to the Sources and the Technique' (University of London, 1949). V.-L. Saulnier analyses both plays in 'Le Théâtre de Barthélemy Aneau', in **Mélanges Cohen,** pp.147-58.

27.   See Gustave Lanson, 'Etudes sur les origines de la tragédie classique en France', **Revue d'histoire littéraire de la France,** 10 (1903),   177-231 and 413-36 (pp.192-94); and Lebègue, p.104.

28.   See Lebègue, pp.151-52.

29.   See Lebègue, pp.145-46, and J. Quicherat, **Histoire de Sainte-Barbe,** 3 vols (Paris, 1860-64), I, 258-59.

30.   In his autobiography, George Buchanan writes that while he was teaching at the Collège de Guyenne, which is to say from 1539 to 1543, 'eas [quatuor tragœdias] enim ut consuetudini scholae satisfaceret, quae per annos singulos singulas poscebat fabulas, conscripserat: ut earum actione juventutem ab allegoriis, quibus tum Gallia vehementer se oblectabat, ad imitationem veterum qua posset, retraheret' (**Georgii Buchanani vita ab ipso scripta biennio ante mortem,** in **Poemata,** sig. A4r).

31.   It has not been possible to date precisely Buchanan's translations and original works for the college theatre, but it is thought that, despite the statement made in his autobiography and quoted in the preceding note, his translation of the **Medea,** published in 1544, does in fact pre-date his stay in Bordeaux by several years. The other three works, however, do indeed date from that period (1539-43),   although they were not published until much later. See I.D. McFarlane, **Buchanan** (London, 1981), Chapter 3 and Appendix A.

32.   See Lebègue, p.245.

33.   On the date of Muret's arrival in Bordeaux, see R. Trinquet, 'Recherches chronologiques sur la jeunesse de M.-A. Muret', **Bibliothèque d'Humanisme et Renaissance,** 27 (1965), 272-85.

34.   See Lebègue, p.159.

35.   Although these plays were written and performed before 1524, they were printed regularly in the 1530s: see Lebègue, p.146. On Ravisius Textor, see also M.E. Cougny, **Des Représentations dramatiques et particulièrement de la comédie politique dans les collèges** (Paris, 1868).

36.   'Formulaire et Institution du colliege de la Trinité de Lion', Arch. munic. de

Lyon, BB.58, fol. 63r.

37. For an analysis, see Saulnier, pp.150-53.

38. There are two in the **Chant Natal,** namely the **Chant Pastoural,** and the second and third episodes of the **Mystere de la Nativité.**

39. See Petit de Julleville, **Les Mystères,** I, 290-92.

40. See Petit de Julleville, **Les Mystères,** I, 251-52. The **Noel mystic** which ends the **Chant Natal** fulfils the function of an epilogue-cum-sermon.

41. See Petit de Julleville, **Les Mystères,** I, 255-61.

42. See Petit de Julleville, **Les Mystères,** I, 268.

43. Gerig, 'Barthélemy Aneau', 1910, pp.196-200, assumes this to have been the case, but Saulnier, pp.152-53, only tentatively envisages such a possibility.

44. See Parfaict, III, 43; La Vallière, I, 111-12; Delandine, p.11; and Brouchoud, p.42.

45. For this exhortation, see above, note 20.

46. There are five **noëls** before the **Chant Pastoural,** the sixth occurs at the end of it, and the final **noël** is placed after the **Chant Royal.**

47. See Alice Hulubei, **L'Eglogue en France au XVIe siècle** (Paris, 1938), p.142.

48. See Henri Chardon's introduction to his edition of François Briand's **Quatre histoires par personnaiges** (Paris, 1906), pp.viii-ix.

49. **Se ensuyvent Les Nouelz Nouvaulx de ce present an. Mil cinq cens et douze dont en y a plusieurs notez a deux parties dont l'une n'est que le Plain Chant. Avecques quatre histoires par personnaiges sur quatre evangilles de L'Advent a jouer par les petis enfans les quatre dimenches dudit Advent. Composez par Maistre Francoys Briand Maistre Des Escolles de Sainct Benoist en la Cité du Mans.** The title is from the introduction to Chardon's edition of the **Farce** (Paris, 1903), p.xi. The printer of Briand's work and place of publication are unknown.

50. Chardon published his edition in three stages: the **Farce** was followed by the **Nouelz Nouvaulx** (Paris, 1904), and then came the **Quatre histoires.**

51. On the **noël,** see Noël Hervé, **Les Noëls français** (Niort, 1905); the Abbé Paul Terris, 'Essai historique et littéraire sur les noëls', **Revue du monde catholique,** 52 (1877), 555-69, 762-68, 831-48; and 53 (1878), 223-33, 740-50; and Henry Poulaille, **La Grande et Belle Bible des noëls anciens,** 3 parts (Paris, 1942-51).

52. See Terris, 1877, p.833; and Poulaille, p.169.

53. On the rival music printers, Pierre Attaingnant in Paris and Jacques Moderne in Lyons, see Daniel Heartz, **Pierre Attaingnant, Royal Printer of Music** (Berkeley and Los Angeles, 1969), and Samuel F. Pogue, **Jacques Moderne: Lyons Music Printer of the Sixteenth Century** (Geneva, 1969).

54. Brouchoud, p.42.

55. Delandine, p.11. Jean Demogeot, **Notice historique sur le Collège Royal à Lyon** (Lyons, 1840), p.6, uses almost the same description.

56. See Hervé, p.30; Poulaille, p.119; and Chardon's introduction to Briand's **Nouelz Nouvaulx,** p.xvii.

57. Herodotus, I, 23-24. Aneau indicates his source in a marginal note (sig. A7r).

58. Gerig, 'Barthélemy Aneau', 1910, pp.282-83. Jean d'Albon succeeded the Cardinal

de Tournon as governor of Lyons in 1542. The fact that the Cardinal was governor of the city at the time the **Lyon marchant** was acted leads Saulnier, p.155, note 31 bis, to believe that it is he who is represented by Androdus, but Gerig's identification seems the more likely.

59.   The solemn entry took place on 24 August 1550. For Aneau's part in its organization, see Arch. munic. de Lyon, BB71, fols 177-200, and CC990, fol. 28r.

60.   Saulnier, p.155.

61.   The allusion is to Guillaume du Bellay's lieutenantship of Piedmont, guarding the gate to paradise, i.e. France.

62.   On this period, see R.J. Knecht, **Francis I** (Cambridge, 1982), pp.289-304.

63.   Aneau mistakenly claims that Wolsey was beheaded. On the reverberations in French literature caused by the deaths of Sir Thomas More and Ann Boleyn, see Georges Ascoli, **La Grande-Bretagne devant l'opinion française depuis la guerre de cent ans jusqu'à la fin du XVIe siècle** (Paris, 1927), pp.60-74.

64.   On the founding of this institution, see J.B. Monfalcon, **Histoire de la ville de Lyon depuis son origine jusqu'en 1846**, 2 vols (Lyons, 1847), I, 601-04.

65.   On this aspect of **rhétoriqueur** versification, see Henry Guy, **Histoire de la poésie française au XVIe siècle**, Volume I, **L'Ecole des Rhétoriqueurs** (Paris, 1910), pp.84-85.

66.   Several of these riddles are quoted by Saulnier, p.155 and note 35.

67.   'I'll make thee eat iron like an ostrich' (**Henry VI**, Part II, IV.x). On this topic, see Beryl Rowland, **Birds with Human Souls: A Guide to Bird Symbolism** (Knoxville, Tennessee, 1978), pp.111-13.

68.   Saulnier, p.156.

69.   **Mots d'Heures: Gousses, Rames. The d'Antin manuscript edited by Luis d'Antin van Rooten** (London and Sydney, 1967); **N'heures, Souris, Rames. The Coucy Castle manuscript edited by Ormonde de Kay** (London and Sydney, 1983).

70.   For further details of the versification, see Saulnier, p.156.

71.   On medieval comedy, see especially Frank, Chapter 24, and Heather Arden, **Fools' Plays: A Study of Satire in the 'Sottie'** (Cambridge, 1980).

72.   Frank, pp.244 and 248.

73.   The outstanding example of political satire in late medieval French theatre is Pierre Gringore's **Le Jeu du Prince des Sotz**, which attacks Pope Julius II. See **OEuvres complètes**, edited by A. de Montaiglon and J. de Rothschild, 2 vols (Paris, 1858-77), I, 295.

74.   The **Dialogus Furor bellicus, Maximilian et Pax** praises the conquering journey of Louis XII through Italy in 1509; the **Dialogus tres Epicuri, Mors** contains allusions to wars in the early years of Francis I's reign, and the **Dialogus Malus, Rumor, Concordia** is based on the betrothal of Henry VIII's daughter, Mary, to the Dauphin in 1518. All three dialogues are published in **Dialogi aliquot Ioannis Ra. Textoris Nivernensis** (Paris, 1534).

75.   See J.-H. Merle d'Aubigné, **Histoire de la Réformation en Europe au temps de Calvin**, 8 vols (Geneva and Paris, 1863-78), II, 245-51.

76.   Aneau's puns do not belong to any of the categories of verbal fantasy distinguished by Robert Garapon in his comprehensive study of the subject, **La Fantaisie verbale et le comique dans le théâtre français du Moyen Age à la fin du**

XVIIe siècle (Paris, 1957), Chapter 2.

77. Frank, p.249.

78. For this occasion Aneau prepared, as well as the 'ystoire d'Androdus', a second 'ystoire' showing the captive wife and daughters of King Darius pleading with Hephaestion, whom they had mistaken for his master, Alexander the Great. See Arch. munic. de Lyon, BB71, fols 187r, 196r and 200v.

79. A full description of this pageant can be found in the contemporary account of the celebrations composed by the lawyer, Benoît Troncy. See **Suytte de la Description des Grands Triomphes faitz à Lyon apres la publication de la Paix** (Lyons, Jean Saugrain, 1559), pp.13-16.

80. Lebègue, p.151; Jonker, p.73; and Petit de Julleville, **Répertoire du théâtre comique**, p.79.

81. On the importance of this passage, which constitutes Aneau's sole open admission to Protestantism, see C.A. Mayer, **Lucien de Samosate et la Renaissance française** (Geneva, 1984), pp.159-61.

82. For the text of this poem, the first line of which, 'Lyon rampant en crouppe de montaigne', became a popular refrain, see Georges Chastellain, **OEuvres**, edited by the Baron Kervyn de Lettenhove, 8 vols (Brussels, 1833-66), VII, 207-12. Aneau seems to have had this refrain in mind towards the end of the **Lyon marchant**, where Verité declares:

> Qui n'est Lyon ne passant, ne couchant,
> Rampant, grippant sa proye rencontree,
> Mais devant tous est le Lyon marchant. (sig. C2v)

83. Petit de Julleville, **Répertoire du théâtre comique**, p.78, and Jonker, p.73, play safe and call it a 'pièce'; Gerig, 'Barthélemy Aneau', 1910, pp.281 and 285, rings the changes with 'play', 'poem', and 'satyre'.

84. Lebègue, pp.107 and 151; Saulnier, p.153, note 29.

85. C.A. Mayer, ' "Satyre" as a dramatic genre', **Bibliothèque d'Humanisme et Renaissance**, 13 (1951), 327-33.

86. See the introduction by H.W. Lawton to his **Handbook of French Renaissance Dramatic Theory** (Manchester, 1949), pp.xiii-xiv.

87. Quoted from Lawton, whose translation is as follows: 'That which is called "satyra" was of the following kind: in it was a composition concerning the failings of citizens, although in a harsh and, as it were, rustic style, yet without any declaration of individual names' (pp.4-5).

88. See, for example, the beginning of Europe's lament (sigs B4r-B4v), and parts of Arion's story (sig. A8v).

89. 'Epistre du translateur au lecteur', **Andrie** (Paris, 1542), quoted from Lawton, **Handbook**, p.37. See also H.W. Lawton, 'Charles Estienne et le théâtre', **Revue du XVIe siècle**, 14 (1927), 336-47.

90. See J.W. Jolliffe, 'Satyre: Satura: Satyros: A Study in Confusion', **Modern Language Notes**, 18 (1956), 84-95.

91. **Ars Poetica**, ll.220-50. Quotations are from the Loeb Classical Library edition of Horace's **Satires, Epistles and Ars Poetica**, edited and translated by H. Rushton Fairclough (London and Cambridge, Massachusetts, 1926).

92. In the 'Préambule du **Quintil Horatian**', written in 1550, Aneau states that he

translated 'toute l'**Art Poëtique,** y a plus de vingt ans, avant Pelletier et tout autre'. See **Le Quintil Horatian sur la defense et illustration de la langue Francoyse** (Paris, Veufve Françoys Regnault, 1555), p.80.

93. Vitruvius, **De architectura,** V, vi, 9, quoted from Margarete Bieber, **The History of the Greek and Roman Theater** (Princeton and London, 1961), p.125. There had been numerous editions of Vitruvius since 1486.

94. The other satyr-play is, in fact, a 300-line fragment of Sophocles's **Ichneutae,** discovered only in 1911.

95. Numerous scholars repeat the Père de Colonia's assertion (II, 668), that Aneau studied Greek at the University of Bourges under Melchior Wolmar, who arrived to teach there in 1529; although this is highly probable, it has not been proved. We do know, however, that in 1543 Aneau's knowledge of Greek was praised by the Consulat of Lyons (Arch. munic. de Lyon, BB 61, fols 75v-76r), and his volume of emblematic poetry published in 1552, the **Picta Poesis** (Lyons, Macé Bonhomme), contains several lines of Greek.

96. The satyrs had equine ears and tails: see Bieber, p.6.

97. The references and quotations are from Arthur S. Way's translation of Euripides's works, in the Loeb Classical Library, 4 vols (London and Cambridge, Massachusetts, 1947), II, 520-91.

98. See above, note 57.

99. **Aeneid,** VIII, l.425.

100. On the **Cyclops** as a satyr-play, see especially D.J. Conacher, **Euripidean Drama: Myth, Theme and Structure** (Toronto, 1967), chapter 18, and the introduction to **Le Cyclope d'Euripide,** edited by Jacqueline Duchemin (Paris, 1945).

101. See ll.41-81, 356-74, 495-518, 608-23 and 656-63. On the metrical variety in the **Cyclops,** see Duchemin, pp.xxvi-xxvii and 3-6.

102. See McFarlane, pp.118-21; A. Pertusi, 'Il ritorno alle fonti del teatro greco classico : Euripide nell' Umanesimo e nel Rinascimento', **Byzantion,** 33 (1963), 396-426 (p.410); and R. Sturel, 'Essai sur les traductions du théâtre grec en français avant 1550', **Revue d'histoire littéraire de la France,** 20 (1913), 269-96 and 637-66 (p.282).

103. As Mayer points out in his article, Roger de Collerye had published, in 1536, a **Satyre pour les habitants d'Auxerre;** but this play has nothing in common with Aneau's **Satyre,** showing rather all the characteristics of a morality, including satire of general failings and personification of abstract qualities.

104. **La Deffence et illustration de la langue françoyse,** edited by Henri Chamard (Paris, 1948), p.42.

105. **Quintil Horatian,** p.103.

TWO

The Dilemma Monologue in
Pre-Cornelian French Tragedy (1550-1610)
Alan Howe

The critical autonomy of French Renaissance tragedy now seems firmly established. Lanson's admonition that to judge the tragedies of the sixteenth century by the criteria normally applied to those of the seventeenth is distorting and unjust to the former[1] has received emphatic support from the two most substantial recent examinations of humanist tragedy, by Richard Griffiths and Donald Stone, Jr.[2] Their detailed studies have underlined how little, beyond a few superficial (and mainly formal) similarities deriving largely from a shared classical tradition, French Renaissance tragedies had in common, in terms either of aspiration or of achievement, with the hallowed masterpieces of the following century. Unmindful of, or indifferent to, the dramatic effects and complex characterization which would typify the genre in the age of Pierre Corneille, with its carefully contrived plots, exploitation of conflict, and penchant for psychological penetration, the Renaissance tragedian is shown to have been concerned primarily with moralizing and rhetoric. His exemplary tales of ineluctable adversity aimed to provide, on the one hand, 'a moral lesson on man's destiny',[3] and, on the other, 'a series of stylistic exercises set in stylized forms'.[4]

It is the primacy of rhetoric for the Renaissance playwright which accentuates most vividly the fundamental difference in the aims and methods that informed the genre in the contrasting periods of Jodelle and Corneille. Griffiths has shown that the humanist writer's training in formulary rhetoric led him to adopt 'an almost operatic technique',[5] whereby speeches were conceived as a series of loosely connected 'set pieces', such as lengthy monologues, developing a single theme or emotion, and stichomythia, which often incorporated an exchange of **sententiae** or of antithetical replies; while these set pieces in turn furnished an opportunity in the other branch of the art, stylistic rhetoric, for the author to deploy his talent for linguistic expansion and stylistic ornamentation.[6] Thus, whereas for his seventeenth-century successor a poetic form would provide the vehicle for drama, for the Renaissance tragedian a dramatic form was conceived principally as the vehicle for poetry.

Now, it is not intended in this essay to contest the main theses of Griffiths and Stone in so far as they identify and elucidate those concerns which were **paramount** for humanist writers.   Nevertheless, to insist, as they do, on isolating Renaissance tragedies so comprehensively from those of the next century, particularly by adducing in the former an unmitigated 'absence of modern dramatic concerns',[7] is to create a major problem for the student of literary history interested in tracing the evolution of the genre and of its techniques. Clearly, by the 1630s a transformation has occurred: writers of tragedy are displaying an interest in the art of plausible characterization, in plot building and the creation of **scènes à faire,** and in effects of suspense and tension. But when, how, in what stages, and in which works did this interest in 'modern dramatic concerns' begin to manifest itself? By what process did the dramatic **poetry** of the Renaissance develop into the poetic **drama** of the Classical era?

The reader of Griffiths's study of Montchrestien (a late exponent of humanist dramaturgy whose plays were not published until 1596-1604) is left to deduce that such a development must have taken place exclusively within the early decades of the seventeenth century, a deduction supported by the hypothesis on 'the fate of the humanist aesthetic' which concludes the volume by Stone.[8]   Yet even if it were accepted that these changes lent themselves to such neat periodization, would it not be surprising if threads of continuity stretching across the two centuries were lacking among successive generations of authors who practised so extensively the imitation and adaptation of earlier models? Indeed, we would maintain that the considerable corpus of tragic drama produced in France between the 1550s and the 1630s[9] offers evidence of a much longer, less abrupt - though certainly very uneven - evolution between Jodelle and Corneille. It offers evidence that, notwithstanding the primacy for the humanist playwright of rhetoric and didacticism, certain of the stock situations and set pieces of Renaissance tragedy, themselves often modelled on or adapted from classical sources, provided models for imitation by later practitioners of the genre. Was it not through the process of being copied, modified and adapted that such models, whose purpose may initially have been purely rhetorical and didactic, began in some instances to acquire a discernible dramatic function, so that gradually, as the result of imitation and experimentation, their potential for dramatic effect was realized and exploited? Was it not in this way, for example, that the stock debates on clemency and rigour in Renaissance tragedy would evolve into the dramatic counsel scene in **Cinna,** or that the conventional messenger's **récit** would be transformed into the fragmented report of Julie and Valère in **Horace**?

It is our contention that this evolution, to which the pages of many little-known and little-talented dramatists bear (often uneloquent!) testimony, not only continues apace in the early decades of the seventeenth century, but can be seen retrospectively to have been prepared, and indeed in some cases to have begun, before the end of the sixteenth. Surprisingly, however, in view of the attention lavished in recent years on other facets of the literature of the baroque period, the detailed history of this evolution still needs chronicling.   The French tragic theatre still awaits an investigation of the type undertaken for English tragedy by Wolfgang Clemen, who sought to show 'how the formal set speech gradually becomes possessed of dramatic life.'[10]   In the meantime, it is in the hope of filling a small part of this large gap that the following study is offered of one type of set piece, the dilemma speech, in tragedies from the Renaissance to the early years of the seventeenth century.

*   *

*

With the notable exceptions of Lancaster, who catalogues many cases of 'psychological struggle' in French drama **after** 1610, and more particularly of Elliott Forsyth, who devotes several pages to its manifestation in plays by Chrestien, Hardy, and the early Corneille, critics have accorded little attention to the emergence and evolution of the 'dilemme tragique'.[11]   Yet moments of inner conflict, of anguished hesitation and urgent choice when a character is torn in a struggle between powerful emotions or ideals, are generally recognized to be a characteristic ingredient of seventeenth-century 'crisis tragedy'.[12]   Corneille observed that 'Les oppositions des sentiments de la nature aux emportements de la passion ou à la sévérité du devoir, forment de puissantes agitations qui sont reçues de l'auditeur avec plaisir';[13]   and his 'grandes pièces' amply illustrate his own resourcefulness and ingenuity in varying the presentation of such 'oppositions'.   In some plays (**Cinna, Polyeucte**), each major protagonist struggles with his own individual dilemma, while in others the major characters all experience a similar conflict, to which they bring either an identical solution (**Le Cid**) or a variety of personal responses (**Horace**).   Their dilemma speeches (most, though not all, of which are monologues) take several forms, from the more passive submission to conflicting impulses to desperate self-exhortation or prayer; and the problem may either be resolved within the speech or appear insoluble. Despite such variations, however, the hallmark of the Cornelian dilemma remains constant: a major character is seized at a crucial moment of urgent choice; his hesitations inspire the sympathy and curiosity of the audience or reader; and their resolution will in most instances have important consequences, not only for the character concerned, but also for the other protagonists and for the outcome of the ensuing action.   The Cornelian dilemma has consequently been considered by Forsyth as having two major functions, 'to establish dramatic tension [...] and to arouse the compassion of the audience for the character concerned';[14]   but it serves additionally, through the opportunity it affords for the examination of motivation, as a catalyst for the **approfondissement psychologique** that is an intrinsic property of French seventeenth-century tragedy.[15]

If the Cornelian tetralogy of dilemma plays marked the beginning of a new, glorious era in French drama, they also constituted, as Forsyth noted, 'the end product of a period of intense dramatic activity' culminating in a new, more dynamic form of tragedy.[16]   Within the narrow context of his own career, Corneille's skilful use of the dilemma may be seen, as that critic has shown, as the 'end product' of renewed experimentation with the theme of inner conflict from 1629 onwards, in several of his early plays.[17]   Within a wider context, however, outside Corneille's career, it may also be viewed as the 'end product' of a development which, as we shall show, began much earlier, and in the course of which the dilemma monologue gradually became invested with an increasingly dramatic role.

*   *

*

Renaissance dramatists can have been no strangers to the theme of inner conflict.   In poetry, a long literary tradition portrayed struggles waging within an individual: 'l'alliance de la haine et de l'amour, le combat du désir et de la crainte, l'oscillation entre le doute et le désespoir',[18] and the opposition between spiritual love and carnal desire, or between reason and passion, had been evoked in sources as diverse as Catullus, Medieval lyricists, and the Petrarchists, sources powerfully conjoined in the **Délie** (1544) of Maurice Scève.[19]   In the theatre, too, moments of hesitation and uncertainty had featured in the two convergent currents of Medieval and Senecan drama, which tended to accentuate respectively choices between moral imperatives and between conflicting passions.[20]

The Medieval morality plays had presented self-division allegorically by using the **Psychomachia** theme of the battle between vices and virtues, with personifications of a wavering character's conflicting impulses disputing possession of his soul.[21]   Vestiges of this treatment would survive into the seventeenth century.   They are found, for example, in the contrastive exhortations that a Fury and an Angel address to a sleeping character in Chrestien des Croix's **Amnon et Thamar** (1608);   and in the prolonged debate, conducted partly in stichomythia, in Montreux's **La Sophonisbe** (1601), in which Gelosses and Misipsa personify the urgings of Massinisse's two incompatible duties to Rome and to his wife.[22]

It was Seneca, however, who provided the concept of the soliloquy in which to express self-doubt and uncertainty.[23] For among the rhetorical set pieces in which his closet tragedies abound, the Latin dramatist had composed introspective monologues of vacillation and deliberation for Andromache, Medea, and Clytemnestra.[24] At some length, these three heroines evoke the balance of irreconcilable pressures acting upon them, and voice their hesitations as they move towards a pressing and painful decision. The last two also mark the climax of their irresolution with images of storms and tides which would later find their way into several French imitations:

> quid, anime, titubas? ora quid lacrimae rigant
> variamque nunc huc ira, nunc illuc amor
> diducit? anceps aestus incertam rapit;
> ut saeva rapidi bella cum venti gerunt
> utrimque fluctus maria discordes agunt
> dubiumque fervet pelagus, haut aliter meum
> cor fluctuatur. ira pietatem fugat
> iramque pietas.   (**Medea**, ll.937-44)

> [...] fluctibus variis agor,
> ut cum hinc profundum ventus, hinc aestus rapit,
> incerta dubitat unda cui cedat malo.
> proinde omisi regimen e manibus meis -
> quocumque me ira, quo dolor, quo spes feret,
> huc ire pergam; fluctibus dedimus ratem.
>   (**Agamemnon**, ll.138-42)

*   *

*

Despite the existence of such models, however, many of the tragedies by major humanist playwrights constitute a barren hunting-ground for the seeker of dilemma speeches. This may perhaps be explained in part by these authors' tendency, noted by Griffiths and attributed to their training in the rhetorical exercise of **prosopopœia**, 'to express a single emotion, a single mood, in one speech'.[25] As Maurice Gras has hinted apropos of Garnier's characters, the expression and examination of each feeling individually and separately precludes their clashing together in a 'conflit intérieur'.[26]

A catalogue of Renaissance tragedies in which the dilemma has no place would include not only La Taille's **Saül le furieux**, a work often praised for its psychological penetration, and the same author's **La Famine, ou les Gabéonites,** a close imitation of Seneca's **Troades** which yet omits any equivalent of Andromache's monologue, but also La Péruse's **Médée**, which, though based mainly on Seneca's version, excludes Medea's hesitations.[27] Nor do Grévin and Jodelle accord much prominence or development to those inner conflicts which implicitly form part of their subjects. In **Didon se sacrifiant,** for example, Jodelle treats an episode from the fourth book of the **Aeneid** which provided ample scope for a dramatist attracted by speeches of vacillation and self-questioning, since Aeneas, on whose decision Dido's fate depended, was placed directly between the conflicting wishes of the gods and of his mistress. Although Jodelle does briefly introduce formulae suggestive of self-division, by employing four lines of antithetical exclamations in one speech by Enée and by using the traditional simile of a bark tossed on the foaming brine in another,[28] both cases immediately follow a display of the Trojan's determination to leave Carthage and accomplish his divinely ordained mission.   Jodelle's lines thus express, not the hesitation which precedes a decision, but the guilt and regret which succeed it. Despite the sensitivity which, in the French Enée, tempers the harshness of 'pius Aeneas', the dramatist faithfully follows Virgil in never allowing his hero to waver in his dutiful resolve to obey the gods and abandon his mistress.

A similar lack of interest in the dilemma is displayed by Grévin.   In Act III of his **César**, inner conflict is but fleetingly evoked when the Emperor responds to the conflicting exhortations, first of his wife, Calpurnie, whose pleas prevail upon him to postpone his visit to the Senate, and then of Décime Brute, who is at hand to reproach him for his cowardice.   Using the Senecan seafaring simile, Grévin summarily expresses César's self-division:

> Je me sens agité, ainsi qu'on voit au vent
> Un navire forcé, que le north va suyvant.
> Madame d'un costé me retient et me prie
> Que j'évite aujourdhuy le hazard de ma vie;
> Brute d'autre costé me propose l'honneur,
> Et je sen dedans moy un magnanime cueur,
> Qui m'empesche de croire aux songes d'une femme.[29]

But it is clear from the last two lines that his decision has already taken shape, and a few lines later (l.794) he is departing for the Senate and inevitable death.   Though César's fate hangs on the decision taken here, his hesitations are but briskly hinted at. The contrast between the brevity of this deliberative monologue, and indeed of the entire scene of persuasion, counter-persuasion, vacillation and decision-making in which it is set, and the lengthy description and discussion of forebodings and dreams which immediately precede it (ll.613-745), furnishes an excellent illustration of the primacy of the Renaissance dramatist's preoccupation with rhetoric and of his corresponding indifference to 'modern dramatic concerns'.

Although such examples lend support to Griffiths's view that 'the Renaissance tragedian [...] is concerned with [...] none of the "inner struggles" so typical of seventeenth-century tragedy',[30] it would be mistaken to assume that sustained dilemma monologues were totally absent from humanist tragedies.   They make interesting appearances in plays by Matthieu and Montchrestien, although these authors contrive nevertheless to employ the dilemma in a manner entirely consonant with the rhetorical priorities of Renaissance dramaturgy.

In Matthieu's long, didactic **Aman** (1589), a summary preceding the third scene of Act III announces that, after Aman has determined to have Mardochée put to death, 'le Poëte [...] descrit le Syndereze d'un homme qui se dechevestre à quelque acte meschant'.[31] There ensues a speech of vacillation extending over more than thirty lines, beginning:

> Il mourra, il mourra, il est force qu'il meure.
> E! non pour s'amender il vaut mieux qu'il demeure,
>   Il est incorrigible, il a l'ame endurcie
> >Le temps de la rigueur des ans ne se soucie:
>   Il fera mutiner contre moy la Province,
> >Un homme seul ne peut honnir l'honneur d'un Prince:
> Je n'ay autre desir que de le veoir défaict
> >Selon la volonté: la loy juge du faict.
>   On peut bien desguiser la volonté secrette,
> >Jamais d'un bon vouloir l'effet on ne rejette:
>   Je ne peux assoupir ma fiere affection
> >L'esprit se doit guider quitte de passion,
>   >Il n'est permis tuer: si est, l'on doit occire
> >Tous les trouble-repos d'un Monarchique Empire.   (pp.75-76)

The remainder of the speech contains the following lines:

> >La vengeance poursuit les actions cruelles,
> >La cruauté poursuit les actions rebelles:
>   >L'homicide ne vit qu'en crainte et en terreur.
> >L'homicide ne craint des hommes la fureur [...]
>   >Le peuple aime le Roy debonnaire et humain,
> >Le peuple craint le Roy sanguinaire et hautain.   (p.76)

It is evident from these extracts - and from a similarly conceived monologue at the end of Act IV of his propaganda tragedy, **La Guisiade**[32] - that Matthieu regarded the clash of conflicting impulses as an opportunity to develop a variation on a favourite Renaissance set piece imitated from Seneca: the **clémence/rigueur** debate (or **agôn**) in stichomythia, in which two characters exchange opposing views in short speeches of identical, or nearly identical, length. Here, unusually, the two voices emanate from within a single character. But the stylized exchange of **sententiae** and of antithetical replies built on word-repetition through which the self-division is expressed is characteristic of the Senecan and Renaissance use of stichomythia.

Exactly the same method of presenting a character's uncertainty is employed (though with greater brevity) by Montchrestien in **La Reine d'Escosse**. In his first two acts, the dramatist gives a sympathetic portrayal of Elizabeth by accentuating her reluctance to accede to demands for Mary's execution. Her first speech shows the English Queen hesitating, unwilling to believe that Mary had plotted against her:

> Mais doy-je tenir vraye une simple apparence,
> Et former un soupçon en certaine creance?
> >Qui croit trop de leger aisément se deçoit:
> >Aussi qui ne croit rien mainte perte en reçoit.
> >Qui s'esmeut à tous vents, montre trop d'inconstance:
> >Aussi la seureté naist de la meffiance.
> >Celuy qui vit ainsi, meurt cent fois sans mourir;
> >Il vaut mieux craindre un peu que la mort encourir.[33]

Here, as in Matthieu's plays, the indecision is conveyed by a stylized 'stichomythic monologue', in which a series of opposing, sententious lines are exchanged by the two discordant inner voices. Composed probably on the eve of the seventeenth century, this variation on a standard set-piece dialogue from the Senecan tradition, while still ostensibly close in spirit to the allegorical personifications of the Medieval moralities, also furnishes a late illustration of the rhetorical orientation of Renaissance dramaturgy.

If these writers' methods of conveying inner conflict may be qualified, like those of their early English counterparts, as mere 'academic pedantry' when judged alongside Seneca's subtler displays of psychological insight,[34] dilemma speeches approximating more closely to those of the Latin dramatist are to be found in several other tragedies published before 1590. Their authors were Pierre de Bousy, Antoine Favre, and - most important of all - Robert Garnier.[35]

*   *

*

It was Ovid, rather than Seneca, who directly inspired the deliberative monologue of over forty lines that Bousy included in his **Méléagre** (1582). In the **Metamorphoses** (VIII, 460-512), Althea's passion to avenge her brothers, slain by her son, was counter-balanced by her maternal affection, so that her eventual decision to burn the brand on which Meleager's life depended was the outcome of a prolonged and anguished inner struggle (presented in both narrative and direct speech) between the conflicting strivings of mother and sister. In common with most other authors who dramatized the story in the sixteenth and early seventeenth centuries - the Italian Gratarolo in his **Altea** (1556), the Englishman William Gager in his neo-Latin **Meleager** (1592), and the Frenchman Jean Boissin de Gallardon in **La Fatalle, ou la Conqueste du sanglier de Calidon** (1618) - Bousy follows Ovid in composing for his Althée a lengthy monologue of vacillation. Passing through numerous **revirements**, his character veers constantly from one decision to its contrary, before resolving finally that her son must die:

Ce Bois Fatalizé que les seurs coupe-trames,
A sa nativité mirent dedans les flames, [...]
C'est luy qui finira et sa vie et mon ire.
  Mais las! que di-je? ou suy-je? encor n'auroy-je pas,
Le cœur de faire aller mon enfant au trespas.
O Bois porte-destin que n'estois-tu en cendre
Quand, fole je couru hors des brasiers te prendre [...]
Toutesfois je fy bien de te tirer dehors,
D'autant qu'il n'avoit fait ceste offense deslors.
Mais aussi fay je bien de luy oster la vie,
Puis qu'il l'a le premier à ses oncles ravie.
  Helas! je ne sçauroy, le maternel amour,
Ne me peut accorder de luy oster le jour.
O freres offensez pardonnez moy de grace!
Le souvenir de vous veut bien que je le face?
Mais ce qu'est une mere à l'endroit de son fils,
M'attendrissant le cœur fait changer mon avis.
  Quoy doncque vivra t'il apres avoir (o crime)
Envoyé l'innocent au Stygien abysme?
Quoy doncque vivra t'il impuny du delict,
D'avoir osé commettre un acte si maudit?
Non, non, il en mourra: La mort est le salaire
De ceux qui comme luy se plaisent à mal faire.
Sus vas-te consumer, Bois fatal, et qu'ainsi
Que tu mourras au feu, puisse-il mourir aussi.
  Que veut dire cela, ô deitez puissantes!
Pourquoy tombe ce Bois hors de mes mains tremblantes?
Las! mon bras que je sen affoiblir peu à peu
N'a pouvoir seulement de le ruer au feu.
O miserable seur! ô malheureuse mere!
Aux freres peu amye, et au fils trop severe!
  Il faut qu'il meure. Non. Mais dieux! auroy-je tort
Si je mettois à mort l'auteur d'une autre mort?
Ouy, Nenny, Ouy, Non auroy ce me semble.
Si auroy, Non auroy: ains droit et tort ensemble,
J'auroy droit de venger mes deux freres occis,
Mais j'auray [sic] tort aussi d'executer mon fils.
Lequel des deux feray-je? Il faut, il faut qu'il meure [...][36]

In less clumsy verses, Favre included a monologue of hesitation and deliberation in his political tragedy, **Les Gordians et Maximins** (1589). In Act II, the elder Gordian weighs his obligation of loyalty and obedience to his prince, Maximin, against his duties to avenge the death of one son, Alexandre, and to support the other, Gordian, in liberating his compatriots from Maximin's tyranny:

Tantost je sens tonner la voix enchanteresse
De mes concitoyens, qui, criarde, me presse
D'accourir au secours, tandis que le malheur
Qui talonne leurs pas d'un marcher prompt, et seur,
Donne encores loisir à mon ame fidelle
De sauver vaillamment ma Cité paternelle:
Tantost, et plus soudain, qu'on ne voit sur la mer
Le pâle nautonier diversement ramer,

> Selon ce que des vents la tempeste orageuse
> Se monstre, ou plus, ou moins, à ses voeux outrageuse,
> Je change mes desseins, je me r'appelle à moy,
> J'accuse le deffaut de ma trop fresle foy:
> Ores je veux vanger le meurtre d'Alexandre,
> Et d'un meurtre nouveau le carnage entreprendre,
> Ores je sens mon cueur plus noble, et genereux,
> De tel acte abhorrir le forfait malheureux:
> L'amour de mon pays, le bien de ma province,
> Le service feal, que je dois à mon Prince
> Bastissent dedans moy contraires fondemens
> D'un combat aveuglé, dont les evenemens
> Vacillent, ebranlez, sur le rond de la boule,
> Qui de noz actions l'incertitude roule:
> Je sens ma volonté prendre double souci,
> Ores vouloir celà, ores vouloir ceci,
> Je pallis, je rougis: Le desir, et la crainte
> Tiennent esgalement de mon ame contrainte
> Les deux extremitez, et ne puis de ce sort
> Decider l'incertain jusqu'au jour de ma mort [...][37]

Though submerged by the sheer quantity of rhetorical set pieces that make up this extraordinarily long play, with its two hundred and thirty-nine pages of political debates and interminable soliloquies, Favre's dilemma provides both a sympathetic insight into the motivation of its speaker and an example of the antithetical style often employed by later authors of dilemma speeches. Like that of Bousy, it also creates temporary uncertainty with regard to the outcome of the dramatic action.

Printed only in single editions in Caen and Chambéry respectively, the tragedies of Bousy and Favre, while notable for providing a foretaste of techniques to be developed by later dramatists, are unlikely to have reached a large readership or to have exerted any substantial influence. Such, however, was not the case with the third author that we have grouped with them, Robert Garnier, the most exalted and prolific of Renaissance tragedians, whose frequently reprinted works would come to rival and supplant Seneca's as models for aspiring playwrights.[38] In Garnier's theatre we may perceive, though curiously it seems to have escaped detection by his commentators,[39] a sustained interest in the dilemma speech and a gradual refinement in its use.

*   *

*

The germ of his more extensively developed dilemmas is already discernible in the closing lines of two of Garnier's earliest tragedies,[40] **Hippolyte** (1573) and **Cornélie** (1574), both of which end with a character debating whether to live or die. Cornélie's simply constructed speech (ll.1909-34) is one less of vacillation than of mere

revirement: sensing that her misfortunes have made her life unbearable, she first opts for death, but then, realizing that her dead would remain unburied, she resolves to live. In a similar situation, Thésée undergoes an additional **revirement**, though his hesitations are but briefly expressed. Having implored the gods in vain to punish him for the death of his son, he urges himself to administer the punishment by taking his own life (ll.2309-50); then he wavers in grief and remorse while debating whether he will suffer more in life or in death:

> Non, tu ne dois mourir: non non tu ne dois pas
> Expier ton forfait par un simple trespas.
> Mais si, tu dois mourir, à fin que tu endures
> Plustost sous les Enfers tes miseres futures.
> Non, tu ne dois mourir: car peut estre estant mort
> Ton beau père Minos excuseroit ton tort,
> Et sans peine et destresse irois de ton offence
> Boire en l'oublieux fleuve une longue oubliance.
> Il vaut donc mieux survivre [...]   (ll.2351-59)

That Garnier invented these lines, which had no precedent in his Senecan source, clearly indicates his early interest in the theme of inner conflict. On the other hand, they occupy only a small section of Thésée's speech, which is a lengthy exercise in **prosopopœia.**   Moreover, Thésée's dilemma, no less than Cornélie's, is of a very primitive type, since it involves a choice of tactics rather than of ideals and impulses. And its impact, like that of Cornélie's speech, is limited by its position as well as its purpose.   For, while giving effective rhetorical expression to these characters' reactions of grief and despair (and, in Thésée's case, remorse), both speeches **follow** the denouement, and the decisions sought can have no effect on the other characters or on the unfolding of the dramatic action.

The subject of **Hippolyte** presented a dramatist with an opportunity, not just of appending a dilemma as a sort of epilogue for a relatively minor character, but rather of situating it in the heart of a major protagonist at a point where the self-division would have serious consequences for the whole development of the action. Such a conflict within the heart of Phèdre would, of course, be central to the treatment of Racine, who considerably magnifies his heroine's sense of guilt. Garnier, too, evokes a struggle within Phèdre between her reason and her passion:

> J'ay tousjours un combat de ces deux adversaires,
> Qui s'entrevont heurtant de puissances contraires.
> Ores cetuy-là gaigne, et ore cetuy-cy,
> Cetuy-cy perd apres, cetuy-là perd aussi:
> Maintenant la raison ha la force plus grande,
> Maintenant la fureur plus forte me commande:
> Mais tousjours à la fin Amour est le vaincueur,
> Qui paisible du camp s'empare de mon cueur.   (ll.735-42)

In its antithetical structure, this speech of self-division, for which once again no model existed in Seneca's **Hippolytus**, foreshadows many later examples. But it lacks the dramatic force of the Cornelian dilemma, because Garnier casts no doubt on the outcome of the conflict. Though the rhetorical patterning may imply the contrary, the adversarial forces are unequal here; for throughout the play, as she admits at the beginning of the speech quoted above (ll.727-34), Phèdre is completely and consistently dominated by her passion. Moreover, that Garnier's principal concern was not subtle psychology and the creation of suspense, but rather rhetorical elaboration, is demonstrated by the manner in which he proceeds to delineate the conflict within Phèdre:

> Ainsi voit-on souvent une nef passagere
> Au milieu de la mer, quand elle se colere,
> Ne pouvoir aborder, tant un contraire vent
> Seigneuriant les flots la bat par le devant.
> Les nochers esperdus ont beau caler les voiles,
> Ont beau courir au mats, le desarmer de toiles,
> Ont beau coucher la rame, et de tout leur effort
> Tâcher malgré le vent de se trainer au port,
> Leur labeur n'y fait rien: la mugissante haleine
> Du Nort qui les repousse, aneantist leur peine.
> La nef court eslancee, ou contre quelque banc,
> Ou contre quelque roc, qui luy brise le flanc.
> Ainsi cette fureur violente s'oppose
> A ce que la raison salutaire propose,
> Et sous ce petit Dieu tyrannise mon cueur.   (ll.743-57)

In this excellent illustration of the Renaissance mode, the seafaring simile is developed at such length that instead of clarifying the psychological battle it usurps the limelight for itself, drawing attention away from the inner drama towards the poetic ornamentation.[41]

Instances of the dilemma increase in frequency in the plays of Garnier's so-called 'second period', which encompasses **La Troade** and **Antigone**. The latter (1580) contains two dilemma speeches, both based on passages in Seneca and both occurring in dialogue rather than in soliloquy. The first, imitated from the **Phoenissae** (ll.369-86), comes in Act II when Jocaste, urged to intervene in the impending battle between her sons, expresses her wavering:

> Pour qui me banderay-je? helas! auquel des deux
> Ma faveur donneray-je, estant la mere d'eux?
> Je ne puis plaire à l'un, sans à l'autre desplaire:
> Faire du bien à l'un, sans à l'autre malfaire,
> Ny souhaiter que l'un ait prospere succez,
> Sans souhaiter aussi que l'autre l'ait mauvais.
>   Tous deux sont mes enfans: mais, bien que je les aime
> D'egale affection, comme mon ame mesme,

> J'incline toutesfois beaucoup plus pour celuy
> Dont la cause est meilleure, et qui a plus d'ennuy. (ll.520-29)

Again, however, this brief inner debate portends little concern for modern dramatic effects. The central issue in this scene, as in Seneca, is not whether Jocaste secretly favours one of her sons, but whether she can act speedily enough to prevent them coming to blows. Her dilemma speech thus constitutes, not a pivotal moment which will give impetus and direction to the action, but the pitiable expression of a mood - that is, an exercise in **prosopopœia** - which actually retards the progression of the action. The second case arrives in Act III, when Jocaste entreats Antigone not to emulate her by committing suicide, but rather to live on and support her father. For Antigone's reply Garnier borrows a dilemma briefly formulated and swiftly resolved in the **Hercules Oetaeus** (ll.1027-30):

> o misera pietas! si mori matrem vetas,
> patri est scelestus; si mori pateris, tamen
> in matre peccas. urget hinc illinc scelus.
> inhibenda tamen est, verum ut eripiam scelus.

but which, in the French play, is inflated to twenty lines (1276-95). Later remembered by Racine,[42] Antigone's dilemma, while resembling those of Cornélie and Thésée in its theme, differs from theirs in its positioning, for Garnier has situated it at a more influential point in the development of his dramatic action.

It is in **La Troade** (1579), however, that we find - again inspired by Seneca - the most extensive and impressive dilemma speech of Garnier's second period. In Act II, faced with Ulysse's threat that, unless Astyanax is delivered to him, he will dismantle Hector's tomb and seize his remains, Andromache views her predicament in terms of an agonizing choice between the living and the dead:

> Hé Dieux, que ferons-nous? mon esprit eslancé
> De deux extremes peurs, chancelle balancé
> Sans sçavoir que resoudre: icy l'enfance chere
> De mons fils se presente, icy les os du pere.
> Las! auquel doy-je entendre? O Dieux des sombres nuits,
> Et vous, grands Dieux du ciel, autheurs de mes ennuis,
> Et vous, Manes d'Hector, saintement je vous jure
> Que rien qu'Hector je n'aime en ceste creature:
> Je l'aime pour luy voir de sa face les traits,
> Et pour ses membres voir des siens les vrais pourtraits.
>   Que je tolere donc? que permettre je puisse
> Qu'on rompe ce tombeau? que lon le demolisse?
> Que sa cendre on respande, et qu'on la jette au vent,
> Ou aux flots de la mer qui ces bords vont lavant?
> Non, qu'il meure plustost. Mais las! t'est-il possible
> Le livrer, pour souffrir une mort si horrible?
> Pourras-tu voir son corps eslancé d'une tour
> Piroüetter en l'air de maint et de maint tour:

> Puis donnant sur un roc d'une cheute cruelle,
> Se moudre, se broyer, s'écraser la cervelle?
>   Ouy, je le souffriray, et pire chose encor,
> Si faire se pouvoit, plustost que voir Hector
> Saquer de son sepulchre, arracher de la biere,
> Et le faire avaler à l'onde mariniere.
>   Mais quoy? cestuy-là vit, cestuy-ci ne vit plus,
> Insensible, impassible, en un tombeau reclus.
> Helas! donc que feray-je en chose si douteuse?
> Au contraire pourquoy branslé-je fluctueuse?
> Ingrate, et doutes-tu lequel des deux tu dois
> Sauver de la fureur du cruel Itaquois?
>   Voici pas ton Hector qui au tombeau te prie?
> Mais voici son enfant qui du mesme lieu crie:
> Tu dois de ton Hector avoir plus de souci,
> Voire, mais cet enfant est mon Hector aussi.
> Or donc, ne les pouvant tous deux garder d'outrage,
> Sauve celuy des deux qu'ils craignent d'avantage.   (ll.939-74)

Ironically, the freedom of choice that Andromache appears to exercise here is illusory, since (as in Seneca) whatever she resolves, Astyanax will be seized, either with her consent or through the sacking of his hiding place.   Nevertheless, Andromache's lengthy wavering at a desperate and poignant moment of decision is significant both for its positioning and the scale of its development - for, while closely following his Senecan source (**Troades**, ll.642-62), Garnier has also expanded upon it.   Moreover, the speech contains many of the formulae - such as the opening allusions to an 'esprit balancé' between 'deux extrêmes', the antithetical structure, and the series of **revirements** - that would become standard in later dilemmas.   In short, the monologue that Garnier composed for Andromache afforded an excellent model for later dramatists interested in exploiting the potential of the dilemma for obtaining those dramatic effects associated with the age of Corneille.

That Garnier was himself aware of, and concerned with, such effects, at least by the second half of his career, is confirmed by one of the plays of his third (and final) period.   The evidence is found, not in **Les Juifves** (1583), which is often singled out for its relatively advanced dramatic technique, but whose depiction of Nabuchodonosor as a totally single-minded avenger permitted no place for self-doubt and hesitation, but rather in his penultimate play, **Bradamante** (1582).   One of the rare sixteenth-century dramas to bear the label of 'tragi-comédie', it was thus differentiated by genre from Garnier's seven other plays.   However, it appeared alongside his tragedies in all of the numerous editions and reissues of his collected works, and it is known to have been read and performed in the seventeenth century.[43] We shall therefore discuss it briefly.

From a few indications provided by Ariosto,[44] Garnier constructs a dilemma monologue which involves an issue of crucial importance to the development of the play, and which is placed at its centre (III.v). Roger has been requested by Léon, to whom he owes his life, to impersonate him in single combat with Bradamante (an excellent swordswoman whom Roger loves and has secretly promised to marry) in order to win her as a wife for Léon. Roger's soliloquy describes the inner turmoil that these circumstances have created, and attempts to resolve his course of action. He begins with an expression of anguished confusion:

> Qui suis-je? où suis-je? où vay-je? ô dure destinee,
> O fatale misere à me nuire obstinee!
> Quel harnois est-ce cy? contre qui l'ay-je pris?
> Quel combat ay-je à faire? Hé Dieu, qu'ay-je entrepris?
> Veillé-je, ou si je dors? sont-ce point des allarmes
> De l'enchanteur Atlant, ou d'Alcine les charmes?   (ll.929-34)

Then a series of antitheses and conceits conveys his paradoxical situation:

> Me voicy desguisé, mais c'est pour me tromper:
> Je porte un coutelas, mais c'est pour m'en frapper:
> J'entre dans le combat pour me vaincre moymesme:
> Le prix de ma victoire est ma despouille mesme.
> Qui veit onc tel malheur? Leon triomphera
> De Roger, et Roger sa victoire acquerra:
> Je suis ore Leon et Roger tout ensemble.
> Chose estrange! un contraire au contraire s'assemble. (ll.935-42)

Regretting that he has not avoided a predicament in which he may cause suffering to both himself and Bradamante (ll.943-58), his first impulse is that, despite his promise, he will not fight (ll.959-64). On the other hand, he is aware of his obligation to Léon: 'Voire mais tu luy est attenu de ta vie' (l.965). However, his debt does not also include Bradamante's life: 'Las! de ma vie, ouy bien, mais non pas de m'amie' (l.966). Nevertheless, it was on Roger's word that Léon had committed himself to the combat, and he cannot therefore go back on his promise (ll.967-70). Thus his provisional conclusion (like Rodrigue's in **Le Cid**) is that he must fight, but that he will allow himself to be killed (ll.971-76). He realizes that this solution is unsatisfactory, however, since not only would he not properly fulfil his promise to Léon (ll.977-78), but Bradamante might also kill herself when she discovered the truth (ll.979-80). He is therefore plunged further into his dilemma. Should he attack her? No, he would be incapable of that (ll.981-84). His final decision is to fight, but merely to defend himself without harming Bradamante (ll.985-86).

Experienced by a major character, developed at length, and placed at a crucial position in the play, this dilemma speech has several of the characteristics of the most memorable seventeenth-century examples.[45] With its series of **revirements** as the hero attempts to come to a vital decision on which the denouement will depend, it not only provides a moment of intense dramatic interest, but at the same time aids the achievement of empathy by enabling the spectator intimately to perceive the feelings and motives of the character involved. It thus reveals that, by the later stages of his career, Garnier could breath powerful dramatic life into a formal set speech for which he had already exhibited a marked attraction in several of his earlier tragedies.

*   *

*

Thus the example of Garnier, whose plays appeared in numerous editions between 1583 and 1618,[46] is likely to have been more influential than has hitherto been acknowledged in popularizing and promoting the dilemma among his successors and emulators.   Also influential, perhaps, was that other paragon of the **derniers Renaissants,** Ronsard, whose third book of **La Franciade** (1572) contained a long evocation (partly imitated from Apollonius of Rhodes) of the hesitations and soul-searching of Clymène.[47]   Whatever its literary antecedents (which, as we have seen, were probably numerous), it is certain that the dilemma enjoyed a veritable vogue in the final years of the sixteenth and early years of the seventeenth centuries. Reflecting the contemporary taste of baroque art and literature for movement, instability, paradox, contrast, and the display of intense emotion,[48] this vogue is evident in the verses of many poets from this period.   To the emotional conflicts cited by Forsyth in lines by Sponde, La Ceppède and d'Aubigné,[49] we may add a similar development of Petrarchan antitheses in an elegy by Philippe Desportes:

> Je ne vous puis haïr quand je vous vois si belle,
> Je ne vous puis aymer vous sçachant infidelle.
> Mes sens sont en debat, mon esprit agité
> Chancele constamment d'un et d'autre costé,
> Et suis si possédé de ma fureur extrême,
> Que je n'ay rien en moy qui s'accorde à moy même.
> Que feray-je à la fin? que veux-je devenir?
> Je ne puis malheureux lâcher ny retenir.[50]

Significantly, these lines, quoted from the 1594 edition of his **Livre premier,** considerably expanded the original version published in editions from 1573 onwards:

> Bien que mille soucis je cache au dedans,
> Animez contre moy de griffes et de dents,
> Exercent pesle-mesle une guerre immortelle,
> Se paissans de mon cœur qui sans fin renouvelle [...][51]

Illustrated here by Desportes's modifications, the contemporary poets' delight in portraying 'cette douloureuse oscillation de la pensée solitaire, ce va-et-vient épuisant de l'âme ballottée entre des émotions contraires',[52] was also shared by several minor and largely neglected dramatists writing in the period between the 1590s and 1610. It is apparent, for example, in Pierre de Nancel's three Biblical tragedies, published in 1607.[53]   In each, as J.S. Street has noted, there appears a lengthy deliberative monologue: 'Hemor hesitates to allow Sichem to marry Dina, Rahab hesitates to betray Jericho [...], and Jahel hesitates to kill her sleeping guest Sisara'.[54]   However, although these dilemma speeches reflect and confirm a general trend in contemporary literature, we would agree with Street that their presence in these overwhelmingly rhetorical and didactic dramas might give 'a misleading impression of the effects Nancel sought by his chosen dramatic technique', for he 'did not seek to derive the plays' substance from the characters' struggles to reach and maintain difficult decisions',[55] and indeed two of the speakers are episodic characters present only in their soliloquy scenes. From the point of view of dramatic technique, more significant examples are to be found in the works of Jean Hays, Nicolas Chrestien des Croix, Jean de Schélandre, Jean Galaut, and Charles Bauter, whose tragedies, as we shall show, collectively constitute an important stage in the evolution of the dilemma speech from a rhetorical set piece to an instrument for achieving dramatic effects.

*   *

*

In **Cammate** (1598), a seven-act revenge tragedy[56] which combines long rhetorical passages with much dramatic movement, Hays depicts in Camma a gentle, tender wife who is transformed into a cruel, calculating widow, thirsting to avenge the murder of her husband by his jealous rival, Sinnoris. Though his heroine is clearly cast in the mould of the Senecan avenger, Hays nuances the stereotyped portrait by providing some insight into her motivation and particularly by revealing, in an important scene of his penultimate act, that her moral scruples and basic humanity have not been completely submerged. It is here that he introduces a monologue of vacillation which was unprecedented in his acknowledged source, Plutarch's **Moralia**, and has drawn little attention from the play's few modern commentators.[57] Having convinced Sinnoris that she will marry him in the Temple of Diana, where she plans to poison him with a 'nectar amoureus', Camma is reflecting on the gullibility of lovers when suddenly she recoils in horror at the thought of her criminal scheme:

> Chetive que je suis, sous quel astre malin
> Ay-je pris ma naissance, helas! de quel venin,
> Quel poison me sera courageus et severe,
> Pour tuer cest Amant, qui m'adore et revere[?]

Quoy? tuer cest Amant, Amour, Amour, Amour,
Abaisse ton bendeau, enlumine ce jour,
Ce jour noircy de mort, de fortune, et d'encombre,
Las? faut-il pauvre Amant, que tu croisses le nombre
Des ames de là bas, que ton cœur amoureus
S'estouffe dans le froid d'un poison rigoureus.
   Cruelle que je suis, ô detestable femme!
O meschante homicide! ô forfait trop infame!   (pp.141-42)

Like Favre's Gordian, Camma links her uncertainty with a general perception of the
instability of human life, and she considers death as a means of escape.   Her
hesitations then continue:

Quoy, tuer cest Amant, mon cœur soyez remis,
>L'on pardonne souvent aus plus fiers ennemis,
>La vengeance ne fut jamais une victoire,
>La vengeance trahit tout l'honneur de la gloire,
>C'est une grand'vertu de sçavoir pardonner,
Encor faut-il, cruel, un poison luy donner,
Plustost tombe sur luy la celeste machine,
Plustost mille couteaus entament sa poitrine,
Plustost les ours sur luy tournent leur cruauté,
Un foudre brouissant tombe du Ciel voûté,
Plustost dessus son chef. O mort trop detestable
>Empoisonner autruy c'est chose miserable.   (p.142)

Her will is weakened by her revulsion, but suddenly there is a **revirement**:

Mais quoy? foible raison, pourquoy t'amollis tu,
D'où vient que mon courage est si tost abatu,
Que je suis ainsi molle, et que la peur me gelle
Dans les veines le sang, dans les os la moüelle.
   O foiblesse trop grande! ô froide affection!
Coüarde volonté[...]   (p.143)

and she gives herself up to her vengeful design.   Although the recourse to **sententiae**
and **adunaton** recalls the rhetorical manner of earlier playwrights, Camma's dilemma
speech serves here quite effectively to cast doubt on the outcome of the plot and to
mitigate the traditional harshness of the avenger's role.

Similar functions are also served by dilemmas introduced into two other revenge
tragedies which, like Hays's play, were published in Rouen by Théodore Reinsart. These
are Chrestien des Croix's **Rosemonde** (1603; republished in 1608 under the title
Alboüin, ou la Vengeance) and **Amnon et Thamar** (1608),[58] works whose dramatic and
psychological qualities have been well elucidated by Elliott Forsyth.[59]

In the first, Rosemonde is transformed much more radically than Camma, from
an affectionate, devoted wife into an unscrupulous avenger who craves her husband's
death and cynically trades her body to further her murderous project. Nevertheless,
Chrestien traces the stages of this transformation in careful detail, allowing his public

to comprehend the causes of the gradual degradation and disintegration of her personality. A crucial moment in this psychological evolution, as well as a pivotal moment in the overall development of the plot, comes in a dilemma monologue in Act IV, in which Rosemonde, having been obliged by her husband, Alboüin, to drink from the skull of her own father, hesitates at length between her need to avenge these cruel indignities and her lingering affection for Alboüin:[60]

> Pourray-je voir tousjours dans la main d'Alboüin,
> Le Crane de mon Pere? ô cœur trop fœminin!
> Coüarde Rosemonde, indigne d'un tel Pere,
> Puis que tu peux souffrir un si grand vitupere.
>   O trop lasche de cœur! trop lente en tes desseins,
> Coupable comme luy d'actes plus inhumains,
> >Car celuy qui permet un crime en sa presence,
> >Comme l'autheur du mal participe à l'ofence.
>   Mais povre femmelette! ou errent tes Esprits?
> Te pleindre de n'avoir encores entrepris,
> Venger ton Pere mort? prendre la hardiesse
> D'ofencer ton Mari qui t'aime et te caresse?
>   Ouy, je mourray plustost que de voir à tous coups,
> Mon Pere contemner par un cruel Epoux,
> Il faut que cette main d'une dague meurtriere,
> Separe de son corps l'ame insolemment fiere.
>   O femme vraiment femme! ô povre! ou songes tu,
> Qu'un desespoir ainsi ton cœur ait combatu?
> Cruelle! pourras tu meurtrir celuy qui t'aime,
> Plus que son cœur, ses yeux, ni que son ame mesme?
> Pourras tu bien ouvrir d'une lame son flanc,
> Et tes foiblettes mains arroser de son sang?
> Dieu détournez de moy ces passions cruelles,
> Qui semblent surjeonner au fonds de mes moüelles.
>   Mais quoy? chetive aussi, pourras-tu voir encor,
> L'os du Chef de ton Pere enchassé dedans l'or,
> Servir à ton Mari d'une ordinaire Coupe,
> Ou il boit quand il est en quelque digne troupe?
>   Je ne le permettray[,] je veux resolument,
> De mon Pere venger la mort absolument[...]
> Il faut, il faut mourir, ou bien venger le tort
> Qu'Alboüin le Tyran fait à mon Pere mort.   (pp.54-56)

A similarly extended monologue, balancing similar sentiments, and placed in a similar position within the play, occurs in **Amnon et Thamar**. In Act IV, following the rape of Thamar by her brother, Chrestien introduces a conflict into the heart of the victim, whose legitimate desire for revenge wrestles with her respect for blood ties. In her lengthy soliloquy (pp.69-71), of which the most important passages have been reproduced by Forsyth,[61] Thamar's thoughts turn initially to revenge. But then she wavers, recalling that the criminal is 'mon sang [...] un autre moy-mesme' and attempting to excuse a crime committed under the tyranny of passion. Finally, there is a **revirement**, as she dismisses her qualms and yields definitively to her longing for punishment and vengeance.

In this second play, the theme of inner conflict is also reinforced by the contest that Chrestien portrays in Amnon between his sexual craving and his sense of honour and shame.   This contest is conveyed, not only by the **Psychomachia**-like debate in which, as we have mentioned, the Fury Mégère and an angel are seen vying to dominate the spirit of the sleeping brother (pp.11-12), but also, both before and after this externalized dilemma, by the anguished outpourings of Amnon himself.   Indeed, his sleep is the physical consequence of the debilitating internal war, expressed in a monologue extending over some 130 lines (pp.5-9), between the 'rage felonne' of his 'ardante flame' and the 'honte mortelle' which holds it in check.   Waking in alarm at the battling voices within him, which have been portrayed allegorically to the spectators, he continues his self-questioning:

> Quelles contraires voix ont touché mes esprits?
> Qui m'ont fait eslancer en dormant mille cris? [...]
> C'est Dieu qui m'advertist; c'est sa sainte parole
> Qui m'ordonne quitter l'amitié qui m'affole [...]
> Helas, je voudrois bien, ô grand Dieu te complaire,
> Mais quoy, pourroy-je bien de l'amour me distraire?
> >Oüy, car Dieu le veut, et l'Eternel ravit
> >Hors du monde celuy qui luy desobeit.
> Faut donc luy obeir; Comment? pourroy-je vivre
> Sans gouster le plaisir de l'amour qui m'enyvre?
> Non, il m'est impossible: Aucun se peut-il voir
> Obliger à l'effet qui passe son pouvoir?
> Non, cela ne peut estre: Et quoy qu'il m'en arrive
> Faut mourir, ou vivant, que par l'amour je vive [...]
> Par force, ou par amour, par art, ou par malice
> Il faut que de Thamar dans ce jour je joüisse.   (pp.12-13)

Thereupon, this last mood imposes itself and silences all his earlier qualms.

A final indication of Chrestien's predilection for the dilemma speech is his invention of one in **Rosemonde** for a secondary character, Pérédée, whom the queen attempts to recruit as an accomplice to her crimes.   His personality follows the same downward path as Rosemonde's, with the dilemma similarly marking the critical point in its evolution, as he is torn between his sense of duty and his fear of death:

> En quel extase suis je! ô Dieu conseillez moy
> Comme je doy sortir d'un si dolent émoy.
>   L'amitié qu'Alboüin estroitement me porte,
> Se presente à mes yeux apres d'une autre sorte,
> Je me sens combatu de la peur du trépas,
> Et que pour m'excuser l'on ne me croie pas,
>   Je ne sçay que resoudre en mon ame affligée
> De deux extrémitez fortement assiegée:
> Comme on voit deux morceaux de fer separément,
> Joindre des deux costez une pierre d'aimant,

De chaque part egaux demeurer en balance,
Ainsi deçà, delà, mon ame ores s'elance.   (pp.77-78)

Thus, although Chrestien's plays still assiduously retain much of the rhetorical and didactic colouring of humanist tragedies, both stand out, as Forsyth has observed, by according 'une place de premier plan aux éléments psychologiques du drame et au débat intérieur qui résulte du conflit de certains sentiments'.[62] And although Chrestien was not, as that critic has claimed, the first French tragedian to exhibit an interest in 'les mouvements contradictoires de l'âme',[63] his sustained use of the dilemma assures him an important place among those who established it as a vehicle for psychological drama.

If the role of Chrestien in promoting the 'débat intérieur' has been well known since Forsyth, no comparable recognition has been accorded to the efforts of Schélandre, Galaut, and Bauter. Of the three, it is Schélandre who, despite his greater notoriety, made perhaps the smallest contribution, since the two dilemma monologues incorporated in his **Tyr et Sidon** (1608) are given to minor characters.[64] Nevertheless, he does situate these speeches at important junctures in the relentless unfurling of the events which, during his first three acts, imperil the happiness of the lovers Belcar and Méliane. One such critical moment occurs in Act II when Eurydice, the Nurse of Méliane's jealous sister, Cassandre, yields to the latter's pleas and promises to serve the cause of her own love for Belcar. After first alluding to the difficulty of her situation (ll.1047-52), Eurydice describes her self-division in a conventional seafaring metaphor:

Que je sens de discours l'un l'autre seduisants!
D'irresolus desirs l'un l'autre destruisants!
Que de flots et de vents dont l'inconstant orage
Submerge ma raison d'un terrible naufrage!   (ll.1053-56)

Then, in the remainder of her speech, she considers whether she should betray Méliane and Belcar or break her promise to Cassandre (ll.1057-64), expressing horror equally at the thought of deceiving the lovers after encouraging their romance, and of abandoning the interests of her 'nourrisson' (ll.1065-76), before she finally concludes in favour of Cassandre (ll.1077-80). The other dilemma monologue is introduced in Act III when, immediately after Eurydice has revealed her plans to release Belcar from prison and unite him, not with Méliane, but with Cassandre, the jailer she has bribed, Thamis, voices his qualms and hesitations (ll.1782-1833). Feeling trapped, he suspects he has been tricked, regrets the inevitable loss of all the honours he had earned, wonders if he will be distrusted by his new masters, and fears the punishment that awaits him if the scheme should fail. Gradually during the course of his speech these doubts are dismissed one by one, until eventually he reconfirms his decision to assist

conflict, and the psychological insight which informs the sympathetic portrayal of the characters. We would therefore concur with Dabney's assessment that 'the author has a clear idea of dramatic struggle and possesses at least the rudiments of the method of psychological analysis of the classical drama'.[70]

The dilemma is also central to the last four acts of Bauter's **La Mort de Roger** (1605; published under the pseudonym of Méliglosse),[71] in which Lancaster has similarly perceived 'a germ of the active and psychological type of tragedy that was to prevail in France a generation later'.[72]   Based on Pescatore's continuation of the **Orlando furioso**, the play has a relatively simple plot: the first three acts prepare the revenge of Ganelon and Alcine against Roger; in Act IV, disguised as his friends, they render his arms inoperative; and in Act V Roger is ambushed and killed. But Bauter manages to produce movement and suspense by exploiting the theme of the hesitations of the enchantress, Alcine, Roger's former mistress, whose desire to punish his infidelity is countered by her continuing love.

Indeed, the dilemma is given an extraordinarily prominent place in this work, and, if Ganelon and Roger are no more than the conventional figures of insensitive avenger and pallid victim, the character of Alcine offers a certain psychological interest. The struggle within her is made apparent from her first appearance in Act II, when, although hoping for revenge and departing with Ganelon in order to 'miner' Roger, she explains that her heart is still occupied by his memory (fols 58v-61v). This dilemma subsequently receives fuller expression in a monologue in Act III (fols 64r-65r). After bemoaning her present unhappiness and recalling her passionate love for Roger, Alcine tries at first to exhort herself to revenge, but is obliged to admit that such urgings do not coincide with her deeper inclinations. She decides, therefore, against espousing Ganelon's cause. But there is a **revirement** as Alcine jealously remembers Roger's devotion to Bradamante. Her deliberation thus ends in irresolution and self-division:

> Helas donc que feray-je en tant d'adversitez?
> Je suis comme un grand pin que les vents irritez
> Escroulent en cent parts, ou comme sur Neptune
> Une nef soubs le train du vent, et de fortune.
> D'oublier mon Roger? mon amour ne le veut,
> De luy faire du tort? mon amitié ne peut.
> De finiir par le temps sa haine, et ma souffrance?
> Ce seroit esperer sans aucune esperance [...]   (fol. 65r)

These words are interrupted by Ganelon, who presses her to act; and though still nurturing the hope that 'Le temps l'amenera, peut estre, à repentance' (fol. 65v), Alcine finally agrees to use her magic against Roger. This decision is not definitive, however, for two scenes later her hesitations are renewed, despite Ganelon's exhortations; and her oscillation is conveyed once again by the traditional seafaring image:

> De cent mille pensers mon esprit agité
> Ne se sçauroit resoudre en ceste extremité,
> La nef n'est sur le dos de l'irrité Neptune
> Des divers accidents du vent et de fortune
> Poussée et agitée en tant tant de façons,
> Que mon esprit se va troublant de passions[.]
> De tuer mon Roger? mon Roger ma chere ame,
> Celuy seul qu'icy bas pour support je reclame?
> Non Gannes, je ne puis, ce seroit m'offencer
> Que vouloir seulement à ceste mort penser; [...]
> Je me turois moy-mesme, et tentant mon bon-heur,
> Helas, j'irois causant mon desastré malheur.   (fol. 68v)

Nevertheless, she eventually submits to Ganelon's political arguments, declaring reluctantly:

> Il faut que ton malheur, ô mon heur, je te trame,
> Il faut, j'y suis contrainte, il convient à ce jour
> Que j'aille desliant des prisons de l'Amour
> Mes esprits enchaisnez, et qu'à fureur ouverte
> J'ailles ores procurer ta ruine et ta perte,
> O Roger mon Roger.   (fol. 69v)

Act IV begins accordingly, with Alcine having used her art to disguise herself and Ganelon as two of Roger's friends. But still she continues to voice her regrets (fols 70v-71r); and her suffering is intensified when they are transported to Rumania to meet Roger, for she can scarcely refrain from throwing herself into his arms. Consequently, Alcine once more hesitates to carry out Ganelon's plan:

> Venue à ce subject, voyant ce beau visage
> J'ay changé maintenant de haine et de courage.
> O Dieu, pourrois-je nuire à ce divin Roger,
> Dont la beauté me vient davantage engager?   (fol. 76r)

Once more Ganelon prevails upon her; and, despite her emotional torment, Alcine begins to use her magic to enchant Roger's weapons.

Bauter has by no means finished with Alcine's suffering, however, for her vacillation is allowed even more extensive expression in Act V. By means of simile and antithesis, the dramatist develops her inner conflict in a long soliloquy:

> Cet amour violant qu'à ce Roger je porte,
> A ce Roy Bulgarin, me poinct en telle sorte,
> Que mon esprit confus ne sçait de quel costé
> Il doit aller cherchant sa douce liberté.
> Ainsi qu'un voyageur qui va par la campagne,
> Que nul homme qui soit ne guide, n'acompagne,
> Trouve un chemin fourchu, il ne sçait quel des deux
> Le prenant le doit rendre en son sejour heureux,

Il demeure craintif, et son ame perdue
Jette de tous costez sa vagabonde veuë
Pour trouver du conseil et avoir quelque frain,
Afin de le conduire, et regir en son train.
Ainsi en mon chemin mille et mille traverses,
Mille desseins nouveaux, mille sentes diverses
Se monstrent maintenant, et si en nulle part,
Où j'aille ores jettant mes yeux et mon regard,
Je ne trouve nul Phare en mon cruel voyage
Dont je pense parer l'effort de mon naufrage.
Ceste desloyauté va mon cœur embrasant,
Sa beauté va mon feu, mon desdain repoussan[t]:
Je m'esgris de fureur contre Roger atteinte,
Je me meurs d'amitié à ce Roger abstrainte:
Mon desdain veut le perdre, et mon fervent amour
Veut que comme mes yeux j'aille gardant son jour.   (fols 79r-79v)

And yet again the dilemma monologue is followed by a scene of persuasion involving Ganelon, after which Alcine finally brings about Roger's death.

La Mort de Roger thus bears at least a superficial resemblance to Marlowe's Doctor Faustus, which has been described as 'in essence a single protracted deliberative soliloquy',[73] since the dramatic interest of Bauter's play is focused almost throughout on the hesitations of Alcine. To achieve this, the author has radically transformed his source-material, and in particular Pescatore's generally unsympathetic presentation of the sorceress.[74] On the other hand, Bauter's somewhat limited conception of his subject deprives his tragedy of the rich psychological texture often obtained in plays based upon the dilemma. Alcine's struggle is a very simple one, essentially a conflict between love and jealousy, with no higher principles or duties involved; and the fact that her faltering is expressed in the same terms throughout, together with the constant recurrence of the formula 'hesitation plus persuasion', induces an effect of monotony and even predictability. Nor is her dilemma enhanced by Bauter's insipid portrayal of the subject of her anguish. Nevertheless, his persistent use of the theme of inner conflict, both in monologues and in conversations, assures La Mort de Roger a niche in the history of the genre as an early example of the 'dilemma play'; and its apparent success, evinced by the publication of further editions in 1613, 1619, and 1620, may indicate that it was familiar to later playwrights.

It was thus Charles Bauter, closely followed by Jean Galaut, who in this period gave fullest expression to a tendency already noted by Forsyth in the plays of Chrestien, and present also in those of Schélandre and Hays. All of these dramatists follow the example of Bousy, Favre, and the later Garnier in giving extended treatment to the dilemma speech. In none of their works is the function of this set speech exclusively or even primarily rhetorical, even though most of these writers (Chrestien in particular, but also Schélandre and Hays) imitate their forerunners in essaying, sometimes laboriously and intemperately, the standard rhetorical exercises of humanist tragedy.   For these 'transitional' works also display an unmistakable interest in modern dramatic effects and psychological motivation, and their authors have learnt to situate their monologues of vacillation and deliberation at points in their plays where both of these interests could be served. Galaut and Bauter go even further, by giving such prominence to the dilemma that it no longer represents simply a **moment** of hesitation: it is prolonged and renewed, it overflows beyond soliloquies into dialogues, and becomes central to the plot mechanics.   These two authors in particular have thus made considerable advances towards the eventual realization and exploitation of the dramatic and psychological potential of a theme which had been transmitted by diverse currents and sources: Petrarch, Ovid, the Medieval moralities, perhaps Ronsard, certainly Garnier, and above all Seneca.   We write 'above all', in spite of the view advanced by Forsyth that, while a tragedy such as **Rosemonde** is clearly Senecan by dint of its set pieces, its didacticism, and its passionate portrayal of revenge, in other aspects of its 'structure interne', such as dramatic movement and psychology, the author 's'est écarté de façon notable du chemin étroit tracé par Sénèque'.[75]   For this surely is to underestimate the importance of another aspect of the rich Senecan legacy - those soliloquies of hestitation and deliberation which offered material for imitation, adaptation, and dramatic exploitation, and which stood at the head of the development which, by 1610, had already established the dilemma as a major ingredient of French dramaturgy.

* *
*

The developments effected by the authors that we have discussed were complemented and reinforced by two of the best tragedies from a more prolific and renowned pen, that of France's first professional playwright, Alexandre Hardy. Although the chronology is uncertain of most of his extant works, which did not appear in print until 1623-28, the best-informed conjectures place several of his tragedies in the early years of the seventeenth century.[76]

For a tragedian whose plays exhibit a strong interest in the creation and depiction of conflict and in psychological motivation, it is ironical that Hardy frequently shuns opportunities afforded by his sources to treat struggles within the heart of an individual.   In **Méléagre** and **Alcméon**, for example, neither his Althée (unlike her namesake in contemporary plays) nor his Alphésibée (based largely on Medea) is allowed the hesitations of their models in Ovid and Seneca, Hardy preferring instead to accentuate the domination and intensity of their unbridled craving for vengeance. Nor in **La Mort d'Achille, Panthée,** or **Coriolan** does he explicitly develop those conflicts suggested by his sources which would have brought patriotism and associated sentiments into battle with honour and humanity for Priam, with amorous passion for Achille, with gratitude for Panthée, and with revenge for Coriolan.[77]   In **Mariamne** and **Didon se sacrifiant,** however, Hardy places the dilemma at the centre of his dramatic action.

In his **Didon se sacrifiant,** which was probably composed before 1609,[78] the **poète à gages** grasped an opportunity that Jodelle had scorned. Like his predecessor, Hardy restricts the subject of his play to that part of Virgil's narrative which dealt with the Trojan's departure from Carthage and its dire consequences for the abandoned queen. But he creates a more dramatically charged situation by beginning at a slightly earlier stage than Jodelle, at a moment of imminent but difficult decision-making **before** Aenée has resolved to set sail. Hardy thereby moulds the Virgilian material into the shape of a crisis tragedy, with the theme of inner conflict promoted to become the starting-point of his drama.   To achieve this, he develops some of the 'vibrant undercurrents of tension' implicit in Virgil's portrayal of Aeneas.[79]   At the same time, the role of the Trojan hero, who in Jodelle's play had been distinctly subordinated to Didon, is expanded by Hardy to the point where he achieves prominence almost equal to that of his unhappy mistress.

Indeed, Hardy's opening lines plunge his reader straight into the inner drama of Aenée. In the first part of his prayer monologue - which is also a modified form of dilemma monologue - a vast oratorical period liberally employing **anaphora** and parallelism amply conveys the intensity of the suffering induced by Aenée's uncertainty, and leads up to his urgent entreaties (to the deities): 'Servez à mon esprit maintenant de conduite' (1.22), and (to Apollo): 'Coule, pere, en mon ame; augure dedans moy, / De soucys devoré, ce que faire je doy' (ll.31-32). The second half of the monologue elaborates on these anxieties, with Aenée weighing the happiness and comfort presently enjoyed by the Trojans in Carthage against the combined attractions and dangers of pursuing the quest for a new Troy (ll.33-50); but he remains painfully irresolute, trapped in his self-division:

> Entre l'obscurité de ce Dedale ombreux:
> Entre le souvenir de nos maux encombreux,
> Et la comparaison de la presente joye,
> Mon esprit agité s'esgare, se fourvoye:
> Chacun d'eux tour à tour me range à son party;
> Je rentre en mesme tems d'où je me voy sorty,
> Semblable au voyageur, qui, la nuit survenuë,
> Rencontre deux chemins, leur addresse inconuë;

De l'un et l'autre pié, il bransle sur tous deux,
Sans qu'aucun il accepte, à l'egal hazardeux.
Ainsi l'infirmité de la nature humaine
Me contraint reclamer vostre main souveraine,
Deffaillant de moy-mesme [...]   (ll.51-63)

This opening soliloquy serves to establish Aenée as a conscientious leader concerned above all with the interests of his subjects.   Indeed, in Hardy's version it is Aenée's sense of patriotic duty, even more than his obligation to the gods, which is subsequently brought into conflict with his loyalty to Didon.

Curiously, however, Hardy curtails Aenée's dilemma before this potentially interesting stage of the battle between conflicting loyalties can be fully exploited. By the end of Act I Aenée's decision has been taken, and thereafter the pressing question is not whether he will depart, but whether before his departure he will justify himself to Didon.   Nevertheless, the dilemma invented by Hardy in his opening lines considerably nuances - and makes more attractive - the personality of his hero; and his **Didon** offers the only example in all the plays that we have discussed of a dilemma monologue placed in the first scene.

The role of the dilemma in **Mariamne** is better known, thanks largely to Forsyth's study of revenge tragedy.[80]   In fact, the play presents two dilemmas - for, like the bribed jailer in **Tyr et Sidon**, Hérode's butler is shown (albeit briefly) 'divisé de pensers' before consenting to transfer his allegiance to Salomé.[81]   But it is the inner struggle of Hérode himself which best illustrates Hardy's mastery of the device.

Hardy introduces Hérode's dilemma in very dramatic fashion.   After placing the king's order for Mariamne's execution at the end of Act III, he suddenly casts the expected denouement into doubt at the beginning of Act IV by causing Hérode to waver and reassess.   However, although presented with the dramatic impact of a **coup de théâtre**, Hérode's monologue of hesitation and deliberation also constitutes the climax of tensions generated and sustained within his heart from the very first act by the searing conflict between love for his wife on the one hand, and a combination of sexual frustration, vindictive spite, and political expediency on the other:

Bourrellé dans l'esprit de passions contraires,
Je ressemble un captif entre deux adversaires,
Un Aigneau que deux Loups terrassent acharnez,
D'une rage de faim cruelle forcenez:
Maintenant cetuy-cy, tantost l'autre l'emporte,
Selon qu'il a donné sa secousse plus forte.
Je sens ne plus ne moins se paistre tour à tour
De mon cœur divisé la vengeance et l'amour:
Le crime m'apparoist d'une femme homicide,
Et d'ailleurs sa beauté divine m'intimide,
M'espouvante, certain que me la separant,

A regret je verray le Soleil m'éclairant,
Qu'apres elle je n'ay chose qui me contente [...]
Bref, que de son salut ma ruine s'éclatte,
Sa perte me conserve, et sa perte me pert.
Que resoudray-je donc en un tel doute offert?
L'absence de ses yeux m'absente de mon ame,
Qui ne vit que des rais de leur jumelle flâme;
Vive, l'impunité son audace accroistra,
Sans fin la trahison en elle renaistra.   (ll.1235-62)

It was probably in Josephus, his main source for the play, that Hardy initially drew inspiration for this monologue. Although the historian scarcely hinted at any hesitation by Herod **after** the sentencing of Mariamne, he did record the king's contradictory reactions on an earlier occasion when his jealousy did battle with his love:

> Il estoit fort fasché voyant le desdaing manifeste de sa femme, contre toute son esperance: et ne pouvoit porter cest ennuy, tant estoit-il espris d'amour: [...] et ne se pouvant tenir en une façon, tantost il estoit transporté d'une affection, tantost d'une autre: tant estoit son esprit esbranlé entre l'amour et la hayne: tellement, que combien qu'il desirast par plusieurs fois punir l'orgueil de sa femme, toutefois l'amitié le retenoit, et empeschoit d'executer ce qu'il avoit entreprins. Or il ne craignoit rien plus, que quand il l'auroit fair mourir, luy mesme ne fust plus griesvement pour celà blessé en son cœur, à cause du regret qu'il auroit d'elle apres sa mort.[82]

Forsyth has pointed out verbal similarities between Hérode's monologue and Pérédée's in **Rosemonde,**[83] and a parallel might also be drawn, at the level of its subject matter and general development, with Alcine's at the end of **La Mort de Roger.**   The conflicting emotions generated by the **odi et amo** theme, common to both Hardy and Bauter, are also expressed in terms remarkably similar to Hérode's in the elegy by Desportes that we have quoted above, and in verses that Desportes's nephew, Mathurin Régnier, published in 1613:

> De contraires efforts mon esprit agité
> Douteux s'en court de l'une à l'autre extremité,
> La rage de la hayne et l'amour me transporte [...]
> Sa beauté me rappelle où son deffaut me chasse;
> Aymant et desdaignant par contraires efforts
> Les façons de l'esprit et les beautez du corps,
> Ainsi je ne puis vivre avec elle et sans elle.[84]

The uncertain date of **Mariamne's** composition discourages vain theorizing about possible imitation. What is clear though is that (apart from the image of the quarry, which in dilemma speeches is unusual) Hardy has developed Hérode's inner struggle in a manner common among poets and dramatists of his time. Nevertheless, in so doing, he creates a potent dramatic impact - by placing the conflict within the heart of an all-powerful character whose decision will affect the lives of others, by positioning it at a crucial moment in the progression of his action, where its resolution will dictate the nature of the denouement, and by using it to bring to a climax an emotional turmoil which had been shown to be potentially explosive throughout the preceding acts. One of the most moving and gripping of early French dilemmas, Hérode's was also the most influential; and its revival in a more modern poetic idiom in Tristan's **La Mariane** would delight theatre-goers during the season of **Le Cid.**

*   *
*

This study makes no claim to comprehensiveness, since it is based on a sample (albeit a large one) of plays of a single (albeit the most important) genre composed between 1550 and 1610. Nevertheless, the evidence that we have assembled reveals that the extended treatment of 'des esprits agitez par des mouvemens contraires', so heartily recommended by the Abbé d'Aubignac,[85] was not an innovation of the age of Richelieu. From sometimes small and sometimes purely rhetorical beginnings, the dilemma had developed to such an extent that by 1610 it had already attached to itself several of the dramatic and psychological functions with which it would be associated from the 1630s onwards.

Its subsequent history between 1610 and 1640 still requires much research, but a few provisional observations may be made. The dilemma will become a commonplace in tragedies published up to 1630,[86] although its sustained treatment occurs infrequently, since these plays tend (with the exception of Théophile's **Pyrame et Thisbé**) to prize spectacle and sensationalism above the subtle nuances of sentiment.[87] These were, in any case, leaner decades for published drama (excepting Hardy's, of course), and for tragedy in particular, which increasingly yielded ground to the newer genres.[88] Brief dilemmas do often find a place in the **romanesque** tragicomedies which supplant tragedy almost completely in the more productive years of 1628-34;[89] but while reflecting a baroque ethos of instability and paradox[90] and allowing the dramatists to display 'des virtuosités de style',[91] the dilemma lacks here the functions that it had assumed in earlier tragedies, for in these tragicomedies the psychology is rudimentary, subordinated to the demands of action-packed plots. It seems, therefore, that the dilemma's fate between 1610 and the early 1630s is one of continuity but also of contraction.

With the relaunching of tragedy in the mid-1630s, the extended dilemma speech will re-emerge, and enjoy such favour in the following years as to become an almost indispensable ingredient of tragic drama.[92]   In this renewal of its vogue, the experience gained by a generation of young dramatists in cultivating dilemmas in the less serious genres may have been a contributory factor, as also perhaps was a rekindling of interest in Seneca. But it should not also be overlooked that Corneille and his contemporaries were familiar not only with 'les exemples de feu Hardy'[93] - whose plays had been kept from publication until almost the end of his long career - but also, in several cases, with some of his less renowned contemporaries whom we have discussed.   Although the circumstances attending the establishment of the 'dilemme tragique' as an outstanding feature of French tragedy in the 'classical' period need fuller investigation, it is likely that a more important debt than has hitherto been realized was owed to the efforts of the now largely unread and forgotten dramatists active in the reign of Henri IV, who had followed the lead of Garnier in experimenting with the theme of a character 'with himself at war'.[94]

NOTES

1.   Gustave Lanson, **Esquisse d'une histoire de la tragédie française**, second edition (Paris, 1927), p.16.

2.   Richard Griffiths, **The Dramatic Technique of Antoine de Montchrestien: Rhetoric and Style in French Renaissance Tragedy** (Oxford, 1970); Donald Stone, Jr, **French Humanist Tragedy: A Reassessment** (Manchester, 1974).

3.   Donald Stone, Jr, 'An Approach to French Renaissance Drama', **Renaissance Drama**, 9 (1966), 279-89 (p.286).

4.   Griffiths, p.37.

5.   Griffiths, p.35.

6.   Griffiths, pp.32-37 and 106-45.

7.   Quoted from Griffiths's chapter heading for pp.62-81; another chapter (pp.82-105) is headed 'Lack of Concern with Non-Literary Matters'.

8.   Stone, **French Humanist Tragedy**, pp.155-204.

9.   A valuable bibliography of these plays appears in Elliott Forsyth, **La Tragédie française de Jodelle à Corneille (1553-1640): le thème de la vengeance** (Paris, 1962), pp.425-72.

10.   Wolfgang Clemen, **English Tragedy Before Shakespeare: The Development of Dramatic Speech**, translated by T.S. Dorsch (London, 1961), p.25.

11.   Henry Carrington Lancaster, **A History of French Dramatic Literature in the Seventeenth Century**, 5 parts in 9 vols (Baltimore and Paris, 1929-42), V, 171, 'Subject Index' under 'struggle, psychological'; Forsyth, **La Tragédie française,** esp. pp.280-82, 341-45, 383-99; and id., 'The Tragic Dilemma in **Horace**', **Australian Journal of French Studies**, 4 (1967), 162-76. A few passing references also appear in Lancaster E. Dabney, **French Dramatic Literature in the Reign of Henri IV** (Austin, Texas, 1952).

12. A useful definition of the 'classical dilemma' is provided by Jacques Scherer, **La Dramaturgie classique en France** (Paris, 1950), pp.66-67.

13. 'Discours de la tragédie', in **Pierre Corneille: Writings on the Theatre**, edited by H.T. Barnwell (Oxford, 1965), p.38.

14. Forsyth, 'The Tragic Dilemma in **Horace**', p.164.

15. In his article 'Rhétorique et dramaturgie: le statut du personnage dans la tragédie classique', **Revue d'histoire du théâtre**, 24 (1972), 223-50, Marc Fumaroli has noted: 'Bien des monologues de tragédies ne sont que des délibérations où les différentes **personae** possibles du même personnage sont tour à tour évoquées; ils [...] font apparaître la pluralité des **personae** incluses comme autant de possibles dans la **dramatis persona** définie au départ [...]. Les conséquences de cette procession des masques à l'intérieur du Masque sont capitales pour comprendre la vitalité du personnage classique [...], et ce que l'on appelle sa psychologie est la vibration même des **personae** possibles qui s'offrent à lui en cours de route, jusqu'à ce qu'il trouve celle qu'appelait sa vocation' (p.241).

16. Forsyth, 'The Tragic Dilemma in **Horace**', p.162.

17. ibid., pp.164-65; and **La Tragédie française**, pp.383-87.

18. Henri Weber, **La Création poétique au XVIe siècle en France de Maurice Scève à Agrippa d'Aubigné** (Paris, 1955; reprinted 1969), p.186.

19. Weber, pp.186-93.

20. See Catherine Belsey, 'Senecan Vacillation and Elizabethan Deliberation: Influence or Confluence?', **Renaissance Drama**, new series, 6 (1973), 65-88. Belsey suggests that in English drama 'Seneca's influence worked in conjunction with the morality heritage to transform the dispute between vices and virtues into the deliberation of a single mind' (p.75).

21. Belsey, p.67; cf. Grace Frank, **The Medieval French Drama** (Oxford, 1954; reprinted 1972), p.155.

22. Nicolas Chrestien des Croix, **Tragédie d'Amnon et Thamar** (Rouen, Théodore Reinsart, 1608), pp.11-12; and Nicolas de Montreux, **La Sophonisbe**, edited by Donald Stone, Jr (Geneva, 1976), ll.1277-1676. Unless otherwise indicated, dates appearing within parentheses in this essay are those of a play's first publication.

23. Belsey, p.67.

24. **Troades**, ll.642-62; **Medea**, ll.895-971; **Agamemnon**, ll.108-24 and 131-44.

25. Griffiths, p.81.

26. Maurice Gras, **Robert Garnier, son art et sa méthode** (Geneva, 1965), p.97.

27. Jean de La Péruse, **La Médée**, edited by James A. Coleman (Exeter, 1985), pp.35-58 offers a detailed study of the play's sources.

28. Etienne Jodelle, **OEuvres complètes**, edited by Enea Balmas, 2 vols (Paris, 1965-68), II, 175 and 193.

29. Jacques Grévin, **César**, edited by Ellen S. Ginsberg (Geneva, 1971), ll.779-85. This editor has shown (p.145, note 104) that the Senecan image was probably borrowed from Muret's neo-Latin **Julius Caesar**.

30. Griffiths, p.75.

31. Pierre Matthieu, **Aman, seconde tragédie** (Lyons, Benoist Rigaud, 1589), p.71. In quotations from Matthieu and other authors subsequently cited, we follow

modern editorial practice in regard to 'i' and 'j', 'u' and 'v', and standard printers' abbreviations.

32.   **Troisiesme édition de La Guisiade** (Lyons, Jacques Roussin, 1589), pp.82-83. A few lines from this monologue are quoted by Forsyth, **La Tragédie française,** p.194.

33.   Antoine de Montchrestien, **La Reine d'Escosse,** edited by A. Maynor Hardee (Milan, 1975), ll.57-64. As this edition shows (p.71), the lines quoted did not change substantially between the 1601 and 1604 editions.

34.   Clemen, p.81.

35.   Among these dramatists, we do not include Jean Edouard du Monin, author of the tragedy **Orbecc-Oronte** (published in **Le Phœnix de Jan Edouard du Monin** (Paris, Guillaume Bichon, 1585), fols 73r-127r). A.T. Gable has written, in his review essay 'Tragic Lament and Tragic Action', **Journal of European Studies,** 3 (1973), 59-69, that the 'heroine is significantly given [...] a dilemma, absent from the Italian model: "Orbecc parlant en soy mesme", not unlike the "syndareze" of Pierre Matthieu's **La Guisiade'** (p.63). But the monologue in question (Act V, fols 122v-123r), which ends with Orbecche frenziedly stabbing her father to death, is less a dilemma speech than a prayer for divine assistance in exacting her revenge.

36.   Pierre de Bousy, **Méléagre, tragédie françoise** (Caen, Pierre le Chandelier, 1582) fols 18r-19r. In his later **Méléagre** (1641), Benserade would go much further than previous dramatists, by introducing Althée's mixture of motherly and sisterly devotion from the very first act and expanding her dilemma to provide the central theme of his play.

37.   Antoine Favre, **Les Gordians et Maximins, ou l'Ambition, œuvre tragique** (Chambéry, Claude Pomar, 1589), fols 20r-20v.

38.   See Raymond Lebègue, 'Succès et influence de Robert Garnier', in his **Etudes sur le théâtre français,** 2 vols (Paris, 1977-78), I, 220-52.

39.   Except for a few brief, undeveloped remarks by Marie-Madeleine Mouflard (**Robert Garnier, 1545-1590,** 3 vols (La Ferté-Bernard and La Roche-sur-Yon, 1961-64), II, 77-78) and Maurice Gras (pp.90 and 92).

40.   We assume that Garnier's plays were written in their order of publication. Mouflard's attempt to establish a new chronology for his works (I, 329-47) is not entirely convincing (see Gillian Jondorf, **Robert Garnier and the Themes of Political Tragedy in the Sixteenth Century** (Cambridge, 1969), pp.28-30). All references to Garnier's plays are to his **OEuvres complètes,** edited by Raymond Lebègue, 4 vols (Paris, 1949-74).

41.   A similar case occurs in Montchrestien's **La Cartaginoise,** where, within a long dream **récit,** Sophonisbe's brief reference to the uncertainty she experienced during her nightmare occasions an equally extended treatment of the familiar seafaring simile (**Les Tragédies de Montchrestien,** edited by L. Petit de Julleville (Paris, 1891), Act I, p.122).

42.   **La Thébaïde,** V.i. Racine replaces Edipe with Hémon, making the subject of Antigone's **stances** a conflict between family loyalty and amorous passion.

43.   See Alexandre Cioranescu, **L'Arioste en France des origines à la fin du XVIIIe siècle,** 2 vols (Paris, 1939), I, 315-17.

44.   **Orlando furioso,** Canto XLV, Stanzas 56-60 and 87-90.

45.   Emile Faguet, **La Tragédie française au XVIe siècle (1550-1600)** (Paris, 1883;

reprinted 1912), pp.232-34, has compared this monologue with Rodrigue's **stances** in **Le Cid.**

46. Editions are listed by Mouflard, II, 472-73, and Forsyth, **La Tragédie française,** pp.437-39.

47. Ronsard, **La Franciade,** Book III, ll.885-1060, in **OEuvres complètes,** edited by Paul Laumonnier and others, 20 vols (Paris, 1914-75), XVI, 214-22.

48. See especially Jean Rousset, **La Littérature de l'âge baroque en France: Circé et le Paon** (Paris, 1954).

49. Forsyth, 'The Tragic Dilemma in **Horace',** p.163, and note 2 on pp.163-64. See also Abraham de Vermeil's sonnet 'Je chante et pleure' (1600), quoted by Henri Lafay, **La Poésie française du premier XVIIe siècle (1598-1630): esquisse pour un tableau** (Paris, 1975), p.224.

50. Philippe Desportes, **Elégies,** edited by Victor E. Graham (Geneva and Paris, 1961), p.87, ll.115-22.

51. ibid., p.85, variants.

52. Weber, p.188 (on Scève).

53. Pierre de Nancel, **Le Théâtre sacré: Dina, ou le Ravissement; Josué, ou le Sac de Jéricho; Debora, ou la Délivrance** (Paris, Claude Morel, 1607).

54. J.S. Street, **French Sacred Drama from Bèze to Corneille: Dramatic Forms and their Purposes in the Early Modern Theatre** (Cambridge, 1983), p.124. The speeches occur in **Dina,** Act III, pp.36-40; **Josué,** Act II, pp.105-09; and **Debora,** Act V, pp.81-85.

55. Street, p.124.

56. Jean Hays, **Cammate tragédie,** in **Les Premières Pensées** (Rouen, Théodore Reinsart, 1598), pp.49-158.

57. Dabney, pp.135-38; Forsyth, **La Tragédie française,** pp.263-64.

58. Both plays are quoted here in the 1608 editions, published together under the title **Les Tragédies de N. Chrestien des Croix** (Rouen, Théodore Reinsart, 1608).

59. **La Tragédie française,** pp.267-89.

60. In his less 'advanced' **Alboin** (1610), Claude Billard avoids tracing any transformation in Rosemonde's character by causing her to hate Alboin throughout. The dilemma that he invents for her servant, Elycie (Act II), resembles the least dramatic cases in Garnier's theatre, since she debates whether or not to end her life.

61. **La Tragédie française,** pp.284-86.

62. ibid., p.289.

63. ibid.

64. We omit from our discussion (**pace** Scherer, p.68) Méliane's prolonged wavering over whether it is her brother or her lover who has the stronger claim to her grief (**Tyr et Sidon, ou les Funestes Amours de Belcar et Méliane,** edited by Joseph W. Barker (Paris, 1975), ll.1317-34), since these lines are concerned, not with what she should do, but with how she should feel. A similarly conceived speech appears in Act III of Montchrestien's **Les Lacènes** (**Tragédies,** pp.176-77).

65. Jean Galaut, **Phalante,** in **Recueil de divers poemes et chans royaux** (Toulouse, Colombiez, 1611), pp.73-147. It has been conjectured - ingeniously, but

unconvincingly - by Albert W. Osborn, **Sir Philip Sidney en France** (Paris, 1932), pp.126-30, that **Phalante** was neither composed by Galaut nor imitated from the **Arcadia,** but that it was a slightly modified version of Antoine du Verdier's lost tragedy **Philoxène** (Lyons, 1567), which in turn was the source of Sidney's episode.

66.   H.C. Lancaster, 'Sidney, Galaut, La Calprenède: An Early Instance of the Influence of English Literature upon French', **Modern Language Notes,** 42 (1927), 71-77 (p.76). The relevant passages of La Calprenède's play are found in I.iii and, more particularly, II.iii.

67.   In Sidney's novel, the tale of Amphiarus (= Phalante) and Philoxenus is told exclusively from the point of view of Helen, who is the narrator **(The Countess of Pembroke's Arcadia,** edited by Albert Feuillerat (Cambridge, 1922), Book I, Chapter 11).

68.   Dabney appears to share this view, remarking somewhat bizarrely that 'Phalante is also in love with Hélène, although his language makes it difficult to discern' (p.244, note 28).

69.   Sidney, p.71. There is no precedent, however, in the English novel for the dilemma expressed in Hélène's monologue.

70.   Dabney, p.245. He also comments: 'The psychological insight and sense of dramatic conflict are more clearly marked than in almost any other play of the time' (p.243, note 28).

71.   In **La Rodomontade, Mort de Roger, tragédies** (Paris, Clovis Eve, 1605), fols 51r-86v.

72.   Lancaster, **History,** I, i, 23.

73.   Belsey, p.86.

74.   See **La Suite de Roland furieux,** translated by Gabriel Chappuys (Lyons, Barthélemy Honorati, 1583). Here, Alcine's reluctance and regrets occur after her arrival in Bulgaria (Discours XXXIX) and after Roger's death (Discours XL). Both in these passages and earlier, she is repeatedly presented as 'la meschante Alcine', 'la cruelle Magicienne', and even '[l']ennemi expresse de tous les Chrestiens', and at one point she declares to Ganes (= Ganelon): 'j'ay plus grand desir de vengeance que vous' (Discours XXXVII, p.362). We cannot therefore agree with Cioranescu's judgement of **La Mort de Roger** that 'les péripéties répètent fidèlement les aventures imaginées par Pescatore; on s'est donc trompé en en attribuant le mérite à Bauter' (I, 323).

75.   Forsyth, **La Tragédie française,** p.278; cf. his comment that 'Bauter a réussi à se libérer presque complètement - tout au moins en ce qui concerne la psychologie [...] et la conduite de l'action - de la tradition purement sénéquienne' (p.314).

76.   Eugène Rigal, **Alexandre Hardy et le théâtre français à la fin du XVIe et au commencement du XVIIe siècle** (Paris, 1889), pp.73-82; Lancaster, **History,** I, i, 42-45; and S. Wilma Deierkauf-Holsboer, **Vie d'Alexandre Hardy, poète du roi, 1572-1632** (Paris, 1972), pp.146-57.

77.   In **La Mort d'Achille,** it is not Achille himself but Nestor who evokes the hero's divided state of mind (ll.201-06 and 267-69). The dilemma formula appears briefly in Coriolan, too (ll.301-03); but, unlike the eponymous hero of Chevreau's later **Coriolan** (1638), whose soul-searching would be extended over two whole acts (III and IV), Hardy's character hesitates, not between revenge and patriotism, but merely over which **tactics** will most effectively achieve his revenge. All references to Hardy's works are to his **Théâtre,** edited by E.

Stengel, 5 vols (Marburg and Paris, 1883-84).

78   Monique White-Boissier, 'La **Didon se sacrifiant** d'Alexandre Hardy et la **Dido, sive amor insanus** de Jacques Tabouret', **XVIIe Siècle**, 32 (1980), 307-12.

79.   R.G. Austin, in the Introduction to his edition of **P. Vergili Maronis Aeneidos, liber quartus** (Oxford, 1955), p.xv.

80.   Forsyth, **La Tragédie française**, pp.341-45, 386-87, 411-12.

81.   II.ii, especially ll.681-84.

82.   **Jewish Antiquities**, Book XV, Chapter 11; quoted from **Histoire de Fl. Josephe, sacrificateur hebrieu**, translated by François Bourgoing, revised by D. Gilb. Genebrard, 2 vols (Paris, Pierre l'Huillier, 1578), I, 493-94.

83.   Forsyth, **La Tragédie française**, pp.343-44.

84.   'Elégie zélotipique', ll.91-93 and 118-21, in **OEuvres complètes de Mathurin Régnier**, edited by Gabriel Raibaud (Paris, 1958), pp.222-23.

85.   **La Pratique du théâtre**, edited by Pierre Martino (Algiers and Paris, 1927), p.306.

86.   For example, Mainfray invented moral qualms for Hercule (I.ii) in his **Tragédie des forces incomparables et amours du grand Hercules** (1616), an adaptation of the **Hercules Oetaeus**; and in the anonymous **Tragédie françoise d'un More cruel** (c. 1613), even the eponymous villain is made to hesitate (Act III) before slaying his innocent child victims.

87.   Two examples: in Boissin de Gallardon's **La Fatalle** (1618), Althée's vacillation (Act III) is considerably less prolonged than in Bousy's earlier, less spectacular tragedy; and in an anonymous **Mort de Roger** of 1624, the author greatly reduces the importance of Alcine's dilemma, allowing her to waver only briefly (Act III) in her determination to punish Roger, and devoting much of his play to the spectacle of the seige of Paris by the Turks. Lancaster, **History**, I, i, 158, notes that between 1619 and 1624 'psychological struggles almost disappear'.

88.   See Lancaster, **History**, I, ii, 760-61; and Scherer, pp.457-59.

89.   Scherer, pp.66-72; Lancaster refers to numerous examples in his 'Subject Index', under 'psychological struggle' (**History**, V, 171).

90.   Rousset, pp.51-78.

91.   Scherer, p.70.

92.   For example, in La Caze's **Cammane** (1641; performed 1639), an updated version of Hays's play, dilemma monologues are created almost mechanically for the main characters (I.vi, II.viii, IV.i); and in Monléon's **Le Thyeste** (1638), even Atrée is allowed one (I.iii)! See also, on the role of the dilemma in the classical period, June Moravcevich, 'Racine and the Classical Monologue', **Kentucky Romance Quarterly**, 19 (1972), 159-82.

93.   Corneille, 'Examen' to **Mélite**, in **Writings on the Theatre**, p.80.

94.   Shakespeare, **Julius Caesar**, I.ii (of Brutus).

THREE

Towards a New Realism:
The Contemporary Staging of Jean Mairet's
Les Galanteries du duc d'Ossone
Philip Tomlinson

During the past fifteen years, Jean Mairet's contribution to the development of French dramatic literature between 1625 and 1642, arguably one of the most exciting periods in the whole history of French drama and certainly a period of rapid expansion and change, has been the subject of quite intense academic interest. Scholarly bibliographical work and a study on the dating of the plays, alongside new editions of a number of them, have been enhanced by a series of books, articles and theses, covering themes, forms, dramaturgy and socio-intellectual biography, the whole forming an impressive corpus of scholarship devoted to the author of **La Sophonisbe.**[1] Rarely, however, has this research dealt systematically with Mairet's work as theatre, treating the plays in the main as literary artefacts subject to the traditional types of critical analysis.

At the same time as attention paid to Mairet has increased, there has developed a huge body of knowledge concerning seventeenth-century French stagecraft and theatre history,[2] which makes it possible to reverse the usual priorities and consider the contemporary dramatic text as background to theatre practice. This essay sets out, therefore, partially to redress the balance of Mairet studies by applying some of the discoveries of the scholarship of stagecraft to one of his plays, the choice having fallen upon the most interesting of his works in terms of the history of seventeenth-century stage practice, inasmuch as **Les Galanteries du duc d'Ossonne** offers us a unique and very individual snapshot of changes in methods of staging occurring during this highly creative and mobile period of theatre history. In particular, the study of **Les Galanteries** from this angle allows us to focus less on the question of how it was done, which has naturally been the major concern of most previous theatre scholarship, than on the aesthetic effects of how it was done.[3]

Mairet's only comedy, first produced at the Jeu de Paume de la Fontaine by the company of Charles Le Noir and Montdory during the Carnaval of 1633,[4] **Les Galanteries** has long been considered avant-garde in the realism of its exploitation of space and of its representation of movement.[5]   The company is better known as the Théâtre du Marais, but it could only have assumed that title on moving into the Marais theatre, which did not occur until 1634, the year after Mairet's comedy was first performed.[6] The custom of calling the company the Théâtre du Marais has led Jacques Scherer to put forward the ill-founded theory that Mairet's realistic approach to the representation of place is due to the Marais stage (where he supposes the play to have been given its first performance), in that its dimensions, so Scherer claims, were broader than those of the Hôtel de Bourgogne, where all Mairet's earlier plays had been performed.[7] It may well be the case that **Les Galanteries** was staged at the Marais, once the company was installed there, but if, in writing his play, Mairet intended it for Montdory's company and he did have a particular stage in mind, then this could only have been that of the Jeu de Paume de la Fontaine, the precise dimensions and features of which are unknown to us.

I have argued elsewhere that Mairet probably had the idea for a comedy on the subject of the Duc d'Ossonne whilst still in the service of Montmorency, and that he may well have brought an outline or even the first three acts with him when he came under the patronage of the Comte de Belin in the latter half of 1632.[8] It would seem doubtful, then, that he should be thinking, at least in the initial stages of composition, of a particular stage, even if from the outset he had Montdory's company in mind. Indeed, as I shall attempt to show, Mairet seems to have designed the play, contrary to the view of Scherer and Dotoli, specifically to suit the narrow tennis-court stage.[9]

Despite the claims made for realism, based uniquely on the text since we know nothing of the original staging, there has been much divergent interpretation and factual imprecision concerning the potential transformation of the text into concrete reality. For instance, Dotoli claims that Mairet gives 'des allusions précises sur les différents lieux' and that he manages to 'débrouiller clairement au spectateur et au lecteur les complexes mouvements des acteurs'.[10] But the alleged clarity and precision must be seriously doubted if so enlightened a reader as Scherer can state on so fundamental a point as the number of places represented by the set that 'quatre maisons' are required,[11] when in fact, as we shall see and as Dotoli affirms,[12] no more than three are called for. The doubt increases if, on a more detailed but no less important point, Dotoli can believe that the door to Flavie's house, on the upper level of which most of the action takes place, is positioned on the facade, fully visible to the audience (see below, Figure 1), thus making a nonsense of the supposedly surprise reappearance of Paulin in Act V, scene vi, as well as creating a number of incoherent visual distractions through inopportune entrances and exits via the door elsewhere in the play.

In Act I, scene v, for example, Paulin arrives at the house of his sister, Flavie, wishing to speak with his wife, Emilie. The previous scene consists of an important monologue delivered from the interior of the house by Emilie and broken off at the arrival of Paulin ('Je l'entends venir', l.283). With the door on the facade, the audience's attention would be distracted from Emilie's words by the visual appearance of Paulin, crossing the stage, opening the door and entering the house. Similarly, in Act IV, scene xii, the audience would witness the arrival at the door of a page, whilst meant to be listening to Emilie and Flavie conversing in an upper-floor room. The servant, Stephanille, would be seen opening the door, presumably enquiring what the page's business is, listening to his response, and perhaps showing him in, only for her to interrupt the upper-floor conversation with what by now would be a perfectly obvious piece of information: 'Un Page du Duc vous demande là-bas' (l.1408). After delivering his message to Flavie, the no doubt blushing actor would then be seen leaving the house, whilst Emilie soliloquizes upstairs, revealing in an important plot development her plan to outwit her sister-in-law. This would again constitute an intolerable, possibly ludicrous, distraction from the action of the play even for a seventeenth-century audience, more tolerant than we of such implausibility. And equally problematic, assuming continuity between scenes, could be Stephanille's instruction to Camille in Act V, scene ii, delivered from an upper-floor window, to wait for her to open the door to him 'sur la porte' (l.1539).

On this evidence at least, the text seems far from clear and precise; and though such matters may be of little significance to the reader of a dramatic text, anxious only to be able to follow the action in the mind's eye, they become of paramount importance when attempting to transform that text, as Le Noir and Montdory must have done, into the physical reality of a theatrical performance. It would seem to be useful therefore to attempt in the first instance to clarify the **mise en scène** required by the text, at least in so far as a reconstitution is possible through close analysis of it, and in the second instance to relate this to what is known of the practical capability in 1633 of meeting these requirements, in the hope that a more judicious evaluation of the degree of innovation involved here may emerge. In what sense can one attribute to the author of **Les Galanteries** 'una sorta di mania scenografica', and does the 'sens du moment de la représentation' allegedly possessed by Mairet consist of more or less than has hitherto been maintained?[13]

To attempt a reconstitution of the staging through a scene-by-scene analysis, a method successfully adopted and adapted for Théophile's **Pyrame et Thisbé**,

Durval's **Agarite** and Rotrou's **L'Hypocondriaque,**[14] would, however, in the case of **Les Galanteries,** prove difficult and possibly tedious in the sheer amount of purely physical description required. Moreover, the starting point provided for the Hôtel de Bourgogne productions by the drawings of Mahelot is lacking here. A more profitable approach may be, therefore, to divide the subject of staging into a number of problem areas of special interest in **Les Galanteries,** so that a more concentrated treatment of each, ranging simultaneously across all five acts of the comedy, can be made. This method will have the advantage, first of obviating the necessity to justify the suggested staging of early scenes by constant reference to, and lengthy explanation of, constraints imposed by the requirements of later scenes, and secondly of allowing the more specific problems of individual scenes to be considered against the background of a more complete visualization of the play as a whole. The problem areas singled out from **Les Galanteries** are: the set and the places represented (**scène simultanée** or **scène successive**);   Flavie's house; communications within the house; communications between house and street, including the question of the **tapisseries** and the upper-level stage; and finally, lighting.

THE SET AND PLACES REPRESENTED

The action of **Les Galanteries** takes place in the following locations:

(a)	the palace of the Duke	(I.i–ii);
(b)	the house of Flavie	(I.iii–v; part of II.ii; II.iii; most of II.iv; III.i; most of III. ii and III.iii; IV.v–xiv; V.v–viii);
(c)	the street outside Flavie's house	(part of II.i; most of II.ii; part of II.iii and II.iv; part of III.i and III.iii; III.iv–v; IV.iii–iv; V.i–iv);
(d)	the house (?) of Camille	(IV.i–ii)

Scherer is not strictly accurate in claiming that 'la totalité des actes III et V se passent chez Flavie', nor in believing that Emilie's house, which he supposes to be the location of Act I, scene iii, is part of the set.[15] The text shows quite clearly that for this scene and the remaining two scenes of Act I Emilie is in the house of her sister-in-law, Flavie: Emilie's husband, Paulin, informs the Duke in scene ii that, on leaving the palace, he is going immediately 'icy près au logis de ma sœur' (l.126); he arrives there in scene v and duly finds his wife.

It is also clear that the Duke's palace and Camille's residence are required for only four scenes, all expository,[16] out of a total of thirty-six, the others all taking place inside or just outside Flavie's house, a space which is itself subdivided into a number of rooms. As Scherer has rightly pointed out,[17] it would be merely a logical extension of the dramaturgic significance of Flavie's house if the **décorateur**, rather than sharing the stage space equally between the various localities of the action in the manner of Mahelot, were to give the majority of it to this one location, thereby focusing the spectator's attention (and, scenographically speaking, inverting the social order, in that a bourgeois residence would visually dominate a ducal palace). Moreover, as well as the quantity of action taking place within Flavie's house, the nature of that action - frequent movement from room to room, up to five actors present within a single room (for example, in Act V, scene viii), one of the rooms containing a bed, which is used and has enough space around it to move in freely - demands that the major portion of the stage space be allotted to it. It would seem, therefore, that in his ground-plan sketch Dotoli (see below, Figure 1) allocates a disproportionate amount of space to the residences of the Duke and Camille.

Indeed, so redundant do these residences become that one wonders if the **décorateur** would trouble to depict them by means of three-dimensional compartments, contenting himself instead perhaps with a simple, and suitably painted, flat placed immediately before the downstage wings, and in front of which the actors would sit or stand when meant to be in either of these two abodes.

This calls into question the assumption maintained up to this point that the staging is a version of the **décor multiple** or **scène simultanée**, with all the places in which the action occurs visible on stage simultaneously and continuously, as in Dotoli's sketch. The textual evidence in support of this view, which is also shared by Scherer,[18] is quite strong. We learn, for example, that Flavie's house stands at a 'Carrefour dont elle fait le coin' (1.495) and that it is only a short distance from the Duke's palace, as is evidenced by Paulin's already quoted line (126), to which the 'C'est tout contre' of the next line adds further proof. Moreover, it is later suggested that Paulin can make his escape from Flavie's house 'par dessus la muraille, / Dans le jardin du Duc' (V.vii, 11.1748-49). Such textual suggestions of proximity lead logically to the conclusion that the two houses stand at the same **carrefour,** and from this it follows naturally that at least for reasons of dramaturgy Camille's house should form a third side of the junction, even though in this case there appear to be no clear textual indications of proximity to it.

Dotoli maintains, however, that the text does provide clear evidence of the proximity of Camille's house. He argues that, since time to be lost between Acts II and III is almost nil and since Emilie is already beneath the window by the beginning of the third scene of Act III, we have to suppose such proximity.[19] But this presupposes that there is chronological continuity between scenes ii and iii, which is not necessarily the case. Moreover, not for the last time in this play, the dramatic fiction clashes here with the scenic reality.

In Act II, scene iv, Emilie arranges with the Duke that the latter will occupy her place in bed next to her sister-in-law, Flavie, whilst she, disguised as a man, escapes Flavie's surveillance to visit her wounded lover, Camille. Flavie eavesdrops on the conversation and, on hearing Emilie mention Camille by name, is exultant to learn the secret of Emilie's scheming (l.678). Seeking further assurance (ll.679-80), she watches Emilie and the Duke descend into the street by means of a silk ladder, and notes the direction in which Emilie sets off, thus acquiring the desired confirmation:

> L'Enigme est expliqué, le chemin qu'elle a pris
> M'arreste au premier sens que j'en avois compris.
> Ma sœur ayme Camille [...]   (ll.688-90)

Emilie's disguise (which would seem unnecessary if Camille's house were merely across the street) and these additional elements of the narrative suggest that there is, on the fictional level, some distance between the two locations, a distance which may be contradicted by their proximity in the physical reality of the stage. Indeed, one wonders where precisely the actress would go at this point.

Meanwhile, the Duke re-enters after dismissing his men and duly takes his place in bed beside Flavie, who thereupon reveals in a feigned dream her passion for him (III.ii). The Duke is delighted to discover that Flavie is not the decrepit old hag Emilie had promised him, but an attractive young woman, prepared to allow him to remain on her bed, though 'dessus la couverture' (l.874) and with the command 'n'entreprenez rien' (l.879) ringing in his ears. At this point, according to the stage direction, the couple disappear behind 'les deux toiles', which are drawn across, leaving the audience and reader free to imagine what happens next. This moment, described by Scherer as 'l'un des plus osés parmi les scènes de ce genre que présentent quelques autres comédies du XVIIe siècle',[20] has caused most readers to imagine the worst and provoked many scandalized comments. But whether the couple 'do' or 'don't' seems to depend on the amount of fictional time which elapses between the end of this scene and the beginning of the next, which features the return of Emilie. She speaks twelve lines, before the Duke appears to help her climb back into the house. If no fictional time elapses and the events are continuous, then the greeting which the Duke addresses to Emilie is full of rich comic irony borne of frustration : 'Ah! Madame vrayment vous demeurez beaucoup' (l.893). But if the Duke's remark is straightforwardly intended and those who have imagined the worst are correct (as they very probably are given the general immorality of the piece), then one is obliged to suppose that some fictional time elapses between the scenes. For, unless the Duke and Flavie are the swiftest of performers, twelve lines plus the time taken to draw the **toiles** and for the actress to make her entrance are surely not sufficient for mutually satisfying completion of the sexual act. And Dotoli's argument, according to which the dramatic fiction itself suggests close proximity between the houses of Flavie and Camille, collapses.

Whatever the case may be, it is certain that a number of other elements here exert upon the likely multiple disposition an enormous strain. First, in Act II, scene ii, the Duke, approaching Flavie's house in the hope of at least catching a glimpse of his beloved Emilie, behaves as if the place were unfamiliar to him:

> Allons donc, en tout cas j'auray cét avantage,
> Que de voir sa maison, ne pouvant davantage.
> Si j'ay bien recogneu je n'en suis guere loin.
> Voicy le Carrefour dont elle fait le coin.
> C'est elle asseurément, j'apperçoy la fontaine,
> Que j'ay prise en plain jour pour enseigne certaine.
> Le balcon, les barreaux, le cul de lampe aussi:
> Enfin plus j'en suis prez, plus j'en suis esclaircy. (II.492-99)

It seems quite implausible, despite the darkness, that the Duke should have any difficulty in recognizing the **carrefour** at which his own palace stands, especially since (as we shall see) he has perhaps only recently emerged from it. And secondly, it seems important to stress that, at least in respect of Flavie's house, the major compartment, there is a significant departure from the traditional way in which compartments were used. Rather than the actor emerging from the compartment and thereby defining the open part of the stage space, as in Mahelot's staging, here all the indoor action, with the possible exception of the small number of scenes taking place in the Duke's and Camille's residences, occurs necessarily **within** the compartment. It would not be surprising to learn, therefore, that the original staging consisted of a fascinating mixture of the old conventionality and a kind of new realism, typical of the restoration of the comic genre in the 1630s, the former corresponding to the traditional use made of compartments representing the houses of the Duke and Camille and the latter to the complete practicability demanded of the compartment representing Flavie's house.

In general, throughout the play the old and the new stand in a state of tension with each other. This tension is already manifest in the dramatist's apparent desire to place the Duke's palace very near to Flavie's house and yet at the same time distant from it to the extent that the Duke is unsure of his whereabouts on approaching it. Mairet shows an awareness of the scenic proximity of the two places, but is not concerned to adjust his dramatic narrative accordingly (an amorous after-dark escapade, the anticipated pleasure sharpened by a sense of danger and of the unknown).[21] The dramatic fiction clashes, therefore, once again with the concrete reality of the stage.

Furthermore, inasmuch as one compartment, dramaturgically speaking at least, completely dominates the other two, and inasmuch as the latter quickly become redundant, one senses that they are almost literally being forced off stage; the temptation to dispense with the old convention and to introduce the technique of the **scène successive** is palpably present, and would undoubtedly be yielded to in a more modern production of the play. Indeed, given the frequent use of **tapisseries** to reveal the interior of Flavie's house, the temptation to employ another kind of **changement à vue** - by striking at the appropriate moment a cloth or **ferme** representing the little-used houses - must have been acutely felt also by the contemporary **décorateur**.[22]

But, in particular, one scene does perhaps illustrate an attempt to fuse the old with the new or, rather, scenographically symbolizes the transition from the one to the other. In the first scene of Act II, a dialogue between the Duke and his friend, Almedor, we are told that Flavie's house is 'à vingt pas d'icy' (1.450), though the precise location of 'icy' has given rise to some confusion. Dotoli supposes that it refers to the Duke's palace,[23] but it is certain that by the end of the scene the two men are in the street, since Almedor expresses his concern at leaving the Duke alone in a public place, where he may fall prey to the whims of a drunk or a madman.[24] Scherer claims that in the course of this scene the two men are expected to 'simuler une vingtaine de pas pour donner l'impression qu'ils ont parcouru le chemin, à la vérité fort bref, qui sépare le palais du Duc de la maison de Flavie', a 'travelling' procedure he compares to Jouvet's technique for the opening scene of Jules Romains's **Knock**.[25] Apparently changing his mind since editing the play, Dotoli then proposes the same solution in **Il cerchio aperto** (p. 173), quoting the same comparison. This is perhaps without realizing that Scherer, too, seems to have changed his mind, since in his earlier **Dramaturgie classique** (p. 179) it was in the next scene, rather than in scene i, that the Duke, alone, moved the twenty paces separating him from Flavie's house.

In truth, Almedor's exit line in scene i, which consists of the wish that the Duke's 'beau voyage' be favoured by 'Amour' (1.477), may well imply that the 'voyage' has yet to be undertaken; but this would be to neglect the evidence of the Duke's lines in scene ii: 'Je ne sçay quoy de doux[...]/ Me force d'achever le voyage entrepris' (ll.489-91). This surely indicates that the journey had begun earlier and that it is now to be completed, the movement recommencing during the next few lines (already quoted).

It would seem plausible, then, that scene i should begin in or before the scenery representing the Duke's palace, from which the actors would then distance themselves by a few paces in order that by the end of the scene they should be seen to be in the street, with the final approach to Flavie's house being completed by the Duke alone in scene ii. It is perhaps significant that, in the early part of this sequence (at the Duke's palace), textual references to location are totally lacking and that they increase steadily over the later part of the sequence (in the street), until they culminate in the descriptive detail lavished on the architectural features of Flavie's house. Mairet literally moves his actors and his audience's eye from the old conventional compartment to the detailed realism of the new, fully practicable scenery. The old is literally being left behind, abandoned as unreal, in favour of the very concrete reality of the new. It is perhaps no accident that the new reality is also in the eyes of the dramatist's hero the potential pleasure dome:

> Cest aymable logis à son premier aspect
> M'emplit tout de desir, de crainte et de respect.
> A le voir seulement ma passion redouble,
> Je sens quelque transport qui me plaist et me trouble.
> Ses effets sont pour moy les signes evidens
> De la divinité qui regne là dedans.   (ll.502-07)

This whole sequence seems, therefore, to constitute as telling a commentary as one could wish on the inadequacy of Mahelot's staging, as seen by a dramatist soon to be writing exclusively, if not already doing so, for the new, rival company.

FLAVIE'S HOUSE

Most of the action of the comedy takes place on the upper floor of Flavie's house, but the precise configuration of this space and the number of fully practicable rooms it contains are less easy to determine than Dotoli's sketch would lead one to believe. Equally problematic are the precise locations within the house of a number of scenes. Up to the end of Act III, it is clear that a bedroom for Flavie and a connecting **cabinet** are required. It is not until the fourteenth scene of Act IV that we learn that there is a second bedroom, which also connects with the cabinet:

> Vous aurez cette chambre et ce lict que voilà,
> Pour moy je passeray dans celle de delà.
> Ainsi ce cabinet fait pour l'une et pour l'autre
> Un passage secret de ma chambre à la vostre.   (ll.1484-87)

But what are the precise implications of Flavie's remarks for the **décor** and the dramaturgy, and do they necessarily mean that this second bedroom is to be represented as part of the set?

Dotoli and Scherer both assume the visible presence on stage of the second bedroom, the former going so far as to relate this late reference to it to the location of early scenes.[26] For instance, he situates Emilie's monologue in Act I, scene iv, in her bedroom, even though we know that until Act IV, scene xiv, Emilie is not allocated a room separate from that of Flavie. Paulin explicitly orders (in I.v, ll.315-26) that during his enforced absence his wife should share the same bed as Flavie, so that the latter may keep close watch over her and thus prevent any night-time assignations.

Nor is there any reason to suppose that in Act I the location of scene iv should be different from that of scene iii, a conversation between Emilie and Flavie, which Dotoli situates in the cabinet. Since it is Flavie, and not Emilie, who exits with an 'Adieu donc' (l.171) at the end of the third scene, why would Emilie suddenly move into a different room to deliver her monologue? Scenes, iii, iv and v of Act I must therefore take place in the same room, which could be either Flavie's bedroom or the cabinet, always assuming that the set depicts merely the upper-floor and not the ground-floor rooms.[27]

The argument that Emilie has not yet been granted a room of her own also precludes initial agreement with Dotoli that Emilie's interview with her father, Basile (IV.v), and her subsequent monologue (IV.vi) take place in her bedroom. Again, unless a ground-floor room could be revealed by suitable movement of the **toiles** (or cloths), which presumably reach ground level, the cabinet may seem to be the appropriate place,[28] with the scene possibly switching at the beginning of scene vii and for the remainder of the act to Flavie's bedroom, the two cloths being opened and closed at the relevant moments despite the absence of stage directions concerning operation of the cloths in the last two acts.[29]

If a second bedroom does form part of the set, it would then be a potentially redundant space, scenographically speaking, at least until Flavie expresses her quoted desire for privacy at the end of Act IV. Even then it may be no more than a question of the actress pointing to it. It becomes potentially a matter of using this space only in Act V, scene v, at which point its use causes problems of a quite different order. The cloth covering the cabinet and on which is depicted the facade of the house must be in the open position at this stage, in order that the action within may be witnessed by the spectators. What, then, are actors who enter one bedroom supposed to do in full view of the audience, whilst the action of the play is going on in the other or in the cabinet, as would be the case at various times in scenes v and vi? For more than four fifths of the play there is no indispensible need for a second bedroom to be represented stage left of the cabinet and, when it may possibly be used, its objective presence on stage may create severe problems of plausibility.[30]

Two solutions seem possible. The first consists of using the cloths in a more subtle and intricate way than indicated by either the dialogue or the stage directions. It would mean that up to and including Act V, scene v, the stage-left cloth covering both the cabinet and the second bedroom would be drawn open at the appropriate moments only so far as to reveal the cabinet, and that it would be drawn fully open to reveal the second bedroom only at the beginning of scene vi, where we have the stage direction: 'Icy Emilie paroist dans sa chambre, prestant l'oreille à la cloison de celle de Flavie, où le Duc et elle sont'. Apart from occasional brief appearances by some actors in the cabinet, the remainder of the play would then take place in the second bedroom, with the stage-right cloth, covering Flavie's bedroom, remaining closed and with the actors making their final exit in the direction of Flavie's room, where a warm fire and a feast await them. The disadvantage of this solution is that, whereas the manipulation of the cloths in Acts II and III is made explicit by clear and comprehensive stage directions, what is here in essence a very technical and special manoeuvre is unsupported by textual evidence and passes without authorial intervention. It also entails the allocation of a not inconsiderable amount of valuable stage space to a little-used room.

The second solution is based on a close analysis of Flavie's already quoted remarks concerning the apportioning of bedrooms in Act IV. Though absolute certainty as to the location of this scene is ruled out by the vagueness of the demonstrative adjectives ('cette chambre et ce lict que voilà', but also 'ce cabinet'), it seems probable, as was suggested above, that in view of the likely switch to Flavie's bedroom at scene vii, all subsequent scenes of Act IV should be played in Flavie's bedroom. 'Cette chambre et ce lict que voilà' would then refer to the room in which the two women are currently conversing, whilst 'ce cabinet' would be 'over there', next to them. Flavie's 'Pour moy je passeray dans celle de delà' would then imply that she intends to use henceforth the bedroom 'beyond', the 'far' bedroom, on the other side of the cabinet, giving up her own room for Emilie's use. The advantage of this solution is first that it reflects very accurately the aesthetics of metamorphosis and change at the heart of the piece, the change of space allocated to the characters corresponding to their willingness to change affections and partners, and secondly that it eliminates entirely the need to represent on stage a second bedroom stage left of the cabinet. Instead, one merely has to imagine the presence of this room in the wings, access to it being gained by a door on the (stage-)left-hand side of the cabinet corresponding to the entrance to what was formerly Flavie's room on the (stage-)right-hand side.

An analysis, based on this hypothesis, of the staging of the relevant scenes of Act V will help prove its practical feasibility. When the Duke climbs into the cabinet in scene iv, the cloth presumably being drawn open at this point, Flavie would enter from the left and, mistaking him for Camille, lead him into her new bedroom in the wings. Emilie would then appear in scene vi, after the opening of the stage-right cloth (also not indicated), in what used to be Flavie's room.[31] During this scene she enters the cabinet: 'Emilie passe avec le flambeau de sa chambre par le cabinet'.[32] There, to her surprise, she finds an embarrassed Camille. They return to her room: 'Repassons dans ma chambre' (l.1580). She calls for Flavie, 'qui est dans sa chambre avec le Duc' (stage direction after l.1605). Flavie then pronounces the following line (1608): 'Que veut ma sœur? sans doute elle a treuvé mon homme'. It is easy to imagine that the line is delivered as she passes through the cabinet on her way to Emilie's room. Once there, she is handed an incriminating letter by Emilie (l.1610). She then returns via the cabinet to her own room, promising to bring a reply (l.1612), which she does almost immediately in the form of the Duke: '[Elle] ameine le Duc' (stage direction after l.1615). Her lines: 'Marchez donc, Stephanille, avec vostre lumiere; / Monsieur, que pour ce coup je passe la premiere' (ll.1616-17) could again be delivered in the cabinet, before she resumes her speech once they have entered Emilie's room (ll.1618-21).

After initial expressions of surprise and recrimination, the scene of joyful pardon for mutual infidelities is interrupted by the servant, Stephanille, who announces the arrival of Paulin, Emilie's jealous husband, at the main door of the house (l.1691). Flavie suggests that, whilst there is no harm in her partner, the Duke, remaining, Emilie's partner, Camille, will have to leave 'par la mesme porte / Que mon frere entrera' (ll.1701-02), though she presumably means at different times and in a manner which avoids discovery. The Duke, however, proposes that both he and Camille should exit in order to carry out a plan he has conceived and which he divulges by whisper to Flavie and Camille only (ll.1702-04), after which Flavie commands: 'Suivez-moy donc'(l.1706).[33] But where do they go?   Or, more precisely, which exit do they take, since they are later said to be in the street, Flavie returning to announce to an alarmed Paulin: 'Camille est là bas dans la rue'(l.1744), whereupon we hear Camille shouting threats from 'derriere le Theatre avec grand bruit' (stage direction after l.1744, realized in l.1745)?   They obviously cannot leave by the door at which Paulin is waiting, and descending into the street via the ladder and running off into the wings seems very clumsy, given that three characters are involved. Moreover, how, if this were the case, would Flavie effect her return? Alternatively, if she were merely to help the men onto the ladder from the cabinet, where would she go while Paulin and Emilie converse in the bedroom (ll.1721-40), before she interrupts them at line 1741?

It is here that an exit into an imagined off-stage bedroom would be particularly useful. It would eliminate the problem of Flavie's re-entrance and the actors would automatically find themselves 'derriere le Theatre'. From there they could quite easily simulate the noise of breaking down the door, an effect called for by lines 1747 and 1753, and convincingly enough for Flavie to complete the Duke's scheme by persuading the gullible Paulin of the presence of his arch-enemy just outside the house. Having seen the actors exit into what for them is a bedroom, the spectators do not need to be persuaded likewise. They can now enjoy the fact of being made party to the ruse, laughing at the comic spectacle of Paulin's total suspension of disbelief in respect of the simulation.

Paulin, in need of a quick escape, accepts Flavie's suggestion that this can best be achieved 'par dessus la muraille, / Dans le jardin du Duc' (ll.1748-49). He makes a hasty exit accompanied by Flavie and his equally alarmed companion, Fabrice. But how? They cannot leave by the main door to the house for the same reason as Camille earlier. The only exit now available is via the ladder into the street, but this time there is little reason to object to the procedure despite the absence of stage directions, since it presents the actors with the opportunity for some facile visual comedy. The spectacle of a half-dressed Paulin, who had returned to Emilie eager to satisfy his sexual urges, and of his panic-stricken servant, Fabrice, scrambling down a ladder and over a wall (which would presumably be represented on stage, probably as part of the Duke's palace) would be irresistible to Mairet's contemporaries, who would be reminded of the farces they so much enjoyed at the Hôtel de Bourgogne. But what becomes of Flavie? Certainly the text demands that she, too, exit at this point, since she reappears on stage - 'Arrivant là dessus' (stage direction after l.1781) - during the course of scene viii.   In all probability she should also climb down the ladder into the street, then help the men over the wall, exiting thereafter into the wings and returning to the house via a backstage entrance. It is important to underline here that none of these problems of exits and entrances during this sequence would be solved by the representation on stage of the second bedroom.

Meanwhile, the Duke and Camille would have emerged from the wings, stage left, at the beginning of scene viii to rejoin Emilie in her bedroom, stage right.[34] With the return of Flavie, the company is complete and they are now free to celebrate the success of their ruse. Stephanille, 'revenant' (stage direction to l.1794), announces that 'tout est prest, / Un bon feu vous attend' (ll.1794-95), and on Flavie's invitation (l.1796) they repair to her bedroom, which would mean that in this **mise en scène** all the actors would, as is fitting at the end of a play, exit into the wings, rather than into an on-stage bedroom hidden by a cloth.

There is nothing therefore in the text which renders impossible such a conception of the staging. Indeed, in many instances it lends scenographic coherence and realistic plausibility to the incomplete and sometimes confusing visualization which the textual references and stage directions would otherwise allow.[35]

In further support of this second solution one can point to the relatively detailed visualization made possible in respect of the first bedroom as compared with the complete absence of any descriptive features for the second. Mairet tells us by a series of textual allusions that the first bedroom contains a practicable bed fitted with 'des rideaux [...] en broderie' (l.561) and a 'couverture' (l.874), that it is furnished with a 'fort bonne chaise' (l.863), which can be made more comfortable with 'un carreau de velours' (l.865), that access to it is available via a number of doors (l.807), secured by 'de fort bons aix et de fort bons verrous' (l.808), that a number of props such as candles, torches, scissors, papers and letters are readily accessible from it, and that, if one assumes that Emilie does take up occupation of the room for Act V, it also boasts a **garderobe** large enough for an actress to undress in (ll.1728-31). Mairet applies the same descriptive realism to the visible parts of the interior of the house as was noted in respect of the exterior. That only the first bedroom is the object of such realistic treatment - note also 'cette chambre et ce lict' as compared with the vague and empty 'celle de delà' - is a sure sign that the second bedroom has no on-stage, visual reality. As with the set and places represented, only the most dramaturgically and scenographically significant elements are done the honour of realism, this notion providing once more, this time in respect of the interior scenes, the key to an understanding of the staging.

It is partly in the dramatist's insistence on the realism and practicability of the **décor** that his stage directions, sometimes infuriatingly inadequate and sometimes superfluous to the modern mind, begin to make sense. The inadequacy stems from the traditional conception of the dramatist's status as a man of letters rather than a man of the theatre. Instructions to actors and stage designers are simply not literature and are to be avoided as destructive of illusion, as d'Aubignac was soon to argue in **La Pratique du théâtre**, insisting that all indications of staging should be included in the dialogue.[36] And indeed such did become the general practice. But the superfluousness often stems, as John Golder has convincingly shown in respect of Corneille's early comedies,[37] from the dramatist's need to stress that the action be confined within the compartment, rather than brought out from it into the no man's land of the open stage, as was the practice with the **décor multiple** system. The repetition of the stage direction concerning Emilie's move into the cabinet referred to above would be a case in point, since Camille's line: 'On vient ouvrir la porte; ô Dieu! c'est Emilie' (1.1577) and Emilie's response: 'Ho, ho, mon Cavalier; que faictes-vous icy?' (1.1578) are sufficient in themselves to make the movement and location of the actors perfectly clear. The same could be said of the stage direction and ensuing lines (quoted below) earlier in the same scene, where Emilie listens at the wall of her room to the conversation next door. What is particularly noticeable is that the stage directions relating to the location of the action multiply rapidly after the transition from the old type of staging (Act I and the first scene of Act II) to the new, that is once the action becomes focused on the centre of realism, Flavie's house. Significantly too, in Act IV, the stage directions disappear completely for the first six scenes, which can be said in the main to conform to the old convention, the action taking place in the more indeterminate spaces of the street and Camille's residence (hence the difficulty experienced earlier in locating scenes v and vi, Emilie's interview with her father and her subsequent monologue), but they reappear in abundance once the action moves clearly into the interior of the house from scene vii onwards. In Act V a similar pattern can be observed: no stage directions for the street scenes (i-iii), but frequent interventions to direct the location and movement of actors from the moment the Duke climbs the ladder to enter the cabinet at the end of scene iv.

If, then, Mairet writes: 'Comme il est entré la toile se tire qui represente une faciade de maison, et le dedans du cabinet paroist' (after 1.555), rather than: 'La toile se tire qui représente une façade de maison, et le cabinet paraît', it is in order to direct the actor to play the scene within the compartment. Similar notes of insistence on realistic practicability can be detected in 'Flavie paroist sur son lict' (after 1.621), or 'Elle escoute à la porte du cabinet' (after 1.624), or 'Le Duc sort par la fenestre' (after 1.947), rather than 'Le Duc sort' or nothing at all. And if Mairet adds 'Il revient' immediately after the Duke has said to himself: 'Retourne au cabinet reprendre le flambeau'(1.784), it is to ensure that the actor should not make some symbolic gesture, which might be necessary were he in the no man's land of the open stage, but that he actually move to the cabinet and return with a torch.

The real, therefore, requires authorial intervention or textual reference; the symbolic is self-explanatory. Mairet's alleged 'mania scenografica' applies merely to those sequences of the comedy corresponding to the new realism.[38]

But the new realism is neither a pure nor yet a perfected technique, and nothing illustrates better the malaise of the dramatist of the 1630s, trapped between his conflicting roles of (traditional) man of letters and (progressive) man of the theatre, than the clash - already noted in respect of the places represented - between narrative idealism and scenic reality at the beginning of Act V, scene vi, a clash created precisely by the disposition of the interior of Flavie's house. It is here, it will be recalled, that Emilie 'paroist dans sa chambre, prestant l'oreille à la cloison de celle de Flavie, où le Duc et elle sont', the stage direction being rendered superfluous by her first lines of this scene:

> Plus j'approche du mur mon aureille attentive,
> Plus le trouble s'esleve en mon ame craintive.
> Dieu! que la voix du Duc se discerne aisément,
> Quoy que ma sœur et luy parlent confusément.   (ll.1568-71)

This is the first indication in the play that the two bedrooms should be envisaged as adjoining, separated only by a dividing wall. It is an idea much easier to accept on a narrative, rather than a scenic, level, since it conflicts somewhat with the image created by the rest of the play of two bedrooms separated (and connected) by an intervening cabinet. For, even if the rooms are envisaged as adjoining only in the upstage end, behind the cabinet, as in Dotoli's sketch, the actress would have to disappear from view in any non-symbolic attempt - which is what the stage direction and the text seem to demand - to listen through a dividing wall. Moreover, with a frontal view of the stage and cabinet (to which, as we shall see, there is a rear entrance, presumably from an imagined stairwell), the audience would have great difficulty in seeing the two bedrooms as adjoining. Nor is the problem solved if only one bedroom is represented on stage, as in my hypothesis. It may be partially eased, however, if the cabinet is seen as being 'built into' the second (off-stage?) bedroom only, rather than protruding equally into both (see below, Figure 2), but it has to be said that Mairet is testing both stage designer and plausibility to their limits here. It would be a case of asking designer and actress simply to make the best of it.

If Mairet suddenly wishes at this juncture that the cabinet should disappear, it is not because the wall he seeks to introduce is part of a consistent scenographic vision, but because it fulfils his need to motivate Emilie's move from the bedroom into the cabinet, where, to the audience's delight and her duplicitous lover's confusion, she may unexpectedly bump into Camille, who is hiding therein. Mairet contrives therefore for her to imagine, on listening to the muffled conversation through the wall, that scandalous revelations are being made about her infidelity, causing her to run via the cabinet to the Duke and her sister-in-law in order to beg forgiveness (ll.1572-76). The aesthetic dynamics of movement, fundamental to the comedy's structure and meaning,[39] have simply prevailed here over the need to visualize scenic reality in concrete terms. Space is expected to adapt itself, as if it were infinitely flexible, to the movement both of dramatic narrative and of actors.

But this is perhaps less a question of an imperfect visualization or of a lack of practical sense on the author's part than of an idealized conception of space, whereby it has the capacity to shed its fixed and immutable reality to become infinitely fluid and transformable, as unstable and shifting as the characters moving within it. Symptomatic of such a conception is the accelerating tendency of the space that is the interior of Flavie's house to subdivide into ever smaller portions. The second bedroom is added, or rather subtracted, as late as the very end of Act IV, and Act V sees Emilie's bedroom suddenly become reduced by a practicable **garderobe** and the cabinet 'contracted' by 'une enfonseure / Dont la tapisserie oste la veue à tous' (ll.1535-36). It is here that Stephanille hides Camille (V.ii), until he emerges into the cabinet (V.v), worried at having heard a man (the Duke) climb into the cabinet and then being led to a bedroom. It is no accident that this increasing fragmentation of space accompanies an intensification of movement both in terms of physical displacement of actors and emotional disposition of characters.

The multiplication and constant metamorphosis of space is perhaps the inevitable result of scenography which attempts to apply naively and literally a realistic technique to a reality perceived as unstable. As evidenced by **Les Galanteries**, the demands of baroque dramaturgy for literalness in the staging, whereby the staging itself becomes a metaphor expressing a vision of the world, are reminiscent of those of modern **nouveau théâtre**, in particular of Ionesco. It is in this sense that the term avant-garde finds its most appropriate application to Mairet. That most of these demands seem realizable, as this analysis has shown, within the narrow confines of the **jeu de paume** stage, for which this play seems specifically to have been designed (and in which the constriction intensifies the animation of movement, rather as it does for flies in a bottle), and also within the technical limitations of contemporary theatre companies, is no small testimony to Mairet's skill as a progressive and practical writer for the theatre.

the Duke's recommendation to Emilie : 'Ne vous hastez pas, l'eschelle est mal-aysée, / Tenez ferme à cette heure, empoignez la croisée' (II.894-95) required no more than a merely symbolic simulation of the gesture?

There can be no sure answers, but the text does provide a suggestion that the window and balcony were intended to be of a free-standing, solid construction placed before the cloth. The stage direction after line 895: 'Icy la toile du cabinet se tire, et paroissent tous deux' implies at least that, having reached the top of the ladder, the actors disappear behind the cloth **before** it is opened, but clearer evidence is perhaps contained in the next stage direction at the beginning of Act III, scene iv: 'Le Duc sort par la fenestre, et la toile se ferme'. If the **toile**-facade is closed after the Duke has stepped through the window, then it is perhaps because the facade and the window are meant to be seen as separate elements. If the window and balcony were merely painted on the cloth, then, with the cloth removed, there would simply be no window to step through and the stage direction - which belongs to that sequence of stage directions already singled out as stressing the requirement for practicability - would be absurd. It would seem, therefore, that one has to imagine one section of the exterior reality remaining permanently in place after the opening of the cloth for interior scenes played in the cabinet. This is perhaps why Mairet, conscious of the possible visual obstruction, specifies through the Duke that the window can be opened (I.510) and has Camille refer to 'la fenestre et la petite grille' (I.1522). Such awareness of the staging problems, so rare in contemporary printed plays, confirms once more the notion that the dramatist intended to use scenographic, as much as literary, means to express his meaning.

But there is a further innovatory departure from normal practice involved here and which has hitherto given rise to little, if any, critical comment. I know of no contemporary French play which calls for so much of its action to be played on an upper-level stage.[43] The demands of **Les Galanteries** in this respect far exceed those of many sixteenth-century comedies, such as **Les Néopolitaines** (1584) by François d'Amboise, in which two-storey buildings are frequently evoked without the action ever taking place within the interior of the upper level. They are equally in excess of the occasional requirement for an actor to appear at an upper-floor window, as in Corneille's **Mélite** (II.viii), an effect easily achieved by placing a ladder behind the set.[44] Nor are these problems posed by **Les Galanteries** solved satisfactorily by transposing to Montdory's theatre the same possibilities as existed at the Hôtel de Bourgogne, where, according to a recent and convincingly argued hypothesis, Mahelot sometimes erected scenery or placed either a bed or 'at least a smaller and possibly more convenient simulacrum' on an extension (at least down the stage-left side) of the **théâtre supérieur**.[45] Moreover, the depth of this second stage, according to the best calculations, was no more than one **toise** (or 1.95 metres) across the back, hardly sufficient for the realistic practicability demanded by **Les Galanteries**.[46] An upper stage of twice that usable depth was erected at the Marais on its reconstruction in 1644, but the dimensions of any upper stage it may have had before that date are entirely unknown.[47] If, however, as John Golder has surmised,[48] the new Marais broadly reproduced the features of the old, and if those other temporary theatres of Montdory's company, at the Berthaut, Sphère and Fontaine tennis-courts, were not markedly dissimilar to the first Marais, then one may legitimately assume the practical capability of staging Mairet's comedy in accordance with its requirements. After all, even though such use of a **théâtre supérieur** remains quite exceptional, it is not unlikely that in its early years Montdory's company would be keen to prove, in staging as in acting and all other respects, that anything the Bourgogne could do, they could do better. By exploiting to the full the **théâtre supérieur** to present a superior form of realistic illusion, again moving his audience's eye upwards away from the inferior, symbolic conventionalism to the new, higher reality, Mairet presented the Marais with the opportunity to 'upstage' its great rival.

LIGHTING

The desire to progress beyond the conventional symbolism of Mahelot's staging to a greater realism is as palpable in lighting, frequently alluded to both in the dialogue and the stage directions, as in all other aspects of the staging. For the numerous nocturnal scenes, Mahelot's star-spangled black cloth is replaced here by genuine darkness lit only by torches or candles often carried by the actors.[49] In stage directions such as: 'Elle pose sa bougie allumée aux pieds du Duc' (II.iii, after l.566), or lines such as: 'Marchez donc, Stephanille, avec vostre lumiere' (l.1616), one detects the same insistent demand for non-symbolic representation as was noted earlier. And once more it is no mere accident that all textual references and stage directions concerning lighting occur when the action is centred on the focus of new realism, Flavie's house.[50] In fact, with the exception of scenes vii-xiv of Act IV, scenes which, perhaps significantly, were found to be problematic in terms of their precise location, all the sequences of new realism occur after nightfall. In **Les Galanteries** reality is an illuminated darkness.

But for scenes played according to the old convention in the open stage space, one can only assume that the stage was lit in the conventional manner. If that were so, what happened at the point of transition between old and new, when in Act I the Duke moves from his palace compartment in scene i and approaches Flavie's house in scene ii?   From the spectators' point of view, it would be impossible to play the initial part of this sequence in pitch darkness; and yet in its final part, and for the rest of Acts II and III, the fiction calls for total obscurity. Given that French theatre companies were unlikely at this date to have at their disposal the relatively sophisticated machinery developed by Sabbattini in Italy and which made it possible to dim the lighting in the course of the action,[51] Mairet's total darkness in this sequence would probably have been more apparent than real, the neutral space in front of Flavie's house remaining lit at least to some extent, perhaps throughout. One may perhaps legitimately surmise, as a rather crude solution to the problem, that the **moucheur** was intelligent enough to fit shortened candles during the interval between the first two acts, so that, as they burned out during the course of Act II, the darkness became progressively established, even though the timing of the change could not be made precise.

The point of major interest here, however, is that the text itself manifests an awareness of such technical limitations, attempting even to turn them to advantage and once more to create, if somewhat awkwardly, a fusion between old and new. On approaching the house, the Duke sees someone he takes to be his adored Emilie's lover descend a silk ladder thrown down from the window, only to ascend and re-enter the house immediately (ll.510-21). But why, he wonders, if it were a lover, would he be leaving at this moment, 'au poinct que les amants / Cuillent les plus doux fruits de leurs contentements' (ll.526-27)? It is no doubt through similar reasoning that the fellow has now returned to the house (ll.528-29). The explanation of this strange behaviour that the Duke then provides is designed specifically to establish spectator illusion, by reconciling illuminated scenic reality with fictional darkness. The light of the open stage space becomes moonlight, which the deluded lover, like the spectators, may have mistakenly perceived as daylight:

> Le gallant est rentré, non, non, c'est un amy,
> Que l'excez du plaisir a sans doute endormy.
> Si bien qu'à son resveil, comme il a veu parestre
> La clarté de la Lune à travers la fenestre,
> Soupçonnant que desja c'estoit le point du jour,
> Il a precipité l'heure de son retour.
> D'où vient que ses soubçons esclaircis à la Lune
> Le voilà qui retourne à sa bonne fortune.   (ll.530-37)

In this way, a possible staging defect, borne of the traditional conventionalism, is integrated into progressive realistic illusionism, Mairet once more demonstrating a scenographic awareness quite extraordinary in a dramatist of this period.

*   *

*

Mairet's only comedy was created at a time when pressure for unity of place within the general framework of the move towards regularity was increasing, a pressure to which Mairet himself had recently contributed by his theoretical preface to **La Silvanire**. **Les Galanteries** is often considered as a momentary deviation from the path of regularity leading to **La Sophonisbe** and the tragedies, an amusing digression or regression into the freedom of the irregular form, consonant with the baroque aesthetics of oscillation between opposite poles. This essay has shown rather that in its exploitation of space **Les Galanteries** intentionally reflects the transition from irregular to regular drama, constituting an experimental crossroads between the two forms. It tends towards disciplined regularity in its concentration of action within a single, well-defined and realistically presented locality, but retains irregular freedom in its continual fragmentation and accelerating metamorphosis of a space to which is then applied a technique of ostentatious decoration.

The staging and its effects have likewise been found to be symptomatic of the transition from the relative freedom of the multiple staging convention with its open, loosely defined locations to a more restrictive and closely defined concept of place. In fact, **Les Galanteries** shows that the move towards concentration of place within an intensified realistic perspective was liable to produce the same kind of effect in relation to space as the move towards unity of time did in relation to plot and the number of incidents. There, the introduction of the rule did not lead automatically to classical simplicity, as is amply proved by the complex web of intrigue of a play like Thomas Corneille's **Timocrate** (1656) or the plethora of incidents in Mairet's own regular tragicomedy, **La Virginie**, composed only a year after **Les Galanteries**.[52] In the case of both unities, until the technique becomes settled and brought under purposeful, rationalistic control, there is initially an explosion, the constricting pressure on place resulting here in animated movement and the fragmentation of space **in perpetuum** into a multiplicity of locations within a single location.

That Mairet chose to confront the problem of well-defined space head-on, where other dramatists simply paid it scant regard, as if it were no concern of theirs, and that the resultant play is a fascinatingly self-conscious experiment in the juxtaposition of two conflicting modes of staging, which dares to comment three centuries before the **nouveau théâtre** on its own theatricality, is a tribute to the writer's courage and progressiveness. That contemporaries and successors failed to follow him down a road successfully opened up for them is no fault of his; events and the strictures of the **doctes,** with their notions of a purely literary theatre, overtook him. But perhaps what this analysis has most importantly revealed is that in its own specific terms **Les Galanteries du duc d'Ossonne,** more possibly than any other play of its era, is as much a theatrical as a literary artefact. The scenography is as vital to its meaning as the text itself, for without its essential staging effects we are unable to appreciate the work in its totality. All we lack therefore is a full-scale, experimental production of this truly rewarding theatrical adventure. If only the financial resources were available...

NOTES

1. Full bibliographical references can be found in the notes to my recent monograph, **Jean Mairet et ses protecteurs: une œuvre dans son milieu** (Paris, Seattle and Tuebingen, 1983), and, for all works on Mairet up to 15 June 1973, in Giovanni Dotoli's excellent **Bibliographie critique de Jean Mairet** (Paris, 1973).

2. For a 'bibliographical image, in résumé', see Tom Lawrenson, 'Holsboer and After: the French Stage and Auditorium in the Seventeenth Century', **Newsletter of the Society for Seventeenth-Century French Studies,** 2 (1980), 65-71 (p.65).

3. A note in my **Jean Mairet et ses protecteurs** (pp.415-17) dealt briefly with the staging of **Les Galanteries.** The present essay expands on some of the ideas contained therein and considerably modifies a number of its conclusions.

4. **Les Galanteries du duc d'Ossonne, vice-roy de Naples,** edited by Giovanni Dotoli (Paris, 1972), pp.27-29. All subsequent line references are to this edition.

5. See Jacques Scherer, **La Dramaturgie classique en France** (Paris, 1950), pp.178-79, and the 'Notice' to his edition of the play in his **Théâtre du XVIIe siècle,** Bibliothèque de la Pléiade (Paris, 1975-), I, 1270-75; see also Dotoli's 'Introduction' to his edition of the play (pp.93-99), and his **Il cerchio aperto: la drammaturgia di Jean Mairet** (Bari, 1977), pp.32 and 159-79.

6. See S. Wilma Deierkauf-Holsboer, **Le Théâtre du Marais,** 2 vols (Paris, 1954-58), I, 24.

7. 'Notice', p.1273.

8. **Jean Mairet et ses protecteurs,** pp.221-30.

9. Given his convincing arguments on the date and place of the first performance in his edition of the play, it is surprising to see Dotoli repeating Scherer's error in his **Il cerchio aperto:** 'Utilizzando per la prima volta la scena del Marais, più larga di quella dell'Hôtel de Bourgogne [...]' (p.170).

10. 'Introduction', pp.94 and 98.

11. 'Notice', p.1273; see also Henry Carrington Lancaster, **A History of French Dramatic Literature in the Seventeenth Century,** 5 parts in 9 vols (Baltimore and Paris, 1929-42), I,ii, 635.

12. 'Introduction', p.94.

13. Dotoli, **Il cerchio aperto**, p. 166; and 'Introduction', p. 97.

14. See T. Lawrenson, 'The Contemporary Staging of Théophile's **Pyrame et Thisbé**: the open stage imprisoned', in **Modern Miscellany presented to Eugène Vinaver,** edited by T.E. Lawrenson, F.E. Sutcliffe and G.F.A. Gadoffre (Manchester, 1969), pp.167-79; T. Lawrenson, D. Roy and R. Southern, 'Le "Mémoire" de Mahelot et l'**Agarite** de Durval: vers une reconstitution pratique', in **Le Lieu théâtral à la Renaissance,** edited by Jean Jacquot (Paris, 1964), pp.363-76; and J. Golder, '**L'Hypocondriaque** de Rotrou: un essai de reconstitution d'une des premières mises en scène à l'Hôtel de Bourgogne', **Revue d'histoire du théâtre**, 31 (1979), 247-70.

15. 'Notice', p.1273.

16. The first two scenes of Act IV are expository in that they set the action, virtually complete by the end of Act III, in motion again through the introduction of Emilie's unfaithful lover, Camille. Several commentators have noted the hiatus in the play's structure between Acts III and IV. For example, Gaston Bizos (**Etude sur la vie et les œuvres de Jean de Mairet** (Paris, 1877), p.162) maintains that 'les deux derniers actes forment comme une autre pièce', a view echoed by Scherer ('Notice', p.1272). I have argued elsewhere (**Jean Mairet et ses protecteurs,** pp.225-30) that it is possible to perform a shortened version of **Les Galanteries** (Acts I-III) without creating a sense of incompleteness.

17. 'Notice', p.1273.

18. 'Notice', p.1273.

19. 'Introduction', pp.94-95.

20. 'Notice', p.1273.

21. See ll.478-509.

22. In the light of this reasoning, the comment by John Golder ('The Stage Settings of Corneille's Early Plays', **Seventeenth-Century French Studies**, 7 (1985), 184-97) to the effect that Mairet's comedy 'cries out for' multiple staging (p.187) is at least questionable.

23. 'Introduction', p.95.

24. See ll.457-70.

25. 'Notice', p.1273.

26. 'Introduction', pp.95-97; 'Notice', p.1274. Dotoli's pages quoted here are also the source of further allusions in this section to his location of scenes.

27. This argument holds good, I feel, at least in terms of the fiction. A more radical alternative for these scenes in terms of the staging is discussed below.

28. A similar alternative to the above in respect of these problematic scenes will be proposed below.

29. After the street scenes at the beginning of Act IV, the cloth covering the cabinet would probably have to be drawn aside for the opening of scene v. It could be closed again after the monologue of scene vi, with the cloth covering Flavie's bedroom opening at the same time for the beginning of scene vii. Based on the assumption that both cloths are closed at the end of Act IV to create the street scene for the beginning of Act V, further suggestions concerning manipulation of the cloths in the last act are made below during the detailed discussion of its **mise en scène.**

estimée', but cannot resist adding: 'il n'y en avoit pas tant de bonnes alors qu'il y en a eu depuis'.[3] **Mithridate** also managed to find its way on to a contemporary list of tragedies favoured by Richelieu[4] and, as Lancaster comments, these must have been 'among the most highly esteemed plays of the day'.[5] As late as 1662 it could still have been making the rounds of the provinces in the repertory of a touring company, for the actors in Poisson's **Le Baron de la Crasse** are prepared to perform it.[6] Aside from a panegyric of La Calprenède penned by an obvious admirer in 1639,[7] there are no other contemporary references to the reception of his plays. Of the eighteenth-century commentators, Maupoint and Léris both describe **Essex** as having had 'un grand succès',[8] and this tragedy remained in the repertory of the Hôtel de Bourgogne until possibly as late as 1647.[9] Going through several editions during the author's lifetime,[10] it also provided inspiration for Thomas Corneille and Boyer when they turned to the same theme during the season of 1677-78.[11] **La Mort des enfans d'Hérodes** was likewise reprinted in 1656 and 1666.[12] And d'Aubignac, in **La Pratique du théâtre,** written in the 1630s and 1640s although not published until 1657, at least remembers **Le Comte d'Essex** and **La Mort des enfans d'Hérodes,** although such favourable comment as he makes is limited to the former.[13] Grenaille's panegyric, written as a preface to his own **L'Innocent malheureux,** describes La Calprenède thus: 'M[r] DE LA CALPRENEDE, pour estre venu des derniers, ne laisse pas de tenir le premier rang' (sig. ẽlv), and comments enthusiastically on four of the tragedies and the tragicomedy **Edouard,** then the latest of La Calprenède's plays. As a young dramatist having composed his first play, Grenaille was perhaps aiming at ingratiating himself with an established and apparently successful playwright and fellow countryman. His remarks nevertheless represent a precious record of one man's reaction to La Calprenède's plays and the criteria upon which his judgements are based serve as a useful indicator of seventeenth-century responses to the drama of the 1630s.

   The recurring tragic situation which La Calprenède chooses to dramatize is sedition, real or supposed, which threatens the welfare of the state and often the life of the monarch. A similarity of approach characterizes his treatment of the various rebellions, whether in Tudor England, pre-Christian Judea, or Visigothic Spain. Indeed, his fidelity to this pattern makes it possible for Lancaster to detail the elements of La Calprenède's 'ideal tragedy':

> According to this system, the ideal tragedy shows an arrest toward the end of the first act, followed by scenes of preparation for a trial that takes place in the third or fourth act. The victim appears in the opening scenes of the fifth act and is led away to be executed behind the scenes. The news is brought to someone deeply interested in the event and comment of some sort ends the play.[14]

Such a schema works with variations for four of the six tragedies: **Jeanne, reyne** d'Angleterre, Le Comte d'Essex, La Mort des enfans d'Hérodes, and Herménigilde. It is a structural formula of which suspense is an integral element. Of the two remaining tragedies, in **Phalante** politics take second place to the love interest, while **La Mort de Mithridate** deals with rebellion but, unlike the tragedies with similar subject matter, does not contain a trial. In both of these plays too, La Calprenède strives to create suspense. In this essay, I shall restrict myself, however, to the study of four of the tragedies in which his manipulation of suspense can be charted from its beginnings through its most effective uses to the final breakdown of the formula of the 'ideal tragedy'. I shall be dealing with **La Mort de Mithridate, Le Comte d'Essex, La Mort des enfans d'Hérodes,** and **Herménigilde.**[15]

The structure of La Calprenède's tragedies is spare and linear. From the beginning there is little doubt as to the end result. The title may give it away, as do the family resemblances between the plays. Problems set in the opening scenes have been logically, inexorably, worked out by the last. The Romans outside the city thirsting for Mithridate's blood have reached the throne room and the dead king by the last scene. The early fears of Hérode's children for their lives have been justified, and the final image is of their corpses littering the stage. Characters even go so far as to predict the catastrophe. As the hero hastens to see Hérode, his wife warns: 'Alexandre, bon Dieu, vous courez au trespas' (**MEH**, I.i, p.7). Herménigilde ultimately gives in to the exhortations of wife and brother, but knows that 'je cours à ma ruîne infaillible' (**Herm**, I.iii, p.18). Indeed, the obstinacy of Herménigilde and Essex contributes to the pervading tragic inexorability, as the one is harangued: '[votre mort] est inevitable, si vous perseverez dans ceste obstination' (**Herm**, III.i, p.52), while the other is warned:

> Vostre obstination visiblement vous traine
> Dans le chemin certain d'une perte certaine. (**CdE**, II.v, p.37)

The tragedy thus often resolves itself into a relentless working out of initial predictions, with the feeling of inevitability underscored by the unscrupulousness of the opposition, the powerlessness of the innocent, or the intransigence of the hero. Refusing to indulge in **péripéties**, La Calprenède destines his tragedies to provide the kind of tragic pleasure described by Alain: 'Le tragique n'est pas dans le malheur réel et imprévu, qui nous vide aussitôt de pensées, mais au contraire dans le malheur attendu, dont on entend les pas, qui arrivera, qui est déjà arrivé, qui fera son entrée comme un acteur'.[16]

And yet superimposed on such ever-present feelings of foreboding are very real attempts at creating suspense. In the four plays under consideration, the pattern is that of the two poles of hero and antagonist, with the other characters of the play the dramatist ensures that these scenes of family confrontation are searingly dramatic.

Pharnace is ambitious and weak. Having accepted Rome's offer of Mithridate's crown, he now stands cowed by Rome's power over him. And yet his great love for Bérénice means that his heart still lingers in Mithridate's camp. He confides to the Roman, Emile:

> Sçache que ma douleur ne vient plus que d'amour:
> Je vis, et toutefois je ne vois plus le jour.
> Privé de mon soleil je suis dans les tenebres,
> Et mon œil n'est ouvert qu'à des objects funebres.
> Emile devant toy je prends les Dieux tesmoins,
> Que cette passion engendre tous mes soins. (II.iv, p.27)

Indeed, Pharnace had a javelin hurled into the city with a letter attached, encouraging Bérénice to leave Mithridate's camp (III.i, p.36). As he reads her reply, just before she appears, he enthuses: 'Tousjours ma volonté dependra de la tienne' (III.ii, p.40). Pharnace's earlier confessions to Emile of his love of Bérénice, his sending the letter, his reactions to the reply entailing a brief reiteration of his passion just before Bérénice's appearance, all inspire hope that Bérénice may be able to sway Pharnace in favour of the family's fate. It is a tenuous hope, discouraged by Mithridate himself, but retained by his daughters, and which we are meant to share. With Bérénice on her way to meet her husband, Pharnace's sister Nise can say: 'J'attends de son dessein un tres-heureux succes' (III.i, p.35). Cautiously optimistic, the other sister, Mithridatie, contradicts her father, putting her faith in Pharnace's continuing love of Bérénice:

> Icy vostre creance heureusement trompée:
> S'il [Pharnace] a peu conserver quelque reste d'amour,
> Permet à nostre espoir encore un peu de jour. (III.i, p.35)

She puts her faith in the power of Bérénice's charms, especially of her eyes, which she describes thus:

> Ils s'arment des attraits qui l'ont faict souspirer,
> Et lancent des regards qui se font adorer. (III.i, p.37)

Enough detail is thus provided by La Calprenède to guarantee that a certain degree of hope is not totally misplaced.

Throughout the interview, it is Pharnace who continues to wear his heart on his sleeve. 'Jette toy dans les bras d'un mary qui t'adore', he urges Bérénice (III.iii, p.45), but she ruthlessly catalogues his crimes. It is Pharnace who is on the defensive, forced to admit his guilt and ultimately to confess that his resolution is steeled by pure, naked fear of what reprisals the Romans might take upon him if he now betrayed them. Whatever we may first have felt to be working in favour of Bérénice's mission, we had not counted on fear of the Romans so galvanizing Pharnace in his resolve.   The act ends with Bérénice vowing that Pharnace will never see her alive again.

Act IV opens with the family now appealing to Mithridate to see Pharnace himself. Mithridate balks at the ignominy of a father having to beg his son for mercy. But Hypsicratée puts her hope in residual filial feeling on the part of Pharnace and even Bérénice ventures to say that perhaps since she saw him Pharnace has started to feel remorse. Under such pressure, Mithridate agrees to appeal to Pharnace. Although we may be sceptical as to the success of his confrontation, as with the previous encounter seeds have been sown by La Calprenède with the aim of maintaining our curiosity.

The possibility of suspense again hinges upon Pharnace's state of mind. We have already seen a Pharnace doubly disturbed, on the one hand by his love for Bérénice and on the other by a guilty conscience with regard to his father. Act II, scene iv, in which Pharnace bared his soul to Emile concerning Bérénice, began with him saying:

> Mais dieux de quels remords je me sens agiter!
> Quel tardif repentir me vient persecuter!
> Je commets un peché qui me rend execrable,
> Et jamais le soleil n'en a veu de semblable,
> Mitridate est mon pere, et c'est mon ennemy. (II.iv, pp.24-25)

He went on to declare: 'J'ay pour plus grand fléau ma seule conscience' (p.25). Immediately before his interview with his father, Pharnace is shown to be wavering. Still consumed by his passion for Bérénice, he has to be told by Emile: 'Reprenés ce grand cœur que vous avez quitté' (IV.ii, p.53). As Mithridate himself appears on the ramparts, Pharnace assures Emile he will remain steadfast but reveals his inner conflict by adding:

> Mais que mon cœur pressé de divers mouvemens
> Garde, avec regret, ses premiers sentimens. (IV.ii, p.55)

La Calprenède constantly works against the inevitability imposed by the play's title. By creating an antagonist torn by divisive feelings and assailed by conflicting pressures, La Calprenède provides us with sufficient grounds at least to hope that one or other of the appeals may be successful. They, of course, are not. True to his reassurances to Emile, Pharnace does not yield to pressure from Mithridate. Although he can tell his father: 'Non, la force du sang n'est pas encore esteinte' (IV.iii, p.62), his hands remain tied by his allegiance to Rome. Neither Mithridate's disappointment and horror at what his son is doing, nor his cynical view of the Roman tactic of using traitors and then abandoning them constitutes sufficient pressure upon Pharnace. The cruellest blow for Mithridate must be his son's admission: 'Je ne suis plus à moy, je despend des Romains' (IV.iii, p.61).

Traditionally, La Calprenède has been criticized for an over-zealous fidelity to history. Unfavourably compared with Racine's **Mithridate**, La Calprenède's version has been regarded as 'une succession de tableaux d'histoire au lieu d'une action dramatique'.[23]   The hero has been said to die 'avec le plus grand respect pour l'histoire',[24] and the play has generally been dismissed since 'l'histoire, fidèlement suivie, ne suffit pas à fonder l'intérêt de la pièce'.[25]   It is La Calprenède's 'Au Lecteur' to **Mithridate** which has been cited as proof of his 'souci de faire œuvre d'historien'.[26] There, Plutarch, Appian, and Florus are mentioned as sources (sig. ẽ1r).   But more interesting than such conventional defence on La Calprenède's part is the freedom he demonstrates in his attitude to his sources.   Far from slavish fidelity to the ancient historians, invention and rearrangement strike one as the keynotes.   For such a pivotal character as Pharnace, let us consider what La Calprenède found in his sources.   In Plutarch, Pompey introduces Pharnaces in the same breath as he announces Mithridates's death to the Roman camp, stating only that the son had rebelled against the father.[27]   In Florus, Pharnaces is instrumental in driving Mithridates to his death: 'la meschanceté de son fils Pharnaces [...] le mit à un tel desespoir qu'il chassa avec le fer, l'ame que le poison n'avoit peu arracher de son corps'.[28]   Appian provides more detail, although Pharnaces is again introduced very late in the story (a page before Mithridates's death) where he 'conspira de faire mourir son pere'.[29]   Characterization is minimal, with Appian the only one to provide a string of possible motives, which all point to fear.   It is left to the dramatist to flesh out the historical facts.   La Calprenède himself confesses to having provided Pharnace with 'les deplaisirs et les remords qu'il devoit avoir de la mort de son pere', although this runs counter to Plutarch, and to having tried to make him 'plus excusable et plus honneste homme qu'il n'estoit' (sig. ẽ1r).   But the transformation from historical figure to dramatic character is even more fundamental.   If the suspense is to be dependent upon Pharnace, his emotions must be engaged and conflicts developed.   He is therefore given an estranged wife in Bérénice.[30]   The confrontations of husband and wife, like those of father and son, are thus of La Calprenède's own invention.   He knows better than to cheat his audiences of the **scènes à faire.**   Such additions all have as their aim the aesthetic rearrangement of history in favour of what is dramatic.   And all around him La Calprenède had examples of his contemporaries working in just this way.   The influence on **Mithridate** of the successful **La Sophonisbe** is clear,[31] and in the 'Au Lecteur' to his tragedy La Calprenède defends Mithridate's suicide by referring to the precedent of Mairet's and Benserade's two recent plays on the theme of Cleopatra (sig. ẽ1r).[32]   Success provides the cachet for even the unhistorical.   La Calprenède can feel fully justified in his invention of Bérénice because, as he writes: 'je ne mentiray point, quand je diray que les actions de ceste femme ont donné à ma Tragedie une grande partie du peu de reputation qu'ell'a [sic] et que celle qui les a representées dans les meilleures compagnies de l'Europe a tiré assez de larmes des plus beaux yeux de la terre pour laver ceste faute' (sig. ẽlr).   La Calprenède therefore falls into the respectable contemporary tradition of choosing an historical subject, of which he honours the essential facts while providing, altering, or elaborating detail for the greatest dramatic effect.   Comparing **Jeanne, reyne d'Angleterre** with Puget de la Serre's **Thomas Morus,** Ascoli has written: 'Il n'y a pas plus de vérité historique, mais plus d'intérêt, de variété, de vraisemblance et de mouvement dans la **Jeanne, reine d'Angleterre** de La Calprenède'.[33]   Throughout his career, 'vérité historique' cedes to 'vraisemblance' and to theatrical qualities.

Concomitant with the criticism on the grounds of historical fidelity, **Mithridate** has been criticized for its 'action insuffisante' or 'le vide de l'action et sa froideur'.[34] La Calprenède defends the creation of some of his 'incidens' by saying that 'la sterilité du subject m'y a obligé' (sig. ã4v).   That built-in slimness led La Calprenède to construct a plot which makes use of confrontations to provide emotional rhythms. The outcome of a play entitled **La Mort de Mithridate** cannot be concealed, but the inevitable nature of the plot is consistently suspended.   Characters are not rigid, and in Pharnace being pulled between different forces and confronted by those with emotional power over him, there is created not only a dynamic emotional tension between characters but also the possibility of change in Pharnace and therefore potentially in the outcome.   Rather than the static clarity of development characteristic of sixteenth-century tragedy, La Calprenède chooses to play with uncertainty and contrasts.   Perhaps another remark of Roaten's on **Le Cid** could be applied to **Mithridate:** 'The persistence of Renaissance attitudes is evident, although they have now become a part of a pattern of artistic forms that is essentially different'.[35]

Having created a stalemate, La Calprenède nevertheless plays upon the audience's curiosity and hopes.   As the play is concerned with attempts to save the family, a rhythm is established of hope inspired by one further attempt, followed by suspense as to whether this appeal will be successful, leading to despair that it has not been but also curiosity as to what the family will do next.   This is the rhythm accompanying the three attempts of the sortie, and the appeals of Bérénice and Mithridate.   Each is dealt with predominantly in one act.   Mithridate takes the decision to fight at the end of Act I. In the opening scene of Act II, he and Hypsicratée are in armour, readying themselves for the fight.   News of the devastation they are wreaking upon the Romans is conveyed to Pharnace by messenger at the end of the

found in the acts on either side of the trial.   In Act II, Elizabeth asks her lady-in-waiting, Lady Cecil, to appeal to Essex to beg for mercy, without letting the earl know that she is doing this on the Queen's behalf (II.ii).   Lady Cecil tries in vain to persuade Essex to save himself (II.v).   In Act IV, Southampton appeals to Elizabeth for his friend's life (IV.iii), and Lady Cecil pays a second, more successful visit to Essex (IV.v). As the rhythm of officialdom pursues its bludgeoningly regular course, suspense is created by the feeling of much desperate scurrying about behind the scenes, as Lady Cecil hurries between the palace and the Tower, between the two poles of Elizabeth and Essex.

Unlike **Mithridate,** however, **Essex** offers the complication of several plot lines interweaving and ultimately fusing. Acts II and IV, for example, also introduce, in the persons of Cecil and Raleigh, further tension on the score of court factionalism. Both are avowed enemies of Essex, to the extent that Southampton even accuses them of conspiracy against him (III, pp.46-47); both are convinced that he is an evil influence upon Elizabeth and dangerous for England; both are determined that he should not escape execution, and both work against him.   After Essex's arrest, Cecil is shown poisoning the Queen's mind against him (II.i).   Dispatched to question Southampton, Cecil reveals his malevolence in a line like: 'Quelque rusé qu'il soit, ma ruse est toute preste' (II.i, p.23).   Later, to ensure that the condemnation to death holds, in the Queen's presence Raleigh counters Southampton's arguments in favour of Essex (IV.iii). All of these characters, with their different motivations and opposing desires all centring on Essex, vie with each other to influence the denouement.

As in **Mithridate,** fundamental to the creation of suspense in **Essex** are the psychological conflicts within the person exercising power, in this case Elizabeth. The two-tiered structure of the play recalls the two roles Elizabeth attempts to fill.   As queen, she sets in motion the official proceedings and then must sit and wait as they take their course; as a woman in love, it is she who instigates the private attempt to save her lover.   Such alternations between Elizabeth's two **personae** are put to the service of suspense.   Which will prevail?   In her monologues she careers from desires for vengeance to heart-rending protestations of love.   Will she relent or not?   A monologue will begin with: 'Tu mourras, tu mourras, monstre d'ingratitude', but thirty-eight lines later she is already saying: 'Ouy, ouy, je sauveray cet aymable ennemy', and eighteen lines further on she is sending Lady Cecil to Essex, thus setting in motion her personal attempt to save him (II.ii, pp.23 and 25).

Her role in the creation of suspense is well illustrated in Acts IV and V.   The major act for suspense is Act IV, its rhythm imposed by appeals to the monarch and to the hero, with the latter's fate fluctuating accordingly.   Psychology has an essential part to play as the burden of suspense falls upon the inner conflicts of both Elizabeth and Lady Cecil as well as upon the personality of Essex. Essex and Southampton have been condemned to death at the end of the third act. The fourth opens with Elizabeth having pardoned Southampton and postponing Essex's execution:

> Si l'Arrest est donné, va dire qu'on differe,
> Que l'on attende encore ma volonté derniere,
> Et qu'on ne haste point ceste execution
> Qu'on ne soit asseuré de mon intention,
> Quoy qu'il ayt entrepris et quoy qu'il m'en arrive,
> Quoy qu'il ayt conspiré, je veux, je veux qu'il vive. (IV.i, p.53)

Although Essex remains in insolent silence, Elizabeth finds that she is still unable to conquer her love. The second scene begins with a deliberate ambiguity on La Calprenède's part. The Huissier announces: 'Le Comte'. Elizabeth, thinking, as the audience must, that the reference is to Essex, cuts him off brusquely: 'Que dis-tu?'. The fuller reply is then given: 'Le Comte Soubtantonne' (IV.ii, p.57). As well as being enjoyable for us, this 'quiproquo-express', as Scherer calls it,[37] is also revealing of Elizabeth's state of mind. Since she has just been thinking of Essex, her reaction is the natural one for Elizabeth taken off guard. No one is there to profit by the betrayal of the woman through her first instinctive reactions, but the suspense of the next scene will be sharpened by our curiosity as to whether in her present state of mind Southampton will indeed be able to appeal successfully on Essex's behalf, or whether Elizabeth will be able to keep up the **persona** of queen she adopts at the end of this scene: 'reprens ce front Royal, / Et cache si tu peux ton estrange foiblesse' (IV.ii, p.57). The use of this 'quiproquo-express' proves yet again that psychological conflicts within the character exercising power are La Calprenède's surest guarantee of suspense. Shadowed by Raleigh, Southampton is unable to have a private audience with the Queen, however. Scene iii becomes a battle for Elizabeth's sympathies. Southampton's appeals to her memory of Essex's attentions in the past are countered by Raleigh's cruel reminders of the earl's recent arrogant treatment of the Queen. It is a battle that Southampton loses. Hesitant when alone, Elizabeth in public shows herself hardened to Essex's fate, to the point of saying that were he to ask for mercy, she would not grant it (IV.iii, p.62). Southampton opens the next scene apostrophizing his friend with 'ta mort est jurée' (IV.iv, p.63). But there remains the tentative hope of Lady Cecil's private appeals to Essex, although we have been told that he has so far remained impervious to her persuasion (IV.i, p.54). Scene v promptly reintroduces Lady Cecil in Essex's cell and reveals the latter's trump card. Just before their arrest, Essex hinted to Southampton that there were strong reasons for his confidence in his power over the Queen:

> J'ay de son amitié de tres bons tesmoignages
> Ou pour en mieux parler j'en ay receu des gages   (I.v, p.15).

Like Lady Cecil, Essex now realizes that time is running out. He hurries to tell her about the ring, 'puis que le temps me presse' (IV.v, p.67). He confides the ring to Lady Cecil, who rushes off saying:

> Ne perdons point de temps puis qu'il nous est si cher,
> Adieu je vay courir ou voler chez la Reine. (IV.v, p.68)

The suspense begins to tighten. Like Elizabeth, Lady Cecil is torn between two possibilities of action. No sooner had the Queen confided in her, than Lady Cecil revealed in the following monologue her deep resentment of Essex, a former lover who had betrayed her and then abandoned her (II.iii). Essex's fate, therefore, now lies in the hands of someone with good reason to be swayed by desires of personal vengeance against him. Lady Cecil's last line to Essex, meant to be a reassurance, thus takes on an ominous ring: 'Le succez en sera tel que je le souhaite' (IV.v, p.69). Nor does hope immediately revive in the monologue which follows. There, resentment battles with the vestiges of love. Although such sentiments as

> Vange toy maintenant, et puis qu'il t'est permis,
> Perds, perds, le plus cruel de tous tes ennemis. (IV.vii, p.[70])

eventually give way to: 'Cedez, ressentiments, à ces restes d'amour' (p.71), the latter is immediately juxtaposed with: 'Mais je voy mon Mary', as Cecil suddenly appears, eerily cognizant of her activities.

As Act IV ends, therefore, its rhythms have led us from a precarious hope as to Essex's fate, dependent upon the still hesitant Elizabeth (scenes i and ii), through increasing despair as Southampton's appeal fails (scenes iii and iv), to the fragile hope that the ring may still save the day (scenes v and vi). A brief sigh of relief is provided by the seemingly secure hope of scene vii, as Lady Cecil overcomes her resentment, before the whole situation is immediately put into limbo once again by Cecil's sudden appearance. Throughout the act, the alternation of hope and fear keeps the audience in a state of 'agréable suspension', to use Corneille's term, just as the end of the act, with Cecil murmuring: 'je cognois vos desseins' (IV.viii, p.72), leaves us on a note of tension and curiosity. Act IV shows La Calprenède aware not only of what Scherer calls 'la valeur dynamique des fins d'actes' (p.206), but also of organizing sequences of suspense wherein the tension is heightened by the contrast with brief moments of respite. This technique is used to great effect in the last act.

Essex walks to the execution block in the opening scene of Act V. There is no last-minute reprieve, although we might well have been wondering if the ring had worked its magic and perhaps a **coup de théâtre** was about to be sprung. Elizabeth is then seen still waiting for 'ce gaige fatal' (V.ii, p.79), and again perhaps we wonder if it might still arrive and, if so, will there be time to halt the execution? All such hopes are dashed as messengers do indeed arrive, but to announce Essex's death (V.iii).

The suspense which continues throughout Act V is now focused upon Elizabeth. Our pleasure is different, though, because we find ourselves in a position of superior knowledge to the Queen. We know the ring has been sent; we suspect that Essex has already been executed by scene ii, while Elizabeth still awaits the ring. We are eager to witness Elizabeth's reaction to the news. In scene iii, with the announcement of Essex's death, La Calprenède satisfyingly puts Elizabeth through a gamut of emotions from shock and distress, by way of sorrow and love, to resentment and hurt. By the end of the scene, thoughts of Essex's scorn and ingratitude have enabled Elizabeth to rise above her grief and even to attain a certain peace of mind. But we are still possessors of information Elizabeth does not have, and even as she prepares herself for the future, we are still curious about her reaction on finding out that the ring was indeed sent. The juxtaposition is brutal. The climax to Elizabeth's spiritual crescendo is a sigh of relief, as she says of Essex's death:

> Il sauve ton Estat, il finit ton martyre,
> Sa perte desormais asseure ton Empire,
> Establit ton salut et donne pour jamais
> A ton regne, à ton cœur, le repos et la paix. (V.iii, p.83)

Immediately, Léonore makes the request:

> Si vous avez pitié de Madame Cecile,
> Madame, pardonnez sa priere incivile,
> Et ne refusez point en cette extremité
> L'honneur de vostre veue à sa fidelité. (V.iv, p.83)

The prospect of this final confrontation further piques our curiosity. As the ring belatedly reaches its destination, handed over by a dying Lady Cecil, Elizabeth faints. With the ring in her hand, she closes the play, her fury at Lady Cecil superseded by despair, as responsibility for Essex's death now weighs heavily upon her.

The ring therefore constitutes an integral element in the play. Hinted at as early as the fifth scene of Act I, it remains in the back of our minds as a last resort Essex can turn to. When he finally does, all suspense is focused on it. Even though it does not save Essex, and although lost from sight during most of Act V, it nevertheless continues to exert a power over the characters, ultimately determining both Elizabeth's and Lady Cecil's fates. Linked to the themes of communication and power, the ring thus serves several purposes. Although the historical sources occasionally hint at the contemporary rumours that Elizabeth wished to pardon Essex and that the causes of her death were linked to that of her former lover, as regards the ring itself La Calprenède's **Essex** represents the first recorded instance of this legend.[38]   In the 'Au Lecteur' to the play, he reassures us: 'Si vous trouvez quelque chose dans ceste Tragedie que vous n'ayez point leu dans les Historiens Anglois, croyez que je ne l'ay point inventé, et que je n'ay rien escrit que sur de bonnes [sic] memoires que j'en avois receues de personnes de condition, et qui ont peut-estre part à l'Histoire' (sig. A4r).   The 'quelque chose' would seem to imply the ring.   La Calprenède appears once again to have been willing to supplement the historical sources when something sufficiently and irresistably dramatic presented itself.

D'Aubignac singles out the denouement of **Essex** for praise because Elizabeth's fate satisfies his tenet that 'la Catastrophe achéve pleinement le Poëme Dramatique' (pp.139-40).   The Frères Parfaict comment that 'le plan est heureux, et bien conduit'.[39]   And Barrière sees it as 'l'une des pièces où son système dramatique apparaît le plus achevé'.[40]   In fact, **Essex** is probably the play in which suspense is most skilfully handled.   Four people have the power to determine the denouement, dependent as it is upon the conflicts in Elizabeth and Lady Cecil, as well as on Essex's personality and Cecil's character.   In **Mithridate**, hope lies solely in convincing Pharnace, as in **Les Enfans d'Hérodes** it depends upon the king.   In **Herménigilde**, although there are ostensibly two people whose decisions affect the outcome, we will see that the responsibility must fall on the king alone.   With the weight of suspense spread over a wider number of characters, the greater complexity of **Essex** ensures that suspense can be maintained to the final scene, something which is not always the case in the later plays.

For his next play La Calprenède seems to have sought to capitalize on Tristan's success by writing a sequel to his triumphantly popular **Mariane**.   **La Mort des enfans d'Hérodes, ou Suite de Mariane** takes up the story fifteen years after his wife's execution, as Hérode now turns against their sons.   Since the last scene of Tristan's play, Hérode's sanity has further degenerated.   Although he is described in the first scene as a bloodthirsty tyrant, La Calprenède immediately counters this description with a monologue of the King himself.   And he is no longer the man he was. From the despotic image established in the first scene, we move in the second to the picture of a broken man, ravaged by remorse, unable to find peace of mind, plagued by counsellors, and preoccupied with death.   His persecution complex persists, and by the end of the scene the whole cycle is beginning again, this time centring upon his two sons by Mariane, Alexandre and Aristobule.

The tragedy depicts the futile attempt of Alexandre and Aristobule to avoid becoming the latest victims of their father's bloody reign.   Suspense is again an essential ingredient, and in this play its effectiveness is even more dependent upon

Hérode's weaknesses than was that of **Essex** upon Elizabeth's conflicts.   Tired and sick, self-pitying and essentially passive, Hérode no longer rules, but is rather ruled by his counsellors.   At the mercy of his court, this former deceiver, prey to constant fears of conspiracy, is now easily deceived.   His brother and sister, Pherore and Salome, as well as his son Antipatre, half-brother to the heroes, scheme to make him believe that Alexandre and Aristobule are conspiring against him.   Such a plot takes easy root, but Hérode's dilemma springs from the fact that he does love these children.   The precarious mental state of the king, torn between the **raison d'état** and love of his sons, the last link with Mariane, endows the play with a desperate uncertainty.

Doom hangs heavy over the play in the atmosphere, the personalities of Hérode and his sons, their past histories and the past successes of the conspirators, as well as in the predictions of disaster.   In the opening scene, Alexandre sees himself and his brother as just the last in a long line of familial murders, including that of his uncle Aristobule:

> Il [Hérode] perd tout ce qu'il creint sans forme et sans scrupule
> Et ce qui fit perir le jeune Aristobule,
> Dans sa gloire naissante et la fleur de ses ans
> Fera bientost perir ses malheureux enfans.   (I.i, p.5)

As in the other plays, attempts are nevertheless made to escape the inevitable.   The traditional appeals are made, with Alexandre's wife Glaphira first going to the source of power, Salome (III.i), and finally to Hérode (V.iii), and with Melas, ambassador of the king of Cappadocia, Glaphira's father, approaching Hérode too (III.iii).   Rather than examining the appeal mechanism, however, it is perhaps of greater interest to look at Acts II and IV, which constitute good examples of La Calprenède's ability to provide suspense at the same time as offering other pleasures.

Act I disposed of one rumour spread by Pherore in order to sow dissension between father and son.   Through the communication of Hérode and Alexandre, and the king's confrontation with Pherore, the rumour that Hérode had designs upon his daughter-in-law Glaphira was exposed as malicious gossip.   As in other plays, the second act brings the opposition into focus, and in this case very swiftly shows their triumph.[41]   What was only talk in Act I becomes tangible here: how dangerous the opposition is, how influential, how unscrupulous.

Act II opens with a discussion which degenerates into Aristobule insulting his dangerous half-brother, Antipatre.   A crisis is approaching.   In scene ii, Glaphira is worried, and Alexandre talks of open warfare.   A brief note of hope hovers in the air as he proposes that they flee.   Preparations have already been made.   As in **Essex**, there is the feeling of a race against time:

> Il se faut donc sauver tandis qu'il est permis,

> Fuir d'une terre ingrate, et de tant d'ennemis. [...]
> Ne faisons point icy de plus longue demeure,
> Ce sejour m'est fatal, il faut avancer l'heure.   (II.ii, p.26)

The next day is therefore set as the date of departure. A love duet between Alexandre and Glaphira provides a moment of respite from the repressive atmosphere and the flurry of activity. The brothers then leave to pay their respects to Hérode for the last time. They will reach him in the last scene of the act. Scenes iii, iv and v are devoted to the conspiracy. Scene iii, although short, carries a shock value by its very position and the contrast it offers with the previous scene. After the talk of 'repos' and 'heureux sejour' (II.ii, pp.26-27), and the hope of the proposed escape, we see another phase of the conspiracy set in motion as Antipatre receives a series of forged letters he has commissioned to implicate the brothers. Scene iv shows Salome deceiving Hérode, further poisoning his mind against his sons, and priming him for the trap which is being set. Therefore, while the brothers are on their way to the king, their fate is being decided by others, and Glaphira's worst fears are coming true. Aristobule set out at the end of scene ii with the words:

> Pour abuser le Roy comme toute la Cour
> Allons tout de ce pas luy donner le bon jour,
> Et luy rendre aujourd'huy la derniere visite.   (II.ii, p.27)

Antipatre, with the letters in hand, ends scene iii saying:

> Cette adresse est extreme,
> Mais sans plus differer allons trouver le Roy,
> Il en sera surpris et trompé comme moy.   (II.iii, p.29)

The race between the factions is on - the one to escape, the other to ensnare. It is a race which, in both cases, has deception as its means and Hérode as its goal. Whoever reaches him first can influence and control him. Scene iv also serves to cover the time while the two groups are **en route**. It is the conspirators who arrive first, in scene v, producing the letters and a suborned witness, so that on their arrival in scene vi the brothers are arrested. The act ends on the triumph of evil, only slightly mitigated by the promise of a trial and the memory that communication between father and son did succeed in the previous act.

This act is particularly effective for several reasons. Despite the relentlessness of the conspiracy, suspense has been maintained by La Calprenède's technique of simultaneous action, used before in both **Mithridate** and **Essex,** and through which the feeling is created that while actions are being performed before us, much activity is going on elsewhere which will also have its effect on the principal action. The impression of rapidity is obtained by a succession of short scenes of short speeches. The violence of clashing emotions is contrasted with interludes of tenderness, producing variations in rhythm and, in the audience, a variety of emotions ranging from curiosity and dread to admiration and pathos, all against a background of mounting tension. Similar techniques will also be responsible for the success of Act IV.

The fourth act contains only two scenes: the trial (IV.i), and its aftermath (IV.ii). The trial itself moves from Hérode's weariness, through Alexandre's cool, calm defence and impassioned argument, to sadness as Alexandre learns his guards have died under torture, before climaxing on the shrill note of Aristobule's sarcasm and anger as he rails at his father for what he sees as a mockery of justice. At the height of this speech, Hérode commands: 'Silence Aristobule', and then addresses the newly-arrived Glaphira: 'Approchez vous Madame' (IV.i-ii, p.68), nicely making the transition from the violence of the first scene to the quieter tone which will initially characterize the second. The speeches become shorter, the tone calmer. Alexandre's resignation to death leads into an interlude of conjugal love in stark contrast to the violence which ended scene i and the confusion which will end the act. The tension is thus briefly suspended before building in intensity again as Alexandre appeals to his father on Glaphira's behalf. As he throws himself on his knees before Hérode, the strain is too much for Glaphira. She faints; her confidante must rush to support her. Touched by the sight, Hérode suddenly wavers. Melas jumps in to win a postponement of the judgement. And the act finishes with the stichomythic adieux of Alexandre and Glaphira. No verdict has been reached, the decision has only been put off, and all still hangs on Hérode's uncertain mental balance. The act ends in that state of 'agréable suspension' which will carry us over the interval and into the final act.

It seems in Act V as if La Calprenède's aim was to prolong the suspense until the last scene. In practice, the brothers being led off to execution at the end of scene ii tends to curtail the suspense, and scene iii seems a curiously muddled and abortive attempt to rekindle it. Our attention is still centred on Hérode as the key to suspense, but with the brothers' fate dependent upon a man as psychologically unstable as Hérode, one realizes how tenuous the hope is. The first scene maintains the suspense, with the brothers back in their prison cell awaiting decisions from above. Summing up in themselves the tension between hope and fear, Aristobule considers Hérode's ostensible change of heart as 'un assez bon presage' (V.i, p.78), while Alexandre reiterates his fears of the opening scene of the play, underlining the impression that in La Calprenède it is but a short step from the first scene to the last. Although the king's **revirement** at the end of Act IV was caused merely by something as fortuitous as Glaphira's faint and the presence of the right person to take advantage of it, Aristobule can still say: 'Sa derniere action de quelque espoir me flate' (V.i, p.77).

Alexandre's speeches, in which he revives the image of an Hérode coveting his son's wife (V.i, p.78; V.ii, p.81), are important for emphasizing the power of Glaphira over the king, necessary to add credence to the third scene.   There, Glaphira appeals to Hérode, who finally grants his sons a pardon at the same time as knowing it is too late, an action which can be seen as a cruel piece of equivocation or ascribed more generously to his aboulia. Suspense must now depend upon whether we believe that Glaphira might arrive in time to save the brothers.   The same technique of simultaneous action and the momentum of the race against time are employed once more, but without the same conviction.   Suspense still seems to have been uppermost in La Calprenède's mind, but its impact is weakened and confused by the arrangement of the scenes, an improved order of which might have placed the second after the fourth.

As marred as the suspense of Act V might be, here, as throughout the play, its attempted creation is totally La Calprenède's and has no precedent in Josephus's detailed but diffuse historical account or in Caussin's more popular tale.[42]   Drama is again responsible for transforming history into something more intense and exciting. Against a backdrop of tension and suspense, contrast and variety are used to full effect, generating Grenaille's enthusiasm, as he writes of the play:

> C'est là qu'on voit ces belles diversitez que causent les passions d'un fils jaloux de son pere, et d'un pere qui est jaloux de ses enfans. La tyrannie et la pitié, l'indulgence et la cruauté y sont meslées avec un si doux temperamment qu'on se réjouit en s'affligeant, et on pleure dans sa joye.
> (sig. ẽ2r)

Perhaps the variety of La Calprenède's production after **Essex** could best be explained by a restless search for an increasingly elusive success. After the sequel to **Mariane**, he reverted to the still fashionable genre of the tragicomedy (**Edouard**), then to a tragedy of a romantic kind not yet attempted by him (**Phalante**), before coming full circle in his last play, where, under the guise of the then popular religious tragedy, he returned to a familiar theme and a familiar source, Caussin's **La Cour sainte**, which had already been used for **Les Enfans d'Hérodes**. But the old formulae no longer work.

The situation of **Herménigilde** is a classic Calprenedian one. Visigothic Spain is ruled by Lévigilde.   The heir to the throne, Herménigilde, has converted from the national religion of Arianism to Roman Catholicism under the influence of his wife, Indégonde, daughter of the King of France. Because of religious persecution organized by his step-mother, Goisinte, Herménigilde has withdrawn from the court with his wife and supporters, and has been defending himself in Seville for the past two years. The play opens as he is persuaded to give up his defence of that city with the promise from his father of a general pardon.   No sooner is he inside his father's palace, however, than he is imprisoned and charged with rebellion. Similar situations have worked before for La Calprenède, but here the new element of religion consistutes a built-in hindrance to all attempts at creating suspense. As before, appeals are made to both father and son.   But since the appeals to Herménigilde involve the renunciation of Roman Catholicism, and we know that Herménigilde cannot become an apostate, his father Lévigilde is really the sole object to be moved. And he is moved again and again, but only so far as to grant pleas for further appeals to his son. The overlay of religion, however, means that this is not far enough. Lévigilde's conditions do not alter: for the good of Spain, his heir must renounce his disruptive new religion; but Herménigilde does not waver in his new faith: 'Mes yeux sont ouverts à la verité Seigneur, [...] et s'il faut mourir pour la querelle de mon Dieu j'abandonneray et le trosne, et la vie sans regret, et je suivray avec joye le chemin qu'il m'a luy-mesme tracé' (IV.i, pp.67-68).

Avoiding any discussion of the central problem, Roman Catholicism **versus** Arianism, La Calprenède dooms his characters to non-communication on this essential matter and his play to stalemate. The reprieves simply allow extra time for Herménigilde to recant, which we know he cannot do. Depriving us of any real confidence that Herménigilde will be saved means that the appeals which form the central acts and constitute an essential element of La Calprenède's dramaturgy can be dismissed by Pascoe as 'seulement l'essai de plusieurs personnes ou de fléchir Lévigilde ou de faire renoncer à Herménigilde la foi chrétienne', and by Loukovitch as 'un seul fait quatre fois répété'.[43]   Both judgements echo Lancaster's remark that 'the second, third and fourth acts could easily be combined into one, for there are frequent repetitions of argument'.[44] Such previously effective means of creating suspense now are grafted on to a subject whose outcome seems determined to remain obdurately inevitable.   If **Herménigilde** was an attempt to renew his appeal with a fashionable religious patina, La Calprenède was unwittingly undermining his own dramatic system.

Though his central characters are locked into their intransigence, La Calprenède nevertheless insists that his play go through the motions of suspense. The air is still full of the perennial themes of trials promised (II.ii, pp.30-31) and of time running out (IV.ii, pp.72-73), as characters hurry to make their appeals. Acts continue to end on a note of curiosity; court factions continue to fight for the mind of the monarch (II.ii-iii, pp.30-33). Hesitations within the character possessing power over life and death still remain the key to suspense. Within, Lévigilde emotional conflicts must be developed upon which the appellants can work. The conflict between king and father must be emphasized so that the audience will feel the ever-present possibility that he may give in to his natural paternal feelings. Therefore, like Elizabeth, Lévigilde is made strong one minute and weak the next.   To his other son, Recarède, he can unwaveringly defend his actions on the grounds of the reason of state and dismiss him with the imperious: 'retirés vous, et ne repliqués point' (II.i, p.25), while in his next speech he will denounce the 'Inhumaines raisons d'Estat' and reveal the father concerned with the fate of his rebellious heir:

> Faut-il que j'affermisse mon Throsne par la perte de ce que j'ay le mieux aymé, et que je cimente de mon propre sang les fondemens de ma Monarchie? [...] Ah! non Levigilde, il vaut mieux hazarder la perte de ton Sceptre, que pancher à celle de ton fils, les considerations de la Couronne sont legeres, si tu les balances avec celles de la nature, et tu ne peus verser le plus pur de ton sang, sans affoiblir ta vie de la moitié.
> (II.ii, pp.26-27)

Goisinte is then introduced to show Lévigilde yielding to his passion for his wife, Herménigilde's fiercest enemy. Although such conflicts and pressures are attempts to make Lévigilde's character the generator of suspense, they are not sufficiently developed.   Lévigilde seems strong enough to combat Goisinte's influence and wise enough to ignore the advice of Atalaric, another of Herménigilde's enemies. Therefore, all the appeals aimed at closing his ears to slander and opening his eyes to Herménigilde's innocence appear unnecessary. Innocence is no longer the question, as it was with the brothers in **Les Enfans d'Hérodes**;   religion is, and within the play Lévigilde has very good reasons to look askance at Roman Catholicism. Nevertheless, he grants concession after concession in order that his son may recant. At the end of Act IV of **Les Enfans d'Hérodes**, it seemed convincing that, with his unstable nature, Hérode should defer judgement under such pressure, but in a similar situation Lévigilde is almost too much in control.   Caussin emphasizes 'la credulité du mal-heureux père',[45] at the mercy of a Goisinte reminiscent of La Calprenède's Salome, assembling plotters and resorting to calumny and forged letters.[46] In diminishing the importance of these elements, La Calprenède is perhaps attempting to avoid too overt a repetition of what he had already done in **Les Enfans d'Hérodes**. Hérode is terribly unstable, just as in **Essex** Elizabeth is terribly torn, and suspense is thus generated by their personalities. In failing to make Lévigilde weak enough, La Calprenède has reduced his effectiveness as an agent of suspense.   The system breaks down since the psychology of the antagonist no longer admits the possibility of his being sufficiently moved.

* *

*

I have chosen to look at suspense in four of La Calprenède's tragedies, but it is such an integral part of his dramatic system and such a sure means of entertainment

that it features in his other plays as well.   Will Roger marry Bradamante?   Will
Rosimène and Clarionte be united?   Will Edward take advantage of Elips or will she be
lost by the plot against her?   Suspense constitutes a natural element of tragicomedy
as the plots of **Bradamante, Clarionte,** and **Edouard** steer towards disaster only to veer
away at the last minute.   With regard to **Edouard,** Grenaille even comments: 'les
Acteurs sont en aussi grande suspension que les Spectateurs' (sig. ĕ3r).   Throughout
the tragicomedies acts end on a question mark, just as they end on a note of curiosity
or anxiety in the other tragedy, **Phalante.**

La Calprenède even resorts - not always successfully - to little artifices to keep
us in suspense.   A plan will be whispered in someone's ear but we will not be let in on
the secret.[47]   The most effective of these devices is the counterplot in **Bradamante,**
wherein Marfise mentions her plan (III.i, p.48) but will confide it only to Renaud. While
she whispers it to him, Bradamante delivers her **stances** (III.ii, pp.50-51), thus
concealing the plan from us.   As they all run off, Renaud promises to tell Bradamante
en route (p.52).   Teasing us with the plan, La Calprenède twice whisks it away from us.
The artificiality of the technique is revealed by Marfise herself, who says to Renaud:

> Vostre sœur n'en sçait rien.
> Quoy qu'aucune raison ne veut que je le cache,
> Je vous en veux parler avant qu'elle le sçache.   (III.ii, p.50).

The only reason is the titillation provided by suspense.   The least successful example
of this technique must be Elizabeth whispering her commands to the captain of the
guards for the arrest of Essex and Southampton, while Alix describes to us her physical
state (**CdE,** I.iii, p.9).   This concealment seems totally unnecessary since Elizabeth's
next speech informs us that Southampton is to be arrested, and although Essex is not
mentioned the object pronouns can refer only to him.   Such a device, even if
ineffectively deployed, nevertheless bears witness to La Calprenède's commitment
throughout his career to the entertainment of his audience.

D'Aubignac comments interestingly on the demands made by such an audience in
the seventeenth century, referring to 'l'humeur des François qui s'ennuyent des plus
belles choses quand elles ne sont point variées, et qui ne désirent que les nouvelles, et
les bizarreries portant quelque apparence de nouveauté' (p.262).   While La Calprenède
does not resort to 'bizarreries', he nevertheless strives constantly to satisfy his
audience's need for variety.   Indeed, the inspiration of La Calprenède's whole dramatic
œuvre might be traced to a quest for both renewal and novelty.   Such is perhaps the
motivation behind his introduction of English themes or his turning to a martyr
subject, or the change from verse to prose in his last play.   Above all, La Calprenède
consistently finds in the psychology of his characters enough **nouveautés,** enough ways

of constantly reviving interest, to keep his audience's attention. Elizabeth is required to be imperiously regal in the first scene of **Essex,** to give way to the woman in the second scene, to rise again to the role of queen in the third, and to dissolve into the heartbroken lover of the fourth.   Such alternations serve both to create suspense and to provide a plum role for an actress.   This is La Calprenède at his best, but similar demands are also placed on the actors playing Hérode or Lévigilde, both torn between the role of monarch and that of father.

Another consideration in the entertainment of an audience is also expressed by d'Aubignac when he writes: 'il est de la beauté du Theatre que tout s'y choque, et produise des évenemens impreveûs' (p.275).   From the four plays under discussion, it can be seen that the unexpected rarely happens in La Calprenède's tragedies. However, tension between dualities is characteristic of his theatre, producing contrasts and variety through the conflict of opposites.   Suspense pulling against inevitability in his tragedies constitutes just one example of La Calprenède following the principle of 'tout s'y choque' without stepping beyond the bounds of the problem he has set for his characters.   On another level, not only do his heroes and heroines clash in their scenes together, but they are often surrounded, as in **Essex, Les Enfans d'Hérodes** and **Herménigilde,** by a divided court whose factions passionately vie with each other for the favour of the monarch, with the life of the hero at stake. Moreover, because he does not always make the **liaison des scènes,** La Calprenède is able swiftly to juxtapose scenes between different groups for the utmost contrast.   Often, as in **Mithridate, Jeanne** and **Les Enfans d'Hérodes,** he introduces one camp in the first scene of a play and immediately satisfies our interest by presenting the second camp in the next scene.   In the case of **Mithridate** and **Les Enfans d'Hérodes,** the first two scenes introduce the two poles around which the action will revolve, the juxtaposition reinforced by making the character presented in the second scene, whether protagonist or antagonist, substantially different from the expectations created of him in the previous scene.   Much pleasure can thus be derived from the contrasts obtained by the sequence of scenes, as we have observed in Acts IV and V of **Essex** and Acts II and IV of **Les Enfans d'Hérodes,** where scenes and acts have their rises and falls, their variations of rhythm and of tone, and their constant renewal of interest, all centred around an increasing tension.   Within scenes, too, alternation between tension and rest can be found, with conjugal love often providing a kind of refuge against the surrounding storm, as in **Les Enfans d'Hérodes** (II.ii, pp.26-27; and IV.ii, p.71) or in **Mithridate,** where the hero's **stances** (V.i, pp.67-68) provide a moment of quiet, lyrical meditation in contrast to the horrors which are to follow.   Such are 'ces belles diversitez' (sig. ẽ2r) that Grenaille admires in **Les Enfans d'Hérodes.**

La Calprenède's preferred structure, his preoccupation with suspense, and with its by-products of tension, variety and contrast, must, at least for most of his career, have ensured satisfaction of that demanding 'humeur des François qui s'ennuyent des plus belles choses quand elles ne sont point variées'.[48]

NOTES

1. Abbé d'Aubignac, **La Pratique du théâtre,** edited by Pierre Martino (Algiers and Paris, 1927), p.38.

2. The dates given are those of the plays' first publication.   It is assumed that the first performances occurred in each case within the two years preceding the date of publication.

3. Tallemant des Réaux, **Historiettes,** edited by Antoine Adam, Bibliothèque de la Pléiade, 2 vols (Paris, 1960-61), II, 584.

4. Guérin de Bouscal, 'Prologue de la Renommee', preceding his **La Mort de Brute et de Porcie, ou la Vengeance de la mort de César** (Paris, 1637), pp.6-7.

5. Henry Carrington Lancaster, 'Leading French Tragedies Just Before the **Cid',** **Modern Philology,** 22 (1924-25), 375-78 (p.377).

6. Raymond Poisson, **Le Baron de la Crasse** (Paris, 1662), p.21.

7. François Chatounières de Grenaille, 'Ouverture générale à toute la piece avec un discours sur les Poëmes Dramatiques de ce temps', prefacing his **L'Innocent malheureux, ou La Mort de Crispe** (Paris, 1639).

8. Maupoint, **Bibliotèque des théâtres** (Paris, 1733), p.81; Antoine de Léris, **Dictionnaire portatif des théâtres** (Paris, 1754), p.89.

9. S. Wilma Deierkauf-Holsboer, **Le Théâtre de l'Hôtel de Bourgogne,** 2 vols (Paris, 1968-70), II, 51.   See also **Le Mémoire de Mahelot, Laurent et d'autres décorateurs de l'Hôtel de Bourgogne,** edited by Henry Carrington Lancaster (Paris, 1920), pp.26-28 and 54.

10. A second Paris edition appeared in 1650, a third in 1651, and a Lyons edition in 1654.

11. Henry Carrington Lancaster, **A History of French Dramatic Literature in the Seventeenth Century,** 5 parts in 9 vols (Baltimore and Paris, 1929-42), IV, i, 148-49 and 152-53.

12. The second edition of 1656 was published in Paris, and the 1666 edition in Antwerp.

13. D'Aubignac, pp.138, 140, and 336-37.

14. Henry Carrington Lancaster, 'La Calprenède Dramatist', **Modern Philology,** 18 (1920-21), 121-41 and 345-60 (p.358).

15. Throughout this essay the titles of the first three plays will be shortened to **Mithridate, Essex,** and **Les Enfans d'Hérodes,** and in act, scene or page references, the abbreviations **MdM, CdE, MEH** and **Herm** will be used.

16. Alain, **Vingt leçons sur les beaux-arts,** second edition (Paris, 1931), p.129.

17. Jean Chapelain, 'Discours de la poésie représentative', in **Opuscules critiques,** edited by Alfred C. Hunter (Paris, 1936), p.128.

18. Pierre Corneille, 'Discours des trois unités', in **Writings on the Theatre,** edited by H.T. Barnwell (Oxford, 1965), p.63.

19. Georges May, **Tragédie cornélienne, tragédie racinienne:** étude sur les sources de l'intérêt dramatique (Urbana, Illinois, 1948), pp.67-71.

20. P.J. Yarrow, 'Montchrestien: a Sixteenth- or a Seventeenth-Century Dramatist?', **Australian Journal of French Studies,** 4 (1967), 140-48 (p.142).

21. Darnell Roaten, **Structural Forms in the French Theater, 1500-1700** (Philadelphia, 1960), p.140.

22. 'Examen' of **Cinna,** in **Writings on the Theatre,** p.116.

23. Pierre Médan, introduction to his edition of Racine's **Mithridate** (Paris, 1925), p.18.

24. N.-M. Bernardin, introduction to his edition of Racine's **Mithridate** (Paris, 1882), p.11.

25. Gustave Lanson, introduction to his edition of Racine's **Mithridate** (Paris, 1888), p.20.

26. Pierre Médan, 'Un Gascon précurseur de Racine: **La Mort de Mithridate** de La Calprenède et le **Mithridate** de Racine', **Revue des Pyrénées,** 19 (1907), 44-63 (pp.48 and 58).

27. Plutarch, **Les Vies des hommes illustres grecs et romains,** translated by Jacques Amyot, newly revised and corrected edition, 2 vols (Paris, 1619), II, 419.

28. Florus, **Histoire romaine,** translated by F.N. Coeffeteau (Paris, 1632), p.73.

29. Appian, **Des Guerres des Romains,** translated by Claude de Seyssel (Paris, 1580), fol. 163v.

30. Mithridate is similarly provided for with Hypsicratée. Neither wife is present in Appian, but the names appear in Plutarch, where Berenice is one of Mithridates's wives while Hypsicratia is one of his concubines (I, 330; II, 416v). See also Lancaster, **History,** II, i, 61.

31. See Lancaster, **History,** II, i, 61.

32. Although 'first acted at about the same time' in 1635 (Lancaster, **History,** II, i, 40), Benserade's **Cléopâtre** was published in 1636 and Mairet's **Marc-Antoine, ou La Cléopâtre** in 1637.

33. Georges Ascoli, **La Grande-Bretagne devant l'opinion française au XVIIe siècle,** 2 vols (Paris, 1930), I, 233-34.

34. Pierre Barrière, **La Vie intellectuelle en Périgord, 1550-1800** (Bordeaux, 1936), p.281; Médan, 'Un Gascon précurseur de Racine', p.48.

35. Roaten, p.141.

36. Jean-François Marmontel, 'Action', in **Eléments de littérature** (1846), I, 78; quoted by May, p.65.

37. Jacques Scherer, **La Dramaturgie classique en France** (Paris, 1950), p.75.

38. For a discussion of the sources, see my article 'The Portrayal of Power in La Calprenède's **Le Comte d'Essex',** **Modern Language Review,** 81 (1986), no.4.

39. Claude and François Parfaict, **Histoire du théâtre françois, depuis son origine**

jusqu'à présent, 15 vols (Paris, 1735-49), V, 479.

40.   Barrière, p.287.

41.   The same technique is used in **Jeanne, Essex** and **Herménigilde.**

42.   Josephus, **Histoire de Fl. Josephe,** translation revised by D. Gilb. Genebrard, 2 vols (Paris, 1627), I, 569-608; and Nicolas Caussin, **La Cour sainte, ou l'Institution chrestienne des grands** (Paris, 1624), pp.627-58.

43.   Margaret E. Pascoe, **Les Drames religieux du milieu du XVIIe siècle, 1636-1650** (Paris, 1932), p.123;   Kosta Loukovitch, **L'Evolution de la tragédie religieuse classique en France** (Paris, 1933), p.300.

44.   Lancaster, 'La Calprenède Dramatist', p.354.

45.   Caussin, **La Cour sainte,** tenth edition (Paris, 1640), II, 472.

46.   Caussin, **La Cour sainte** (1640), II, 448-49.

47.   As well as on the occasions discussed here, the technique is also used twice in **Edouard** (III.i, p.36; IV.i, p.55).

48.   D'Aubignac, p.262.

FIVE

Spanish *Honor* and French *Poltronnerie* in the Plays of Paul Scarron
John Trethewey

Everyone knows that honour is a major theme in Spanish Golden-Age theatre. Its presence is felt, not only in those plays which have been labelled 'honour plays', but in practically everything, from tragedy to farce, in which a social order and social **mores** are evoked as a background to, or a framework for, the action. Scholars argue about the extent of its influence in real life, but of its importance as a dramatic theme there can be no doubt. Lope de Vega's well-known lines from his **Arte nuevo de hacer comedias en este tiempo,**

> los casos de la honra son mejores,
> porque mueven con fuerza a toda gente,[1]

reflect the opinion of more than a generation of Spanish dramatists.

Such a preoccupation with honour can seem bizarre to foreigners, when it takes the form, for instance, of a bewildering casuistry (as in the Rosaura sub-plot of Calderón's **La vida es sueño**) or of a clinical study of apparently insane and self-defeating cruelty (in the same author's **El médico de su honra**). Nevertheless, in general it is accepted as a powerful motif capable of generating strong dramatic conflict, and consequently strong emotional response in an audience. A sense of honour, whether it manifests itself on stage as a private, personal code of conduct or as a preoccupation with public reputation, is depicted as a great motivator, as having its sects, its dogmatic extremes, its advantages and its drawbacks, its force for social cohesion or disruption, its alliances and conflicts with other codes, all of which material is capable of being fashioned and moulded by dramatists into a spectacle which can stir any emotion.

Historically, as a dramatic theme, honour had its rise, its moment of ascendancy, popularity and maximum exploitation, and its inevitable decline. It had the happy fortune of achieving the height of its expression in the works of some of Spain's greatest dramatists, such as Lope de Vega, Rojas Zorrilla and Calderón, which happy fortune, however, meant that honour was regarded inevitably as an essentially **Spanish** preoccupation - not to say obsession - by foreigners, who built their Spanish stereotypes to a large extent on the examples provided by these prestigious writers.

The details of the popular French view of the Spaniard need not concern us here,[2] but what **is** important, where the study of Paul Scarron is concerned, is the attraction of Spain in seventeenth-century literature and drama as a source for character, themes, settings and 'local colour'; and naturally the theme of honour was taken up, being regarded as a characteristic which distinguished the Spanish from other nations. At times in the seventeenth century, French literature gives the impression of being a mere derivative of that of Spain, as if the native tradition had become stale and dreary to the public. Charles Sorel, in **Les Visions admirables du pélerin de Parnasse** (Paris, 1635), gives us a satirical portrait of Lope de Vega, making of him a swaggering braggart, fiercely proud of his output of 'pour le moins deux mille Comedies' and scornful of French attempts to emulate him. But, as is frequently the case with Sorel, the satire is double-edged, and there is no little truth in Lope's claim, concerning the French, that 'ils ne sçauroient dresser une Comedie qu'ils n'ayent pris le patron sur quelqu'une des miennes',[3] and many Spanish dramatists, famous and obscure, could have made a similar claim. Cioranescu states that Rotrou's **La Bague de l'oubli** (from Lope's **La sortija del olvido**), played in 1629, is 'la première imitation française de la comédie espagnole', and he goes on to cite seventy-two translations and adaptations in the forty-four years between the date of that play and Molière's death.[4]

Scarron's theatrical output therefore, like the Spanish tales in his **Le Roman comique** and like his **Nouvelles tragi-comiques,** was following a fashionable trend. It comprises nine completed plays, seven comedies and two tragicomedies, published between 1645 and 1663, the last two - a comedy and a tragicomedy - published together posthumously.[5] Only **Le Prince Corsaire,** his very last play, does not have an identified Spanish source. Furthermore, unlike, for instance, Pierre Corneille in **Le Menteur** and **La Suite du Menteur,** he made no attempt to disguise their provenance, but retained all the Spanish trappings - names, settings, manners - as well as the complexity of the Spanish plots and the mixture of comic and heroic so uncharacteristic of the work of writers imbued with the ideals of French classicism (such as d'Ouville, who subjected his Spanish raw material to fearsome cuts and reshapings to make it conform to the unities).

Scarron's concessions to French conventions were simply the use of the five-act framework (replacing the three Spanish **jornadas**) and the alexandrine couplet with the occasional soliloquy in another verse form (never used seriously, nearly always a burlesque of some identifiable model, or self-mockery on the part of the reciter). He also affixed the French genre labels, comedy or tragicomedy, to material which had known no such categories. The distinction between these two genres was, however, important to him, as we shall see. The theme of honour is naturally part of the cultural baggage which he took over from his Spanish models, and which he retained with the Spanish atmosphere and settings that were so attractive to him and his time. Nevertheless, Scarron was no mere translator, and every single model that he chose for adaptation is stamped with his personal style and character so that these plays are as representative of him as are the burlesque poems and **Le Roman comique**.[6] There is, furthermore, in all these plays, a division between those elements - of character, plot or setting - which can in their several ways be labelled **romanesque**, and those which are farcical and burlesque. This duality is characteristic also of **Le Roman comique**,[7] but naturally, in his drama, Scarron takes care to achieve a **theatrical** effect by their interaction. It is undoubtedly true - and French classicists were aware of it - that farce, unless it is severely rationed or kept somehow apart from serious action, possesses the dangerous ability to 'contaminate' it and thereby to mock it. Such contamination occurs in several of Scarron's comedies, though plainly, it must be added, with his full knowledge and consent.

Scarron's plays can be divided, if one abandons chronological order, into a number of categories and sub-categories according to their content. First of all there are the two tragicomedies, **L'Ecolier de Salamanque** and **Le Prince Corsaire**, both complex **comedias de capa y espada** in which noble characters work out their destinies according to principles dictated by the code of honour. The genre label is important: it indicates that an audience must be made seriously concerned for these heroes and heroines and for their ultimate safety and reconciliation. There is no comic element in **Le Prince Corsaire**, and that in **L'Ecolier de Salamanque** is confined to the occasional joyful antics and comic-cowardly protests of a **gracioso**, Crispin, and his exchanges with two maids, Béatrix and Lisette, none of which affects the course of the main action.

All the other plays, as we have said, are comedies, but two of them, **La Fausse Apparence** and **Jodelet duelliste**, are again comedies of intrigue, and there is a fairly clear division between serious and farcical action. The first play most resembles **L'Ecolier de Salamanque** in that the comic element is confined to the largely choric comments and exclamations of Cardille, a valet, and the main action presents a complexity and an uncontaminated seriousness which absorbs the audience's attention and sympathy. **Jodelet duelliste** is different in that the farce action has a separate sub-plot of its own which alternates with the main, more serious one.[8] The effect is again to preserve the central action from the undermining influence of farce.

The remaining five comedies all have one important feature in common. The expression **comedia de figurón** is used in Spanish to describe this sort of play in which the action is dominated by one grotesque character round whom the intrigue develops. One can however in Scarron's case subdivide this category into a group of two plays in which the grotesques are genuine - **Dom Japhet d'Arménie** and **Le Marquis ridicule** - and three in which the eccentric behaviour is a mask put on to suit a temporary situation. In one of these last, **L'Héritier ridicule**, this behaviour is a deliberate and successful piece of action, and in the other two, **Jodelet, ou le Maître valet** and **Le Gardien de soi-même**, it is the accidental result of placing an 'actor' of very limited ability in a role for which he is completely unsuited. In all five of these comedies the farce element dominates and subverts the serious. I propose now to study in more detail all these plays in the order in which I have named them.

*   *
*

Scarron's two tragicomedies are by no means his worst plays. **L'Ecolier de Salamanque** maintains pace and tension and variety of action without losing clarity. Chance may have too big a part in the unfolding of the action, for those with classical taste, but that is a constant feature in Scarron's theatre, and one in which he resembles his Spanish mentors. This play is perhaps his most Spanish, with its Toledo setting and its overriding preoccupation with honour.

The code, as it informs this tragicomedy, is quite a complex one, and various of its admirable subtleties are revealed to us in the course of the action. We are for instance confronted with Dom Félix, an irascible, hasty old man with a tetchy concern about expense and the follies of youth. One might be tempted to see in such an assemblage of imperfections a potential comic **senex**, but one would be wrong. The presentation of these traits has a definite, serious moral purpose in the play. Dom Félix is an honourable man but his faults bring him anguish and suffering. Likewise his daughter, Léonore, who is passionate and headstrong.

The cause of all their pain and anger is the Comte who appears, at the opening of the play, to be about to abandon her, a fate which would bring dishonour to her and her family (without however dishonouring the Comte: he enjoys traditional male immunity). The intention of the dishonoured Léonore will be to follow the Comte everywhere implacably, a living reproach, until he consents to marry her. The father however seeks revenge through his son Dom Pèdre, the **écolier** of the title. The Comte is of course misunderstood. His sense of honour is so fine-tuned that not only is he a man of perfect civility, as well as of perfect valour, he is also one who cannot tolerate anything less in those he encounters. Loss of temper, displays of anguish, are treated therefore with a polite 'refusal to co-operate'. He exposes his pedantic concern for coolness and equanimity when explaining to the enraged Dom Félix why he cannot accede to his demand that he marry Léonore:

> Pour me la faire prendre, il fallait me prier,
> Non pas me quereller, non pas m'injurier,
> Je ne fais rien par force, et fais tout par prière;
> Aux humbles, je suis doux; aux fiers, j'ai l'âme fière [...]
> Pensez-y mûrement, et que je me retire. (I.iv, p.76)

Dom Pèdre, the son, absent at the beginning of the play, and therefore not **au fait** with recent family history, proves to be a character exactly moulded to elicit the admiration of the Comte, even though (with an eye for symmetry) he is secretly making love to the Comte's sister. As irony piles upon irony in the course of the action, and as revelation succeeds revelation to test the generosity and self-possession of each, we realize that these two are in the end fated to be brothers-in-law. Various subtleties of the code of honour are revealed to us on the way. The plot decrees that the Comte should not learn too soon who his adversary is, and Dom Pèdre must therefore refuse to reveal the name of his father, because (aphorism) 'le nom d'un offensé ne se révèle point' (II.ix, p.89). Furthermore, although the two have already ample grounds for fighting each other, Dom Pèdre must first attend to 'other business' (finding and punishing the seducer of his sister) because, until it is accomplished,

> [...] aussi bien me vaincre est un exploit honteux,
> Que je n'ai point d'honneur, puisqu'on l'ôte à mon père.(II.ix, p.89)

Such ideological subtleties are not tainted for us by the presence of any laughable traits in these central characters. Humour is kept in its place, in the role of the **gracioso** Crispin.[9]

One last quirky feature of the code of honour is worth mentioning here, since it is first illustrated in this play. It is the fact that once Léonore's seducer has agreed to marry her, her 'fault' is as if it had never been. There is no Christian dimension to complicate matters: the word 'sin' passes nobody's lips. At the end, the placated Dom Félix can even see her passionate adventure, dispassionately, as a sort of gamble which paid off:

> Tout n'a que bien été,
> Hasardant votre honneur vous l'avez augmenté. (V.vii, p.128)

Similar feelings motivate the characters in **Le Prince Corsaire**, and, even though they are not Spanish, but Cretan, similar subtleties complicate their lives and render them more exciting. The hero Orosmane, who is the unconventional prince of the title, is the enemy of Amintas, and yet the two are admirers of each other's valour and integrity as were the Comte and Dom Pèdre. A fight to the death between them is constantly postponed by some scruple or other, so that in the end the fact that they are brothers can be revealed, together with other happy coincidences. Thus, Amintas will help his imprisoned enemy to escape because the latter, having previously defeated him in single combat, has spared his life. This act is not simple gratitude, however, but a logical move dictated by the code:

> [...] je te dois la vie et l'honneur me conseille
> De rendre à mon vainqueur une grâce pareille,
> Pour reprendre sur lui, sans passer pour ingrat,
> L'honneur que m'a fait perdre un malheureux combat. (IV.ii, p.469)

Orosmane, for his part, is also at pains to make it clear that, as far as he is concerned, this changes nothing in their basic antagonism:

> N'espère pas pourtant
> Qu'en me tirant des fers de ton injuste père,
> J'en sois moins ton rival, ton cruel adversaire.   (II.vii, p.476)

The wicked, cruel father of the two, Nicanor, despite his villainy, receives the obedience and respect of Amintas throughout, since the latter knows he is his son, but Orosmane too, on discovering his own relationship, expresses regret for his exploits against him, and asks humble pardon of a man who, but a few moments before, was a 'tigre affamé de sang' (V.ix-x, pp.485-87). The absolute, mystical power of the family head over its members is such that it can instantly bring a cruelly wronged rebel to submission, though at the same time another mystical power - dramatic expediency perhaps - finally converts the father to regret and reconciliation.

Honour motivates the women in this play too. In the case of Alcione it is obviously from a concern for public reputation that she, the younger sister of Elise, rejects Amintas who has turned to her after he has himself been spurned by the older girl: 'Je ne puis accepter ce qu'un autre refuse' (II.i, p.452). Admittedly, she suspects that he has not yet rooted out of his heart his love for Elise, but even so,

> [...] quand il changerait, le pourrais-je estimer?
> Pensant gagner mon cœur, il perdrait mon estime,
> Et son amour pour moi me paraîtrait un crime.   (II.iii, p.457)

To yield to him would be to 'trahir la fierté de mon cœur' (p.458). Elise, on the other hand, sure of the love of the hero Orosmane, vies with him in a sort of loving contest of **générosité**. 'Vous n'avez rien à craindre', says Orosmane (V.vi, p.482), which elicits the gentle rebuke:

> Que tu me connais mal, si tu crois que mon âme
> Dans le péril s'étonne [...]

And Orosmane, in his next speech, chides her: 'Jugez mieux d'un cœur où vous régnez'.

One can imagine for them a happy lifetime of such sweet mutual remonstrations.

The code of honour informs both these plays, therefore, and its illustration is the stuff of various **péripéties**.   No jarring note of doubt mars the serene certainty of these aristocratic protagonists, since honour is the morality by which they live. Crispin's timorous protests in **L'Ecolier de Salamanque** are those of a lesser mortal and only serve to offset the admirable intrepidity of his superiors.

It is hard to decide why **La Fausse Apparence** (from a play by Calderón) is not also labelled 'tragicomedy'.   The social class of the central characters appears to be the same as of those in **L'Ecolier de Salamanque**, and the role of Cardille, the play's **gracioso**, is similar to that of Crispin.   The code is once more upheld against those who would seek to flout it, or who misinterpret it.   The play begins with a seduction once again, but this time the young lady's downfall is only supposed.   As the other Calderón example, **El médico de su honra**, shows us, however, supposition can be a motive for action as impelling as facts where matters of honour are concerned.   Dom Carlos's reserve towards Léonore is not just the manifestation of ordinary jealousy, but is in addition the posturing of a man who cannot contemplate uniting himself with a woman on whom the slightest public suspicion has fallen.   Seeing himself as obliged to protect her (since she is in danger from her enraged father), he is determined to marry her off to the person who, he believes, is responsible for her downfall, 'pour rendre à ton honneur quelque sorte d'éclat' (IV.vi, p.425), a duty which adds further twists to an already complicated plot.   This complexity possibly explains the genre label because, although finally in the play honourable integrity is vindicated, we are more likely to be preoccupied (or indeed bemused) by the intricacies of the action than by the illustration of niceties of the code.

There can be no doubt about the genre of **Jodelet duelliste**.   Jodelet's appropriating of an entire sub-plot to himself is enough to establish not only a strong comic element, but also, for the first time, the disruptive presence of farce.   As the title indicates, Jodelet, a valet, wishes to take the usual course to avenge an insult received.   Much simple amusement is to be derived from the alternating bouts of ludicrous bravado and abject cowardice that he displays, and perhaps rather more sophisticated amusement from the attempts at casuistry which he rehearses with the audience:

> Mais avait-il la main toute ouverte ou bien close:
> Un coup de poing est plus honnête qu'un soufflet:
> Je m'en veux éclaircir; quoique simple valet,
> Je suis jaloux d'honneur autant ou plus qu'un autre.   (II.ii, pp.202-03)

Nevertheless, honour is not mocked by Jodelet's antics.   He is plainly a foolish servant attempting to imitate his betters, and while his sub-plot parallels on a burlesque level the scheming and the real duel that take place in the main action, the very fact of the clown's plot being a separate element in the play prevents it from contaminating real honour, or really honourable characters.   Even Jodelet's fame and extra-dramatic status as a popular **persona** who has appeared in many plays and scenarios are not enough to enable him to influence a main action in which, after the opening scene, he has very little part.

The main action is comedy of a different, complementary nature and is concerned with the attempts of a truly dishonourable man - liar and seducer - to trick his way to respectability and a wife, and the tricks that the sympathetic faction employ to defeat him.   Their deceptions, however, subvert their moral status and prevent them from being the advocates or defenders of honour. In consequence their actions do not parallel, on a higher, serious plane, the antics of Jodelet.

The intermittent intrusion of a **figuron**, Dom Gaspard, also destroys any serious mark that the code of honour might make in the play. He is a swaggering soldier who loves two women and jealously challenges any man who approaches either. The main action of the play is not in fact serious, but satirical, the seducer Dom Félix being a comic 'stage villain' and his adversaries only **relatively** innocent and honourable.[10] Honour's reputation is perhaps saved (despite Jodelet's intermittent antics) by Dom Félix's mockery of it in exchanges like:

JODELET

Vous êtes donc menteur?

DOM FELIX

Oui, j'ai l'honneur de l'être. (I.i, p.194)

and by his enthusiastic embracing of every dishonourable vice - infidelity, deceit, cruelty, discourtesy - except cowardice, this last being reserved for Jodelet.

Dom Gaspard prefigures in his way the central characters of **Dom Japhet d'Arménie** and **Le Marquis ridicule**. All three, despite their absurdities, are men of consequence whose actions and opinions influence others. Dom Japhet is perhaps the least influential because, despite his wealth and retinue, his reputation as former court jester makes him a sort of permanent unofficial fool and the butt of everyone's satirical attacks.   His attitudes and claims justify this. He is vain, a bellicose coward,[11] given to excessive display of all kinds, speaking a burlesque **galimatias** composed of a colourful mixture of archaisms and neologisms, and believing himself 'venu de père en fils du puîné de Noé' (I.i, 1.31). The rest of the cast, servants, equals, superiors, is engaged in either baiting him or using him, including the hero, Dom Alphonse, the heroine, Léonore, and the heroine's uncle, the Commandeur. In fact, so much ingenuity goes into the persecution and deception of the ex-jester that the modern spectator must remind himself that such an attitude to madness is commonplace in Renaissance and seventeenth-century literature.

Scarron has, however, seen to it that, because this grotesque has so little real power, he can occasionally be banished from the stage so that a serious, if simple, plot can develop.   To this end, the hero Alphonse is allowed to spend the night which intervenes between Act IV and Act V with the heroine.   Seduction is a motif that appeals to Scarron, as we have seen, but here the seduction of heroine by hero takes place in mid-action and must be vindicated morally before the end of the play, a task which is easily accomplished.

According to **romanesque** conventions, if a loving couple have privately exchanged vows which they intend to keep, then they have the right to feel above reproach when they consummate their rather irregular union.   Scarron assumes that the audience will recognize the convention and bestow their unreserved sympathy on Alphonse and Léonore.   He does not share the strait-laced scruples of classical theorists and practitioners on this score.   Nevertheless, the lovers do create problems for themselves with Léonore's irate uncle, the Commandeur, who proposes to put the young man to death.   His objection to their night of love is not in fact due to abhorrence of an illicit union, but to a supposed betrayal of her social status by his niece, since he knows Alphonse only as the secretary of the ludicrous Dom Japhet. Once the young man's nobility and respectability are established, the Commandeur, like Dom Félix in **L'Ecolier de Salamanque**, accords instant, absolute, all-obliterating forgiveness.   There has been no transgression, merely a misunderstanding.   The Commandeur thought the family had been dishonoured, but he was wrong.   As he admits to Léonore, she has not erred: 'Votre choix vous excuse' (V.v, 1.1438).   The subtleties of the code of honour are not ignored, therefore, in this **comedia de figurón**. They enjoy, as it were, equal and separate status with the antics of Dom Japhet, and survive contamination from his disruptive presence, partly as a result of the play's careful structuring, and partly by the ex-jester acquiring the mystical status of community madman.

One cannot be equally confident of being able to isolate the burlesque content of **Le Marquis ridicule**.   The play contains, from the point of view of honour, an exemplary character, a young lady of perfect integrity.   'J'ai de l'honneur', says Blanche, as she resists the beloved Dom Sanche throughout Act II, repressing her feelings for him because her father destines her for another, Dom Blaize Pol, the Marquis of the title.   Whatever his faults, says Blanche, 'pour l'aimer, il suffit qu'il serait mon époux' (I.i, p.15), and however eloquently Dom Sanche (younger brother to Dom Blaize) pleads his case, her heart appreciates honour as much as it does love:

'Mon cœur [...] m'apprend mon devoir' (I.iv, p.17). In Act IV, she still insists, with reference to the absurd Dom Blaize, 'puisqu'il est approuvé de mon père, il me plaît' (IV.i, p.36).

Unfortunately for Blanche and her equally honourable lover, they are surrounded by farce figures and others whose characters seem composed of a mixture of sense and nonsense. The Marquis is an unredeemable grotesque whose eccentric ways are the antithesis of every noble quality. His concern for honour is reduced to an inordinate terror of cuckoldry, which causes him to fear the prospect of union even to the blameless Blanche. He is in spite of this the preferred suitor, and his impulses and hesitations regarding marriage are the mainspring of the play's complex central plot. At the same time, there is another eccentric in the play, pursuing a sub-plot of her own which has its effects on the main action. Stéphanie is a 'femme d'intrigue', and she is beautiful: Dom Sanche himself tells us so (I.iii, p.7). But while lacking scruples, she also lacks cunning, so that her scheming deceives only those who are as absurd as herself. The valet Merlin finds her not only 'franche fripponne' but also 'faible de cerveau' (p.8). When, therefore, Dom Sanche admits that he is often to be found at her lodgings - 'Ma paresse souvent m'y retient tout un jour' (p.7) - we begin to doubt, not his integrity perhaps, but certainly his wisdom. We also feel that Blanche, if dutiful, is lacking in spirit, accepting as she does the prospect of a husband of the quality of Dom Blaize, and we wonder at the wit of a father who can propose such an alliance. And indeed, when we meet Dom Cosme, we find him elderly, and so vacuously affable that he will react in no way to the angry goading of Dom Blaize - 'un doux à triple étage', the latter irritably calls him (IV.v, p.47) - until late in the action, when a sudden outburst of rage achieves an added comic effect by contrasting with what has gone before.

In the midst of this gallery of grotesques (not to mention a number of idiosyncratic servants), it is impossible not to feel that the 'noble' responses of Blanche and Dom Sanche are, of dramatic necessity, accompanied by a certain comic primness of response, an excessive concern for the proprieties, that these lovers are in fact a trifle grotesque themselves.   Dom Sanche cannot react against his absurd elder brother, Dom Blaize, but remains submissive despite every provocation. When Dom Cosme makes his sudden bland admission (important to the plot) of having once kept a mistress whom he had abandoned when she was with child (IV.iv, p.44), we note that neither Blanche nor Dom Sanche show the slightest reaction. The revelation is an enormity which cannot be taken in by them (as it can by Stéphanie, who makes use of it).   They do not so much act on principle as remain spinelessly inactive, and are therefore, with their scruples, part of the comic scene. At last, in a play by Scarron, we find Spanish honour's eminent status as the motivator of heroic actions and high ideals clearly undermined by the corrupting contact of farce.

L'Héritier ridicule is a comedy in which the grotesque element is juxtaposed not so much with the shallow primness of a superficial **romanesque** as with characters who display considerable bitterness. As in **Jodelet duelliste**, there are no truly honourable characters present. The hero, Dom Diègue, decides to test the fidelity of the woman he loves, Hélène, by pretending poverty and by throwing a seemingly richer suitor (his disguised valet, Filipin) in her way, and on discovering she is a 'femme intéressée' turns his test into a revenge, seeking to humiliate and isolate his former mistress. At the same time, it is his new mistress, Léonore, wishing to win him for herself, who points out Hélène's cupidity, suggesting the test and triumphantly attending the final humiliation, which is conducted ritualistically by the three men involved, who each pronounce a vindictive eight-line rejection speech with identical first and last lines (V.iv, ll.1539-62). Ironically, the theme of 'honour lost and to be retrieved' is invoked only by the defeated Hélène: 'Je ne manquerai pas de parents en Espagne' (l.1563), 'Ma vengeance, ou ma mort, / Me mettront en repos, avant que le jour passe' (ll.1570-71).

The rest of the action involves two eccentrics, a major one (Filipin, alias Dom Pedro de Buffalos) and a minor (Dom Juan). The latter is a variant of the traditional rival in love, affecting violent emotions and embarking on headlong courses of action which inevitably lead nowhere. Dom Pedro is the imitation **héritier**, set up to tempt Hélène. Filipin's portrayal of this absurd figure reminds one at once of Dom Japhet and Dom Blaize Pol with their mixture in language and comportment of outmoded tradition and feverish innovation, their swaggering bravado which scarcely hides cowardice, and their constant need for reassurance concerning their status, illustrated identically in all three cases by the treatment meted out to an unfortunate lackey. These exaggerated manifestations in Dom Pedro of social insecurity should be too much for an intelligent woman to pretend to believe in, even for ulterior motives. Despite her beauty, therefore, Hélène is also reduced to a caricature, to little more than an emblematic figure representing self-interest. Having no champions, honour is not mocked in this play as it is by the wan figures of Dom Sanche and Blanche in **Le Marquis ridicule.**

With **Jodelet, ou le Maître valet,** we leave both bitterness and **romanesque** behind and enter a realm of pure fantasy. This may not at first be evident on a reading of the play. We find at the opening a young nobleman, Dom Juan, who is aware that it is his responsibility to restore the family honour by avenging the death of a brother and the seduction of a sister. That sister, Lucrèce, appears to foreshadow the Léonore of **L'Ecolier de Salamanque** in that she too, we find, feels obliged to follow her fickle lover, Dom Louis, through the world like a reproachful shadow until he will agree to marry her. We also find this same Dom Louis involved in machinations which threaten to compromise the virtue of Isabelle, Dom Juan's intended bride. The main action of the play is launched by Dom Juan's exchanging roles with his valet so that he may be in a better position to spy on Isabelle.

All this would have the air of a standard **comedia de capa y espada**, were it not for the involvement of farce: once again the famous **enfariné** Jodelet is present, this time in a position to subvert not only the serious action of the play, but also the assumed values that underlie that action.

Jodelet is not alone in this subversion, however. One tried and trusted technique which Scarron uses in this comedy to amuse the audience is the introduction of deliberately anomalous French details into what otherwise is recognized as a wholly Spanish setting and action. Dom Fernand, Isabelle's father, to whose unsavoury habits – 'il crache / Plus fort qu'aucun qui soit dans Madrid que je sache' (II.i, p.265) – the servant Béatrix has already introduced us, displays a senile (and anti-illusory) habit, which becomes evident as soon as he appears (II.ii), of giving a running commentary to the audience on his own utterances to the other characters. He amuses us a few moments later with his preoccupation with the **literary** quality of the distressed Lucrèce's speeches when she enters to ask for protection, and our amusement is redoubled by his sudden admiring cry that 'Ces vers sont de Mairet!' (II.iii, p.268), both 'vers' and 'Mairet' drawing particular attention to themselves because they show Dom Fernand again slipping dangerously out of his dramatic role as head of a Spanish household to become for a few seconds a French literary dilettante speaking to a French audience. He is thus suddenly closer to that audience than to the Spanish action, which is momentarily frozen and distanced. Poor Lucrèce must not react to this outburst in any way: indeed she must not even know that it is taking place. It is outside her time-scale and on a plane which has nothing to do with her, and therefore it undermines, from the audience's point of view, the earnestness of her plea for pity and concern. She is no longer (if she ever was) a genuine Spanish damsel in distress, but a caricature whose protestations need not be taken seriously. Henceforth also, Dom Fernand's **real** involvement in the action must be regarded as suspect. Even though we get no more such textual lapses from him, we are on the look-out thereafter for hints (textual or gestural) of extra-dramatic commentary or irony.

Dom Fernand's momentary lapse is nevertheless exceptional in Scarron's theatre, for characters of his status and importance usually stay within the illusion. In most (but not all) conventional comedy, it is generally left to the valets, the servants of both sexes, the grotesques to ingratiate themselves in some extra-dramatic fashion with the audience. Here, that task falls to Jodelet. Ugly, **poltron**, servile and foolish, he is by any realistic standards woefully miscast in the role of his master. That the latter should contemplate the exchange, that any other character should be taken in by it, places the action firmly in the realms of fantasy. That fantasy is further emphasized by Jodelet's displays of scepticism with regard to what is happening to him in this Spanish dramatic setting, a scepticism which he shares with his French audience and which draws them closer to him.

Such sceptical moments have various forms. As Jodelet the clown, he can react to the audience by taking note of their laughter:

> Ils rient tous, ma foi! Rient-ils de m'entendre?
> Est-ce que j'ai tenu quelque propos de fat?   (II.vii, p.275)

On the dramatic plane, such exclamations are proof to the Spanish characters that Jodelet is mad. His madness confers on him a kind of immunity when he behaves or speaks in a manner contrary to aristocratic ideals. Thus, when, in the guise of Dom Juan his master, he insults and shocks Dom Fernand or Isabelle, his remarks are diplomatically ignored. At the same time, however, many such remarks are made to the audience, especially those spoken at the expense of Dom Fernand, who, we already realize, is fair game for derisive comment. Therefore, when, in Act II, Scene vii (pp.274 ff.), Jodelet treats his prospective father-in-law with jeering contempt and impatience (wishing as quickly as possible to get his hands on his promised bride), we are regaled with remarks about the old man with which we can readily agree: 'le beau-père a de l'air d'un chat-huant', 'Quoi! toujours ce vieillard! [...]   maudit soit le fâcheux', etc.

As for cowardice, Jodelet does not have the persuasiveness and eloquence of a Falstaff, but his **poltronnerie** is nevertheless given the status of being a valid point of view for one in his position. We laugh at his language but at the same time we do not reject what he says in, for instance, his soliloquy composed in stanza form:

> Que béni soyez-vous, Seigneur,
> Qui m'avez fait un misérable
> Qui préfère l'ail à l'honneur.   (IV.ii, pp.296-97)

Jodelet's solitary observations are the commonplaces of any homily against honour: better to be small and secure than great and an easy target for the blows of fortune; how absurd to kill someone or be killed for a slap on the face; the pleasures of this life are not worth giving up for a point of honour. The language enlivens them and contributes to our good-humoured sympathy with him.

The **servante** Béatrix too, to a smaller extent, has her links with the spectators, and even, like Dom Fernand, her moment as a French textual commentator towards

SIX

Love and Politics in Corneille's *Agésilas*
Stephen Scott

In a remark that seems particularly appropriate to his later plays from **OEdipe** (1659) to **Suréna** (1674), Doubrovsky writes of Corneille's dramatic output that 'il n'est guère d'œuvre illustre, et tant de fois commentée, sur laquelle il reste tant à dire'.[1] Whilst the early comedies and several plays of the 'middle period', from **La Mort de Pompée** (1644) to **Pertharite** (1652), have inspired widespread interest and comment, there still exists only one full-length study of the later plays, which itself dates back almost forty years.[2] Indeed, of these later works, only **Sertorius, Attila**, and **Suréna** have appeared separately in modern editions.[3]

In the few paragraphs devoted to the later plays in the various histories of French literature, it is normally implied that since they were, as far as we can tell, relative contemporary failures they can now be dismissed for that reason. In attempting to account for this failure, even those critics most familiar with the plays have often offered superficial explanations. Since political themes continue to feature so prominently in the later works, it has frequently been assumed that the plays failed because such concerns were irrelevant to the domesticated courtiers of an increasingly absolutist Louis XIV: Corneille, refusing to comply with the new taste for **romanesque** tragedy, represented most successfully by his brother Thomas and by Philippe Quinault, simply went out of fashion. Even a critic of the standing of Nadal can say of the later plays that they represent 'les formules et les images que son intelligence du théâtre, et peut-être aussi un entêtement tranquille, continuaient à répandre sur la scène; ce n'était le plus souvent que replâtrage et recettes de métier'.[4] The problem with such summary analyses is that they are not so much an interpretation of the plays as a post-mortem: the plays' contemporary failure is the starting point for further criticism. It is not therefore surprising that criticism has often obscured some of their most interesting and important aspects. This is not to say that the particular characteristics of the later works have not been identified: the problem is that they have more often than not been simply stated rather than elaborated. Whilst it is no doubt true that the later plays are characterized by an interest in the intrigue of matrimonial politics, by the relative failure of the formerly triumphant 'hero', by the compromising of the ethos of **générosité,** and by a sense of social disillusionment that results in the demand for the respect of the solitary individual over and above the imperatives of the group, it also remains true that the meaning and interrelatedness of these elements have still to be properly investigated.   How should they affect our understanding of Corneille in terms of his earlier work and preoccupations, and in terms of the change in social outlook and literary production that followed upon the aristocratic failure of the Fronde and the arrival of Louis XIV's majority?   This is the central question to which critics of the later plays should address themselves.

Agésilas may appear an odd choice for such a study in that commentators seem agreed that it represents a departure from the plays of the later period. The use of **vers libres,** the artificiality of the play's 'happy ending', the stylized **tendresse** of the young **amants,** Cotys and Spitridate, the **enjouement** of Aglatide and the **préciosité** of Mandane, amongst other factors, led Georges Couton to style the play a 'tragédie gaie'[5] and to venture the opinion that **Agésilas** represents an attempt on the part of Corneille to imitate the prevailing fashion in **romanesque** tragedy.[6]   Almost all subsequent critics of the play have followed this lead.   So Nadal sees in **Agésilas** an illustration of 'l'amour tendre et galant à la manière de Quinault et de Thomas Corneille, amour aussi éloigné du politique que de l'héroïque, et qui répond à une des formes de l'amour précieux';[7] and Lockert writes that **Agésilas** 'was doubtless meant to compete with the purely romanesque dramas of Quinault, which had culminated in **Astrate** a year earlier and were all the vogue while **Sophonisbe** and **Othon** were finding few admirers'.[8] But, as Doubrovsky notes in an unpublished critical edition of the play, this emphasis on the love interest in **Agésilas** has almost completely obscured discussion of the play's political interest.[9]   Indeed, critics tacitly acknowledge this fact by revealing a certain degree of embarrassment at the obvious presence of a strong political element in the play.   However radical this 'departure' might be, Corneille, it is implied, remains very much himself to the extent that the two aspects - love and politics - are simply not harmonized. Lemonnier writes: 'Au troisième acte le ton se hausse ou plutôt se guinde par l'introduction de la politique.'[10] Other critics have sought to justify their neglect of the political themes by claiming that they are completely obscured by the love interest[11] or, rather absurdly, that they do not exist.[12]

This critical neglect of the political aspect of **Agésilas** should, I think, make us pause before accepting what has come to represent an established consensus on the play, a 'traditional' interpretation.   It would, moreover, seem highly unlikely that Corneille, who refers contemptuously to the **romanesque** writers as 'nos délicats' and 'nos enjoués', and who attacks them in several of the prefaces to the later plays as well as in his **Lettre à Saint-Evremond**, should seek to imitate them in **Agésilas**. Exponents of the 'traditional' interpretation must also explain how Corneille came to write such a light **romanesque** work at a time when, as Doubrovsky has shown, he was depicting in his other plays (including those immediately before and after **Agésilas: Othon** and **Attila**) the tragedy of the collapse and degradation of the **éthique aristocratique** that had been so painfully consolidated in his earlier work.[13]   And if Corneille was satisfying contemporary taste, why was **Agésilas** such an unmitigated disaster whilst **Othon** and **Attila** enjoyed a far better reception?[14]   Indeed, why, if one accepts the traditional view, does Corneille call his play a tragedy instead of a 'comédie héroïque', a term coined by him as far back as **Don Sanche d'Aragon** (1649)?

For critics like Nadal[15] and Bénichou[16] who, in spite of the evidence cited above, encounter no problems in reconciling Corneille's **amour héroïque** with the **amour tendre** of a Quinault, the traditional interpretation can be consistently, if erroneously, maintained. For those who assert, however, like Doubrovsky and Adam, that Corneille opposes this exaggerated form of **romanesque** love in his later plays, there remains a nagging sense of contradiction. Thus Adam states that 'Corneille a pris, dans ses tragédies historiques, le contre-pied de la tragédie galante',[17] and he cites the evidence adduced above. He nonetheless asserts that with **Agésilas** Corneille was pandering to popular taste: 'A l'époque d'**Œdipe**, Corneille put être sans injustice considéré comme un écrivain précieux. Il l'était à nouveau en 1666, lorsqu'il écrivait **Agésilas**'.[18] What makes this thesis improbable is, of course, the very anachronistic position it reserves for the latter play. Doubrovsky shows, in fact, how unlikely it is that Corneille imitated Quinault; the influence was rather in the opposite direction.[19] The later plays represent, on the contrary, 'une contre-offensive' on the part of Cornelian heroism.[20] Thus, for Doubrovsky, **Agésilas** again constitutes an anachronism in the context of the later works; but if it follows the prevailing fashion, it is only in order to parody it.[21] Corneille's first audiences were, moreover, not to be fooled: the very artificiality of the triumph of heroism at the end of the play represents an implied critique of the **société mondaine**.[22] So one of the critical problems of the traditional interpretation, the play's unequivocal failure, is finally explained, if a little too ingeniously.[23] Doubrovsky's interpretation does have the merit, however, of striving to place **Agésilas** in its manifold context and is for that reason more satisfactory than the traditional one. It seems to us, however, that it is only by looking more closely at the neglected political aspect of the play, and by examining its relationship to the love aspect, that a solution to these critical problems is likely to be found. In this respect, we agree strongly with Doubrovsky's view that 'dans ce cas see how **Agésilas** participates, in a most illuminating way, in what Bénichou has shown to be the great debate of so much of the literature of seventeenth-century France in the post-Fronde period.[25]

Pelous has shown how the 'demolition' of the hero was accompanied between around 1655 and 1670 by a complementary demolition of the conception of love that had been generally espoused by writers up to that time, a conception set forth most influentially in **L'Astrée**, but which had its roots in medieval courtly love.[26]   The heroic 'synthesis' of Rodrigue can be seen simply as an attempt to reconcile the spiritualized, sublimated Platonic love of the idyllic shepherds of **L'Astrée** with a contingent, complex social reality.[27]   Indeed, as Pelous shows, this attempt at a reconciliation between love and the world was the dream of all seventeenth-century writers on the subject until what he terms the 'schisme galant' sought to undermine the 'orthodoxie romanesque' in the 1650s.[28]   The **galants** were opposed to **tendresse** in all its forms, both the sublimated form exemplified in the novel and the heroic form exemplified in Corneille and other dramatists of the 1630s and 1640s;   they sought therefore to strip love of what Pelous calls its 'idéalisme moralisant', to demystify it and to insist instead on the lover's right to the happiness and fulfilment of physical gratification.[29]   In this context, **préciosité** is seen as a revolt on the part of a number of women, unwilling to play the **galant** part of the **coquette,** who saw **galanterie** as an extremely dangerous threat to their hard-won status and dignity which were wholly dependent upon the supremacy they were able to exercise in the field of love.[30]   As both Bénichou and Pelous demonstrate, then, the idealism that motivates Cornelian drama, in both the public (political) and private (amorous) spheres, was under increasing attack by the 1660s: in both spheres the cult of **générosité** is replaced by that of what might broadly be termed **intérêt.** The consequence, in its most extreme form, is Corneille's Persian tyrant, in whom a quasi-legalized social hierarchy is replaced by the anarchy of Machiavellianism, and in whom the official status of love as belonging inseparably to the same value system is overturned in the name of 'caprice', of immediate gratification and the consequent degradation of woman.   Yet were the enemy to be so self-evidently 'without', the integrity of the heroic world would not be so radically threatened as we find it to be in **Agésilas.** The heroic citadel has been penetrated and a disguised enemy stalks within.

* *

*

Lysander has understandably been viewed first and foremost as a political adventurer, but this emphasis has led to his analysis of love being somewhat obscured.

In fact, he has a good deal to say on the subject, including what are virtually his first words in the play:

> Je sais trop que l'amour de ses droits est jaloux,
>   Qu'il dispose de nous sans nous,
> Que les plus beaux objets ne sont pas sûrs de plaire.
> L'aveugle sympathie est ce qui fait agir
>   La plupart des feux qu'il excite.
> Il ne l'attache pas toujours au vrai mérite:
> Et quand il la dénie, on n'a point à rougir.   (II.ii, ll.541-47)

Here Lysander provides a perfect example of **galanterie** as defined by Pelous. Love, he says, often contradicts conventional morality and in so doing dissociates itself from the concept of 'mérite', the aim of which, we have seen, was to impose a sort of moral **askesis** on love, to bring it within the systematization of the **éthique généreuse**, to 'collectivize' it. Thus the form of love Lysander describes here is a pre-ethical love, in the sense that it fails to transform the subjective nature of passion into an objective value. For Lysander, love can dispense with 'mérite' (objective value of the clan) since it possesses its own intrinsic criteria which, being particular to it, are eccentric, thus individualistic. Consequently, **galant** love is not always motivated by 'mérite' or 'les plus beaux objets', but is governed on the contrary by an 'aveugle sympathie' which takes no cognizance of pre-established values: 'il dispose de nous sans nous'; such a love is fiercely and imperiously independent: 'l'amour de ses droits est jaloux'. Since the lover's capitulation to passion is thus seen as inevitable, Lysander is able to absolve him of any moral responsibility: 'Et quand il la dénie, on n'a point à rougir'. Such a fatalistic view of love stands, of course, in diametrical opposition to Rodrigue's heroic synthesis.

When he appears with Cotys in Act II, Lysander goes so far as to assert that love is legitimized by the extent to which it is able to gratify instinct. In thus employing the **généreux** language of legitimacy, he completely inverts the **éthique généreuse**; since instinct henceforth constitutes the sole arbiter of morality, a 'foi' that has taken no cognizance of it can be legitimately revoked:

> Ne traitez pas, Seigneur, ce nouveau feu de crime:
> Le choix que font les yeux est le plus légitime,
> Et comme un beau désir ne peut bien s'allumer
> S'ils n'instruisent le cœur de ce qu'il doit aimer,
> C'est ôter à l'amour tout ce qu'il a d'aimable,
> Que les tenir captifs sous une aveugle foi,
>   Et le don le plus favorable
> Que ce cœur sans leur ordre ose faire de soi
>   Ne fut jamais irrévocable.   (II.iv, ll.591-99)

Galant love rests primarily, then, on establishing a disjunction between 'les yeux' and 'le cœur'. In the light of what we have noted already, it should not surprise us to learn which of the two predominates for Lysander: 'les yeux [...] instruisent le cœur de ce qu'il doit aimer'. So it is that a passion that is not 'aveugle' - that is, one which suppresses 'la vue' or 'les yeux' - represents the very negation of love: 'C'est ôter à l'amour tout ce qu'il a d'aimable'. One can imagine the horror that such a conception of love must have evoked among the Précieuses for whom this sort of anarchic libertinage represented the **galant** enemy that they were trying to combat. For Lysander denies to woman the sexual prerogatives he so willingly accords to man; so we are returned to the pre-heroic stance of the misogynous Don Diègue. If the 'cœur' of man must be free and untrammelled, that of woman (he speaks here of his daughter Aglatide) must submit to the will of the male:

> Surtout ne craignez rien du côté d'Aglatide:
> Je puis répondre d'elle, et quand j'aurai parlé,
> Vous verrez tout son cœur, où mon vouloir préside,
> Vous payer de celui qu'elle vous a volé.   (II.iv, ll.616-19)

Pelous shows how the more frivolous **galant** writers continued to use the linguistic categories of the 'orthodoxie romanesque' for the purposes of ironical word-play: 'Cette image [tendre] de l'amour, à laquelle la société mondaine a cessé d'adhérer, va longtemps encore pourvoir à ses divertissements: de l'héritage "tendre" elle ne retient que ce qui peut servir à ses menus plaisirs'.[31] In the character of Lysander, however, Corneille points out the perniciousness of this attitude: the amoral reality of 'caprice' comes now to don the ethical language of **générosité**, even usurping its very categories of thought. This deliberate confusion that Lysander exploits in this scene should put us on our guard: to say that the **foi amoureuse** can legitimately be revoked in the name of sexual **intérêt** is but a short step from saying that the **foi généreuse**, between king and subject, can itself legitimately be revoked in the name of political **intérêt,** which is nothing other than Machiavellian tyranny. Thus it is that in the case of Lysander we witness the dual ascent of the **galant** and of the tyrant; for we are soon to learn that the Spartan general is not only a **galant** in love, but also a rebel in politics.

Lysander is politically subversive in that he seeks to undermine that ethical concept of old which constituted the very corner-stone of the aristocratic social order, which provided it with both its metaphysical justification and its establishment in practise, the concept of **sang:**

> Nous avons trop longtemps asservi sa couronne [de Sparte]
>   A la vaine splendeur du sang,
> Il est juste à son tour que la vertu la donne,
> Et que le seul mérite ait droit à ce haut rang.   (II.v, ll.700-03)

Hence Lysander would establish another disjunction, this time between, on the one hand, birth or 'sang' and, on the other, virtue or 'mérite'. For the aristocratic ethos, however, such virtue depends absolutely on birth: the notion of a bourgeois participating in the moral value of **mérite** is inconceivable in Cornelian drama. We have already seen how, in fact, the concept of **mérite** operates within a very particular context, that of the **éthique généreuse**: the hero proves his **mérite** and wins **estime** (in love) or **gloire** (in battle) through proving his moral conformity. Once a disjunction is forged between **sang** and **mérite**, therefore, it is easy to perceive the extent of the threat posed to the aristocratic order, in regard to its metaphysical justification and its social dominance. Significantly, then, Lysander performs the part normally reserved in Cornelian drama for the **fourbe infâme**: for him, as for an Euphorbe **(Cinna)** or a Martian **(Othon)**, virtue or **mérite** becomes synonymous with the pursuit of self-interest, with the Machiavellianism that Corneille has always shown to be totally inimical to the preservation of political harmony. It is typical of Lysander that in the social sphere, as in the sphere of love, he should seek to invert the two mentalities to the point where each comes to symbolize its antithesis. Thus he reduces blood, the corner-stone of the old ethos, to what he calls 'la vaine splendeur du sang' (l.701), hence to the level of the vulgar bourgeois whose only preoccupation is with purely external appearances. Yet, astonishingly, no sooner has he asserted the moral superiority of this **mérite embourgeoisé** than he goes on to discuss the details of his 'ligue', or his 'harangue', with the conspirator Cléon (II.v): the collapse of the **éthique généreuse** issues not in the awesome manifestation of a liberated virtue, but in Machiavellian intrigue and subversion. Whilst maintaining the façade of the old **générosité**, the ethos to which this term refers is fatally relativized by Lysander. In Act II, scene iv, he had urged upon Cotys the obligations of **honneur** (ll.626-27); alone now with Cléon, he can let the mask drop:

> Je prends pour l'attacher à moi
> Ce qui s'offre de plus utile. (ll.670-71)

Henceforth the hero becomes an actor and an intriguer whose only motivation is self-interest:

> D'un emportement indiscret
> Je ne voyais rien à prétendre. (ll.672-73)

*   *

*

Lysander's daughters, Elpinice and Aglatide, are themselves no strangers to the mask. Neither ceases to proclaim her total loyalty to the old ethos, which they both translate by the concept of **devoir**. Each seeks to outdo the other in asserting her duty to her father and her concomitant refusal to surrender to amorous temptation. But in the three scenes where they appear together (I.i, II.vi, and II.vii), each does her best to penetrate the other's mask in order, simultaneously, to show herself to be the sole upholder of the old ethical claims. The tone of these verbal duels is in fact one of the frankest comedy.   Faced with Spitridate's amorous supplications, Elpinice had protested haughtily that 'Je ne sais aimer ni haïr' (II.iii, l.286) and 'Je ne sais qu'obéir' (II.vi, l.740); in the presence now of their father, Aglatide will seek to expose her sister by means of heavy, comic sarcasm:

> Vous ne savez que c'est d'aimer ou de haïr,
> Mais vous seriez pour lui [Spitridate] fort aise d'obéir
> (II.vi, ll.748-49)

This comic tone stems from the ironical reduction of the women to the same level of bourgeois 'naturalism' that we have analysed in the case of Lysander. Elpinice has already demonstrated in Act I how, despite her pose of the 'grande dame glorieuse', she has in fact substituted for her heroism of old the **mondanité** of the comic **amante**. If she loves Spitridate, it is not because he has 'dazzled' her with his heroic prowess, not because she 'esteems' him for his **mérite,** but simply because he is her ideal of the **honnête homme,** of the consummate **mondain.** As **honnêteté** comes to replace heroism, a tone of cosy, comic naturalism replaces the proud grandiloquence of former heroines:

> Car enfin Spitridate a l'entretien charmant,
> L'œil vif, l'esprit aisé, le cœur bon, l'âme belle.   (I.i, ll.41-42)

It is therefore hardly surprising that Elpinice, like her father, should repudiate the essentials of the **éthique généreuse.** She substitutes for the idealism of **générosité,** which bases itself on the recognition of collective values, a 'naturalism' founded on the primacy of the individual considered in his personal uniqueness and particularity.   For the idealist ethos of the **généreux** she substitutes the bourgeois cult of the **personne** with its implications of a possible disjunction between birth and quality, between **sang** and **mérite.**   Discarding the whole system of heroic love founded on the concept of **mérite/estime,** she goes so far as to suggest a possible antithesis between love and respect:

> Moi, je m'éblouis moins de la splendeur du rang,
> Son éclat au respect plus qu'à l'amour m'invite.   (I.i, ll.136-37)

Once again, we see how those whose only concern is with individual happiness enter into conflict with the **éthique généreuse** which depends crucially on the acknowledgement of communal bonds. In order to pursue their own self-interest, these individualists override, as they must, the corner-stone of **généreux** society, the concept of **sang.** The result, on the political level, is the anarchy of rebellion and

Machiavellianism. On the personal level, it is the devaluation of love and the decadence of an unbridled, self-indulgent sensibility. The coincidence of these two 'moments' represents the point at which Cornelian heroism has been irremediably vitiated.

* *

*

On one level, Aglatide is a 'pure ambitieuse' and is therefore representative of a type found in several of the later plays. The crown, for example, ceases to be a symbol of the ethical grandeur of the monarch, being reduced to a mere object of vanity. The cult of **gloire** is replaced by that of **gloriole**:

> La couronne, Seigneur, orne bien une tête.
> Je me la figurais sur celle de ma sœur,
>   Lorsque Cotys devait l'y mettre;
> Et quand j'en contemplais la gloire et la douceur,
>   Que je ne pouvais me promettre,
> Un peu de jalousie et de confusion
> Mutinait mes désirs et me soulevait l'âme.   (II.vi, ll.783-89)

'Et quand j'en contemplais la gloire et la douceur': Aglatide's ambition is pure cupidity in the sense understood by a generation deeply imbued with neo-Augustinian ideas. Indeed, the Jansenists linked this cupidinous ambition with the triumph of the obscure instincts of nature, with a perverted sensuality. For Aglatide, the corollary of this cupidinous desire for domination is the unbridled jealousy which 'Mutinait mes désirs et me soulevait l'âme'.[32] Elpinice is quick to exploit this admission and to reveal the full extent of the sordid reality:

> La gloire d'obéir à votre grand regret
>   Vous faisait pester en secret.   (II.vi, ll.792-93)

It is remarkable how often in this scene each sister urges the other to tell **(dire)** the truth. In a world where language has become a tool of intrigue and manipulation, this invitation represents a real danger of which both of them are clearly aware. In urging each other to be frank, they seek to force each other into committing an irreparable error, into letting the mask slip:

AGLATIDE

> Je sais que c'est ma sœur à qui va cet hommage,
> Et quelque chose encor qu'elle vous **dirait** mieux.

ELPINICE

> Ma sœur, qu'aurais-je à **dire**?

AGLATIDE

A quoi bon ce mystère?
Dites ce qu'à ce nom le cœur vous **dit** tout bas,
Ou je **dirai** tout haut qu'il ne vous déplaît pas.   (ll.742-47)

Je n'ai pas besoin d'interprète,
Et je vous en **dirai** plus, Seigneur, qu'elle n'en sait.   (ll.754-55)

Que **dites**-vous ma sœur, qu'osez-vous hasarder,
Vous qui tantôt...?   (ll.795-96)

Pour bien m'aider à **dire** ici mes sentiments,
Vous vous prenez trop mal aux vôtres.   (ll.798-99)

ELPINICE

Achevez donc, ma sœur: **dites** qu'Agésilas...

AGLATIDE

Ah! Seigneur, ne l'écoutez pas:
Ce qu'elle vous veut **dire** est une bagatelle;
Et même, s'il le faut, je la **dirai** mieux qu'elle.

LYSANDER

Dis donc. Agésilas...   (ll.810-14)

'Dire mieux' is ultimately equivalent, then, to 'mentir mieux'. To do this, Aglatide employs the mask of her so-called 'enjouement', which is the mark of a very particular form of coquetry.[33]   This is the mask she dons in order to convince her father that she remains uniquely attached to her filial duty and that she is indifferent to love. In the scene we have been discussing, Elpinice almost succeeds in forcing this mask to slip, but Lysander has been roundly deceived. He has already informed Cléon that

Aglatide est d'humeur à rire de sa perte:
Son esprit enjoué ne s'ébranle de rien.   (II.v, ll.724-25)

As Elpinice's probing becomes more threatening in the sixth scene of Act II, Aglatide has increasing recourse to the mask. Faithful to her 'enjouement', she belittles her former liaison with Agésilas, calling it a mere 'bagatelle' (l.812). She endeavours to counter the damaging effect of her admission of jealousy by denigrating the real bitterness of her feelings, which she claims is but a coquettish affectation that Lysander should not take too seriously; after all, she suffered only 'un peu de jalousie' (l.788), only 'quelques ennuis' (l.803), only 'un petit chagrin' (l.804).   Aglatide's 'enjouement' in fact conceals a cruel reality, that of jealous ambition and consummate deceitfulness.

It is also, however, a reality of the utmost mediocrity. In the short scene that follows (II.vii), Elpinice substitutes for her sister's 'petit chagrin' her own interpretation and talks of her 'chagrin trop juste' (l.836);   she revels in her triumph by conveying to Aglatide that she knows only too well that her sister's 'inépuisable enjouement' is but a facade.   Aglatide responds to this thinly-veiled attack by philosophizing, by making of her 'enjouement' a sort of **sagesse**.   She is thus led, paradoxically, to take her careless coquetry extremely seriously, which is itself the proof of its falsity and its failure.   This 'philosophy' is, moreover, of the most unheroic kind;   flat, resigned and prosaic, it is a form of hedonism whose pleasures are yet utterly banal:

> Je sais comme il faut vivre, et m'en trouve fort bien.
> La joie est bonne à mille choses,
> Mais le chagrin n'est bon à rien.   (II.vii, ll.839-41)

A philosophy therefore of the mean, of the **juste milieu:**   in short, a sub-heroic, bourgeois philosophy.   Whilst the heroic urge demanded and imposed confrontation and challenge, a sense of the quest for, and the conquest of, experience, Aglatide's **sagesse** is based only on a cosy complacency, a need for **repos** and the resigned acceptance of the status quo.   She represents an extreme development of the comic naturalism that has surreptitiously corrupted the high idealism of old:[34]

> Ne perds-je pas assez, sans doubler l'infortune,
> Et perdre encor le bien d'avoir l'esprit égal?
> Perte sur perte est infortune,
> Et je m'aime un peu trop pour me traiter si mal.   (II.vii, ll.842-45)

*   *

*

In the end it will be left to the 'illustre Persane', Mandane, to struggle for the restoration of the old order and for the right of woman to her former dignity. The fourth act of the play can be said to belong to her.   In two long interviews, with her brother Spitridate (IV.ii) and with her lover Cotys (IV.v), she refuses to be intimidated by these **capricieux** and makes instead a resolute and moving appeal in favour of the **éthique généreuse**.   According to Pelous, as we have seen, it was to the Précieuses that the task fell of defending the old ethos against the growing influence of the **galants** in the 1650s and 1660s.   What is particularly interesting with regard to these two scenes in **Agésilas** is that they provide an illustration of this contemporary debate and allow us better to define Corneille's own position.

Spitridate's aim in Act IV, scene ii, is to force his sister into a hasty marriage with Agésilas in order that he may win Elpinice.   Faced with her brother's attempts at intimidation, Mandane resolutely asserts the right of woman to equality:

SPITRIDATE

Inexorable sœur!

MANDANE

Impitoyable frère,
Qui voulez que j'éteigne un feu digne de moi,
Et ne sauriez vous faire une pareille loi!

SPITRIDATE

Hélas! considérez...

MANDANE

Considérez vous-même...

SPITRIDATE

Que j'aime, et que je suis aimé.

MANDANE

Que je suis aimée et que j'aime.   (ll.1391-96)

In responding to this demand Spitridate reveals himself to be every inch a Persian and every inch a **galant:**

N'égalez point au mien un feu mal allumé:
Le sexe vous apprend à régner sur vos âmes.   (ll.1397-98)

Mandane reacts angrily to this and, in the style of the militant Précieuse, rises up against the emotional slavery to which the **galant** seeks to reduce woman, and accuses men of being inconstant and libertine. At this point, the play must have reached a height of topicality for its first audiences:

Dites qu'il [le sexe] nous apprend à renfermer nos flammes,
Dites que votre ardeur, à force d'éclater,
S'exhale, se dissipe ou du moins s'exténue,
Dont le joug odieux ne sert qu'à l'irriter.   (ll.1399-403)

As a true heroine of the old school, Mandane intends to sacrifice her love and urges Spitridate to do the same. In so doing she asserts a fundamental principle of the heroic enterprise. To the fatalistic complaint of her brother: 'N'aimer plus! Ah! ma sœur', she replies: 'J'en soupire à mon tour, / Mais un grand cœur doit être au-dessus de l'amour' (ll.1420-21).

What is doubly interesting and significant in this respect is that Mandane goes on, as Spitridate had done in his long speech in Act II, to link explicitly the language of tyranny and slavery with the heroic degradation of Persia. She declares that in abandoning himself to the cult of amoral love, hence to sexual **intérêt,** Spitridate behaves as a slave. In abandoning themselves to the cult of political **intérêt,** Agésilas and Lysander behave as tyrants. Again Corneille renews the conventional language of **tendresse** by investing it with an ironical function: the 'fers' and the 'châines' are the symbols of political slavery and social humiliation, but, in the language of **tendresse**, they are also the symbols of the tyranny of the senses to which Spitridate has submitted in demanding satisfaction at any cost of his love for Elpinice.   This particular tyranny entails as an inevitable consequence the tyranny of political **caprice**:

> N'avons-nous secoué le joug de notre Prince
> Que pour choisir des fers dans une autre province?
> Ne cherchons-nous ici que d'illustres tyrans,
>   Dont les chaînes plus glorieuses
> Soumettent nos destins aux obscurs différends
>   De leurs haines mystérieuses?   (ll.1426-31)

Greece and Persia thus come to offer mirror-images of each other.   The only difference is that the Persian vision is better disguised at the Greek court: 'chaînes' are no less humiliating for being 'glorieuses', nor tyrants less odious for being 'illustres'! All of these characteristics are in fact summed up in Spitridate, the very character who had so roundly condemned them in his long speech at the beginning of Act II.

A similar debate is initiated in the fifth scene of Act IV. Cotys begs Mandane to marry him; she refuses, since to do so would be to risk being banished with Spitridate to their native Persia, the result of which would be inevitable disgrace:

> Comme il [le tyran persan] nous traitera d'esclaves révoltés,
> Le supplice l'attend et moi l'ignominie.   (ll.1632-35)

Mandane therefore opposes the possibility of such ignominy with the necessity of a sacrificial choice:

> Serait-il d'un grand cœur de chercher à périr,
>   Quand il voit une porte ouverte
> A régner avec gloire aux dépens d'un soupir?   (ll.1621-23)

It will be by sacrificing the consummation of her love that she will prove it and sustain it.   She thereby allies herself with Rodrigue's **amour-valeur**.   Love can be consummated in the world only so long as it accords with the higher imperatives of the **éthique généreuse**:

> Seigneur, je vous aime,
> Mais je dois à mon frère, à ma gloire, à vous-même.   (ll.1624-25)

If need be, she will guard against the disgrace of returning to Persia by committing suicide. In the meantime, however, she intends to safeguard her love and to prove its ethical basis by striving to reconcile it with her **gloire** and with her concern for Cotys's safety. It will be by means of 'sacrifice' and 'malheurs' that she will triumph over a malevolent destiny. This acceptance of misfortune in no way betrays any form of capitulation on Mandane's part; rather, it represents a sort of synthetic sublimation by means of which what is most deeply noble and human accords itself the status of an incorruptible value in the face of a hostile contingency:

> C'est ce que je saurai prévenir par ma mort,
> Mais jusque-là, Seigneur, permettez-moi de vivre,
> Et que par un illustre et rigoureux effort,
> Acceptant les malheurs où mon destin me livre,
> Un entier sacrifice de mes vœux les plus doux
> Fasse la sûreté de mon frère et de vous.   (ll.1636-41)

Cotys replies that love constitutes his 'unique bien': he turns his face against what he calls Mandane's 'mesure' and against everything that risks injuring his love (ll.1641-46). He seeks in fact to dissociate love from the world, from that 'mesure' demanded by the fact of contingency. He therefore seeks a return to the idealized world of the pastoral, of **L'Astrée**: he wants to transport love to the realm of an impenetrable idyll which exists in an almost mystical sphere, beyond the reach of contaminating reality. In this respect, Cotys represents the **amant tendre,** a type with which the audiences of Quinault and of Thomas Corneille were well familiar. What Cotys overlooks, from the Cornelian viewpoint, is that this 'mesure' which he so vehemently criticizes represents the only way of confronting the real world and of resolving those conflicts which potentially are fatally destructive of human dignity. This refusal is a refusal of conflict, thus a refusal of reality, even of life itself; from Cotys's refusal of conflict ensues the temptation of death. What we might call the **tendre** mortido, which surrenders to the deadly force of nature, replaces the heroic libido, which sought the resolution of conflict by means of the synthetic paradox of sacrifice. It is significant that the **tendre** Cotys should point to the survival of Mandane's 'raison' as proof of her indifference:

> Laissez, laissez périr ce déplorable Roi,
> A qui ces intérêts dérobent votre foi.
> Que sert que vous l'aimez, et que fait votre flamme
> Qu'augmenter son ardeur pour croître ses malheurs,
>   Si malgré le don de votre âme
>   Votre raison vous livre ailleurs?   (ll.1648-53)

A love that is 'malheureux' - that is, one which sacrifices the 'ardeur' of immediate gratification - represents in Cotys's view a logical contradiction. Unable to face the fact of a painful and ambiguous reality, he seeks to escape it by falsifying it; he begs Mandane to hate him:

> Armez-vous de dédain, rendez s'il est possible,

Votre perte pour lui moins grande ou moins sensible,
Et par pitié d'un cœur trop ardemment épris,
Eteignez-en la flamme à force de mépris.   (ll.1654-57)

Cotys's **tendresse** is clearly not far removed from Spitridate's **galanterie:**   whilst
galanterie represents a subversive refusal to integrate love with the moral system of
générosité, tendresse represents the failure to achieve this heroic goal owing to the
triumph of an overwhelming sensibility which, unrequited, tends towards destruction.
Again Mandane counters this **tendresse** with her **précieux** heroism:

Vouloir ne plus aimer, c'est déjà n'aimer plus,
Et qui peut n'aimer plus ne fut jamais capable
          D'une passion véritable.   (ll.1661-63)

But the **tendre** Cotys is incapable of ever imagining such a love; like Spitridate's **amour
galant,** his **tendresse** is utterly superficial:

L'amour au désespoir peut-il encor charmer?   (l.1664)

For Mandane, it is the capacity of love to suffer, and even to grow in spite of
this suffering, that is evidence of its authenticity. In this she follows Rodrigue: the
capacity to suffer sacrifice is proof of the reality of love, that is of its ethical
foundation.   Cornelian heroism, based on the existentialist pursuit of **générosité,** can
be said to be opposed to most metaphysics: it aims at the most complete integration of
the person in the context of a very definite world. It shares, though, with **préciosité** a
realistic suspicion of love which is a potential source of disruption and chaos.   As far
as possible, sexual passion is tamed by being integrated with the **éthique généreuse.**
Should such integration fail, however, love is sacrificed in order, paradoxically, that it
may survive: Corneille's own **préciosité** is aimed at the retention and protection of the
ethical status of love by means of its sublimation. If metaphysics is thus invoked **in
extremis,** it is always in the service of the existentialist ethos that is **générosité.** So it
is that we can speak of Mandane's **héroïsme précieux:**

L'amour au désespoir fait gloire encor d'aimer,
Il en fait de souffrir et souffre avec constance,
Voyant l'objet aimé partager la souffrance.
Il regarde ses maux comme un doux souvenir
De l'union des cœurs qui ne saurait finir.   (ll.1665-69)

She ends by accusing Cotys of the **amour-propre** and the **intérêt** that are at the root of
galanterie. She calls this preoccupation with one's own 'plaisirs' a form of 'bassesse',
for Cotys's **tendresse** is but the forerunner of the tyrant's **galanterie:**

Et comme n'aimer plus quand l'espoir abandonne,
C'est aimer ses plaisirs et non la personne,
Il [l'amour véritable] fuit cette bassesse, et s'affermit si bien
Que toute sa douleur ne se reproche rien.   (ll.1670-73)

* *

*

Agésilas shocked its first audiences with its dramatic innovations, most notably with the prosaic fluidity of its **vers libres.**[35] Not the least of these, however, is the fact that the play's eponymous hero does not appear until the third act. It is nonetheless true to say that the action of the play centres on the King of Sparta. It will be for him to sort out the various couples of lovers and the outcome of the play will depend on his treatment of Lysander: with which of the two visions represented in the play, Greek or Persian, will he choose to ally himself? On this choice will depend the fate of Greece and the cause of its justice.

Agésilas does, in fact, make a promising start. He is fully aware of the role played by self-interest in Lysander's behaviour; in pursuing an alliance with Cotys and Spitridate, the Spartan general is aiming more at his own benefit than that of the State:

> Votre intérêt s'y mêle en les prenant pour gendres,
> Et si par des liens et si forts et si tendres
> Vous pouvez aujourd'hui les attacher à vous,
>   Vous vous les donnez plus qu'à nous.   (III.i, ll.909-12)

In taking into account the role of **intérêt,** Agésilas is aware too that whilst, as Starobinski has shown,[36] the hero of old used language to project and parade his deepest self, the hero of the new world of this play uses it instead as a vehicle of disguise. The triumph of self-interest, that seeks to safeguard itself by adopting the appearances of **générosité** whilst betraying its substance, issues in the reign of intrigue. It is in the knowledge of this that Agésilas alludes to Lysander's desire to retreat from the public world of court into the world of private solitude:

> Cependant cet exil, ces retraites paisibles,
> Cet unique souhait d'y terminer leurs jours,
> Sont des mots bien choisis à remplir leurs discours:
> Ils ont toujours leur grâce, ils sont toujours plausibles,
>   Mais ils ne sont pas vrais toujours,
> Et souvent des périls, ou cachés ou visibles,
> Forcent notre prudence à nous mieux assurer
>   Qu'ils ne veulent se figurer.   (III.i, ll.878-85)

The old relationship between king and subject, which depended on respecting a mutually sworn **foi,** is therefore vitiated in its very essence: in this new environment, the king has to become the ever-watchful guardian over a subject who has forfeited his trust. From the moment that self-interest replaces **générosité,** that an individualistic and anarchic **caprice** replaces a collective and ascetic ethic, the king's only function is to 'prévoir', to 'regarder' (ll.893-94), to be vigilant and to act with 'prudence'. This breech in the relationship between king and subject represents an acute danger to the cohesion and security of the State; the hero's **élan** on which the king formerly relied for safeguarding and enhancing the State's integrity must now be restrained and held in suspense. Even the hero's 'grands services' become suspect:

> Le service est bien grand, mais aussi je confesse
> Qu'on peut ne pas bien voir tout le fond du projet.   (ll.907.08)

As we have noted, the new hero has even dared to mount an assault upon the concept of **sang** which constituted the very foundation and guarantor of the **éthique généreuse**. In the past, **sang** alone could suffice to guarantee the subject's good faith, his sincerity, his **grandeur d'âme,** in short his status as a **généreux**. But this is no longer the case; faced as he is with the omnipresence of intrigue, the king has to demand tangible proof of his subject's loyalty:

> Vous ne nous laissez aucun gage:
> Votre sang tout entier passe avec vous chez eux.   (ll.924-25)

Thus the concept of **sang,** too, is reduced to a tactic in intrigue, in the game of domination and possession. In this new world, given over to factions, **sang** is an instrument of politico-familial solidarity rather than the symbol and guarantor of socio-ethical solidarity: it is in marrying his daughters to Cotys and Spitridate that Lysander will use his **sang** to increase his personal authority and advance his own interests. Here lies the importance of the theme of matrimonial politics that critics of the later plays have so often noted but rarely explicated: the concept of **sang**, being used to enhance and further individual interest, is itself **embourgeoisé.**[37] Thus we see the extent of the significance of Lysander's attempt to subvert the existing order: Xénocle reminds us (III.ii, ll.1106-12) that, in insisting on 'mérite' and 'les grands services' as the sole criteria of election to monarchical rule, Lysander strikes at the very foundations of the system. The possibility of a distinction between **mérite** and **sang** depends on a fluid social structure that is everywhere linked in this play with the reign of anarchy and Machiavellianism.

Faced with this radical encroachment upon his prerogatives, Agésilas demands the restoration of the traditional relation:

> Si vous m'avez fait Roi, Lysander, je veux l'être.
> Soyez-moi bon sujet, je vous serai bon maître,
> Mais ne prétendez plus partager avec moi
>   Ni la puissance ni l'emploi.   (ll.994-97)

For Agésilas, **gloire** is linked with the practice of justice which leads to the harmonious functioning of the State; justice is linked with 'douceur' and is opposed to

the brutality, sensuality and cupidity of **caprice**. Again, we recall the dichotomy
Spitridate had drawn in Act II:

> J'ai tiré de ce joug les peuples opprimés,
> En leur premier état j'ai remis toutes choses,
> Et la gloire d'agir par de plus justes causes
> A produit des effets plus doux et plus aimés.   (ll.1024-27)

Agésilas is perfectly conscious, then, of the extent of the threat that Lysander poses
to the Greek ethos and of the course he must take to counter it. Yet, at the end of this
same act, we find him reduced to complete disarray: 'Que ma confusion, que mon
trouble est extrême!' (III.iv, l.1270).   Even earlier, he had hesitated to act when
confronted, in the form of Xénocle's 'copie', with the certain proof of Lysander's
treachery. He had attributed this hesitation to the exercise of his 'prudence':

> J'ai peine à démêler ce qu'il faut que je fasse,
> Tant la confusion de mes raisonnements
>   Etonne mes ressentiments.   (III.ii, ll.1121-23)

But a few lines later he adds that he is hesitating out of feelings of 'reconnaissance'; it
seems now to be more a question of his debt of personal friendship towards Lysander:

> Je sens que ma reconnaissance
> Ne cherche qu'un moyen de le mettre à couvert.   (ll.1128-29)

He hastily dismisses this consideration, however, and attributes his hesitancy to the
'rational' question of political necessity: Sparta is 'un état populaire' that would resent
any action he might take against his illustrious general (ll.1136-56). Faced with this
confusion on the part of Agésilas, what are we to make of the reasons for his
uncertainty?

      What is most remarkable in this respect is the highly ambivalent nature of
Agésilas's feelings towards his general. On the one hand, he is resentful and jealous of
Lysander, who has placed him on the throne and even now continues to exercise such
influence over Sparta that, next to him, Agésilas feels but a 'fantôme éclatant' (III.i,
ll.978-87).   And yet, in spite of these feelings and of the very real threat Lysander
poses to all that he holds so dear, Agésilas remains haunted by the idea of
'reconnaissance'. In spite of his lucidity and of his grasp of the **éthique généreuse**,
Agésilas suffers from a deep sense of his own inadequacy. It is for this reason that he
is ultimately unable to take decisive action against Lysander. Dazzled, like everyone
else, by the military and political prowess of this ageing hero, Agésilas takes flight
from the necessity of challenging him. He excuses himself from such action by
accusing himself, very significantly in the light of what we have said of the use of
'legal' language in the play, of 'ces injustices / Dont vous avez raison de vous

mécontenter' (ll.1034-35). Consequently, Agésilas remains a theoretician of monarchy: he lacks the confidence to make of this theory a militant reality.

Lysander is quick to seize on his king's vulnerability. It is in accusing himself of 'injustices' that Agésilas makes his greatest mistake; whilst he has a firm grasp of ethical theory, Agésilas is clearly very insecure concerning his own personal status in relation to this theory. Lysander exploits this insecurity by using the language of 'justice' to imply that Agésilas, like all **capricieux**, is in fact endeavouring to manipulate these absolute terms so that they serve his own self-interest. If Hercule's blood serves to enhance Agésilas's power, it serves also, it seems, to condemn Lysander's daughters to ignominy:

> Il est le sang d'Hercule en elles comme en vous,
> Et méritait par là quelque destin plus doux,
> Mais s'il vous peut donner un titre légitime
> > Pour être leur maître et leur Roi,
> C'est pour l'une et pour l'autre une espèce de crime
> > Que de l'avoir reçu de moi.   (ll.856-61)

The result of this is Agésilas's swift capitulation. In trying to appease Lysander and to parry these accusations which increase his sense of his own hated vulnerability, he succumbs completely to his general's bourgeois vision, claims that his demand for a 'récompense', hence for equivalence, is justified, and promises him all he requests. He thereby contradicts everything he had formerly upheld concerning the proper relationship between king and subject:

> Il nous serait honteux que des mains étrangères
> Vous payassent pour nous de ce qui vous est dû.
> Tôt ou tard le mérite a ses justes salaires,
> Et son prix croît souvent, plus il est attendu. [...]
> Vos filles sont d'un sang que Sparte aime et révère
> Assez pour les payer des services d'un père.
> Je veux bien en répondre, et moi-même au besoin
> J'en ferai mon affaire, et prendrai tout le soin.   (ll.1066-79)

* *

*

In resolving to give up Mandane to Cotys, to marry Aglatide and to pardon Lysander, Agésilas will claim in Act V that he has overcome the conflicting emotions inherent in his 'faiblesse' in order, like Auguste, to inaugurate the triumphant reign of a fortified **générosité**:

> Mais enfin il est beau de triompher de soi,
> > Et de s'accorder ce miracle,

> Quand on peut hautement donner à tous la loi,
> Et que le juste soin de combler notre gloire
> Demande de notre cœur pour dernière victoire.
> Un Roi né pour l'éclat des grandes actions
>   Dompte jusqu'à ses passions,
> Et ne se croit point Roi, s'il ne fait sur lui-même
> Le plus illustre essai de son pouvoir suprême.   (V.v, ll.1982-90)

Thus Agésilas describes this 'triomphe' in terms of the triumph of **générosité** over nature: it is in sacrificing the compulsions imposed by this nature that the hero transcends it in order to acquire the authentic voice of the monarch. In dazzling others with his show of **grandeur d'âme**, the triumphant hero inspires others to a similar act of magnanimous self-sacrifice.   So Agésilas sees his act of clemency as an act of affective sacrifice: in pardoning Lysander he overcomes the hatred and the desire for vengeance that have haunted him throughout, and in giving up Mandane he overcomes the power of instinct.   His ultimate victory will consist, then, in conquering the two strongest, most extreme of passions: love and hatred.   Even Auguste was not confronted with so taut a conflict:

> J'aime, mais après tout je hais autant que j'aime,
> Et ces deux passions qui règnent tour à tour
> Ont au fond de mon cœur si peu d'intelligence
> Qu'à peine immole-t-il la vengeance à l'amour,
> Qu'il voudrait immoler l'amour à la vengeance.   (ll.1938-42)

Yet what we witness at the end of **Agésilas** is not the triumph of authentic **générosité**, but the final consolidation of appearance and of the mask.[38]   The whole of the crucial scene vi, the keenly anticipated interview between Agésilas and Lysander, is based upon the triumph of the lie.   Lysander enters to ask Agésilas to allow Cotys to marry Mandane.   As he has given his word to Cotys, Lysander declares that his 'gloire' (l.1963) and his 'honneur' (ll.1966 and 1973) depend on the conclusion of their marriage. Appealing to his 'trente ans de service' (l.1974), he reaffirms his loyalty to his king: 'N'exigez rien de plus d'un père, / Il a tenu toujours vos ordres à bonheur' (ll.1970-71). Agésilas knows of course that this is a flagrant attempt at subterfuge: Xénoclès has just provided him with documents (V.i) which prove Lysander's treachery beyond doubt. Yet, astonishingly, Agésilas, instead of exposing his general's egregious lies, actually corroborates Lysander's testimony.   When Lysander begs him to be allowed to carry his honour to the grave, Agésilas reassures him:

> Oui, vous l'y porterez, et du moins de ma part
> Ce précieux honneur ne court aucun hasard.
> On a votre parole, et j'ai donné la mienne,
> Et pour faire aujourd'hui que l'une et l'autre tienne,
> Il faut vaincre un amour qui m'était aussi doux
>   Que votre gloire l'est pour vous.   (ll.1975-80)

In drawing a veil of oblivion over Lysander's misdeeds, Agésilas conspires in his crimes; in vindicating Lysander's lies, he invites his general to perform the same favour for himself. With quite outrageous cynicism, he even goes so far as to allow Lysander to feign a **générosité** that has in fact been irrevocably traduced. Transformed by the sudden adoption of the mask, his own capitulation will pass for the affirmation of his kingly authority and Lysander's Machiavellian deceitfulness for the fidelity of the true subject. Agésilas's act of 'clemency', by means of which he is able to pose as the incarnation of a triumphant and revitalized **générosité,** represents in fact the ultimate appeasement of Lysander and his surrender to the world-view of tyrannical **caprice.** From the beginning of scene vii, in which we are supposed to witness his apotheosis, we find Agésilas meekly asking of his general: 'Eh bien! vos mécontentements / Me seront-ils encore à craindre?' (ll.1995-96).   Indeed, one can scarcely speak of Agésilas's 'clemency' since the person who is the recipient of this mercy fails to make any admission of guilt. If Lysander regards himself as guilty, it is only of having been found out:

> Je suis coupable,
> Parce qu'on me trahit, que l'on vous sert trop bien,
> Et que par un effort de prudence admirable,
> Vous avez su prévoir de quoi serait capable
> Après tant de mépris, un cœur comme le mien.   (ll.2009-13)

'Un cœur comme le mien': Lysander's attitude has not changed. He uses the same language as in Act III; his so-called admission of guilt is in fact a self-apology. If he seems to submit to Agésilas, it is not because he has been dazzled (as Emilie was) by some act of moral brilliance; all that is 'admirable' in Agésilas is his 'prudence': that is, the degraded idea of the monarch that Lysander had outlined in Act III. Whereas in **Cinna** Auguste's act of clemency had represented a revolutionary break with a mediocre past, Agésilas's pseudo-clemency and Lysander's pseudo-repentance merely represent a continuation of the debased status quo. Agésilas concludes by echoing the maxims of Cléopâtre;[39] even **gloire** is a fluid concept that can apply equally well to the criminal as to the hero:

> Ce dessein toutefois ne passera pour crime
> Que parce qu'il est sans effet,
> Et ce qu'on va nommer forfait
> N'a rien qu'un plein succès n'eût rendu légitime.
> Tout devient glorieux pour qui peut l'obtenir,
> Et qui le manque est à punir.   (ll.2014-19)

In the end it is Agésilas who confesses and submits. On the basis of appearances alone, he convinces himself that the world has not changed whilst he has repudiated the very substance of the monarchical ethos; he indulges in this elaborate charade in order to save face. He even protests against an admission that Lysander has not made: 'Non, non, j'aurais plus fait peut-être en votre place' (l.2020), and confirms Lysander's opinion of himself: 'Il est naturel aux grands cœurs / De sentir vivement de pareilles rigueurs' (ll.2021-22). He even admits that the king can owe a debt to his subject. In so doing, he implicitly confirms the equivalence in this relationship that Lysander has sought throughout:

> Dites-moi seulement avec même franchise,
> Vous dois-je encor bien plus que vous ne me devez?   (ll.2032-33)

Thus he tacitly requests Lysander's collaboration in the reign of appearances. Significantly, from the point of view of the play's 'legal' language, he again blames himself for his 'injustices' and praises Lysander's 'grands services'. In doing this, he acknowledges the replacement of the **éthique généreuse** by the bourgeois cult of **mérite**. So the terms of the **généreux/capricieux** debate are inverted: to demand the **généreux** relationship between king and subject is to be unjust, and 'les grands services' performed solely for the benefit of personal self-interest are condoned. It would be difficult to conceive of a more complete revolution in the values that Agésilas had articulated in Act III:

> Reprochez-moi plutôt toutes mes injustices,
> Que de plus ravaler de si rares services.
> Elles ont fait le crime, et j'en tire ce bien
> Que j'ai pu m'acquitter et ne vous dois plus rien.   (ll.2047-50)

In marrying Aglatide, Agésilas will formally renounce the old ethos:

> S'ils [vos services] ont su conserver un trône en ma famille,
> J'y veux par mon hymen faire seoir votre fille:
> C'est ainsi qu'avec vous je puis le partager.   (ll.2055-57)

We have already commented at length on the central rôle played by the various concepts of **sang** in **Agésilas,** on how these represent and reflect the two great historical ideas that here confront each other. In Act III, scene i, Agésilas had insisted on the **généreux** concept of **sang** which we termed socio-ethical, whilst Lysander had sought throughout to replace this by the domesticated, familial concept which substitutes for the old social ethos the new bourgeois cult of individual self-interest. In his last speech in the scene that we have been analysing in Act V, Agésilas reiterates what he had said in the third act concerning the relationship between king and subject: it is for the king to command and the subject to obey. In short, kings 'aiment qu'on leur doive, et ne peuvent devoir' (l.2062). This openly contradicts, of course, all that Agésilas has said and done in this same scene. As we have seen, all that he now seeks to do is to save face; whilst repeating these **généreux** formulae, he lets it be known that he has, in fact, betrayed the substance of the ethic to which they refer. It is in this context that the word 'gendre' in the last line partakes of a shattering and bathetic irony: Agésilas does not demand that Lysander treat him as a 'roi', the word we would have expected had we been taking him seriously, but as a 'gendre', as a member of his own family. The king, embracing explicitly now the politico-familial concept of **sang,** capitulates formally to the bourgeois and simultaneously self-destructs:

> Prenons dorénavant, vous et moi, pour objet,
> Les devoirs qu'il faudra l'un et l'autre nous rendre:
>   N'oubliez pas ceux d'un sujet,
>   Et j'aurai soin de ceux d'un gendre.   (ll.2067-70)

In such a context, the general expressions of joy which conclude the play (V.ix) ring decidedly false. The marriage of Agésilas and Aglatide is one of political necessity in a cynical and debased political environment. The play ends with the celebration of the death of the **éthique généreuse.**

* *

*

In this essay, we have sought to show how **Agésilas,** far from representing a 'brusque temps d'arrêt'[40] in the decline of the hero, is in fact firmly anchored in the context of the general concerns of Corneille's later plays as a whole. We hope thereby to have substantiated the views of those critics who have raised some doubts with regard to the traditional interpretation.[41] The concerns of the later works are themselves rooted in contemporary reality: Corneille's art remains a subtle and acute reflection of the various social and literary currents of his time. **Agésilas** shares with these other works the central theme of the fate of the idealistic **éthique généreuse** in a new and hostile social climate, where a creeping **embourgeoisement** substitutes for the moral order and harmony of **générosité** the amoral chaos of an ethos based entirely on the pursuit of individual interest. As we have tried to demonstrate, this phenomenon has important consequences on both the public (political) and the personal (amorous) levels: **tendresse** (in the character of the 'délicat' Cotys) and **galanterie** (especially in the characters of the 'enjoués', Spitridate and Lysander) are seen as the corollaries, on the personal level of love, of the triumphant bourgeois cult of **intérêt** which, on the public level of politics, is explicitly linked with tyrannical Machiavellianism. The two forms of female response to these linked developments are analysed in the characters of Aglatide and Mandane. These responses are also grounded in contemporary reality. Aglatide, the comic **coquette,** is apolitical and seeks simply to beat the **galant** at his own game; in winning Agésilas at the end of the play, she can be said to have succeeded, but only at the cost of reducing the **éthique généreuse** to the level of a sort of anti-ethos based on cynicism, deceitfulness and defensive mediocrity.   The alternative response is that of the Précieuse and is represented in the play by Mandane: she calls for the restoration, on the personal level, of Rodrigue's **amour-valeur** and, on the public level, for the vigorous defence of the monarchical ethos.   It is significant that she does not speak again in the play after her challenge to Agésilas in Act V, scene iv, and does not join in the celebrations of the final scene.   Her defeat makes **Agésilas** a deeply pessimistic work.

Corneille, then, far from seeking to imitate the despised Quinault, remains admirably loyal to the ethos reflected in his earlier work and consolidated there only on the basis of heroic struggle, trial and occasional tragedy.[42]   As recent criticism has stressed, however, Corneille was an essentially modern writer, constantly innovating, revising and experimenting.   He himself asserts as much in the 'Au Lecteur' to **Agésilas:**   speaking of the artistic principles of the Ancients, he says that 'Leurs règles sont bonnes, mais leur méthode n'est pas de notre siècle, et qui s'attacherait à ne marcher que sur leurs pas ferait sans doute peu de progrès, et divertirait mal son auditoire'.[43]   **Agésilas** testifies very clearly to Corneille's own keen observation of his contemporary social and literary environment and to his continuing preoccupation with testing out the **éthique généreuse** in ever new and more complex environments. The tragedy of **Agésilas** is the tragedy of the later works as a whole: in the degraded environment of the 1660s, the formerly hallowed **éthique** is cynically manipulated, betrayed and ultimately reduced to a decorative function.   In playing such a role, its fate parallels that of the domesticated aristocratic courtiers of an increasingly absolutist Louis XIV: as Agésilas capitulates to Lysander, he ensures his own destruction and that of an aristocratic class with its ethos, traditions, culture and history. **Agésilas** participates in the artistic transposition of this epochal process.

NOTES

1.   Serge Doubrovsky, **Corneille et la dialectique du héros** (Paris, 1963), p.26.

2.   Georges Couton, **La Vieillesse de Corneille** (Paris, 1949).

3.   **Sertorius,** edited by Jeanne Streicher (Geneva, 1959);   **Attila,** edited by Marcel Autrand (Paris, 1959); and **Suréna, général des Parthes,** edited by José Sanchez (Bordeaux, 1970).

4.   Octave Nadal, **Le Sentiment de l'amour dans l'œuvre de Pierre Corneille** (Paris, 1948), p.318.

5. Couton, p.127.

6. Couton, p.112: 'L'humeur gaie d'**Agésilas,** fort extraordinaire dans une pièce qui porte le sous-titre de tragédie, pourrait bien signifier que la pièce souhaitait obtenir les suffrages d'une cour galante et se mettre à l'unisson de la gaieté environnante'.

7. Nadal, p.23.

8. Lacy Lockert, **Studies in French Classical Drama** (Nashville, 1958), pp.92-93.

9. 'L'**Agésilas** de Corneille' (unpublished doctoral dissertation, University of Paris, 1964), p.138.

10. Léon Lemonnier, **Corneille** (Paris, 1945), p.244.

11. Nadal, p.240: 'On y suit bien entre Agésilas et son général Lysander un conflit d'autorité où se profile l'ombre d'un complot. Mais l'intrigue galante recouvre tout, même le long plaidoyer politique du troisième acte'.

12. René Bray, 'L'Introduction des "vers mêlés" sur la scène classique', **PMLA,** 66 (1951), 456-84 (p.468): 'C'est une tragédie de tendresse, une comédie sentimentale à fin heureuse. Corneille se rapproche de Quinault, dont l'**Astrate** vient de triompher. Il abandonne la politique et l'héroïsme pour la galanterie'.

13. Doubrovsky, **Corneille,** pp.337-427.

14. That **Agésilas** was such a disaster cannot be doubted: see Doubrovsky, 'L'**Agésilas** de Corneille', pp.8-11.

15. Nadal, p.234: 'Ni Thomas Corneille, ni Quinault, dans la plupart de ses œuvres, ni Boyer, ni même Racine jusqu'à **Andromaque,** n'ont de l'amour une conception fondamentalement différente de celle de Corneille'.

16. Paul Bénichou, **Morales du grand siècle** (Paris, 1948; reprinted 1973), p.58: 'L'amour des romans tourne aussi souvent au sublime, que le sublime de Corneille tourne à la galanterie: l'un ne va guère sans l'autre'.

17. Antoine Adam, **Histoire de la littérature française au XVIIe siècle,** 5 vols (Paris, 1948-56), IV, 228.

18. Adam, IV, 227.

19. Doubrovsky, 'L'**Agésilas** de Corneille', pp.53-54.

20. ibid., p.48.

21. ibid., p.153: 'Corneille ne s'accommode au goût public, que pour tourner en dérision la morale régnante'.

22. ibid., pp.152-53: 'Au moment où la classe aristocratique a cessé d'être une force historique, où l'existence nobiliaire, confinée à la vie d'apparat, est condamnée à se détériorer, le noble jouit désormais de lui-même sur le mode mythologique. Ne pouvant plus être dieu de chair, il se vit comme dieu d'opéra, justifié et supporté par la beauté de sa propre mélodie. Tel est bien, dans **Agésilas,** le sens de ce curieux infléchissement du tragique vers le lyrique'.

23. ibid., pp.153-54: 'Son Arcadie ne dépayse, que pour poser plus cruellement les problèmes. C'est cette contradiction intime qui, déroutant ou heurtant les contemporains, explique, plus que toute cause extérieure, l'échec total d'**Agésilas:** c'est elle qui fait, aujourd'hui, l'intérêt d'une tentative originale'.

24. ibid., p.138.

25. Bénichou, pp.155-80, on 'La Démolition du héros'. As we will see, the concepts

place est raisonneur, héroïque et sans faiblesse en un temps où on aime la faiblesse. [...]   Il y a chez lui du puritanisme, voire même du don quichottisme à lutter ainsi obstinément pour la cause perdue d'une tragédie héroïque et d'un monde moral sans faiblesse' (p.266).

43.   Corneille, **Writings on the Theatre,** edited by H.T. Barnwell (Oxford, 1965), p.169.

SEVEN

'Marine Chassée': A Reconsideration of the Dramatic Structure of Lesage's *Turcaret*
Richard Parish

If certain common critical emphases could be said to have done a disservice to classicism, it would probably be in their advancement of too static or formulaic a view of its structures. Jean-Louis Backès writes in a recent book on Racine that 'à force de décrire le système dramatique de Racine, le personnage, le monde racinien, on finit par perdre de vue un trait caractéristique du poète: son goût pour l'expérimentation',[1] and such a judgement could well be applied both to other major dramatic writers of the seventeenth and eighteenth centuries, comic and tragic, and to dramatic developments over the period as a whole. The dynamism of the classical writers emanates less from their belief that they have found the perfect marriage of form and theme than from their conviction of the value of striving to attain it. When we think of the period cursorily, certain individual authors inevitably come to mind, for a variety of reasons, and not least for the amount of their corpus that remains studied and staged. However, when we look at it historically, we do not find that their deaths or retirements leave the stage bereft of other writers ready to pursue the same goal. In some cases the demise of a talent may seem to leave the eventual direction of its successors unclear, and this is no doubt what causes us to talk of post-Molière comedy, as if comedy somehow stopped and started again, with **Le Malade imaginaire** as the turning point. But the experiment still goes on, perhaps in some cases all the more vigorously, albeit in a more dispersed fashion; thus after Molière we hear not about one successor, but rather see that the continuing tradition, immeasurably enriched if for a time somewhat eclipsed by a single writer, re-emerges and moves forward.[2]

Among those writers contributing to its progress in the early eighteenth century, Lesage might be seen as typifying the continued exploration of the potential of comedy; if we leave aside his non-dramatic works, we find translations and adaptations of Spanish comedies, the first two of which are preceded by an important theoretical preface; a small number of, broadly speaking, social comedies written directly in French; and then the vast output of the **théâtre forain**. Lesage, too, would be characteristic of such figures in that just one or two of his plays remain relatively well known. In his case, it is **Turcaret** (1709) that is singled out for popularity, both among his plays and among comedies of the period. Yet the same play has been the object of a good deal of disparagement, on account primarily of its irregular construction, and particularly with regard to the use made by its author of secondary characters. So could it be that its very irregularity carries some attraction, as F.-X. Cuche, in a brilliant article on the play,[3] may be taken to imply? Or are the perceived defects simply overlooked, so that we enjoy the best elements of an experiment which, taken as a whole, did not come off? Above all, what is Lesage contributing to the continuing vitality of dramatic form and the comic medium?

If we begin by collating critical assessments of **Turcaret**, we find a degree of negative accord among the play's more recent commentators.   Concluding his introduction to Lesage's three major French plays,[4] Maurice Bardon, for example, identifies **Turcaret**'s two principal weaknesses as, first, the **soubrette** Marine and her 'rôle d'utilité': 'ne valait-il donc pas mieux ne pas nous la montrer,' he asks, 'ne pas nous intéresser à elle?' (and more recently Cuche writes, albeit from a different standpoint, that 'tout l'épisode de Marine est d'une totale gratuité');[5] and secondly, the other minor roles: 'plus gratuits encore, sans nécessité même pour l'action, sont les rôles de Flamand, du marquis, de Madame Jacob, de l'usurier Rafle'. T. Lawrenson, introducing his edition of the play, describes a 'pointless **remue-ménage**' as prevailing, but goes on to suggest that this is 'an intentional part of the comedy which must be accepted if the play is to be fully enjoyed'.[6] Finally, Bernard Blanc, in his edition, summarizing thereby a variety of degrees and kinds of scepticism on the matter, remarks quite simply that 'la structure de la pièce n'est pas très claire'.[7]

It is perhaps worth asking, therefore, with these areas of criticism particularly in mind, how far it is possible to agree with a view of the kind expressed so forcefully in his article on **Turcaret** in 1932 by C.S. Gutkind: 'Man komme nicht mit dem üblichen Argument, Lesage habe keine Komödie konstruieren können! Es genügt ein Blick auf die von ihm 1707 gefertigte Intriguenkomödie "Crispin rival de son maistre", um die Unhaltbarkeit dieser Ansicht sofort zu erkennen'.[8] This is undeniable, and a further glance, this time at **Le Point d'honneur** (1702), his adaptation of Francisco de Rojas's **No ay amigo para amigo**, would only serve to confirm such a verdict. True, **Crispin** is a one-act, **Turcaret** a five-act play, but this cannot alone account for the disparity between the tautness of the earlier work and the apparent randomness of the later. Some closer examination of these elements of 'gratuité' will therefore serve as a starting point for our reading of the play.

THE MARINE EPISODE

There is little room to contest that, **prima facie**, the role of Marine is structurally eccentric. She is on stage for the first seven scenes of the first act, during which period she is cast in high relief, and then is never seen again. She fulfils superficially the simple function of reporting La Baronne's extravagances and infidelities to Turcaret, and thus of triggering off the so-called 'scène de la casse' (II.iii).[9] One view of her which it seems fair to challenge, as does Cuche, is that of Antoine Adam, which would see her as the only 'honnête et sympathique' character in the play.[10] There is indeed an aspect in which her moral or immoral ambitions are different from those of her successor, but her parting line, 'je ne veux pas qu'on dise dans le monde que je suis infructueusement complice de la ruine d'un financier' (I.vii, ll.433-35), makes it difficult to disagree with Cuche's gloss on it: 'Il nous étonne qu'on ait pu considérer Marine comme échappant à la corruption'.[11] But he too refuses to give her any real function in the play's development, proposing rather that this formal irregularity in the first act constitutes one of the ways in which 'les structures de la comédie traditionnelle éclatent'.[12] We too shall argue that the function of Marine is related to the enlargement of comic structures, both in the first act and at a later stage, but in a more gradual and self-conscious process of change than is suggested by 'éclatement'.

Considering that we see her for such a short time, we obtain a reasonable characterization of Marine (**pace** Blanc, who writes: 'Marine, la première soubrette de la Baronne, a tenté de s'opposer à sa maîtresse, énonçant une morale cynique; cela aurait pu lui donner une personnalité, si elle ne disparaissait si tôt de la scène').[13] She is frank, and has difficulty in hiding her feelings: 'je ne puis me taire' (I.i, l.3), 'je ne puis me contraindre' (I.vii, l.421); she speaks on an equal footing with her mistress, in which respect she shares the relative ease and familiarity which characterize exchanges of this kind throughout the play, but adds to it on occasion a note of patronizing disapproval, which does single her out: 'Vous mettez ma patience à bout' (I.i, l.6); 'Eh! que m'importe, après tout, que votre bien s'en aille comme il vient?' (I.iii, ll.227-28). She does not hesitate to give instructions: 'Ne le recevez pas' (I.ii, l.105), and becomes morose when disobeyed. The tone which she displays with others, too, shows no place for subtlety or politeness, unless her own interest is likely to be served - compare her 'Bon jour et bon an' to Frontin ('d'un air brusque') (I.ii, l.101), or her **répliques** to Le Chevalier (I.vii), with her farewell to the generous Turcaret: 'Adieu, monsieur; je suis votre très humble servante' (I.v, ll.373-74). She opposes the prodigal tendencies of La Baronne: 'je vous vois dans la nécessité de [thésauriser]' (I.i, ll.9-10) and the world of gamblers (the tone which is indicated by her references to 'un petit

that the apartment of La Baronne should also serve as a meeting place, a place of passage, and Frontin and Lisette encourage this function. Lisette, upon her appointment, immediately occupies herself with an action symbolizing welcome: 'Vous savez qu'on soupe ici?', La Baronne asks her, and then orders: 'Donnez ordre que nous ayons un couvert propre et que l'appartement soit bien éclairé' (III.iii, ll.1046-48), and Lisette leaves to attend to it (in contrast to Marine's departure from stage to engage in a retentive action). During her absence (Turcaret being already present), Le Marquis and Rafle both arrive. Later on, Lisette introduces Furet (IV.vi, ll.1694-95), encourages Madame Jacob in her sale: 'Vous n'y perdrez pas; madame est généreuse' (IV.x, l.1845), welcomes Flamand (V.iii, ll.1985-87), admits her curiosity with respect to Madame Turcaret (V.v, l.2052), and announces Turcaret for the recognition scene (V.x, ll.2198-99). In other words, without causing the arrival of all these characters, she facilitates for her mistress, in the end beyond the latter's wishes (as Cuche says, 'il arrive souvent que le jeu dépasse celui qui s'y est donné et se retourne contre lui'),[34] the succession of visits which prepares the climax. The spirit which prevails, therefore, after the installation of Lisette, and with the help of Frontin and of chance, is one which favours movement and openness as a means to disorder and the seizing of the opportunities that randomness provides. It is a philosophy that takes the risks that the present moment affords and conceives of the future as open-ended.

So far, then, we would propose a possible view of the play as consisting of two mirror-image prologues, followed by a three-act **comédie d'intrigue,** with the whole also functioning as a five-act comedy. Lesage had, after all, already adapted one Spanish play, **Le Point d'honneur,** into both a three-act and a five-act version, and he writes at the beginning of the later (and only extant) three-act piece: 'Je l'accommodai au Théâtre Français, et la fis représenter à Paris, au mois de février 1702. Elle était en cinq actes, mais je l'ai réduite à trois, pour la rendre plus vive'.[35] Might he not have tried to have the best of both worlds in **Turcaret?**

The next way we would propose of looking at the opening acts of the comedy must be seen as overlapping with, rather than contradicting or exactly complementing, the previous one. It would be to suggest that Lesage proposes two partial comic structures within a third comprehensive framework (the five-act play, **Turcaret**). Both depend on Marine.

The first is the project we have already evoked as enunciated by her at the end of the first scene as the 'grand ouvrage' (I.i, ll.69-77). This would, if ever realized dramatically, have been a simple, one-act comedy, with one of two possible endings: either a marriage for money between La Baronne and Turcaret (hardly **per se** a plot with endless comic potential); or a fleecing of Turcaret followed by his departure, and by a decent marriage by La Baronne to someone else of higher rank. Both of these rather harmless comic variants would demonstrate that money and birth are no longer related, and that a charming young widow can get what she wants. The first would be a relatively anodine piece, with a happy ending for both main characters; the second would have a little more edge, and would make a satirical point, but as it is presented seems too sequential to provide much comic overlap (nothing of the eventual marriage being woven into the fleecing of Turcaret theme). The satirical point of this would emanate from the portrayal of ordered social change governed by money with, in the second version, La Baronne's return to the clan showing that blood is thicker than water; and such a second version would also make the point implicitly that even the wits of the lesser aristocracy can still outstretch the financial astuteness of the emergent **bourgeoisie**. It is the way Marine would like to see the plot develop, but in one sense it is already too late, and the acceptance by La Baronne of the note from Frontin in the following scene leaves little doubt that this development will not take place. At all events, it would have provided Lesage with a much more limited comic subject, deprived of the element of disorder which will characterize both the other partial comic structure and the overall one. It would rather lead to the sort of 'maison triste' in which Lisette had been working before she got bored. Finally, either denouement which it would admit would, by serving as the conclusion to a plan conceived for the future and then realized in dramatic time, represent a **terminus ad quem**. It would be a static denouement, suggestive of, because capable of, no further comic development.

The second partial comic structure is more developed within the play, and culminates in the 'scène de la casse' (II.iii), of which Cuche writes that 'on pourrait dire que la pièce ne commence véritablement qu'à [cette] scène'.[36] The plot, as it is already worked out, is that Marine tries to get her own back on her mistress who has disobeyed her, and in so doing gives rise to the (fully expected) outburst of Turcaret; La Baronne in the meantime has recovered the diamond, Turcaret is penitent and duped, and La Baronne is in a stronger position than before. For the scene to have been a self-contained denouement, however, it would also have been necessary to re-introduce the character of Marine, rescue the **billet au porteur**, and dismiss Le Chevalier. In this way, the latter's further involvement in the play would be thwarted, La Baronne would be in possession of all the scattered objects (while still being in a position to gain more and more from Turcaret by virtue of his need to make amends), and Marine would recant, congratulate her mistress on her skill, and be re-instated. Such a denouement would constitue a restoration of the **status quo ante** in terms of relationships, but with the promise of further material gains to come; it would thus at once provide a conclusion, and be indicative of a restorative and progressive comic structure, positing the repetition of the past in the future against the static view of post-dramatic time implicit in the first hypothesis. Finally, it would, like the 'grand ouvrage', make the satirical point that the nobility could still outwit the **bourgeoisie,** and partially vindicate the 'morale de Marine', whilst leaving enough room on both sides for accommodation. Of course this development is also impossible, because the **billet au porteur** and Marine have both irretrievably vanished, and the involvement of Le Chevalier and Frontin is already well advanced; we have only to compare the degree of precision contained in the latter's plans at the end of Act II with those of Act I to realize how much progress has been made. This is, however, Marine's last scene in one sense, and it is appropriate that Lisette does not figure in it at all; but La Baronne's turning of Turcaret against Marine, not all of which is strictly necessary for her escape, leaves no room for the possibility of Marine's reinstatement.

These two hypothetical directions suggested by early parts of the play in which Marine is involved further underline another way in which her departure points to an épanouissement, both in terms of **dramatis personae** and of satirical implications. Such embryonic developments are characterized by the potential for certain types of comic conclusion, which are however not realized because, running through them, there are destructive counter-tendencies which will progressively come to the surface as the play moves on. The five-act **Turcaret** depends on events portrayed in these first two acts which prevent them from having a simpler denouement. The Marine episode points beyond its own limitations to areas of the greater comic scope of the play as a whole, which in the end makes its satirical point, not by the portrayal of isolated and regulated social movement within however tenuous a hierarchy, but by a disordered and generalized upheaval. Her presence in the first act allows Lesage to indicate areas of contemporary social critique within relatively precise bounds, and then to develop them by means of more expansive comic devices. The satire will emanate from the implied power of change to generate its own movement, resulting in the suggestion of **perpetuum mobile** which is contained in the denouement. The progress of the play is from the particular to the general, from a **comique de caractère** to a **monde à l'envers,** from a conception of comedy whose stylization lies in the simple, the predicted, the stated, the delimited to another conception, still stylized, but altogether bigger and looser, which depends on the complex, the unexpected, the random, the turbulent. It is now time to consider the other secondary characters, with a view to elucidating this further.

THE SECONDARY CHARACTERS

It is necessary merely to glance at the **dramatis personae** of **Turcaret** to see that, compared with the previous two French plays of Lesage (**La Tontine** having been written before **Turcaret**), there is a considerable expansion in both the number of characters involved and the diversity of relationships between them (though here again the fact that the previous plays are much shorter obviously makes a difference). In both these plays, a tight knot of characters works out its internal resolution. Even in the larger-scale Spanish plays there is a more closely interwoven texture of relationships (although with a small number of peripheral figures)[37] and a maximum of twelve characters (in **Don César Ursin**). **Turcaret** is, then, quite simply Lesage's most ambitiously populated play. Bardon, we recall, singles out for their 'gratuité' the characters of Flamand, Le Marquis, Madame Jacob, and Rafle, to which we would add Furet and Jasmin. The criteria for drawing up the extended list are simply that these characters are supplementary to the three couples which make up the centrally interwoven sextet: that is, La Baronne and Le Chevalier, Turcaret and Madame Turcaret, Frontin and Lisette. Within this group, it is evidently Madame Turcaret who figures least on stage, but her important concealed role as La Comtesse to some extent compensates for this absence in the first four acts.

Before beginning to consider these secondary roles, two points must rapidly be mentioned: first, in the context of what we have already suggested, their presence largely follows the establishment of Frontin and Lisette; and secondly, the presence of Jasmin need not detain us for long. As the functions of servant figures such as Marine, Frontin and Lisette are so significant in the whole comic intrigue, some kind of more minor figure may be charged occasionally with simple duties, such as announcing arrivals, when these cannot be executed by another character. The purely expedient role of Jasmin, 'petit laquais de la Baronne', is of this order.

It is not only as Lesage's most populated play that **Turcaret** goes beyond his previous writing for the theatre, and in examining the extended **dramatis personae** we would propose to take into particular account the other ways in which Lesage endows his play with an extended framework of reference. These are the sometimes overlapping extensions of pre-dramatic time and off-stage business.

Turcaret begins **in medias res,** with the eponymous financier already involved with La Baronne. The first line of the play refers to the preceding day, and the immediate past, real or invented, is essentially the business of the first two scenes. As the play develops during the third and subsequent acts, however, so the revelation of the past which preceded its opening is gradually effected. Without there being any exactly schematized development, it is possible to chart a retrospective extension of pre-dramatic time as the play progresses; and it is the extension of the **dramatis personae** which causes this revelation. Turcaret is the principal victim of this process, and each of the four characters of Le Marquis, Rafle, Madame Jacob and Flamand plays a particular role in confronting him with the history from which he is trying to escape by virtue of his social mobility. Le Marquis's function, therefore, in reminding him and La Baronne that he was 'laquais de mon grand-père' (III.iv, l.1142) and that he has 'des revendeuses à sa disposition [...] même dans sa famille' (III.iv, ll.1134-35) is the first painful encounter. Le Marquis also alludes to Turcaret's financial practices (anticipating Rafle): 'C'est l'usurier le plus juif' (III.iv, l.1088) for La Baronne's benefit. This aspect is above all exposed in the Rafle scene (Act III, scene vii), a meeting which brings us abruptly forward to the more recent past; and here (now anticipating Madame Jacob's revelation) we also learn of his wife's presence in Paris. (It is perhaps worth noting that this scene takes place exclusively between Turcaret and Rafle; with them, only the audience at this stage knows of the detailed circumstances of the financial background, thus allowing a greater element of surprise to be expressed by characters on stage at Frontin's revelation of Turcaret's arrest in Act V, scene xiv). Madame Jacob is the next to appear, and reveals, confirming the remark of Le Marquis, her own relationship to Turcaret. She then complains that he does nothing for her or her family and, most important, tells La Baronne of the existence of Madame Turcaret, separated ten years ago from her husband, and kept away from Paris by a pension. She further reveals to the disquiet of La Baronne, and now anticipating Flamand, that 'il a toujours quelques demoiselles qui le plument', giving rise to La Baronne's hesitant reply: 'Oui, cela n'est pas tout à fait...' (IV.x, ll.1932-33 and 1936-37). Finally, Flamand makes it implicitly clear, too, that the favours accorded by Turcaret to his minions depend on their patroness's relationships to him: 'le commis que l'on révoque aujourd'hui pour me mettre à sa place, a eu cet emploi-là par le moyen d'une certaine dame que M. Turcaret a aimée, et qu'il n'aime plus. Prenez bien garde, madame, de me faire révoquer aussi' (V.iii, ll.2027-31).

In these four different but related ways, therefore, Turcaret is reminded of his distant undistinguished past and of his recent financially incompetent or dishonest circumstances; La Baronne of his origins; and La Baronne and Lisette told of his financial reputation, of his wife's existence, and of the implications of his various amorous exploits. His past is thus both elucidated for an audience in readiness for his final humiliation, and presented to him - and partially to certain other characters - as a prelude to it. All these characters represent an actualization of Turcaret's past because they are all provided with a point of reference vis-à-vis both of Turcaret and of pre-dramatic time. So, although he would wish to refute it (saying, in Act III, scene iv, 'Le passé est passé; je ne songe qu'au présent'), this compositely revealed past becomes progressively more present. In the scenes which are devoted to them in Act III, scenes iv and vii, Le Marquis and Rafle establish the contours of Turcaret's secrets, and indicate the major concealed areas of the play's reference. Then, in the last act, as is appropriate to the comic build-up, the remaining aspects of his past are presented to him with increasing rapidity. As Lawrenson says, albeit perhaps concentrating too much on one scene: 'The supper party, in a sense, is to represent Turcaret's past catching up with him';[38] he is thereby made aware of the trap that he is in, and the efforts of the 'associés' do no more than make it function effectively and rapidly: 'Nous envisagions le plaisir de le ruiner; mais la justice est jalouse de ce plaisir-là; elle nous a prévenus' (V.xiii, ll.2311-13). Turcaret is furthermore not unique in being exposed to unwelcome revelations in the last act, since Madame Turcaret is humiliated when her social pretensions are punctured by Madame Jacob: 'M. Briochais, votre père, était pâtissier dans la ville de Falaise' (V.viii, ll.2169-70); and Le Chevalier, too, is embarrassed by the arrival and revelation of the true identity of the 'comtesse' whom he had so generously sacrificed to La Baronne. These scenes function, too, as minor parallels, or pointers, to the end.

These four characters, therefore, by their referential function to a pre-dramatic past, cause an incursion of this past into the past-denying present of Turcaret, Madame Turcaret, and Le Chevalier. Even La Baronne learns of things which offend her **amour-propre** and perhaps her aspirations; she emerges, ironically, as also transitory and replaceable in the affections of Turcaret, and as the rival of a pseudo-'comtesse' whose favours seem as easily distributed as her portraits.

Closely related to the question of pre-dramatic time is that of off-stage business, and it should first be noted in this context that if the number of characters to apear on stage is large, the number simply mentioned is also important. Again, as the play progesses, Lesage attributes a growing role to this wider cast, and the world of **Turcaret** increasingly appears as one that is indirectly composed of various milieus and societies, each containing a considerable element of the specific; the play points to these outside worlds with which it is indissolubly linked. Seen in one light, then, all the characters present or mentioned in **Turcaret** would find their place on a sliding scale of dramatic actualization, of presence and absence, distance and proximity. At one end is La Baronne who, after all, is **chez elle,** and is on the stage for the majority of the time, and at the other, for the sake of argument, the 'cuisiniers' of Madame Turcaret, in Normandy, who, always assuming they exist, 'tirent les viandes si à propos, qu'un tour de broche de plus ou de moins, elles seraient gâtées' (V.vi, ll.2099-2100). Between these two extremes lies a whole iceberg of fictional characters, only the very tip of which is exposed in **Turcaret**. The confines of the point at which this tip emerges are also made clear, just as are the chronological confines of the play's reference: Furet and Rafle, with the exception of one scene each **chez** La Baronne, conduct their affairs (of which we are nevertheless told a certain amount) elsewhere; they just make it (albeit vitally so) into the **dramatis personae**; just left out are, for example, Turcaret's 'créanciers', who in the last scene of the play are clearly on the very threshold of entering La Baronne's apartment. Between these limits, those characters who spend a substantial amount of their time on stage are linked to the outside world in two ways: by their periodic sorties into it, about which we are often told, and by the incursion, through other characters, of the exterior into the stage world. Here again, it is Turcaret who is provided with the most extended context: we know of him that he leaves to go to 'une de nos assemblées, pour m'opposer à la réception d'un pied-plat' (I.v, ll.368-69); he proposes to invite to supper one M. Gloutonneau, a poet, who 'mange et pense beaucoup' (II.iv, l.870); immediately after the 'scène de la casse', 'je cours chez Dautel, vous acheter...' (II.iv, l.871); he has just bought land, to 'faire bâtir un hôtel' (III.iii, l.1059); he is 'abonné à l'Opéra', and so on. Turcaret furthermore seems to inhabit more milieus than the other characters who appear, and the socially referential range of the secondary quartet also serves to illustrate the extent of these parts of his life, Le Marquis giving the aristocratic point of view, Flamand that of a dependent, Madame Jacob that of a member of the family, and Rafle that of a colleague. He is thus defined and contextualized by them and, therefore, in the end, humiliated by them. It is of course the scene with Rafle which provides the most central definition of Turcaret's status in a detailed and precise way. The exterior of his present is, it goes without saying, no more salubrious than his past, and this scene exposes the full reality of the financial activities on which the whole plot is based; at the very centre of the play there is revealed the rotten infrastructure on which it is built, a revelation which prepares us for the final collapse of Turcaret, not ultimately because of his social, but because of his financial, exposure. Lesage's play is constructed with this context at the centre, radiating, if such a word may be used, throughout its texture, a context which in the last act overtakes all the other humiliating revelations to ensure his defeat. The overall defeat is, however, greater than this particular arrest; Turcaret is defeated by the becoming present of what had been past or absent. It is therefore appropriate that the final humiliation itself be inflicted off-stage; Turcaret is no longer acceptable in the milieu he had come to frequent, and he returns to the society that underpins the play, into the infrastructure represented by Rafle. The triumph of the here and now, of the present, in other words, is underlined by Turcaret himself becoming absent, absent because re-absorbed into his own past.

Frontin, too, has and manipulates a context. He has a variety of outside connexions and meetings (though some are invented): he visits the 'agent de change' (IV.i, ll.1492-94); speaks of a 'maître maquignon qui est mon neveu à la mode de Bretagne' (III.x, ll.1448-49), who will provide a carriage; and mentions a 'vieux coquin de ma connaissance' (IV.i, ll.1515-16), who of course turns out to be Furet.

Two points deserve mention here. The first is the interaction of random extension and random selection in Lesage's play. Of the five affairs brought forward by Rafle, only one is the cause òf Turcaret's downfall:

RAFLE. L'affaire est sérieuse et pressante.

TURCARET. On l'accommodera. J'ai pris mes mesures: cela sera réglé demain.

RAFLE. J'ai peur que ce ne soit trop tard.   (III.vii, ll.1269-73)

In this way, the dramatist both provides the broader context for his character, but also chooses from it one particular aspect which eventually serves to defeat him. Or again, it is Furet who is brought on stage to contextualize Frontin as opposed to the 'agent de change' or the 'neveu à la mode de Bretagne', who could equally well have appeared. Furet's scene is indeed used to bring out Frontin's underworld connexions (we recall from Act IV, scene i (ll.1527-28) that he 'a presque toujours eu un logement dans les maisons du roi, à cause de ses écritures') and makes him in one sense representative of this underworld. What Lesage thereby appears to be underlining, however, is not the randomness of the extension of his **dramatis personae** as much as the randomness of selection: these characters are no more than representatives, and Furet is no more the whole of Frontin's life off-stage than Rafle is that of Turcaret. Such characters point to the incompleteness of the picture which Lesage is able to paint by such brief appearances **chez** La Baronne. They serve to indicate, in varying degrees, the links which connect the apartment to the worlds which meet there; but the links remain, as in reality, inconsistently present or absent. If we compare Frontin and Le Chevalier, for example, we find that Frontin's range of contacts is wide, but it extends horizontally only and at one remove from the stage company - in other words, his other named contacts belong to the same world as Furet. The milieu of Le Chevalier is, however, extended by the presence of Le Marquis (aristocratically a superior title), which in turn refers to that of his aunt who, to judge from her wealth and jewels, is, at least financially, better placed again. We could, then, see Le Chevalier's links with an external society as moving vertically.

This is a narrow distinction, however; the main point it illustrates is that secondary characters point beyond themselves to tertiary characters who are in turn contextualized or extended in a variety of ways. Some of this tertiary information contributes as well to furthering the characterization of the secondary characters, as we have seen. But a good deal of it is apparently entirely incidental: the life of Madame Jacob, for example, is depicted as consisting of the struggle to look after her idle husband and 'famille nombreuse', and in working as a 'revendeuse' and match-maker; she is connected to La Baronne by the shadowy but temporarily impoverished figure of Madame Dorimène. Here, then, Lesage gives a good deal of context which seems to be more or less picturesque and nothing more. Elsewhere, Madame Turcaret, technically a primary character but a late arrival on stage, depicts in a few brief speeches the small-time provincial **mondanité** which mimics the Parisian **salons**: 'On joue chez moi: on s'y rassemble pour médire' (V.vi, ll.2093-94), and so on. All of this provides an extended, and apparently extensible, context for the events which take place in La Baronne's apartment.

The second point worthy of mention, and associated with this idea, is that Furet and Rafle make no appearance in the fifth act; at the same time, they are more than cameo-figures. Having the status of representatives and no more, they nevertheless represent a facet of the two financial wizards of the play (whose reigns, as far as we know, succeed each other) that is crucial and common, namely the world of small-time financial criminality. They thus underpin the play's ethos, and are as necessary as they are dispensable; other characters could have performed the functions they perform, but they or their putative replacements are vital for an understanding of the play's infrastructure, and when Turcaret returns into it, it is not surprising that Rafle is nowhere to be seen. (And we could imagine, in post-dramatic time, a Furet playing a Rafle-like scene to Frontin.) For the time being, in the vital present moment that concludes the play, it is Rafle who comes to represent the world of projects failing or on the wane, and Furet those that are thriving and promise for the future. Finally, La Baronne, with her apartment, provides a meeting place for all the milieus and combinations of milieus which her visitors represent. For the duration of the play her world becomes a cross-roads of provincial life, town life (both high and low) and the underworld. In one sense, the whole play is her context. And, for the duration of her employment by La Baronne, Lisette is also **chez elle**, predominantly concerned with her contribution where she is, rather than with external comings and goings (she is on stage throughout from Act IV, scene vi, to the end of the play).

By indicating some of the extent of Lesage's theatrical population, we would suggest that far from choosing extra characters to add, arbitrarily, to a limited maximum, Lesage has sought in his play to depict an extended society of considerable breadth and variety, vigorously peopled with sketched-in characters who help to give it precision and colour, but from which he brings onto the stage just the number of secondary figures necessary to point to the ways in which primary characters relate to it and it to them. These primary characters emanate from, and in most cases return to, a network of little societies which had, during the latter part of the play at least, fed the transitory dramatic society of which La Baronne was at the centre. They forge the link between the **comédie de mœurs** and the **comédie de caractère(s)**, but Lesage indicates by their inconsistent contribution the jagged if relatively clear edge to the line which divides the stylization of the classical play from the more naturalistic depiction of a freer genre. Comparisons between **Turcaret** and the novel have been made (M. Spaziani describes it as a 'vera "tranche de vie" contemporanea trasferita dal romanzo sulla scena',[39] and Lawrenson suggests in his introduction to **Crispin** that **Turcaret** demonstrates that 'episodic reality' is better suited to a novel than a play),[40] but a closer look at this external reality may make it easier to reconcile it with the dramatic genre. Those details of conversation and characterization without which, there is no doubt, the denouement could still have ensued quite convincingly relate to the placing of **Turcaret** and Turcaret in a larger context; and it is the mode of incursion of this context which socially and financially defeats Turcaret, and satirically and generically defines **Turcaret**. Given this function of secondary characters in the definition and in various aspects of the humiliation of the hero, therefore, it would have made them more arbitrary if we had known less about them, and their incidental context allows them to emerge as rapidly but effectively characterized figures. Just as with Furet, they are dispensable, in that other characters could have fulfilled the roles they play, but necessary, in that they bring on to the stage, represent and make present the absent or the past, and so arrest and then reverse the movement forwards.

Thus in the last five scenes, and after the stage has become maximally crowded (Act V, scene x), it is rapidly depopulated. Scene x of the last act completes the humiliation of Turcaret. La Baronne pointedly concludes the preceding scene with one last territorial challenge to Madame Turcaret: 'Songez que vouz êtes chez moi' (V.ix, ll.2272-73), and Jasmin arrives to announce the 'associés' of Turcaret. Thereafter, the network of relationships rapidly disintegrates; as Blanc puts it, 'les alliances se défont'.[41] Turcaret, we will soon learn, is not to reappear, and the Turcaret tribe (Madame Turcaret and Madame Jacob) follow him. La Baronne is alerted to some of the truth, and she too leaves, making a final comparison between Marine and Lisette: 'J'ai chassé Marine parce qu'elle n'était pas dans vos [Le Chevalier's] intérêts, et je chasse Lisette parce qu'elle y est...' (V.xiii, ll.2341-43). Le Chevalier and Le Marquis return to their usual pastimes, a little scarred we must suppose: 'Allons souper chez le traiteur et passer la nuit à boire' (V.xiv, ll.2348-49). And Frontin and Lisette remain alone on stage.

Two things have happened, therefore. First, the multiplication of characters present on stage has ended with a variety of embarrassing discoveries resulting from their contact; the welcoming, expansive 'complaisance' of Lisette has contributed to an explosive accumulation, containing the capacity for its own destruction, of which the catalyst is the arrest of Turcaret. After this brief hiatus, movement is resumed, but now in most cases it is backwards into past roles; only Frontin and Lisette suggest a continuing movement forwards. Secondly, and although it is apparently La Baronne who dismisses Lisette, it is, in terms of the occupation of the stage/apartment, Lisette who dismisses La Baronne. Her feeling of unease is betokened by her retreating into an inner part of her apartment, escaping from the place of confrontation, and seeking a kind of reassurance by defining her rightful place more closely. Both these factors illustrate how Frontin and Lisette, by encouraging turbulence and movement, have created a self-destroying dynamic. This movement has concentrated progressively towards a centre, and, upon destroying itself, has left a temporary vacuum which Frontin and Lisette now set about filling with the present moment.

CONCLUSION

We have suggested a number of factors which may permit a more structured reading of **Turcaret,** in the light of, rather than despite, its more notorious irregularities. These are:

(a) the possibility of seeing the Marine episode as standing in some kind of role as a prefatory commentary on the rest of the play, be it as one of two complementary prologues and the counter-prologue to Lisette's emergence, or as a means of positing and rejecting certain comic treatments of a theme;

(b) the elements of mobility and openness which, although present throughout the play and to some extent in pre-dramatic time, are particularly encouraged by Lisette's 'complaisance' and so become increasingly significant in Acts III-V;

(c) the functions played by pre-dramatic time and off-stage business, and the relationship of secondary characters to these;

(d) the possibility of seeing in Lesage's apparent arbitrariness a demonstration of the use of multiple levels of characterization, and thereby of a more extended framework of stylization;[42]

(e) the eventual triumph of the present moment against the planned future and the rejected past.

In developing this last point, we would suggest that Lesage, in positing and rejecting two types of comic denouement (the static and the restorative/progressive), and inaugurating in their stead a comic structure whose fully-realized denouement is destructive and recreative (Frontin and Lisette rise phoenix-like from the ashes...), is at the same time drawing our attention to the process. But he is not, in this third play, **Turcaret**, thereby trying to represent naturalistically the larger world. By the jagged line which he draws between a more naturalistic extension and the more closed stylization of the classical comic stage, he is pointing to the outside world that the stage represents, but doing no more than that. The characters chosen to represent this outside world still function within the apartment of La Baronne, in other words on stage. The definitive denouement of **Turcaret** is no more naturalistic than the rejected ones; it just uses and refers to a wider spectrum of external reality in the construction of its comic devices. Turcaret is relatively safe within an enclosure, even one where he is socially **dépaysé**, so long as it remains closed. Once it is opened, however, he becomes threatened, since his absence and his past consequently become the here and now.

But of course once Lesage employs a greater range of characters in his play, who in their different ways are also embarrassed or humiliated by the denouement, the implications of the satire become wider. The putting to flight of a whole spectrum of characters at the end of **Turcaret** implies a much more anarchic, explosive potential in the meeting of the categories of people he portrays, and a much more fragile triumph. The self-conscious selection points to the stylization of comedy; but the clear function of the characters **qua** representatives suggests at the same time their universal significance. If Lesage goes beyond the simple comedy of character(s) in **Turcaret**, he is still far from any more naturalistic approach that would anticipate the **drame**, as well as being exempt from writing the sort of comedy of manners that Blanc describes as being 'destinée principalement à ses contemporains'.[43] If the **dramatis personae** up to Act III, scene iii, could have carried two satires of the financier, Lesage writes neither of these. However, by the nature of his treatment of the secondary characters and their **rapport** with the outside world, he makes it equally clear that he is writing a satire. Satirized in his play is the tendency of increased mobility (here financial and social) to create its own dynamic, to contain the potential for destruction and self-destruction, but to conceal at the same time a regenerative energy; and in this play about social movement, which is also a satire of mobility, it is the most cunning who triumph within dramatic time ('Frontin sort gagnant du jeu parce qu'il est le plus habile tricheur').[44] In this structure, it is the secondary characters who serve particularly to contribute the past and the absent (in other words, that from which characters have moved away in time or place) to the present which prevails after their defeat; but the past and the absent will not stay away for long, of course, and the triumph of the here and now, of Frontin and Lisette, is by its very nature transitory. The present moment triumphs at the end of the play only because it is the present moment, for the time being free of a past. It triumphs by virtue of the past's capacity to overtake those who had seen themselves as freed from it, and in contrast to a circumscribed view of the future that has now also been dismissed into the past; but the present moment does not prevail without drawing attention as it does so to the ephemeral nature of its triumph. In one way Don Cléofas was right, of course, to ask: 'Les bonnes dispositions de Frontin ne font-elles pas assez prévoir que son règne finira comme celui de Turcaret?'.[45]   Yet the acknowledgement of this would not allow us to agree with Gutkind's rather quaint phrase that the play is 'Ohne Happyend, freudlos'.[46] Only if we take a Marine-like stance, and refuse any complicity to Frontin and Lisette, is such a view possible; and only if we fail to observe that minute but vital difference between our reaction to a comedy's ending and our subsequent reflections on its implications. The celebration of the present **is** the happy ending.

We would, therefore, bring Marine and the other secondary characters together in concluding that she serves, in negative ways, to indicate the ultimate direction and bounds of the satire, and that they serve to establish the fine equilibrium which that direction requires, between a broader depiction of a period and its societies on the one hand, and a stylized comic treatment of it on the other. Lesage talks of something similar in the 1700 Preface when he writes of the Spanish theatre and his adaptations of it that 'j'ai gardé un milieu entre les libertés de leur théâtre, et la sévérité du nôtre'.[47]   Two other critics in particular also comment on this: P. Voltz, who acknowledges that 'Lesage ne renonce ni aux plaisirs de la comédie d'intrigue ni aux procédés classiques de stylisation',[48] and again Gutkind: 'Er [Lesage] folgt damit dem ewigen Gesetz aller grossen Komik, deren Wesen eben in dem endlosen, unlösbaren Widersinn zwischen Wahrheit und Wirklichkeit beschlossen liegt'.[49] Thus his satire is as wide-ranging as he can make it, but not, **pace** Lawrenson, 'splitting at the seams'.[50] Without the secondary characters and Marine, it would have been less, not more, balanced, and it would have been a different kind of play. What **Turcaret** has to say about eighteenth-century society has already been amply exposed. What can perhaps be added is the light it throws on its own comic denouement. In recognizing the triumph of the present moment against a certain past and a certain future, the attitude of the audience as the curtain falls is one of an acknowledged ephemeral complicity. Things will go wrong again, and in such an ending other comedies, as yet unwritten, are implied. But just for a moment, time is defined by the present, and the momentary freedom to laugh without fear of the past or the future is realized. The comic denouement of destruction and recreation both implicates and releases its witnesses, and thus achieves the balance of association and dissociation on which so much theatre depends.

NOTES

1. Jean-Louis Backès, **Racine** (Paris, 1981), p.28.

2. It is not possible to provide a general résumé of the works either of Lesage or of his contemporaries, but the following table may serve as an **aide-mémoire:**

    > 1672, Molière, **Les Femmes savantes**
    > 1673, Molière, **Le Malade imaginaire**
    > 1687, Dancourt, **Le Chevalier à la mode**
    > 1696, Regnard, **Le Joueur**
    > 1697, Dufresny, **Le Chevalier joueur**
    > 1700, Lesage, **Théâtre espagnol** (Preface, **Le Traître puni, Don Félix de Mendoce**)
    > 1702, Lesage, **Le Point d'honneur**
    > 1707, Lesage, **Don César Ursin** and **Crispin rival de son maître**
    > 1708, Lesage, **La Tontine** (first performed in 1732 as **Arlequin colonel**)
    > 1708, Regnard, **Le Légataire universel**
    > 1709, Lesage, **Turcaret**
    > 1709, Destouches, **Le Curieux impertinent**
    > 1713, Lesage, **Arlequin, roi de Sérendib**
    > 1714, Lesage, **La Foire de Guibray**
    > 1720, Marivaux, **Arlequin poli par l'amour**
    > 1720, Marivaux, **La Surprise de l'amour**
    > 1723, Marivaux, **La Double Inconstance**
    > 1732, Lesage, **Arlequin colonel** (written in 1708 as **La Tontine**).

3. F.-X. Cuche, 'La Formule dramatique de **Turcaret** ou le rythme et le jeu', **Travaux de linguistique et de littérature**, 10, 2 (1972), 57-79.

4. Lesage, **Théâtre: Turcaret, Crispin rival de son maître, La Tontine**, edited by M. Bardon (Paris, 1948), pp.xxii-xxiii.

5. Cuche, p.74.

6. Lesage, **Turcaret**, edited by T.E. Lawrenson (London, 1969), p.9.

7. Lesage, **Turcaret**, edited by B. Blanc (Paris, 1973), p.19. All references to **Turcaret** in the text are to this edition.

8. C.S. Gutkind, 'Lesage's Komödie "Turcaret" ', **Zeitschrift für französische Sprache und Literatur**, 55 (1932), 308-24 (p.320).

9. So called by Lawrenson in his edition of **Turcaret**, p.11. It seems a useful shorthand.

10. Antoine Adam, **Histoire de la littérature française au XVIIe siècle**, 5 vols (Paris, 1948-56), V, 294.

11. Cuche, p.78.

12. Cuche, p.73.

13. Blanc, p.21.

14. Cuche, p.62.

15. Cuche, p.75.

16. Lawrenson, **Turcaret**, p.11.

17. Lawrenson, **Turcaret**, p.11.

18. This seems at least likely to have been possible. In his **The Comédie Française, 1701-1774: Plays, Actors, Spectators, Finances,** in **Transactions of the American Philosophical Society,** 41 (1951), 591-850, Henry Carrington Lancaster writes: 'The poorer members of society could not often afford the price of admission even to the parterre, though they came when there were free performances and were represented at other times by the lackeys and coachmen to whom Lesage refers as occupying the third tier of boxes' (p.594).

19. Cf. Bergson: 'Le comique [...] s'adresse à l'intelligence pure' [...]. Le rire cache une arrière-pensée d'entente [...] presque de complicité, avec d'autres rieurs, réels ou imaginaires' **(Le Rire** (Paris, 1969), pp.4-5).

20. Blanc, p.21.

21. Scene xi **(Théâtre,** p.211).

22. These are, in chronological order, and with their sources: **Le Traître puni** (Francisco de Rojas, **La traición busca),** 1700; **Don Félix de Mendoce** (Lope de Vega, **Guardar y guardarse),** 1700; **Le Point d'honneur** (Francisco de Rojas, **No ay amigo para amigo),** 1702; **Don César Ursin** (Caldéron, **Peor está que estava),** 1707. The first two are described as translations, the third as a translation-adaptation, and the last as an adaptation. The first two were published in The Hague in 1700 as **Le Théâtre espagnol, ou les Meilleures Comédies des plus fameux auteurs espagnols traduites en français,** preceded by the frequently quoted Preface. They are all reprinted in Lesage, **OEuvres choisies,** 16 vols (Paris, 1810), XI, 335-536 and XII, 1-168. These plays have received a detailed study in A. Kamina, 'Le Théâtre de Lesage et la "comedia" espagnole', **Revue de littérature comparée,** 43 (1969), 305-19. The Preface is reproduced in H. Cordier, **Essai bibliographique sur les OEuvres d'Alain-René Lesage** (Paris, 1910), pp.237-40; and in M. Spaziani, **Il teatro minore di Lesage** (Rome, 1957), pp.167-69.

23. I.i; **OEuvres choisies,** XI, 338-39.

24. I.iv; **OEuvres choisies,** XII, 95-96.

25. I.vii; **OEuvres choisies,** XII, 103-04.

26. F.L. Lawrence, **Molière: The Comedy of Unreason** (New Orleans, 1968), pp.14-15.

27. III.viii; **OEuvres choisies,** XII, 132.

28. V.x; **OEuvres choisies,** XII, 167-68.

29. Cordier, p.239. The Preface is not paginated in the 1700 edition. I have modernized spelling in quotation from it.

30. A. Kamina in her article emphasizes the increasingly important role in the Spanish plays of servants in indicating and underpinning the direction of the action.

31. Cuche, p.64.

32. Bardon, p.xx.

33. Cuche, p.77.

34.   Cuche, p.62.

35.   **OEuvres choisies,** XII, 1.

36.   Cuche, p.74.

37.   Notably the characters of Galindo and Le Sicilien, both inventions of Lesage, who appear only in the fifth act of **Le Traître puni** and the third of **Le Point d'honneur** respectively.

38.   Lawrenson, **Turcaret,** p.8.

39.   Spaziana, p.45.

40.   Lesage, **Crispin rival de son maître,** edited by T. Lawrenson (London, 1961), p.21.

41.   Blanc, p.19.

42.   J. Dunkley, in **'Turcaret** and the Techniques of Satire', **British Journal for Eighteenth-Century Studies,** 2 (1979), 107-22, writes: 'One might also consider **Turcaret**'s plot-structure as reflecting the ancient **satura,** in so far as the inclusion of certain scenes and subordinate characters is less a logical necessity dictated by the plot than an authorial method of amplifying the spectator's knowledge of the protagonist's' (p.112).

43.   Blanc, p.13.

44.   Cuche, p.67.

45.   Lesage, 'Critiques de la comédie de **Turcaret** par le Diable boiteux', reproduced by Blanc, pp.149-53 (p.152).

46.   Gutkind, p.322.

47.   Cordier, p.239.

48.   P. Voltz, **La Comédie** (Paris, 1964), p.101.

49.   Gutkind, p.323.

50.   Lawrenson, **Crispin,** p.21.

EIGHT

Jacques Autreau's *Le Naufrage au Port-à-l'Anglais* and the Nouveau Théâtre Italien
Richard Waller

> C'est la première pièce où cette troupe d'**Italiens** parla françois **à Paris**.
> L'affluence de spectateurs commençoit à diminüer; les amateurs de la
> langue **italienne** ne pouvant suffire à deffrayer le spectacle, ils voulurent
> donc imiter les anciens comédiens **italiens** congédiez en 1697.
> Véritablement, cette pièce-cy est dans le goust du Théâtre de **Gherardi:**
> caprices, intrigue liée sans suitte, dissonances, badinage, corps
> étrangers, scènes détachées et burlesques, lazzis, obscenitez, nuls
> caractères, nuls mœurs, de l'italien en françois, et leurs dialogues furent
> fort meslez de langue **italienne,** comme il paroist par l'imprimé. Tel que
> cela est, cela réüssit beaucoup.[1]

The Marquis d'Argenson's note gives a comprehensive summary of the place
traditionally occupied in the history of the French theatre by **Le Naufrage au Port-à-
l'Anglais, ou les Nouvelles Débarquées:** a play of no outstanding intrinsic merit which
nevertheless (succeeds, and) succeeded, by its extensive use of French, in reversing the
declining fortunes of Luigi Riccoboni's Italian theatre company when it opened the
1718-19 season. What follows is an attempt to evaluate the importance of the play in
the context of the situation of the Italian players in the early years of their return to
Paris and, in so doing, perhaps to show that d'Argenson's thorough-going criticism of
its literary qualities is both excessive and narrow.

THE CONTEXT

The company assembled by Riccoboni (at the request of Philippe d'Orléans,
Regent of France) in 1716 was not as well balanced as it might have been. The ideal
composition had been stated in a ruling for the old troupe, drawn up in the name of
Louis XIV's daughter-in-law about 1684, the first article of which read:

> Que ladite troupe demeurera toujours composée de douze acteurs et
> actrices, sçavoir: de deux femmes pour jouer les rooles sérieux; de deux
> autres femmes pour les comiques; de deux hommes pour jouer les rooles
> des amoureux; de deux autres pour les comiques; de deux autres pour
> conduire l'intrigue et de deux autres pour jouer les pères et les
> vieillards.[2]

Strictly speaking, Riccoboni's company consisted of only ten actors and actresses, listed here in the same order as in the 1684 document: Elena Balletti (Flaminia) and Zanetta Benozzi (Silvia), officially described as first and second **amoureuses;** Margarita Rusca (Violette); Luigi Riccoboni (Lelio) and Antonio Balletti (Mario), first and second **amoureux;**   Tomasso Vicentini, otherwise known as Thomassin (Arlequin), and Giacomo Raguzini (Scaramouche); Giovanni Bissoni (Scapin); Pietro Alborghetti (Pantalon) and Francesco Materazzi (the Docteur). The total of twelve was completed after a fashion by Ursula Astori, a full member of the troupe but employed principally as a singer and available for utility roles, and her husband Fabio Sticotti, capable of playing small roles for which he was paid **ad hoc.** Although Violette paired neatly with Arlequin, Scaramouche was not a traditional **zanni** figure and had no natural partner (at its suppression in 1697, the old troupe could boast a Pierrot and a Spinette as well as an Arlequin and a Colombine).[3] With only one **intrigant,** in the person of Scapin, the company was therefore a little short of comic actors - shorter, indeed, than appears on the surface, for acting talent was distributed even more unevenly.

Nicolas Boindin and Thomas-Simon Gueullette, well-informed, objective but well-disposed, even enthusiastic observers of the company's beginnings, are in reasonable agreement over the lack of ability of both Scapin and Scaramouche. Gueullette is the more tolerant of Scapin, contenting himself with dismissing him with faint praise: 'un comédien passable, assez bien facé',[4] while Boindin descends to heavy irony: 'je croy pourtant que je puis oser soûhaiter que son visage prît quelque part dans ce que sa bouche exprime'.[5]   Boindin is only slightly less critical of Scaramouche: 'Si l'on pouvoit perdre l'idée de l'ancien Scaramouche, peut-être prendroit-on plus de plaisir à voir celuy-cy';[6]   Gueullette castigates him as 'un intrus dans la troupe', relates the story of how he bribed his way into the company and describes how, 'malheureusement', the Regent and his mother were so delighted with Scaramouche's playing of 'un rôle de femme ridicule' that Orléans revoked an order to send to Naples for a replacement.[7]   What with Pantalon's utterly incomprehensible Venetian dialect and the Docteur's acting so subtle that 'il n'y a que les bons connoisseurs qui rendent justice à son mérite', it would seem that the cards were stacked against the new arrivals. Boindin even had a number of reservations concerning other actors. On Lelio: 'il luy manque des graces Françoises.   [...] Les mauvais plaisans disent de luy que c'est un fort bon Comedien battu à froid', while in 'les sçenes de tendresse [...] il affecte un ton piteux qui n'est pas du goût de bien des gens'; on Mario: 'il a les hanches trop hautes; il marche mal et ne parle (s'il m'est permis de hazarder cette expression) que **par courbettes';** on Flaminia: 'bien, mais fort maigre' and not only does she speak too fast, but 'elle a la voix aigre et par consequent désagreable'; as for the singer, she is 'ny bien faite ny jolie. Je ne puis goûter sa voix, et sa façon de chanter n'est pas plus de mon goût; je vous dis mon sentiment avec d'autant plus de liberté qu'il m'a paru jusqu'à present que celuy du Public est tres conforme au mien'.[8]

But there were things going for them as well. Part of Boindin's adverse criticism was a reaction to what he saw, no doubt correctly, as an unreasonable **engouement**: for example, Lelio may not be the greatest actor there had ever been, but he was the equal of the best. He admits, among other concessions, that Flaminia is a very intelligent actress and that Violette's vivacity is appreciated by the audiences[9] (Gueullette agreed: 'pas une grande actrice, mais elle ne déplaisait pas au public', and he saw Ursula Astori with different eyes: 'fort belle femme').[10] Above all, there was the excellence of Thomassin and the promise of Silvia, the latter being 'fort bien faite', her style 'tout à fait noble' and 'elle entre vivement dans la passion'.[11] Nor can their standing have been harmed by the public knowledge of the protection they enjoyed of the Regent, who allowed them the use of the stage of the Opéra (which was in his own palace, the Palais-Royal) while the old Hôtel de Bourgogne was undergoing final preparations to restore it to its former use as the Italiens' theatre. But the principal factor in their favour was their novelty value, tinged with nostalgia for their predecessors. The presentation of the Italiens was completely different from that of their main rivals, the actors of the Théâtre Français, a distinction well summarized by Dubois de Saint-Gelais in that first year, 1716:

> Chez les Italiens, les personnages sont toujours les mêmes, le dialogue n'est ni composé ni préparé; ils se passent de mœurs, de caractère et ne sont point assujettis aux règles dramatiques. Ils se contentent de faire un plan pour former les rôles, et aux représentations chaque acteur doit trouver sur-le-champ ce qu'il convient de dire: en sorte qu'à cet égard les comédies italiennes ressemblent plutôt à des conversations concertées. La vivacité de l'intrigue, les incidens et le jeu font le reste et soutiennent toute l'action; ainsi le degré de perfection de ces trois points fait celui de la comédie italienne: ce qui montre qu'elle n'est comparable qu'avec elle-même, et que son genre est singulier et n'est propre qu'à elle.[12]

The French public was particularly conscious of the actors' skill in extemporizing their dialogue (even today a bone of contention among theatre historians) and it was soon put to the test. On 25 July 1716, the company presented its first play not already part of the repertoire (it was also Riccoboni's first original comedy), **L'Italien marié à Paris**. Its success and particularly 'la manière dont Lelio et Flaminia dialoguaient leurs scènes' raised doubts about whether the actors really were performing 'à l'impromptu'.[13] Consequently, a number of French men of letters, among them Houdar de La Motte, Dufresny and Boindin, conspired at the Café de Gradot to produce a French canvas which was eventually provided by Rémond de Sainte Albine with the help of La Motte. Under the title of **L'Amante difficile**, it was performed on 17 October the same year as a five-act comedy. According to the **Mercure de France**, the players effected the transformation with ease, 'sans en avoir fait une seule répétition, et seulement après avoir écouté avec beaucoup d'attention le sujet bien détaillé par le Sr Lélio'.[14] One senses probable exaggeration here (particularly as the **Mercure** report dates from 1731, when a new version by La Motte was performed), but the anecdote serves its purpose in demonstrating one aspect of the impact of the Théâtre Italien on its early audiences. It is also instructive to compare d'Argenson's comments with those of Dubois de Saint-Gelais: the characteristics of the Italian theatre which they identify are substantially the same but the Marquis condemns them from the standpoint of the norms of the traditional French theatre, whereas the contemporary judgement argues strongly for an acceptance of the new form as entirely **sui generis**.

The other novel element is the obvious one: the medium of Italian which transmitted the novel dramatic form. Whatever later problems the language caused, there is no doubt that in the early days it was a positive factor in the popularity of the company. Boindin records how, at the beginning, everybody 'projette d'apprendre l'Italian', how teachers of the language are looking forward to a busy future and how booksellers are searching in the corners of their shops for Italian books covered in dust from years of neglect.[15] It became the fashion to take your Italian interpreter with you to the theatre, and the **Mercure** played its part by printing a monthly story in Italian for its readers to practise on.[16] A further advantage became apparent only later, when French began to be introduced: it was found that much that passed muster in an Italian garb appeared in poor taste, or simply unamusing, when put into French.[17]

The popularity of the company in its early days is undeniable, even if the loss of the first official register means that it is not possible to quantify it or measure its limits with anything like scientific rigour. We do possess substantial information on the very first performance, at the Palais-Royal, on Monday, 18 May 1716. Contemporary sources show that it was common knowledge that receipts topped 4,000 livres[18] and an early historian, who appears to have had access to the lost register, states the precise figure of 4,068 **livres**.[19] That this sum represented a full house is also clear from more than one contemporary account: as early as three hours before the official start of the performance, the only places to be had, according to Gueullette, were in the **parterre**.[20] The audience probably numbered about 1,400.[21] One way of looking at these figures is to compare them with later performances by the Italiens. Such a method certainly demonstrates how impressive was this first audience: the takings were exceeded only twice during the period up to the fusion with the Opéra Comique in 1762 (and that in a theatre accommodating about 300 more spectators).[22]   More to our purpose, though, would be to make a comparison with the Italiens' principal rival, the Théâtre Français. Since the Italiens' first performance was given on the stage of the Opéra and at a date when neither of the great fairs with their theatres was operating, the public had a straight choice between the two companies. Against 4,068 **livres** from 1,400 spectators, the Français could muster but 276 **livres** from 161 spectators.[23]   The following day, with the help of a new one-act comedy by Dancourt and with the competition reverting to the Opéra, the Français recovered to 579 **livres** and 10 **sous** from 382 spectators. On the Wednesday, with the Italiens back and with a new play, the Français were down to 164 **livres** from 111 spectators, whereas, according to Buvat, the Italiens played 'avec même foule' as on the Monday.[24]   Neither played the next day, but on the Friday, a rest day for the Italiens for religious reasons, the Français recovered again to 629 **livres** and 10 **sous** from 410 spectators. The figures for the Italiens are impressive also in the wider perspective of comparison with the Français for the preceding month, that is, for the whole of the new season until the arrival of the Italiens when the only competition was provided by the Opéra. In that time, the three greatest numbers of spectators were 1,017, 850 and 750, with corresponding receipts of 1,9531.10s., 1,6161.10s and 1,3341 (all for Molière's **La Princesse d'Elide**).

From this point, however, the figures for the Théâtre Français are no longer sufficiently unequivocal to be of service. Audience and receipts for 23 May, when the Italiens put on their third new play in as many performances, were greater than for the day before, when the Opéra was occupying the Palais-Royal stage. It might be expected, if the competition remained serious, that the Français audiences would pick up on Fridays, and one Friday in June did indeed attract 431 spectators, the highest number for the whole of the month. Attendances for the other three Fridays, however, were no better than average (100, 60 and 48). In July, a new element entered the picture with the opening of the Saint-Laurent fair. On 24 July, another Friday, the Français audience was again only 48 and this time there is an explanation: a new play by Lesage and Fuzelier, **Arlequin Hulla,** performed by the widow Baron's troupe at the Saint-Laurent fair, and with the added attraction of a new Colombine making her début in it.[25]   From now on, for four months of the year, four theatres vied for the patronage of the Parisian public and, without figures for three of them at any one time until 2 June 1717, the decline of the Italiens cannot be plotted with any accuracy.

We are reduced to relying on the testimony of one or two contemporaries whose opinions may well be deceptively subjective.   Boindin notes what we might well expect: 'grand monde' at the opening of the Hôtel de Bourgogne on 1 June 1716.[26] Nearly two months later, Buvat comments sardonically: 'Les comédiens françois commencent à mourir de faim depuis ceux qui sont venus d'Italie, et, sans le savoir-faire de leurs femmes, ils seroient déjà enterrés'; seven weeks later still, he is quite categorical: 'les comédiens italiens se maintiennent en crédit et augmentent en monde tous les jours'.[27]   More than three weeks before Buvat's last announcement, however, and for the first time in over four months, the Français actors began paying themselves a share of the receipts, and an upturn in their fortunes could indicate a falling-off in those of their competitors.[28]   Apart from a dismissive comment by Saint-Simon,[29] we have no evidence of an abrupt change. More likely is a gradual decline, its cause being probably precisely the factor which most evidently accounted for the initial popularity: the novelty value provided by the difference between what the Italiens offered and what the French public was used to. As the novelty wore off, so that same characteristic of difference and strangeness ceased to be attractive and began to repel. The criticism was, of course, present from the beginning in certain sections of the public: the quotation from Saint-Gelais was a summary of those elements of the Italian theatre which were resisted by, no doubt, the more consciously literary of the critics. It was evidently merely a matter of time before the attitude spread to the general public. In his third **Lettre** on the Théâtre Italien, bearing an **approbation** dated 25 January 1718, Boindin notes not only the decline and a reason for it but also indications that the decline has been arrested:

> pendant un certain temps, j'ai trouvé de l'éloignement entre nos nouveaux Comediens et le Public; mais insensiblement nous nous en sommes approchés; et pour peu qu'ils soient d'humeur à faire la moitié du chemin, en engageant nos Auteurs à composer peur eux des Pieces dans nôtre goût, je suis très-persuadé qu'ils pourront donner de la jalousie aux autres Theatres.   (p.4)

But he had already noted in his second **Lettre** (**approbation** dated 18 August 1717) the need to correct the other novel element, the medium of Italian, which was now keeping audiences away. He proposes the engagement of the son of the last Arlequin of the old troupe:

> ce seroit pour lors qu'ils pourroient larder leurs Pieces de François, ce qui en donneroit l'intelligence à ceux qui n'entendent pas l'Italien, et qui leur attireroit beaucoup de monde, sur tout les femmes qui abandonnent insensiblement ce Theatre.   (p.15)

The wheel would appear to have come full circle: the un-French elements of the new theatre, both literary characteristics and language, now conspire to threaten the future of Riccoboni's enterprise.

THE ROLE OF 'LE NAUFRAGE AU PORT-A-L'ANGLAIS'

After the production of **Le Naufrage**, Boindin advised the Italiens to cultivate its author because, he said, 'selon moi le succés de leur theâtre en dépend',[30] a statement which would appear to imply imminent collapse if the advice were not followed. Autreau's first editor claimed that the play 'eut par son succès la gloire de fixer à Paris ces Comédiens qui méditoient alors leur retour en Italie'.[31] This comment was picked up by at least two later historians who embroidered considerably. Léris rendered it thus:

> Le merveilleux succès qu'elle eut, fixa à Paris ces Comédiens, qui méditoient leur retour en Italie, parce que leur Théatre étoit devenu désert par l'épuisement de leurs pieces Italiennes, plusieurs fois reprises, et dont d'ailleurs peu de personnes se soucioient, faute de les entendre.[32]

Desboulmiers, whose work appeared only ten years after Pesselier's edition of Autreau's theatre, presents the case in its most extreme form:

> Les Comédiens Italiens, malgré leurs soins et leurs efforts continuels pour attirer le Public à leurs Spectacles, n'avaient pû l'y fixer; on convenait de leurs talens; on approuvait leur zele; mais on n'allait point à leurs représentations: les Dames qui avaient montré le plus grand empressement d'apprendre la langue Italienne, ne garderent pas long-temps cette résolution, et leur émulation s'évanouit avec la nouveauté; leur désertion entraîna naturellement celle des hommes, et les Comédiens étaient réduits à parler souvent dans le désert.
>   Désespérés de voir leurs travaux si mal récompensés, ils méditoient leur retraite en Italie, lorsqu'un Auteur Français eut le courage de travailler pour eux; son essai réussit, et le succès du Port-à-l'Anglais ramena les Spectateurs en foule, et fixa les Comédiens en France.[33]

We have here evident borrowings from Boindin, and perhaps the **Mercure**,[34] as well as from Pesselier, plus a quantity of not implausible extrapolation from Desboulmiers himself. The question is, how close is it to reality? The Parfaict brothers explicitly contradict Pesselier, inserting a parenthesis into his account, immediately after the passage quoted above: '(Ce fait est très douteux, et ces Comédiens pensoient seulement à faire un voyage en Angleterre)'.[35] Gueullette, the contemporary who maintained the closest personal as well as professional contact with the theatre and its actors, makes no mention of a special crisis, and his comment on **Le Naufrage** in the list he gives of the company's early repertoire, often with fairly extensive comments, is simply: 'Comédie française de M. Hautreau. Imprimée'.[36] Antoine d'Origny, in his **Annales du Théâtre Italien** of 1788, limits his comments to purely aesthetic considerations.[37] The accounts kept by the company for every performance provide additional, although still not conclusive, evidence. The problem here is that the first surviving register covers a relatively brief period before the opening of **Le Naufrage** (from 2 June 1717) and there is a further gap beginning a mere twenty-five nights after the first performance of **Le Naufrage** and continuing until 30 May 1721. Moreover, they do not supply all the information a historian would like.

They are, nevertheless, more informative than they appear from the text published by Clarence Brenner. Information on receipts and attendance (which is what Brenner supplies) does not tell us anything about profit and loss. The registers do tell us that much. Expenses are itemized, net profits given and also the share received by the actors with the carried-over remainder. The figures do not appear to show a desperate situation. In 223 performances (all we have figures for) up to, but not including, the first night of **Le Naufrage,** the company failed to make a profit on only twenty-two occasions. This figure is, moreover, slightly exaggerated by the fact that every deficit was sedulously carried over to the following performance when a small profit might not be sufficient to cancel it out. The greatest deficit for one night was 751.5s.6d. The share distributed to each actor was zero on seventy-two occasions, which might appear disastrous were it not that the Français **received** shares on only eighty-five occasions throughout the same period while performing seven nights a week as against the five or six of the Italiens.[38] Evidently, this is far from being the whole story. The Français, or many of them, were in receipt (if probably irregular receipt) of pensions, whereas the Italiens depended almost entirely on box-office takings. Also, the Français were used to living with a huge debt. Such was not the case with the Italiens, who were left with a bill of about 100,000 **livres** after the initial repairs to the Hôtel de Bourgogne. Unlike their competitors, they were conscientious debtors and had paid it by 1719.[39] In the latter months of the 1717-18 season, this repayment may well have been a burden. They appear to have met the debt by allowing for at least one more share than there were shareholders and by devoting to it at least part of the balance remaining on every profitable night.[40] Again, these figures are by no means conclusive, but it seems unlikely that, however high their morals, the actors would have continued to pay off so large a debt if they were dying of hunger. The story of heavy financial pressure forcing a projected retreat to Italy may well be exaggerated.

The messianic quality of **Le Naufrage** also seems to have been overstated. The play was certainly a success: it had ten, probably eleven performances[41] over a period of 26 performing nights, and by the 1760s it had proved itself among the score or so most performed plays in the repertoire,[42] but its financial impact in April and May 1718 does not appear to have been remarkable. The ten performances for which figures are available attracted 3,741 spectators who paid an average of 609 **livres** per performance, providing a total share of 150 **livres** for each actor and a total balance of

3641.0s.6d. By way of comparison, the seven performances of **Colombine avocat pour et contre** (a revival from the old troupe) in the preceding February and March attracted 4,177 spectators at an average of over 1,000 **livres** per performance, a share of 295 **livres** and a balance of 2951.2s. Moreover, unlike **Le Naufrage, Colombine** was performed during one of the fairs and so was subject to greater competition. Nor does Autreau's play appear to have helped attract audiences to other performances: of the remaining eleven nights, no fewer than nine produced a zero share for the actors.[43]

Such is the external evidence for the impact made by **Le Naufrage** on the life history of the new Italian troupe. There remains the problem of its importance in the evolution of the repertoire of the company between the canvases of the traditional **commedia dell'arte** and (to take the touchstone by which the Italiens' contribution to French literary history is usually measured) the comedy of Marivaux. If the question is posed in terms of progress in the concept of character, then the answer has to be that it is of very little importance. It may also be that some claims (particularly those made in the eighteenth century) for its role in effecting a change from more superficial characteristics from the Italian to the French may have been overstated. It is nevertheless in this field that we must make our investigations.

The introduction of French elements into the Italian repertoire appears to have been made surprisingly rapidly. Riccoboni presented his Italian canvas **L'Italien marié à Paris** little more than two months after the company's arrival, on 25 July 1716. The plot centres on the jealousy of Lelio, married to a wife who, although herself Italian, has adopted French attitudes towards relationships between the sexes in normal social life. It is not a case of an attempt at a Moliéresque comedy of character (the jealous husband or lover and its variant, the possessive uncle or brother, are a mainstay of the **commedia dell'arte** plot). It is rather that the siting of the play in France to the point of including a visit to the Comédie Italienne and the Tuileries, and the explicit inclusion of French **mores** demonstrate a willingness to develop and evolve, perhaps an indication that Riccoboni was well aware that he could not for long depend on the novelty value of the purely Italian character of his offerings. The **Mercure** was very complimentary about the play, which it considered 'dans toutes ses parties une Comédie digne de tous les applaudissemens qu'elle a reçûs',[44] but it was not the immediate forerunner of a host of others moving in the same direction. The road to **Le Naufrage** and beyond is marked by a number of stages, quite widely spaced. The conditions required for the evolution were, first of all, French authors to present canvases which, even if they were to be performed in Italian, would provide a text more in keeping with French taste and **mœurs** than the traditional repertory; secondly, the actors to acquire the ability to speak French convincingly or, failing that, the addition to the troupe of an actor or actors who were francophone; thirdly and eventually, French authors to present complete plays in French to be performed in French. These aspects have been carefully analysed by Xavier de Courville,[45] so little is required here beyond a summary of his findings and an attempt to highlight the chronology.

The next stage after **L'Italien marié à Paris** was the combined French effort, related above, which planned and finally produced **L'Amante difficile** on 17 October 1716.[46] There appears to have been no French spoken at its performance, but Courville perceives in it the beginning of a passage from the comedy of intrigue of the Spanish type to an embryonic psychological comedy. Another long gap precedes **Arlequin secrétaire public** (17 May 1717), a failure dismissed by Gueullette as a 'pièce mauvaise et nouvelle, présentée aux comédiens par un inconnu'.[47] The 'inconnu' was presumably French,[48] as was the author of the equally unsuccessful and unknown **Les Pères rivaux de leurs fils** (19 August 1717).[49] Between the two, Lelio presented his **L'Italien francisé** with a plot centred on a character whose francophilia leads him to exaggerate the faults of the Italians as well as the virtues of the French. D'Origny, in a typical comment combining irony with a play on words, comments: 'la mauvaise conduite de l'**Italien Francisé** trouva son excuse dans l'intention qu'avoit l'Auteur [...] de captiver la bienveillance de la Nation'.[50] There is even evidence that some French was spoken: Boindin writes that one scene between Lelio and Flaminia was a reply in French to his earlier criticism that Flaminia's delivery was too rapid.[51] The play was performed on 30 June with some success, and not long afterwards a more direct attempt was made to demonstrate a willingness to effect a **rapprochement.** After a performance of **Arlequin bouffon de cour** (which would have been either 28 July or 26 September),[52] Thomassin addressed the audience in a mixture of French and Italian and recited La Fontaine's fable **Le Meunier, son fils et son âne.** He then asked whether he should act in future in French or in Italian. That a member of the **parterre** is supposed to have replied: 'Parlez comme il vous plaira, vous ferez toujours plaisir' is neither here nor there; the point of the anecdote is the concern the company was feeling about the French-Italian problem.[53] It may also show that the problem was felt particularly acutely because their best comic actor by far was unable to speak good French, a fact underlined by Boindin who, as late as his fourth letter (completed about the end of 1718), said of Arlequin: 'il faut qu'il s'en tienne à son bergamesque, jusqu'à ce qu'il se soit rendu intelligible dans nôtre langue'.[54] The solution (or one solution) was not now long in coming.

On 11 October 1717, Dominique (Pietro-Francesco Biancolelli), born in Paris in 1681 and with a long experience of playing Arlequin in French in the provinces and the

Paris fair theatres, made his début as Pierrot in **La Force du naturel.** The play was a failure and Dominique was not appreciated in his new role,[55] but a step had been taken which was to accelerate the movement towards French, for not only was Dominique a fluent French speaker and a fine actor, he could also write, and he contributed immediately with a prologue and a few scenes in French for **La Force du naturel.** Shortly before his arrival (and evidently part of the same movement which engaged him), was performed a three-act comedy, **L'Education perdue,** based on a French canvas by Charles-Antoine Coypel. This play appears to have contained a far greater proportion of French dialogue than **L'Italien francisé** and, as far as our clear evidence goes, to have been the first play since Lelio's work to incorporate any substantial quantity of French. According to a manuscript description seen by the Parfaict brothers, it contained in French a complete role (Flaminia), part of a role (Silvia), and a scene between Flaminia disguised as a man and the Docteur disguised as a woman.[56]

It would seem that about this time a watershed was reached. The last six months of the 1717-18 season (October to 2 April) saw a marked increase in the French element in the repertoire with a particular concentration from January 1718. During this period, beginning with 4 October, about twenty-two plays were performed which were new to the company's repertoire.[57] Of these, we have evidence of seven in which French authors had a hand (Coypel, Fréret, Coutelier and Gueullette),[58] at least two of them having some of the dialogue in French.[59] Three others contained scenes in French contributed by Dominique[60] and two represent a new departure: a return to the repertoire of the old troupe.[61] **Colombine avocat pour et contre,** by Fatouville, was first performed in 1685 but the complete text was available in Gherardi's **Le Théâtre Italien.**[62] Most of the text is in French (a greater proportion, indeed, than the scenes of **Le Naufrage** which were delivered in French), but there is no reason to suppose that when the new company presented it, on 20 February 1718, it was performed precisely as published. The probability is rather that more Italian was used than in the printed version. Nevertheless, that there was a considerable amount of French appears evident from an anecdote related by Boindin, who found himself at the first performance next to a 'gros marchant'. His neighbour was agreeably surprised at understanding the dialogue, exclaiming: 'Mais ils parlent pourtant Chrétien, et l'on m'avoit dit que non'.[63] The merchant was not the only spectator to be delighted by what he saw and heard, nor yet the most important. The young Louis XV saw it on what was probably the second night and, according to Buvat, 'a ri comme il n'a jamais fait'.[64] Probably in spite of himself, Riccoboni had been forced, by the demand for French and by the disinclination of French authors of note to provide him with suitable material to supplement the creative activity of Dominique, into the retrograde step of dipping into the work of his predecessors. The approval of both commoner and prince would appear to indicate that the die had been cast.[65] Before the season ended, recourse was had again to the old repertoire, though **Le Banqueroutier** (also by Fatouville) was less advanced a text than **Colombine** in that the Italian element was sufficiently divorced from the French for the 'scènes françoises' alone to be printed by Gherardi.

The next step was, it seems, inevitable, provided that an author could be found to effect it: a new play, by a French author, which would serve the Regency public as the works of Fatouville, Regnard, Dancourt and Dufresny had served the middle period of Louis XIV's reign. **Le Naufrage**, in spite of the quantity of dialogue which was delivered in Italian when it was first performed, has no serious rival as the claimant to have made the break-through. There was, moreover, no great rush to follow Autreau's example. The next play at all comparable to **Le Naufrage** in its length (three acts) as well as in the preponderance of French dialogue did not appear for another five months.[66] Its author, Fuzelier, was a regular contributor to the fair theatres and thus did not have to combat the prejudice that other established dramatists appear to have found impossible to overcome. It is not until 1720 that Marivaux and Delisle de La Drevetière start their dramatic careers, like Autreau, with the Italiens. In the meantime, Riccoboni depended largely on Dominique and Gherardi for his French dialogue and was far from being able to abandon the traditional Italian repertoire.

THE PLAY

The play itself presents a deal of internal evidence for a situation in which the Italiens needed to woo an audience. So pervasive is the intention, indeed, that it gives the work a complex unity that belies its episodic structure. Autreau took a practical problem and, making a virtue out of necessity, converted it into thematic material which gave an added dimension to a play which would otherwise have been little more than an amalgam of a number of elements taken from the Italian tradition and exemplified by both the old and the new companies. Such a view of the work, in spite of Jacques Truchet's commendation in his Pléiade edition, has not been generally promulgated. D'Argenson explicitly denied it any unity at all and, nearer our own times, Xavier de Courville damned it as 'plutôt un innocent dessert qu'un mets de consistance',[67] while Gustave Attinger was even more dismissive: 'c'est une comédie française, la première du nom. Ne lui demandons aucune autre signification'.[68] So the case has to be argued.

As we have seen, both the success and the decline in favour of the Italiens were to a large extent the consequence of the element of difference - strangeness, 'foreign-ness' - which at first attracted and then repelled. In 1718, their problem, and consequently Autreau's problem, was to make the strangeness acceptable now that its novelty value had worn off. The extreme form the strangeness took was, of course, incomprehensibility: the language barrier. Ultimately, this presented an insoluble problem, for the simple reason that parts had to be provided for actors with little or no French. Autreau therefore started out with the hard fact of a flawed artefact, a hermaphrodite of a play, half French and half Italian. He appears to have decided that since he could not destroy the strangeness, he would play upon it, accentuate and diversify it, appeal in ways of varying degrees of directness to the audience to understand and accept it, familiarize the audience with it.

The play opens with a prologue in which Flaminia and Silvia, representing themselves (they address each other by name) and robed in dressing-gowns, discuss the situation.[69] They express their fears that the French audience, however indulgent, may not appreciate their attempt to speak throughout the play in French and will be more critical of a French author than they would be of an Italian. Flaminia emphasizes their inadequacies in comparison with the old troupe: 'des Italiens naturalisés en France depuis plus de trente ans, et qui avaient d'excellentes actrices françaises' (Prologue, scene i). This is the direct approach, with Flaminia referring to Lelio as 'mon mari' and, two scenes later, talking to Arlequin of his wife, thereby making the audience aware of Lelio, Arlequin and Violette as real people behind their dramatic **personae**. In this way, the five most important members of the company are presented as human beings and the audience is forced into a position of complicity, or at least of sympathy with the Italiens' dilemma. An extension of this technique is pursued at odd moments during the play proper. Elena Balletti was considered as something of an intellectual and also, as we have seen, too much on the thin side. Both these attributes are accorded Flaminia in the play and the nascent rivalry between the two principal actresses is perhaps hinted at, on the same plane of intellectual and physical qualities, when Silvia contrasts her own position: 'Ho, je n'ai que faire d'esprit, moi, j'ai de l'embonpoint' (II.xv). Also, Pasquella's condescending injunction to Arlequin, 'retire-toi d'ici, petit roquet. Cela n'est pas plus haut que ma jambe, et cela veut faire l'entendu' (I.ix), aims beyond the character to the diminutive Thomassin behind the mask.

The second scene of the prologue introduces an entirely invented character, Trafiquet, described as 'courtier du Parnasse'. In another situation, Trafiquet's role would have been taken by the supposed author, but the real author is, as Silvia has informed us, French, and Mario has an Italian accent, hence the foreign 'broker' to act as intermediary between author and actors. Again, Autreau underlines the situation: Trafiquet is taken by Flaminia to be the author, Trafiquet denies both function and nationality, and Flaminia insists: 'Il est vrai qu'il a l'accent un peu baroque aussi bien que nous' (Prologue, scene ii).   The name is not unique in the Italian theatre.   It appears in Regnard's **La Coquette** (performed by the old troupe in 1691 and published by Gherardi) where the character has no particular identity beyond the traditional role of a father.   Autreau, however, particularizes the role as part of the familiarizing function of the play.   Whereas Regnard probably meant to designate by the name no more than a member of the merchant class, adopting the verbal sense of 'to trade, deal, traffick, or drive a Trade, to buy and sell', Autreau evidently uses both this sense and the more specific one of 'trafiquer des Billets, des Lettres de Change'.[70] Autreau's Trafiquet 'agiote du papier comique' and compares the sub-standard type of play which is all the Italiens can expect to be offered with the 'quincaille' that traders are taking to Louisiana.   He recalls the rigorously contemporary Mississippi Company of John Law established the preceding August.

The plot and structure of the three-act play which follows the Prologue are ostensibly within the Italian tradition.   The plot consists of two young couples (the Comte de Trinquemberg and Flaminia, the Chevalier de La Bastide and Silvia) attempting to come together, hindered by an old couple (a possessive father, Lelio, and an old **gouvernante**, Pasquella), who are opposed by a pair of servants (Arlequin and Violette); the structure is largely conditioned by a female **intrigant,** a provincial opera-girl named Tontine, who imagines various ways of effecting the union of the two couples, thereby creating a series of otherwise unconnected episodes.   The characters, moreover, can make no claim to psychological realism.   This is how d'Argenson viewed the play and it is a justifiable view as far as it goes.   But it does not go far enough. All three elements, plot, structure and characters, have the common characteristic of the juxtaposition of the foreign and the strange with the French and the familiar.   It is true that Lelio, before departing for Paris, leaves instructions to Pantalon to make sure that his daughters speak to nobody, true also that Pasquella has to be prevented from drinking to enable her to keep an eagle eye on the girls and that Violette is to keep close to them (I.iv).   But none of these material obstacles is real.   Pantalon is on the side of love, Arlequin and Violette feel on common ground with the girls and Pasquella is immediately given drink. The real obstacle is the girls' invincible timidity which is the direct consequence of their 'Italian-ness'; they are over-conscious of their cultural inferiority, of their inability to engage in amorous dalliance in a French context. This timidity results from a dual Italian disadvantage: they have been kept shut away from male company and they belong to a nation whose attitude towards love is unrefined, nay barbarous (much satirical play is made of the latter view as mistaken, French love-making having made considerable strides away from the ethereal manners of **L'Astrée**). Such a feeling of inferiority cannot be compensated for by intelligence (II.v) and leads to the added fear of an inability to attract through physical qualities (II.xv). The solution is found in a dual **rapprochement**. Tontine demonstrates that the difference between the two nations' concept of love is not as great as the girls have thought and the two men are discovered not to be complete strangers, one being a former acquaintance and the other a distant relative by marriage (II.xvi). Such a denouement, particularly as it is in effect reached by the end of the second act, may be weak in terms of a dynamic plot but it is thematically very satisfactory.

All the characters (with the exception of Tontine who will be discussed separately) are particularized by their place of origin in a manner both varied and consistent which transcends the mere advisability of adapting the roles to the actors' poor or non-existent French. The most straightforward situation is where Italian characters speak in Italian. This applies, as far as may be judged from the not always comprehensive indications at the head of every scene, invariably to Violette, perhaps invariably to the girls' aunt Cecilia (but not when she sings), almost invariably to Arlequin, probably invariably to Pasquella. In the case of Violette and Arlequin, the language element is also adapted to the plot. Violette is finally acceptable to Pantalon as a serving girl because her lack of French will force her to be, for a woman, unnaturally discreet (III.ii) and Arlequin attempts a few words of French only when he tries himself out in a sort of rehearsal of his new job as a waiter (III.v). Riccoboni's rather better knowledge of French allows him to speak whichever language is the better suited to the scene he appears in at a given moment. At the further extreme, Flaminia and Silvia, the 'nouvelles débarquées' of the sub-title, speak only French. It is of considerable interest that the two **amoureuses**, who are most commonly endowed with very little characterization beyond being young, personable and in search of a husband of similar age and looks, provide the focal point of the play with their predicament centred on cultural and linguistic alienation.

If the situation had permitted, Autreau would doubtless have given Flaminia and Silvia two pure-blooded young Frenchmen as their counterparts, thus climaxing the play with the romantic fusion of the two nations, the ideal resolution of the French-Italian dilemma. Such a solution being precluded by the accents of Mario and Scapin, he took the opportunity to present two quite different linguistic characterizations for two parts which, even more than those of the **amoureuses**, were traditionally unparticularized. The Chevalier de La Bastide is French enough to embody the girls' fears of French cultural superiority. He is, however, a Frenchman with a regional accent (from Marseilles) which is specifically remarked upon by Flaminia (II.xv) and whose first language may indeed not be French, since he at one stage prefers the

Provençal 'quauque ren' to 'quelque chose' (III.ix). It may be surmised that Mario did his best to speak with as little accent as possible, for there is but the one Provençal expression and no orthographic indication of peculiarity of accent. Nor is there any oddity of style or character; he is no Bailli du Maine or Gascon braggart. In no way a comic character, he demonstrates that it is not necessary to speak pure French with a pure Ile-de-France accent to be an upright young Frenchman. His companion, the Comte de Trinquemberg, presents a different case altogether: a German barely capable of pronouncing correctly a single syllable or of producing a correct part of speech, let alone a complete clause. His delivery is by far the most outlandish of the play, much more so than the Italian of other characters because it is murdered French. And yet, Trinquemberg's role is essentially no more comic than that of the Chevalier. He is presented as no less acceptable a partner for Flaminia than is the Chevalier for Silvia. In terms of the problematic situation of the Italiens, Autreau is showing that if a Provençal and a German are acceptable **amoureux**, then the Italian troupe is an acceptable Parisian company. A similar purpose, but effected differently, is served by the Chinese **opérateur** or mountebank, more foreign than Provençal, German or Italian, to whom is given a long speech, of frequently brilliant word-play, containing a lesson on the dangers of attaching too much importance to the envelope of language:

> Gardez-vous bien, illustre assemblée, de juger mal de ma science, par mon accent et par mon baraguoin. Il est permis à un médecin étranger de parler mal la langue française; et ne croyez pas qu'elle guérisse de rien, puisqu'en France même les médecins ne s'attachent qu'à parler bon grec et bon latin, et sont très souvent, aussi bien que moi, des ignorants en bon français. Vous devez au contraire bien augurer d'un médecin qui vient de loin, puisque la rhubarbe, le séné, la casse, le gayac, le bézoard, et les meilleures drogues de la médecine viennent comme moi des extrémités de la terre.   (II.ix)

Finally, with Pantalon, Autreau adopts a different approach again, for here he deliberately avoids any attempt to fit the 'foreign-ness' of the actor to the part. The inn-keeper of Le Port-à-l'Anglais is the one indigenous Frenchman among the cast. Not excluding Tontine, he is the one character who really belongs to the scene in which the action is set[71] and, with the exception of two **lazzis** shared with Arlequin in the first act, nothing in the role, either in his character or in his speech as it appears in the printed French, is other than appropriate to the proprietor of a rather dubious establishment situated conveniently and discreetly just outside Paris. And yet he is called Pantalon and speaks entirely in Italian (or rather, no doubt, in his incomprehensible Venetian dialect). Autreau would seem to be turning a Nelsonian blind eye to the problematic French-Italian situation.

There remains the mysterious character of Tontine, described as a 'fille d'opéra de campagne', who is teaching the girls' aunt Cecilia to sing in French and has been included in the outing to Le Port-à-l'Anglais 'parce qu'elle inspire partout la joie' (III.iii). She opens the play rehearsing to herself Lully and Quinault's grand opera **Armide et Renaud** and closes it with a sung parodic 'prologue à l'italienne' of her own invention. In between, she orders the plot in ways both Italian and French. It is her idea to disguise herself and the Chevalier as peasants in order to help the latter approach the girls (I.i) and she manipulates the **opérateur chinois** scene to the same end and equally unsuccessfully (II.viii): two eminently Italian episodes. On the other hand, her attempts to reason Flaminia and Silvia out of their inferiority complex (II.xvi) and to tempt Arlequin into Pantalon's service (III.ii) are much closer to the more rational and discursive French tradition. She stands out as the only 'French' character to speak French and as a female **meneur d'intrigue** who is not an eponymous **commedia dell'arte** character. Traditionally, the latter role is filled by a **zanni** such as Mezzetin or Trivelin, occasionally a **suivante** such as Colombine. Moreover, it is not immediately evident who could have played the part. Most of the characters present no problem. The roles of Lelio, Flaminia, Silvia, Arlequin, Pantalon and Violette are eponymous and the **Mercure** gives the actors in the cases of Trafiquet (Mario), Trinquemberg (Scapin), La Bastide (Mario again) and the **opérateur chinois** (Lelio); Pasquella, a burlesque old woman, was presumably played by a man, probably Scaramouche (perhaps the part seen by the Regent?) and Cecilia, who sings at the end, will have been played by Ursula Astori. No woman remains to take the part of Tontine who was, indeed, undoubtedly played by the same Dominique who had but recently joined the company.[72] That the part was played by a man is suggested by the text itself. In the musical ending, Tontine asks Cecilia to sing 'tous les airs de broderie' because she herself has a cold, one of those colds 'qui grossissent plus la taille d'une voix' and, in explaining why she spoke rather than sang her part, an editorial notation uses the masculine form of a word which had a perfectly good and current feminine form: 'l'acteur qui fait Tontine, se défiant de sa voix, n'a pas osé la chanter' (III.xi). A combination of considerations makes Dominique the only possible candidate:

(a)   he was the only member of the troupe to speak sufficiently good French;

(b)   in his fourth **Lettre**, which contains details of plays performed between November 1717 and December 1718, Boindin says of Dominique: 'nous lui avons vû jouer dans une Piece nouvelle le rôle d'une fille d'Opéra avec beaucoup de finesse et de grace' (p.10);

(c)   the register for the first night contains the following entry: 'Nollo d'abito per il sig Domenico',[73] which shows not only that Dominique was a member of the cast but also that his costume was considered exceptional (the actors being responsible for their own costumes by statute).[74]

It seems quite clear that the part was played absolutely straight. The only hint in the text is the reference to the deepening of the voice quoted above. Boindin indicates the delicate portrayal of a young female personage and the **Mercure** treats the part in so matter-of-fact a manner that Tontine is the only one of the principal non-eponymous characters whose creator is not identified. Dominique's Tontine transfers to a figurative plane the thematic problem of rendering the strange acceptable and familiar.

It needs to be said that, in all probability, there is nothing absolutely original in **Le Naufrage** if its constituant parts are considered separately. They are practically all to be found in earlier comedy and particularly in the repertoire of the old troupe as preserved by Gherardi. The name Trafiquet had already been used; prologues with the actors representing themselves and appealing more or less directly for the audience's favour existed;[75] an **opérateur** glides swiftly through Molière's **L'Amour médecin** from which Autreau's Arlequin quotes a line[76] and, perhaps more significantly, in Fatouville's **La Fille savante** (performed by the old troupe in 1690), Arlequin disguises himself as one and indulges in a bout of punning not dissimilar to the verbal acrobatics of Autreau's character;[77] there may be no earlier Chinese **opérateur**, but there is a 'Docteur Chinois' in Regnard and Dufresny's **Les Chinois** of 1692. Even Dominique's **tour de force** is not unique: Boindin says of Mario that 'l'habit de femme lui est fort avantageux, il y paroît avec des graces qu'on trouve rarement dans un homme quand il est sous ce déguisement'.[78] And one could go on... Autreau's achievement is to have collated, inflated and diversified all these elements so that they became aspects of a whole which is greater than its parts.[79]

Trafiquet's parting advice to Flaminia and Silvia was 'surtout mettez bien votre Arlequin dans son jeu; en voilà assez jusques à ce qu'il sache parler français'. The injunction is, of course, obeyed, the first victim being Trafiquet himself, his dramatic brokerage paid for in blows. A number of **lazzis** follow: Arlequin pretends to break a leg in jumping in feigned joy (I.iv); he makes great play, to the physical discomfort of Pantalon, with the alcoholic remedy to the injury (I.v); he initiates a free-for-all with Pasquella (I.ix); he enacts a peace treaty with bottles of wine as its articles (II.iv); he performs 'des lazzis d'admiration' during the Chinese **opérateur**'s speech (II.ix) and in the same scene empties his pockets to see if the mountebank's 'orviétan' has filled them with money. His traditionally gluttonous and bibulous nature is exploited to the full as he describes Violette as 'une belle treille, une vigne délicieuse, chargée d'un fruit qui me tente' (I.ii) and particularly in an extended scene which sees him torn between love for Violette and the culinary advantages of employment in Pantalon's inn

(III.ii). He bids fair, indeed, to destroy the structure of the play. Autreau, at least to some extent, solves this problem by extending Arlequin's characteristics to other parts of the play, making of food and drink a pervasive image. To begin with, an additional culinary element is introduced into Arlequin's own world with the creation of a (distant) rival in the form of an apprentice pastry-cook, allowing Violette to counter Arlequin's temptations in Pantalon's service ('Poulets, dindons, fricassées, matelotes, vin à la glace') with a vision of her own ('Petits pâtés, tartelettes, biscuits, confitures'). Tontine's down-to-earth nature is also expressed in part in terms of food. As the lovers begin to overcome their inhibitions, she sees the necessity for one dining table, not two (II.xvii), takes the trouble to oversee the menu and accompanies Pantalon to the kitchen (II.xviii), sees no better seal to set on a lovers' agreement than a meal: 'allons à table confirmer ces alliances' (III.xi). It is to fill the gap while waiting for the meal that Tontine composes and helps perform her prologue parodying Campra and Danchet's **Camille reine des Volsques**, much of which concerns food and drink:

> Accourez et mangez en ces lieux à grands frais
> Brochets, tanches, carpes et vives.
> Habitants de ces lieux, phaétons de ces chars,
> Chantez, dansez, buvez de toutes parts.

As the song progresses, the **topos** becomes figurative:

CECILIA

> Un amant, avec ce qu'il aime,
> En ces lieux fait un bon repas,
> Si Comus en fait un carême
> L'Amour en fait un mardi gras.

TONTINE

> Pour l'épouse jeune et gentille
> Qui s'échappe et fait le plongeon,
> Nous gardons la carpe et l'anguille;
> Maris, avalez le goujon.

Moreover, the view of love presented by the play is explicitly expressed in the same terms. Love is described as a boy who, in former times, 'n'avait presque plus de corps' and was afflicted with 'inanition' because 'on ne le nourrissait de rien'; now, however, 'il a repris chair', 'il se fortifie tous le jours'; instead of 'les jolis vers, les galants madrigaux, les tendres élégies' which used to give him a migraine, he is now regaled only with 'des vaudevilles gaillards ou des chansons à boire'; he has abandoned the pastoral countryside of **L'Astrée** and is now to be found in the provinces of Burgundy and Champagne (II.xvi).

Finally, and most significantly for our **propos**, the play opens and closes with the food image applied to the work itself and to its audience. Before passing to his Mississippi image, Trafiquet employs a lengthy culinary metaphor for the difficult situation in which the Italians find themselves:

> Le public ressemble à présent à un convive qui est sur la fin d'un repas. Il y a longtemps que le repas dure. Quand il se mit à table au commencement du siècle passé, il se contentait des plus grosses viandes. On lui a servi depuis les mets les plus friands et en abondance, dont il s'est rempli avec volupté. Il en a jusqu'au nœud de la gorge. Et quand on lui en offrirait encore de pareils, ce qui n'est presque pas possible, je ne sais s'il en serait touché. L'appétit lui manque, vous dis-je.
>
> FLAMINIA. Que lui faut-il donc à présent pour le ragoûter?
>
> TRAFIQUET. Il lui faut des liqueurs violentes, des mets d'un goût extraordinaire et bizarre, de ces drogues que l'on vend à la foire, du pitrepitre, de la mortadelle, de la poutargue; ou bien de ces choses légères que l'on donne au dessert, pour ne point charger l'estomac, et pour amuser seulement: des cornets par exemple, ou de la crème fouettée; et c'est de ce genre-ci qu'est la pièce que je vous donne.
>
> (Prologue, scene ii)

The last words of the play, the last verse of Tontine's prologue, are sung by Arlequin, dressed in his new French costume of 'garçon de cabaret':

> Nous servons, pour vous satisfaire,
> Moitié chair et moitié poisson.
> Si vous faites mauvaise chère
> Pardonnez au nouveau garçon.

The dominant image and the dominant theme come together in the words and appearance of the principal actor. It is a very French ending, as d'Argenson should have appreciated.

NOTES

1. R.-L. de Voyer de Palmy, Marquis d'Argenson, **Notices sur les œuvres de théâtre,** edited by H. Lagrave (Geneva, 1966), volumes XLII and XLIII (with continuous pagination) of **Studies on Voltaire and the Eighteenth Century,** p.699.

2. Emile Campardon, **Les Comédiens du roi de la troupe italienne pendant les deux derniers siècles,** 2 vols (Paris, 1880), II, 226. The principal official documents concerning the Italiens in the eighteenth century are published in this work. The odd gap is filled by Xavier de Courville, **Luigi Riccoboni dit Lelio,** 3 vols (Paris and Geneva, 1943-45). All references to this, the supreme work in the field, are to the second volume, **L'Expérience française (1716-1731),** in the reprint by Slatkine (Geneva, 1969). Useful supplementary information is to be found in Guy Boquet, 'La Comédie italienne sous la régence: Arlequin poli par Paris (1716-1725)', **Revue d'histoire moderne et contemporaine,** 24 (1972), 189-214. Much first-hand documentation is supplied by Thomas-Simon Gueullette, **Notes et**

JACQUES AUTREAU AND THE ITALIENS 221

souvenirs sur le Théâtre-Italien au XVIIIe siècle, edited by J.-E. Gueullette (Paris, 1938) and, especially, Nicolas Boindin to whom is attributed four separately-paginated **Lettres historiques sur la Nouvelle Comédie Italienne** (Paris, 1719). The particular interest of Boindin is that his **Lettres** form what is almost a running commentary on the first two and a half years of the troupe's history in Paris and he has been heavily exploited in the present essay. The most comprehensive (and usually correct) information on individual plays and, less importantly, authors is furnished by Claude and François Parfaict, **Dictionnaire des théâtres de Paris**, 7 vols (Paris, 1767), used here in the reprint by Slatkine, 2 vols (Geneva, 1967). Other information on plays, authors and the history of the troupe can be found in Antoine de Léris, **Dictionnaire portatif, historique et littéraire des théâtres** (Paris, 1763; reprinted Geneva, 1970); Antoine d'Origny, **Annales du Théâtre Italien depuis son origine jusqu'à ce jour**, 3 vols (Paris, 1788; reprinted Geneva, 1970); the first volume of **Le Nouveau Théâtre Italien, ou Recueil général des comédies représentées par les Comédiens Italiens Ordinaires du Roi**, nouvelle édition, 10 vols (Paris, 1753; reprinted Geneva, 1969); [Jean-Auguste Julien, known as] Desboulmiers, **Histoire anecdotique et raisonnée du Théâtre Italien depuis son rétablissement en France jusqu'à l'année 1769** (Paris, 1769; reprinted Geneva, 1968). Though not always infallible in identifying the dates of first performances or alternative titles for the same play in the early years, Clarence D. Brenner, **The Théâtre Italien: its Repertory, 1716-1793** (Berkeley and Los Angeles, 1961) remains an indispensable tool. The 304 volumes of registers on which it is based are catalogued, somewhat confusingly, in the library of the Paris Opéra as **Registres de l'Opéra-Comique, 1716-1856: historique, règlements, décrets, comptes;** the tenth volume contains the earliest extant records of **recettes journalières,** covering the period from 2 June 1717 to 30 May 1718.

3. The composition of the old troupe in 1697 is given by Campardon, II, xxiv-xxv; the best description of the new troupe is by Courville, pp.19-25.

4. Gueullette, p.36.

5. Boindin, first **Lettre**, p.12.

6. ibid., p.14.

7. Cited by Parfaict, VII, 689.

8. The source for the remainder of this paragraph is Boindin, first **Lettre**, pp.8-17.

9. ibid., pp.14-17.

10. Gueullette, p.38.

11. Boindin, first **Lettre**, pp.9-11 and 15-16.

12. Dubois de Saint-Gelais, **Histoire journalière de Paris (1716-1717)** (Paris, 1885), pp.30-31.

13. Desboulmiers, I, 161-62.

14. Quoted by Courville, p.117.

15. Boindin, first **Lettre**, p.29.

16. ibid., pp.34-35.

17. ibid., third **Lettre**, p.11 (on the occasion of Dominique's début in **La Force du naturel,** 11 October 1717).

18. The round figure is supplied both by Philippe de Courcillon, Marquis de Dangeau, **Journal,** edited by E. Soulié and others, 19 vols (Paris, 1854-1860), XVI, 382 (18

May 1716), and by Jean Buvat, **Gazette de la Régence**, edited by E. de Barthélemy (Paris, 1887), p.82.

19. D'Origny, I, 29.

20. Gueullette, p.27; also Dangeau, XVI, 382 ('jamais salle de comédie ne fut plus pleine') and Buvat, p.82 ('Lundi les comédiens italiens jouèrent sur le théâtre de l'Opéra et prirent autant qu'on y prend').

21. See Henri Lagrave, **Le Théâtre et le public à Paris de 1715 à 1750** (Paris, 1972), p.86: 'la salle de l'Opéra peut recevoir de 1.300 à 1.400 spectateurs, et peut-être plus'. Subsequent details concerning theatre capacity are taken from the same source.

22. On 29 January 1742 and 24 March 1751 (4,446 **livres** and 4,227 **livres** respectively). Unless otherwise stated, all such information is from Brenner.

23. This and all subsequent information on receipts and attendances at the Théâtre Français is from Henry Carrington Lancaster, **The Comédie Française, 1701-1774: Plays, Actors, Spectators, Finances**, in **Transactions of the American Philosophical Society**, 41 (1951), 591-850.

24. Buvat, p.82.

25. Parfaict, I, 249. The text is a shortened version of an entry in the same authors' **Mémoires pour servir à l'histoire des spectacles de la foire**, 2 vols (Paris, 1743), I, 188-90.

26. Boindin, second **Lettre**, p.16.

27. Buvat, pp.97-98 (27 July) and p.115 (18 September).

28. Lancaster, pp.651-52 (after 17 May, the actors' share remained at zero until 26 September).

29. Dangeau, XVI, 382 (Saint-Simon adds a comment on the **comédie italienne**, 'qui d'abord fut à la mode, mais dont les ordures dégoûtèrent les honnêtes gens. Elle tomba fort, malgré ses appuis, et toutefois elle nous est demeurée jusqu'à présent').

30. Boindin, fourth **Lettre**, p.36.

31. **Oeuvres de Monsieur Autreau** [edited by Charles-Etienne Pesselier], 4 vols (Paris, 1749; reprinted Geneva, 1973), I, xiii.

32. Léris, p.360.

33. Desboulmiers, I, 196.

34. The **Mercure's** account of the play contained the following: 'les Dames qui fréquentoient peu ce Théatre auparavant, parce qu'elles se trouvoient dépaysées, en ont été si contentes, qu'elles n'ont pas fait un des moindres ornemens de la Scéne' (May 1718, p.105).

35. Parfaict, III, 487.

36. Gueullette, p.88.

37. 'Si l'intrigue en paroît foible, le dialogue en est vif et agréable. On y rencontre des Scenes bien faites et de bonnes plaisanteries. Les divertissemens en sont jolis, et la musique est remplie de graces et de gaieté' (I, 49).

38. For half the period we are considering here (until Tuesday 16 November 1717), the Italiens rested on Tuesdays as well as Fridays.

39. The sum and its repayment are mentioned in an 'acte de société' drawn up by the

Italiens and dated 27 October 1719 (Campardon, II, 241).

40. Until the arrival of Dominique in October 1717, the register shows twelve shares for eleven actors; from 11 October, fourteen shares are recorded (one extra for Dominique and perhaps another for the male singer Théveneau who was taken on at about this time).

41. The registers do not supply a title for the play performed on 1 May; the likelihood is that it was **Le Naufrage**. The recorded figures for attendance and receipts are just below average for the ten stated performances.

42. According to my count, Brenner records eighty performances by then.

43. The figures for shares and balances are taken direct from the register; those for attendance and gross receipts from Brenner.

44. Quoted in Parfaict, III, 226; the play is discussed at some length by Courville, pp.67-73.

45. Especially in his Chapters 6 ('L'Abandon de la langue italienne') and 8 ('Exercices français').

46. ibid., p.118.

47. Gueullette, p.84.

48. The Parfaict brothers, who probably based their information on Gueullette, describe it as a 'canevas françois' (I, 282).

49. 'Cette pièce est d'un auteur français inconnu' (Gueullette, p.85); 'Canevas Italien [**sic**] en trois actes, d'un Auteur François **Anonyme**, représenté une seule fois' (Parfaict, IV, 103).

50. D'Origny, I, 43.

51. Boindin, second **Lettre**, p.6.

52. The September date seems the more likely: it is closer to what seems to have been a critical moment about the beginning of October, and Thomassin may well by then have heard rumours of the imminent engagement of Dominique of whom he was initially very jealous (see Gueullette, pp.30-31).

53. The incident is related by Desboulmiers, I, 185-86.

54. Boindin, fourth **Lettre**, p.9.

55. See above, note 17 and the text to which it relates.

56. Parfaict, II, 366. It appears to have been performed only twice, on 4 October and 23 October (Brenner); Parfaict, II, 367, says 23 October only.

57. The lack of daily accounts for the first year, the difficulty of distinguishing between two plays of similar titles and one play with more than one title make it impossible to be precise about the number, given the present state of research in the matter. These problems are well illustrated by Brenner who, to give but two examples, confuses **Pantalon banqueroutier vénitien** (first performed 18 October 1716) with **Le Banqueroutier** (by Fatouville, first performed by the new troupe 24 March 1718) and wrongly distinguishes **Diables sont les femmes** (first performed 23 June 1717) from **Rebut pour rebut** (first given as an alternative title for the same play 25 November 1717).

58. The French element was, in most cases, limited to a canvas in French which the actors, under Riccoboni's direction, turned into an Italian play. The plays in question, with the date of their first performance are:
Coypel, **L'Education perdue**, canvas, 4 October.

Coypel, **Les Effets de l'absence,** canvas, 7 October (Brenner), 5 March (Parfaict), not given in the register (Courville, p.120, note 1).

Fréret, **La Force du naturel,** adapted from the Spanish of Moreto, 11 October.

Coypel, **L'Impatient,** canvas, 23 October.

Coutelier, **Arlequin corsaire africain,** canvas, 5 January.

Gueullette, **Les Comédiens par hasard,** canvas, 15 January.

Coypel, **Les Avantages de l'esprit,** canvas.   This play is something of a mystery in that Parfaict gives the first performance as 9 September and Gueullette as 9 October, but it appears to figure nowhere in the register.

59.   Besides **La Force du natural,** they are **L'Education perdue** and **Les Comédiens par hasard.**

60.   Besides **La Force du naturel,** they are **Les Ignorants, ou les Fourbes par intérêt** (16 October), **La Métempsychose d'Arlequin** (19 January) and **L'Amante hypocrite** (23 January).

61.   Fatouville's **Colombine avocat pour et contre** (20 February) and **Le Banqueroutier** (24 March).

62.   The edition used here is **Le Théâtre Italien de Gherardi,** 6 vols (Amsterdam, 1721).

63.   Boindin, fourth **Lettre,** p.34.

64.   Buvat, p.238 (25 February).

65.   Honesty forces us to treat Boindin's testimony with a dash of scepticism, however. The Prologue (in French) of Fatouville's **Le Banqueroutier** has Arlequin in the role of a hostile critic at a play performed by the Italiens. The first scene was in French, and Arlequin relates the effect it had on one member of the audience: 'Un Bourgeois, qui n'avoit jamais été à la Comédie Italienne que ce jour-là, s'est tourné vers moy, et m'a dit d'un ton fort sérieux: Je m'étonne qu'on dise que l'on n'entend point les Comédiens Italiens, voilà une Scêne dont je n'ay pas perdu un petit mot' (Gherardi, I, 113).

66.   **L'Amour maître de langues,** performed 18 September and described by Gueullette as a 'pièce française et italienne' (p.90). It may even be that the French element did not become preponderant until Fuzelier modified it considerably the following May (see Courville, p.138).

67.   Courville, p.125.

68.   Gustave Attinger, **L'Esprit de la commedia dell'arte dans le théâtre français** (Paris, 1950), p.362.

69.   The text used is the most accessible, the first edition as edited by Jacques Truchet for the Pléiade **Théâtre du XVIIIe siècle,** 2 vols (Paris, 1972-74), I, 339-94.

70.   Both quotations are from Abel Boyer's **Dictionnaire royal, françois-anglois et anglois-françois** (Amsterdam, Rotterdam and The Hague, 1726), 'Trafiquer'.

71.   That the recognizably French setting should have a foreign element in its name (and be emphasized by providing the title of the play) is evidently part of the same pattern.

72.   Courville (p.123) gives the actor who played Tontine as 'Dominique certainement'; he is followed by Boquet (p.205) who simply states parenthetically: 'Dominique en travesti'. Neither attempts a demonstration of the identification.

73. **Registres**, X, entry for 25 April 1718. The cost of hire is given as five **livres**, but the figure is crossed out and ignored in the addition of expenses. The item does not appear again.

74. The fourth article of the 1716 **règlement** contains the following: 'Et pour ce qui regarde le trouve robbe, chaque camarade, soit sérieux ou comique, sera obligé de se pourvoir à ses dépens de tous les habits qu'il [sic] peut avoir besoin' (Campardon, II, 232).

75. For example, Louis Biancolelli's **Arlequin misanthrope** of 1696 (Gherardi, VI, 297-378), where Arlequin objects to playing a part so alien to the tradition of his character.

76. 'Oh la grande puissance de l'orviétan!' (II.ii).

77. Je suis [...] un Operateur infaillible pour les fractures de la raison, pour les dislocations de l'esprit, pour les entorses du bon sens, et généralement pour tous les mauvais plis qu'un cœur peut prendre ou par ignorance ou par temperament' ('Scène du Professeur d'Amour', Gherardi, III, 77-78).

78. Boindin, third **Lettre**, p.13.

79. One specific item of originality has been claimed for the play by Stanley Schwartz in a workmanlike study of Autreau's dramatic works, 'Jacques Autreau, a Forgotten Dramatist', **PMLA**, 46 (1931), 498-532 (p.511): '[Autreau] introduced a character which, as far as the writer has been able to ascertain, was a distinct novelty at the time, namely, a German who speaks French with a decided accent'. This may be so, though the Italiens had earlier put on **Arlequin feint baron allemand** (21 August 1716), and Mario 'jouait à merveille le rôle de français, d'italien et d'allemand' (Gueullette, p.81) in **Les Stratagèmes de l'amour** (26 November 1716). More important, perhaps, is Trinquemberg's being a 'real' German. There is, indeed, only one use of disguise in the play (Tontine and La Bastide dressed as peasants and providing another example of non-standard French), a definite dilution of an Italian tradition.

NINE

Tragedy in the Service of Propaganda:
Voltaire's *Mahomet*
Ahmad Gunny

As is well known,[1] French tragedy in the early part of the eighteenth century was hampered by the rules, tradition and notions of decorum which prevented dramatists from experimenting freely on stage. Its development was also hindered by the conservative taste of the public who frowned on whatever was new and unusual. These factors may have encouraged a tendency amongst some playwrights, including Crébillon and Voltaire, to rely on the great models of Corneille and Racine who were admired and sometimes servilely imitated. Imitation was not in itself a serious weakness, as it was widely practised and cultivated as an art in the eighteenth century. What was objectionable was that it took little account of the spirit of classical tragedy, distinguished at its best by subtle pyschological analysis of character. Instead, emphasis was placed on the unexpected, **coups de théâtre,** mistaken identities and horrible crimes so characteristic of tragedies of the period 1700-1715. For example, in Crébillon's **Atrée et Thyeste,** which was performed in 1707 and was often compared with Voltaire's **Mahomet,**[2] Atrée plans to punish his brother Thyeste by using the latter's son to kill him. Moreover, in his desire to renew tragedy, Houdar de La Motte even wrote an **OEdipe** in prose in 1726.

Voltaire was acutely aware of the problems besetting the French stage in that period. That is, perhaps, why one finds in the public and private utterances of the playwright who was aspiring to be Racine's successor not only some interesting observations but also some suggestions as to how these problems could be solved. In one sense, although no theorist of the theatre, Voltaire says enough on tragedy in his prefaces, **dissertations, discours, épîtres** and in his correspondence to justify his own attempt to renew Aristotle's **Poetics.** Even his earliest pronouncement on tragedy can illuminate his practice as a playwright. In the **Lettres sur OEdipe** (1719), for instance, he acknowledges the simplicity of the Greek theatre, but points out that this very simplicity is synonymous with aridity and does not provide scope for a modern play in five acts. Therefore Corneille, argues Voltaire, had to make good this deficiency in **OEdipe** by falling back on his inventive powers. Voltaire criticizes the Thésée-Dircé episode which Corneille invented in his play, because he sinned against decorum by allowing Dircé to hurl abuse at her mother and was also guilty of **invraisemblance.** Lack of verisimilitude is understandable when one is hampered by the bizarre events of certain tragic subjects. In such cases, one must aim at being interesting rather than precise. Part of the significance of the **Lettres sur OEdipe** lies in the young dramatist's defence of the rights of poetic licence and invention. Voltaire was to continue to give us his thoughts on French tragedy right up to the end of his long career. More important for our purpose, however, is what he thought of it at the time of **Mahomet, ou le Fanatisme,** the play on which he spent so much time between 1739 and 1742.

In view of the attitude Voltaire had adopted in the **Lettres sur OEdipe,** there is some justification in the claim he made in his private letter to Jean Baptiste Sauvé La Noue of 3 April 1739 that he had been critical of French style in tragedy for the past twenty years. La Noue was the right person to write to about **Mahomet,** for Voltaire had the play performed by him in Lille subsequently and told d'Argental after the performance that La Noue, 'avec sa phisionomie de singe, a joué le rolle de Mahom bien mieux que n'eût fait Dufrene' (Best. D2477, 5 May 1741). In his letter to La Noue (Best. D1966), he quotes lines from various parts of **Mahomet second** which the actor-playwright had sent him. He shows admiration for the dazzling display of imagination everywhere in the play, while acknowledging that too much daring is out of place in a tragedy. But then, have not the French been 'un peu trop timides'? If a polished courtier and a young princess can use simple and graceful language, it seems to Voltaire that certain foreign heroes - of Asian, American and Turkish origin - can speak in prouder, more sublime accents. Voltaire likes the daring, metaphorical language of Mahomet II, arguing that all other nations appreciate striking imagery and reproach the French with a poetry that is too prosaic. He says he is not asking dramatists to go beyond nature: he simply wishes it to be strengthened and made more beautiful. This paves the way for a stylistic criticism of Racine's **Bajazet,** some seventeen lines of which are quoted, from one who claims to be a great admirer of Racine.

Voltaire wonders if Bajazet's style is written in anything but the tone of a Frenchman 'qui s'exprime avec élégance et avec douceur'. What he is looking for in Bajazet's language is something more virile and passionate. With regard to the subject matter of **Mahomet second,** Voltaire applauds the changes which La Noue, following precedents, brought to the historical character of the hero. In his words, 'une fausseté qui produit au théâtre une belle situation, est préférable en ce cas à toutes les archives de l'Univers; elle devient vraye pour moi puis qu'elle a produit la situation aussi frappante que neuve et hardie de Mahomet levant le poignard sur une maitresse dont il est aimé' (Best. D1966). Voltaire believes that there are new subjects for tragedy and even new genres to be created. In any case, he would be 'bien à plaindre si je perdais le goust de ces bautez parce que j'étudie un peu d'histoire et de phisique'. It seems that, by writing this letter, Voltaire wanted to continue his defence of poetic creation begun in the **Lettres sur OEdipe** and to justify his tampering with history in his own play of **Mahomet**.

Granted that a beautiful situation on stage is preferable to the dryness of history and that a dramatist has every right to modify history to suit his purpose, how did Voltaire go about it in **Mahomet** and what did he achieve? In the preface to **Mariamne** in 1725, he had argued that one of the fundamental rules is to depict heroes as they were, or rather as the public imagines them, for it is easier to influence people by using the ideas they have than by giving them new ones.[3] But the public also wants characters that arouse pity. So if the latter are disagreeable, it is clear that they should be softened, for it is necessary to think of one's public even more than of one's hero and not to follow history blindly, if one's aim is to move. If Voltaire had practised in **Mahomet** what he preached in the preface to **Mariamne**, **Mahomet** could have been a different and probably more successful tragedy. As many in the audiences that watched performances of **Mahomet** at Lille and Paris and many of the readers of the play no doubt considered the Prophet a lecherous villain in real life,[4] it would have been quite in order to tone down his character in the play. There were good precedents for this course of action. Thus Racine claimed in the first preface to **Andromaque** that he had softened the character of Pyrrhus as portrayed by Seneca and Virgil. Voltaire seems to have done the reverse. Privately, he admitted that in his play he had made Muhammad appear worse than he was. In a letter to Frederick the Great, for example, he said he knew that he could be reproached with being overzealous in making Mahomet commit a crime that Muhammad did not in fact commit and that 'Mahomet n'a pas tramé précisément l'espèce de trahison qui fait le sujet de cette tragédie' (Best D2386, 20 December 1740). At the time of **Mahomet**'s successful revival in 1751, Voltaire wrote to his niece, Madame Denis: 'Il n'appartenait assurément qu'aux musulmans de se plaindre, car j'ai fait Mahomet un peu plus méchant qu'il n'était' (Best. D4597, 29 October 1751).

In his letter to Frederick, Voltaire concedes that history simply records that Muhammad took away the wife of Seide,[5] one of his disciples, and that he persecuted Abu Softan (i.e. Abu Sufyan), whom he calls Zopire. What history of the Arabs was Voltaire reading? It has been suggested that for certain aspects of Mahomet's character, Voltaire drew both on Henri de Boulainvilliers's **Vie de Mahomed** (1730) and Jean Gagnier's **Vie de Mahomet** (1732).[6] In Boulainvilliers is to be found the idea of a meeting between Muhammad and Abu Sufyan, leader of the Meccans and inveterate enemy of the Prophet, at the suggestion of the latter's uncle, Al Abbas. Al Abbas persuaded Abu Sufyan to find the Prophet, acknowledge him as his lord and embrace Islam. As soon as Omar saw the old enemy of the Prophet, he ran to Muhammad to ask him for permission to kill Abu Sufyan. Permission was refused, and Muhammad subsequently persuaded Abu Sufyan to become a Moslem. More significant details of the surrender of Mecca and of Abu Sufyan are given by the Arab historian Abul Feda (1273-1331), who devoted chapters of his **General History** or **Annals** to the life of Muhammad. In 1723, Jean Gagnier, Professor of Arabic at Oxford, edited extracts of the work in Arabic with a Latin translation entitled **De Vita et rebus gestis Mohammedis.** To challenge Boulainvilliers's account of Muhammad in his **Vie,** Gagnier gave an expanded French version of his Arabic-Latin biography in 1732. From the original source (Abul Feda), we learn that Muhammad granted protection to Abu Sufyan on the intervention of his uncle, who also persuaded him to give some privilege to the new convert. Muhammad decreed that whoever took shelter in Abu Sufyan's house would be spared.[7] This additional information, as well as Boulainvilliers's, is authenticated in a much earlier biography of the Prophet, respected by Moslems, that written by Ibn Ishaq (702-68).[8]

A reading of these biographies may at first give the impression that they do not contain much material for drama. On the other hand, if he had planned to cast Mahomet in the Aristotelian mould, Voltaire would have found enough material from Boulainvilliers's work.   In particular, he could not avoid noticing Muhammad's generosity towards his principal enemy and his qualities as a leader. He also knew that Aristotelian tragedy required a hero with some outstanding qualities, but with some central flaw in his character to be placed in circumstances which would widen this flaw until it brought his downfall. In **Mahomet,** the hero, far from having any outstanding qualities, appears like a scheming, ambitious and wicked tyrant. It is not just the Moslems who have grounds to complain. In a different way, the modern reader too has legitimate cause for complaint. The character Mahomet is overdrawn: hardly any redeeming trait is to be found in this cruel monster.

It is true that Voltaire had altered the early versions of the play where Mahomet appeared triumphant and unrepentant right up to the end. He decided to make the hero feel remorse in Act V, scene iv. If we are to believe what he says to Cideville, 'tout le monde a exigé absolument quelques petits remords à la fin de la pièce pour l'édification publique' (Best. D2515, 19 July 1741). It seems, however, that Mahomet's last-minute remorse is simply an after-thought and is not fully integrated with his character.   Nothing that Mahomet had said or done previously would lead one to believe that he was capable of such an emotion. His remorse appears at best like a passing impression and not a permanent trait of character. And Cideville may well have made the most apposite comment when he suggested to Voltaire:

> Pour les remords de Mahomet je persiste à les croire contre l'idée que nous avons de son caractère. N'est-ce pas un illustre fourbe qui se joue de dieu et des hommes? Comment accorder ce portrait avec des Remords? Si les plus grands coquins en ressentent, c'est bien en passant, ces remords ne les effleurent qu'à peine - ainsy je n'en voudrois absolument point à la fin parce-que La fin est comme L'achèvement du Tableau et le spectateur en emporte trop l'idée.
>
> (Best. D2521, 7 August 1741)

However grateful Voltaire may have been to his friend for suggestions regarding the play, he did not accept his advice on Mahomet's remorse, which remained in the final version. Yet Cideville felt that there was in **Mahomet** a novelty worthy of Voltaire's genius.

Voltaire himself thought that the tragedy was 'sinon dans un bon goût, au moins dans un goût nouveau' when he wrote to Frederick in 1739 (Best. D2048, c. 20 July 1739). He dared suggest that he had scored a first for depicting superstition and fanaticism on stage. He repeated the suggestion in a later letter to Frederick (Best D2106, c. 1 November 1739). **Mahomet** even led him to disparage his other play, **Zulime,** for in his letter to the d'Argentals, he declared: 'Quand Mahom. ne serait joué que 7 fois en caresme je le ferois imprimer par ce qu'il y a plus de neuf, plus d'invention, plus de choses, dans une seule scène de ce drôle là, que dans toutes les lamentations amoureuses de la faible Zulime' (Best. D2162, 16 February 1740). He claimed that, whereas the danger of love (the theme of **Zulime**) is a trite subject, the danger represented by fanaticism (the subject of **Mahomet**) is quite new. In his letter to Cideville (Best. D2221, 5 June 1740), Voltaire showed how conscious he was of the eternal problem of the writer seeking originality when he exclaimed: 'Heureux celuy qui trouve une veine nouvelle dans cette mine du téâtre si longtemps fouillée et retournée!'. He wondered whether he had indeed struck gold from this vein.

Considering that large claims have been made by or on behalf of Voltaire that **Mahomet** is highly original, it might be worth examining if there is any truth in this opinion and to what extent. **Mahomet** is, of course, only one of the plays in which, in his attempt to renovate the French theatre, Voltaire decided to widen geographical frontiers instead of sticking to the Greco-Roman world, as happens much of the time in French classical tragedy. Voltaire was thus able to depict the customs of other times and far-away places. In **Zaïre** (1731) he had set the scene in Palestine and the timing of the action was that of the Crusades, in **Alzire** (1736) we are transported to Peru, in **Zulime** (1740) the action is set in North Africa, while **L'Orphelin de la Chine**

(1755) takes us to China. In the preface to **Les Scythes** (1765), Voltaire explained what he had been doing in **Tancrède** and these above-mentioned plays in order to satisfy the public taste for novelty: 'un amateur du théâtre a été forcé de mettre sur la scène l'ancienne chevalerie, le contraste des mahométans et des chrétiens, celui des Américains et des Espagnols, celui des Chinois et des Tartares' (M.VI, 267).

One of Voltaire's achievements in **Zaïre** was perhaps to set Moslem against Christian **mores**. Admittedly, Montesquieu had done the same exercise earlier: not on stage, but in his 'espèce de roman', the **Lettres persanes**. Even from the point of view of décor, **Mahomet** cannot show much originality: the action of **Zaïre** and **Mahomet** takes place in broadly the same area of the world. Earlier, **La Henriade** had seen the culmination of attacks on the intolerance and fanaticism of Roman Catholics. The character Mayenne in the epic has even been called a previous incarnation of the impostor.[9] Moreover, Voltaire had denounced fanaticism, both Moslem and Christian, in **Zaïre**. The denouncing of Moslem fanaticism only in **Mahomet** does not appear particularly original. Where, then, does the originality of **Mahomet** lie? It is perhaps in the subtle attack on Christianity which is not directly mentioned. There are only the vaguest of resemblances between the life and words of Jesus and those of Muhammad. Voltaire's hero enters Mecca 'l'olive à la main' (II.ii), and he tells Omar:

> Tu connais quel oracle et quel bruit populaire
> Ont promis l'univers à l'envoyé d'un dieu.   (II.iv)

Many eighteenth-century critics took **Mahomet** to be a general attack on religion, not a specific attack on Christianity. Thus the Abbé Le Blanc, writing to the Président Bouhier, commented: 'La Politique y est pour le moins aussi maltraitée que la Relligion, c'est le triomphe du Déisme ou plustôt du Fatalisme' (Best. D2635, 13 August 1742). If a particular religion was being referred to, it was Islam. For in eighteenth-century thought, Islam was often described as a form of deism, its guiding principle being fatalism.[10] In a surviving fragment of a letter from the Procureur Joly de Fleury to the Lieutenant de Police Marville, there is reference to **Mahomet** as a 'comédie où quelques-uns des **messieurs** ont été, et qu'ils disent contenir des choses énormes contre la religion' (Best. D2634, 11 August 1742). Two days later and before he had read the play, Joly de Fleury was writing in the same vein when reporting to Marville about what he had heard from people who had been to see the performance in Paris: 'Voici ce qu'on m'a dit: C'est l'énormité en fait d'infâmies, de scélératesse, d'irréligion et d'impiété: et c'est ce que disent ceux même qui n'ont pas de religion [...] On m'en a tant dit que j'en oublie la moitié: que vous faites triompher l'irréligion et les crimes' (Best. D2638). Even when he had read the play, Fleury came to the same conclusion. In his 'Observations sur le **Mahomet** de Voltaire', written as a result of a request from the Lieutenant de Police, he described as 'Comble de l'impiété et de l'irréligion' the following lines spoken by Mahomet in Act II, scene v:

> Oui; je connais ton peuple, il a besoin d'erreur,
> Ou véritable ou faux, mon culte est nécessaire.

With regard to the rest of this scene, Fleury thought it was worthy of a man 'qui n'a point d'idée de ce que c'est que Dieu'.[11]

César de Missy, to whom Voltaire had offered the right to have an edition of his collected works including **Mahomet** published in London (Best. D2648, 1 September 1742), seems to have been taken in by Voltaire. He said he found it strange that the play should be on trial as if it were attacking the Christian religion 'pendant qu'elle enlève aux ennemis de cette même Religion un de leurs lieux-communs favoris, qui est de faire de Mahomet un Personage digne d'être mis en opposition ou en parallèle avec Jésus-Christ'. In his view, only the enemies of Christianity and not good Christians have legitimate grounds for complaint, for **Mahomet** represents the foundation of Mohammedanism as a work of fraud and violence. This leads Missy to ask: 'Qu'est-ce que cela peut avoir de commun avec le Christianisme, dont le premier établissement s'est fait, non-seulement avec la meilleure foi et la plus grande douceur du monde, mais par une patience portée au delà de toutes les bornes naturelles que la Morale pouvoit lui prescrire?' (Best. D2689, 18 November 1742). Despite what Missy thought, the parallel between Christ and Muhammad was being made by a discerning few who knew the play. Chesterfield told Crébillon that under the guise of Mahomet, Voltaire was really attacking Christ. He was surprised that nobody had noticed the parallel when **Mahomet** was first performed in Lille, in 1741. He had even met there a good Catholic 'dont le zèle surpassait la pénétration, qui était extrêmement édifié de la manière dont cet imposteur et ennemi du Christianisme était dépeint' (Best. D2653, 6 September 1742).

Of course, in the first part of the eighteenth century, the parallel between Christ and Muhammad was fairly familiar. It was drawn by writers such as Meslier in his **Testament.** To these two figures was added that of Moses, especially in manuscript writings that had a wide circulation like the **Traité des trois imposteurs.** In such works, the comparison was obvious. It was not so in **Mahomet,** where Voltaire improved on the technique of Jurieu and Bayle.[12] For whereas the latter denounced the Catholics openly by praising Moslems, Voltaire made his own denunciation discreetly, so discreetly in fact that he mystified the majority of his readers and playgoers. Much of what he says in his private correspondence - one is struck by the abundance of letters or references regarding **Mahomet** between 1739 and 1742 - does not provide the right clue about his real intention in the play.[13] For this, one has to go to a contemporary pamphlet about which Voltaire says little,'Du fanatisme'. It often appeared as a short essay with other miscellaneous pieces before it finally became a dictionary article. How typical of Voltaire that his attack should be conducted in two different **genres**!

When 'Du fanatisme' was first published in 1742 in an authentic collective edition in the **OEuvres mêlées de M. de Voltaire,**[14] it was immediately preceded by another essay entitled 'Remarques sur l'histoire' with which it was linked. Indeed, it came under the general heading 'Remarques sur l'histoire'. In the 'Remarques' proper, Voltaire suggested that history should be seriously studied at a time when it became really interesting, that is, towards the end of the fifteenth century. Why that particular period? It was then, according to Voltaire, that one no longer found 'prédicateurs chimériques, ni oracles menteurs, ni faux miracles, ni fables insensées'. The pamphlet 'Du fanatisme' shows a real affinity with **Mahomet, ou le Fanatisme** and may be regarded as a continuation of the war waged on fanaticism and false miracles in the play. After its success in Lille, **Mahomet** was performed in Paris on 9 August 1742 with the approval of Cardinal Fleury. But it was withdrawn in the face of opposition from the Jansenist party led by the Procureur Joly de Fleury. Voltaire complained to Cardinal Fleury about the part played by the 'cabale des convulsionnaires, c'est à dire ce qu'il y a de plus abject dans le rebut du genre humain', in getting his play withdrawn (Best. D2644, 22 August 1742). In another letter to Cideville about **Mahomet,** he noted that 'les bonnes gens ont cru que l'on attaquait St Medard et monsieur St Paris' (Best. D2649, 1 September 1742).

In the pamphlet 'Du fanatisme', as in **Mahomet,** Voltaire does attack the 'convulsionnaires'. Indeed, there is little to distinguish the activities of the 'Protestant géomètre', Nicolas Faccio (referred to in the pamphlet) and his associates, the Camisards or 'French prophets', from those of the Jansenists on the tomb of the deacon Pâris. Faccio and his friends had been prosecuted at the charge of the French churches in London and been condemned by the queen's bench to the pillory as common cheats and impostors. In their attempt to bring a dead man back to life with their 'très pieuses contorsions', they may also be compared with Mahomet's disciples who are thus described by Phanor in Act I, scene i, of the play:

> En ces murs même une troupe égarée,
> Des poisons de l'erreur avec zèle enivrée,
> De ses miracles faux soutient l'illusion,
> Répand le fanatisme et la sédition,
> Appelle son armée, et croit qu'un Dieu terrible
> L'inspire, le conduit, et le rend invincible.

Faccio's miracle turns out to be false and Voltaire pours contempt on his naive supporters who believe that resurrection could occur infallibly under certain circumstances. Likewise, in **Mahomet**, Voltaire is particularly successful in proving how Mahomet's miracle is bogus. In Act V, scene iv, just when the villain is about to be unmasked, he appeals to God to judge between him and Séide: 'De nous deux, à l'instant, que le coupable expire'. Séide falls dead, but his death is due to no miracle. Omar had seen to it that Séide took a poison which caused slow death. The people naturally believed that Heaven had worked in Mahomet's favour.

In seeking Cardinal Fleury's support, Voltaire did not hesitate to stigmatize the Cardinal's enemies, the Jansenists. What he did not tell him was what he had written about other Roman Catholics elsewhere. In the printed text of 'Du fanatisme', he denounced not only the miracles of a Protestant mathematician and the superstition of Islamic sects, but also the saints of the Roman Church and the Pope himself. In the surviving manuscript of the text, the attack against Christ, the disciples and the saints is even clearer and fiercer.[15] For instance, the line 'annoncer publiquement qu'ils ressusciteraient un mort dans tel cimetière que l'on voudrait' of the printed text is different in the manuscript. In the latter, the phrase 'au nom de Jesus Christ' is added after 'mort'. Where the published text has 'Ils disaient: Les vrais disciples doivent faire des miracles', the manuscript reads 'Ils disaient Jesus Christ a promis à tous les vrays disciples qu'ils feroient [...]'. If the line of the edited text: 'De simples saints de l'Eglise romaine, qui n'étaient point géomètres, ont ressuscité beaucoup d'honnêtes gens' is biting enough, that of the manuscript: 'St François, St Dominique, St Jean qui n'estaient que des papistes ont ressusciter [sic] beaucoup d'honnêtes gens' is even more damaging to Rome. With regard to the idea that the Pope is anti-Christ, both the printed text and the manuscript attribute it to Newton, who is purported to have found it in the Apocalypse.

It is the pamphlet 'Du fanatisme' that properly justifies the identification of Christ and the Roman Catholic Church with Muhammad and Islam. Another pamphlet intimately connected with **Mahomet** was first published on its own under the title 'De l'Alcoran et de Mahomet' in an authentic collective edition in the **OEuvres de Mr. de V.**[16] and subsequently became Section Two of the article 'Alcoran, ou plutôt le Koran' of the **Dictionnaire philosophique**. Although it was to a large extent a justification of the 1748 edition of **Mahomet** and, like 'Du fanatisme', a continuation of the war waged on the charlatan Mahomet in the play, it does not lend itself to the same double interpretation as 'Du fanatisme'. The importance of the latter lies in the fact that it provides Voltaire with a springboard from which to launch his massive attack on miracles in the **Dictionnaire philosophique**. In the **Dictionnaire**, he simply had to multiply examples to show the connexion between pagan, Islamic and Biblical miracles, which became devalued in the process. In the interval, he had developed his technique of drawing similar parallels in the Leningrad, Pierpont Morgan and Picci notebooks.[17]

However, is there a sense in which **Mahomet** can be regarded not merely as 'philosophical' propaganda but also as belonging to the mainstream of French classical tragedy rather than its margins? As in the case of **Zaïre**, Voltaire, in spite of his desire to be original, remains close to the seventeenth-century theatre at times in **Mahomet**. Linguistic borrowings or parallels from Racine and Corneille are plainly visible in **Mahomet**.[18]   Mahomet's use of 'premier degré' in his declaration: '[...] mon culte épuré / De ma grandeur naissante est le premier degré', from Act II, scene v, of **Mahomet** recalls that of **Cinna** (I.i, ll.11-12). Séide's 'main saintement homicide' (II.vii) and Palmire's 'tes mains saintement homicides' (II.iii) echo lines from **Athalie** (IV.iii). Palmire's curses against Mahomet in Act V, scene ii, though perhaps not as striking as Camille's in **Horace**, nevertheless have a similar ring. The following lines in particular:

> Puissé-je de mes mains te déchirer le flanc
> Voir mourir tous les tiens et nager dans leur sang!
> Puissent la Mecque ensemble, et Médine, et l'Asie,
> Punir tant de fureur et tant d'hypocrisie
> Que le monde, par toi séduit et ravagé,
> Rougisse de ses fers, les brise, et soit vengé!

can be matched by Camille's verses in **Horace**:

> Puissent tous ses voisins ensemble conjurés
> Saper ses fondements encor mal assurés!
> Et si ce n'est assez de toute l'Italie,
> Que l'Orient contre elle à l'Occident s'allie;
> Que cent peuples unis des bouts de l'univers
> Passent pour la détruire et les monts et les mers!
> Puissé-je de mes yeux y voir tomber ce foudre
> Voir ses maisons en cendre, et tes lauriers en poudre. (IV.v)

Jean-Jacques Rousseau took a different view in his **Lettre sur les spectacles.** He thought that in the scene between Zopire and Omar (Act II, scene v), Voltaire surpassed even the greatest masters of French classical tragedy. Corneille and Racine are not specifically named in Rousseau's criticism, but one must assume that even they could not produce such a scene. Rousseau declared: 'Je n'ai jamais ouï faire de cette scène en particulier tout l'éloge dont elle me paraît digne, mais je n'en connais pas une autre au théâtre français, où la main d'un grand maître soit plus sensiblement empreinte, et où le sacré caractère de la vertu l'emporte plus sensiblement sur l'élévation du génie'.[19]   He felt that the scene was so skilfully constructed that Mahomet, without losing any of his superiority, was nevertheless eclipsed by Zopire's commonsense. Only a great author, according to Rousseau, could have opposed two such characters. More restrained, but sounder perhaps, was Joly de Fleury's evaluation of Palmire's speech in Act III, scene ii, which he described as 'Monologue très beau'.

This monologue has certain affinities with that of the heroine in **Zaïre** (Act III, scene v). Palmire and Zaïre stress their confused state of mind, Palmire being both attracted to and repulsed by Mahomet. Where Zaïre laments:

> Quoi! dans ce trouble extrême
> L'univers m'abandonne ou me laisse à moi-même!

Palmire expresses even more complex feelings:

> Délivre-moi, grand dieu! de ce trouble où je suis.
> Craintive je te sers, aveugle je te suis.

Yet is is Zaïre's tragic dilemma that strikes one as being more Cornelian. Her divided loyalties come out more clearly, in terms that echo Sabine in Corneille's **Horace** (Act III, scene i):

> Hélas! suis-je en effet Française ou Musulmane?
> Fille de Lusignan, ou femme d'Orosmane?

It seems that there is less poignancy too in Palmire's doubts when she says:

> J'invoque Mahomet, et cependant mon cœur
> Eprouve à son nom même une secrète horreur.
> Dans les profonds respects que ce héros m'inspire,
> Je sens que je le crains presque autant que Zopire.

On the other hand, as Joly de Fleury pointed out, the monologue of Séide in Act III, scene vii, is beautiful. Séide expresses in delicate touches the pathos of a character who has to

> Immoler un vieillard de qui je suis l'otage,
> Sans armes, sans défense, appesanti par l'âge!

After a slight hesitation, he decides to kill Zopire. However, Séide's resolve is but a pale imitation of Corneille's Horace. His words,

> Enfin Dieu m'a choisi pour ce grand sacrifice
> J'en ai fait le serment, il faut qu'il s'accomplisse,

seem flat when compared with those of Horace:

> Rome a choisi mon bras, je n'examine rien.
> Avec une allégresse aussi pleine et sincère
> Que j'épousai la sœur, je combattrai le frère. (II.iii)

Although keen on innovation, especially with regard to action, Voltaire tried to stick to some of the conventions of French classical drama. Despite his bewilderment in the **Discours sur la tragédie** that heroes and heroines should be allowed to commit suicide on stage, but prevented from killing anyone there, in **Mahomet** he observed

French classical **bienséances**. He refused to allow a murder to take place before the eyes of the spectators. Séide actually goes behind the altar where Zopire is in order to strike him. Yet the act of killing was not perfectly executed, as the wounded Zopire rose from behind the altar to meet his children. Perhaps Voltaire was following the example of Euripides's Hippolytus who appears on stage wounded. At any rate, he refers to this situation in the 'Cambridge Notebook' (**Notebooks**, p.107). By making Séide strike Zopire behind the altar, Voltaire uses a technique which shows closer affinity with the practice of **Zaïre** where the heroine falls in the wings, while Orosmane stabs himself on stage. In his three-act tragedy, **La Mort de César** (1735), Voltaire appears to have been more daring in this respect. He reached a compromise between showing the murder of Caesar on the stage, as happens in Shakespeare, and giving an account of the death of the character, as usually happens in French classical tragedy. He ensured that the shouts of the conspirators who are behind the stage and performing the murder are heard by Dolabella who is before the audience.

One may also find in **Mahomet** the polarization so characteristic of the tragic heroes of Corneille and Racine. There can be no **via media** for the character who sees every situation in terms of black and white: choice hardly exists. Thus at the end of Act I, scene iv, Zopire proudly rejects Mahomet's offer of pardon conveyed by Omar, and says instead: 'Préparons son supplice, ou creusons mon cercueil'. Zopire again scorns the proposal, personally made to him by Mahomet, that if he accepts to serve him as Prophet, Mahomet will give him back his son Séide and will marry his daughter Palmire. He gives an unequivocal reply:

> Mais s'il faut à ton culte asservir ma patrie,
> Ou de ma propre main les immoler tous deux
> Connais-moi, Mahomet, mon choix n'est pas douteux. (II.v)

As far as the unities are concerned, it is doubtful whether **Mahomet** is classical in its observance of them. The action of the play is set in Mecca and it is true that the vague stage direction appears to convey a semblance of unity of place. But one wonders where precisely the action takes place: changes of scene, if not specifically indicated, may be safely assumed. It is unthinkable that the characters, with their varied backgrounds and interests, could be meeting in the same place. It is clear, for example, that at the end of Act IV, scene iii, when the stage direction reads: 'Le fond du théâtre s'ouvre. On voit un autel', we are being introduced to a part of Mecca where Zopire usually prays to his heathen gods, which must be different from where Mahomet, Omar and other Moslems meet. Moreover, although the action of the play is only an episode in the capture of Mecca by Mahomet, so many things happen that it is hardly likely that one day would suffice to cover all these events.

Mahomet is totally unconvincing when compared with Zaïre. The portrayal of female psychology in **Zaïre** is much more successful, and even if the play has defects, it, much more than **Mahomet,** can claim to represent the mainstream of classical tragedy. In **Zaïre,** there is certainly an element of propaganda when in Act I, scene i, Voltaire preaches through the heroine that geography and one's education in early childhood are the sole determinants of one's religion. This propaganda is, however, under control most of the time and the tragic destiny of Zaïre predominates. In **Mahomet,** on the other hand, it is the propaganda against fanaticism and religious hypocrisy that predominates at the expense of tragedy. In his ridiculous love for Palmire, Mahomet appears more like a character of comedy than tragedy. Voltaire himself likened Mahomet to Tartuffe when he wrote to Frederick: 'Mahomet n'est icy autre chose que Tartuffe les armes à la main' (Best. D2386). He expanded on this idea in his letter to César de Missy when he said:

> C'est Tartuffe le grand; les fanatiques en ont fait suprimer à Paris les représentations, comme les dévots étouffèrent l'autre Tartuffe dans sa naissance. Cette tragédie est plus faitte je crois pour des têtes anglaises que pour des cœurs français. On l'a trouvée trop hardie à Paris parce qu'elle n'est que forte, et dangereuse parce qu'il y a du vray. J'ay voulu faire voir par cet ouvrage à quels horribles excez le fanatisme peut entraîner des âmes faibles conduites par un fourbe.   (Best. D2648)

From beginning to end, the play produces the effect of a pamphlet on spectator and reader alike. Reading **Mahomet** is to a certain extent like reading the pamphlet 'Du fanatisme'.

It is not the fact that **Mahomet** violates some rules that ensures its relegation to the margins of French classical tragedy. It is rather because it lacks its essential element. The character Mahomet is not only completely devoid of the finer traits of psychology, but he also sins against verisimilitude. With all his defects and without any qualities in the play, it is hardly credible that he should have had a following. Mahomet can be viewed as a Satanic figure without any of the graces of Satan. This is rather surprising, as Milton's **Paradise Lost** remained constantly in Voltaire's thoughts in the late 1730s and in 1740 Voltaire even wrote **Pandore,** which was described by Madame d'Aiguillon as an opera 'à la Milton' (Best.D2219, c. 4 June 1740).[20] Yet Mahomet often uses an epic tone of speech.[21] This is particularly true of Act II, scene v, where he unveils his plans to Zopire. It is clear that what he has in mind is the destiny not only of himself, but of Arabia and the whole world:

> Si j'avais à répondre à d'autres qu'à Zopire
> Je ne ferais parler que le dieu qui m'inspire;
> Le glaive et l'Alcoran, dans mes sanglantes mains,
> Imposeraient silence au reste des humains [...]

20. See my book, **Voltaire and English Literature** (Oxford, 1979), volume CLXXVII of **Studies on Voltaire and the Eighteenth Century,** pp.131-33.

21. See T.W. Russell, **Voltaire, Dryden and Heroic Tragedy** (New York, 1946), p.135.

22. Voltaire himself says so in the 'Avis de l'Editeur' which he wrote to the 1743 edition of **Mahomet,** published in Amsterdam. See M.IV, 99.

23. See Mitchell, p.19:   'But in this effort [to achieve elevated style], in the emphasis on stage settings, in the introduction of historical material, Voltaire helped point the way toward the Romantic tragedies of Hugo'.

TEN

Diderot and Racine
Derek Connon

> On a halcyon day it is merely a monument,
> In navigable weather it is always a seamark
> To lay a course by   (T.S. Eliot)

Like Hugo's **Préface de 'Cromwell'**, Diderot's two great dramatic treatises (the **Entretiens sur 'Le Fils naturel'** and **De la poésie dramatique**) have an air of theatrical iconoclasm. They seek to overthrow the values and traditions of pre-existing French theatre in order to replace it with their own revolutionary form of drama. Both authors overstressed the novelty of their innovations by claiming foreign sources whilst neglecting to mention those of their immediate French predecessors to whom they owed many of their ideas: Hugo praises Shakespeare, but makes no reference to the fact that many of his own ideas had already been expressed by Diderot; Diderot writes at length of his debt to eighteenth-century English authors and to writers of Greco-Roman antiquity, but makes little reference to the works of La Motte, Nivelle de La Chaussée or Madame de Graffigny (although, perversely, he does stress the importance of the very minor play **Silvie** attributed to the equally minor author Paul Landois, whose principal claim to fame is as the addressee of the brilliant and superbly insulting letter by Diderot published by Grimm in the **Correspondance littéraire**).[1]

One important difference between the two writers is, however, that Racine, that foremost representative of the classical tradition that both innovators were trying to replace, was one of the principal **bêtes noires** of Hugo, whereas Diderot was far from rejecting the works of such an illustrious predecessor even though he does question the contemporary value of his literary school. He did in fact admire all three of the great seventeenth-century dramatists.

His admiration for Molière is perhaps the least surprising: even if we no longer accept the simplistic generalization that Molière's plays depict the value of the reasonable middle way ('La parfaite raison fuit toute extrémité', as it is expressed in **Le Misanthrope**), it is nevertheless true that in his greatest plays -particularly **L'Ecole des femmes**, **Le Tartuffe** and **Le Misanthrope** - important social problems are under discussion, a factor which should make them particularly attractive to the creator of the family unit and eventually destroy it, in **Iphigénie** the threat comes from outside the family which struggles to protect itself and is ultimately successful. This tends to underline the domestic aspect of the plot at the expense of its more universal political and amorous aspects. The role of Agamemnon does show a conflict between the duties of paternity and kingship, but Clytemnestre is almost entirely depicted as a mother rather than a queen, and Achille is far more important as fiancé than as warrior. Significantly, **Andromaque,** the only other play of Racine to concentrate on a positive aspect of the family, shared **Iphigénie's** popularity with the eighteenth-century public. But **Andromaque** concentrates only on a single domestic emotion, and although it explores this in considerable depth, we are never given the same impression of a whole family unit.

This situation can be confirmed by statistical comparison: **Andromaque** contains 86 uses of the word 'fils' as compared to 72 occurrences of 'fille' in **Iphigénie**[10] (**Mithridate** with 52 uses of 'fils' and **Phèdre** with 51 are the only other tragedies of Racine to have more than fifty uses of either word), but **Iphigénie** heads the lists for uses of 'mère' (28 occurrences, **Britannicus** is close behind with 26, but **Andromaque** has only 12) and 'père' (65 occurrences, **Mithridate** has 50 and **Andromaque** 33).[11] That is to say that **Iphigénie** contains more references to members of the family unit than any other of its author's works, thus drawing attention to its characters' functions as members of the family rather than as independent individuals.

Iphigénie herself typifies another role much loved in the imaginative literature of the eighteenth-century fiction, particularly the **drame** and its precursors: she is the virtuous, innocent victim who is persecuted by external forces.   There are many possible variations on this theme: the situation is all the more touching if the victim goes willingly to her fate in order to protect her persecutors; generally she is spared by a providential last-minute reprieve.   Diderot used the type for Sophie in **Le Père de famille,** but there are countless other examples throughout the century, such as, for instance, La Motte's Inès de Castro, Voltaire's Zaïre and Nanine, Madame de Graffigny's Cénie, Beaumarchais's Eugénie and, closest to Diderot's heart, Richardson's Clarissa and Landois's Silvie.   The type was to find its extreme form in the person of Sade's Justine.

We have briefly mentioned the often providential nature of the denouements of the **drame** and its precursors.   The tensions of the plot are more often than not resolved by a recognition scene or some other form of **coup de théâtre.**   Such scenes may well be more realistic than the ancient **deus ex machina,** but they are scarcely less gratuitous, and rarely more credible.   It is surely, above all, this characteristic of which Barthes is thinking when he refers to the 'mauvaise foi' of the **drame,** for although the author would have us believe that the characters receive their just reward because of their actions during the course of the play, as often as not they receive it despite those actions. This is certainly the case with Diderot's **drames**: the plots of neither **Le Père de famille** nor **Les Pères malheureux** could be unravelled without their concluding recognition scenes, and, although the tensions of **Le Fils naturel** have already been resolved before the final reunion, that last scene is needed to prevent the play ending in the same melancholic mood as **Bérénice**.

And **Iphigénie**, too, ends with a recognition scene which, although of a different type, has exactly the same effect of saving the victim and reuniting the family: Eriphile discovers her true identity and takes Iphigénie's place as victim. Faced with the choice between the alternative conclusions of the traditional versions of the myth, Racine rejected the brutality of the human sacrifice which, whilst being the logical tragic conclusion to the play's action, would seriously infringe the **bienséances**. He rejects, too, the fantasy of the **deus ex machina**, the intervention of Artemis which is found in versions by, amongst others, Euripides and Rotrou. Instead, he makes use of a third option, found in the relatively obscure poet Tisias, in which it is a second Iphigénie who dies on the altar. Since Eriphile stabs herself on discovering her true identity and also has a motif for her suicide, her frustrated love for Achille, Racine avoids any problems of **bienséance**. This solution, however, undermines the tragic impact of the conclusion by providing the domestic plot with a happy ending, and Racine further reduces the force of Eriphile's fate by having her behave so odiously towards Iphigénie in the final acts that we are presumably intended to feel that she has got her just deserts. And, interestingly, this fortuitous happy ending undermines the tragic impact of this play in just the same way that similar conclusions were to damage the didactic intentions of the **drame**, since the characters, spared the consequences of their actions, learn nothing from their experiences, are in no way enriched by the events of the drama. Alain Niderst's comments on this aspect of Racine's play are of particular interest, since they could equally well be applied to **Le Père de famille**:

> Qu'apprennent-ils au dénouement tous ces braves gens, qui peuplent le devant du théâtre? Rien qu'ils ne savaient déjà dans le fond. Qu'ils sont de braves gens. Que les dieux sont justes et raisonnables, malgré quelques apparences. Et qu'il suffit de leur faire confiance, de s'abandonner naïvement à leur volonté, pour voir tomber tous les obstacles, et se résoudre les problèmes les plus graves.[12]

And yet, despite the striking resemblances between this denouement and similar scenes to be found in the **drame**, it must in certain respects have been a disappointment to Diderot, for another aspect of this work which must have appealed to him is its strong strain of brutality. It is one of the stranger paradoxes of Diderot's theatre that, whilst he frequently criticizes in his theoretical works the limitations imposed by the **bienséances** and imagines with relish the scenes of unbridled primitive sex and violence he would like to see on stage, his plays are in general very well behaved. The scenes where Diderot was criticized for being too **osé** are such timid innovations as d'Orbesson's prayer over his new-born child rather than scenes in which 'les dieux altérés du sang humain ne sont apaisés que par son effusion; où des bacchantes armées de thyrses s'égarent dans les forêts et inspirent l'effroi au profane qui se rencontre sur leur passage; où d'autres femmes se dépouillent sans pudeur, ouvrent leurs bras au premier qui se présente, et se prostituent' (DPV, X, 401; **OE,** p.261). We will find examples of such violence in **La Religieuse** or in **Le Plan du 'Shérif',** but not in any of his completed theatrical works. The reason is clearly that, despite his protestations, the **bienséances** were as firmly entrenched in his own subconscious as in that of his contemporaries, and, unlike so many of his other works, the **drames** were not composed for posterity or a small circle of the cultural élite, but for performance. And since these same strictures limited not only Diderot but also his predecessors, it is clear that few plays in the French repertoire would be able to answer this desire for stage violence. So it is that he had an extreme liking for those occasions in Racine's plays on which violence and brutality broke through the veneer of seventeenth-century refinement: such passages of physical violence as the narrations of Théramène or Ulysse[13] proved particularly to his taste.

Iphigénie revealed the primitive instincts of its protagonists by, in particular, its treatment of the theme of human sacrifice. Indeed, so attractive does Diderot find this theme that when writing about the play he tends to overemphasize it. In a letter to Sophie Volland concerning Aaron Hill's play **The Fatal Extravagance,** Diderot's plot summary makes this work's catastrophe much more bloody than it in fact is: in Hill's play, the central character's intention to kill not only himself but also his wife and children is thwarted by the intervention of an uncle and he dies alone; in Diderot's version, this last minute reprieve is suppressed and the plan succeeds.[14] One would not expect Diderot similarly to misrepresent a play like **Iphigénie,** which would be much more familiar to his readers than Hill's work, and yet, though he never specifically rewrites the plot of Racine's tragedy as he does that of **The Fatal Extravagance,** he underplays the final recognition scene so much that all of his comments about the catastrophe tend to suggest that Iphigénie does die on the altar. Curiously, the clearest example of this comes in another letter to Sophie Volland in which he is replying to her criticisms of the play; he could not therefore have been in any doubt about his reader's knowledge of its plot. This tends to suggest that any apparent misrepresentation of Racine's, and possibly also of Hill's, denouement stems not from a conscious desire to mislead his reader, but from his own subconscious hankering for the violence of the more bloody, and also more logical, ending. His summary of the plot in his letter, which is designed to show how skilfully the character of Agamemnon is drawn, begins with the words: 'Un père immole sa fille par ambition' (Corr. III, 237), and ends: 'Cependant il est sur le point de ravir sa fille au couteau, lorsque Eriphile dénonce sa fuite aux Grecs et à Calchas qui la demande à grands cris' (Corr. III, 237-38). No mention is made of the recognition scene and so such a retelling would leave the untutored reader in no doubt that Eriphile's treachery results in the immolation of Iphigénie spoken of at the outset. Other examples of the same tendency are more allusive or ambiguous, but often make the same implication, as for instance the following reference in the **Discours de la poésie dramatique**, in which, as in the above letter, the sacrifice is spoken of as a fact rather than a possibility: 'Celui qui sacrifie sa fille peut être ambitieux, faible, ou féroce' (DPV, X, 375; OE, p.234). Or this summary of the narration of Ulysse found in the **Entretiens sur 'Le Fils naturel'**, in which the identity of the dead princess is unspecified: 'L'air obscurci de traits. Une armée en tumulte. La terre arrosée de sang. Une jeune princesse le poignard enfoncé dans le sein' (DPV, X, 142; OE, p.151).

The conclusion of **Iphigénie** must have provoked very mixed feelings in Diderot, the poet in him longing for the horror and violence of the truly tragic ending that is found in the earliest versions of the tale in Antiquity, while the moralist and creator of the **drame** must have approved of the softened ending used by Racine which allows the family to be reunited. The role of Agamemnon seems also to have given him cause for concern. Diderot's admiration for his father is well known and, although it is nowhere more apparent than in the **Entretien d'un père avec ses enfants**, the **drames** too are dominated by the glorification of the father-figure. In consequence, as is shown throughout the letter to Sophie Volland quoted above, he finds the image of an Agamemnon who would coldly allow the sacrifice of his daughter highly disturbing and, in consequence, strongly approves Racine's attempts to make him into as sympathetic a character as possible. Indeed, in that same letter, he pushes his own efforts to vindicate the Racinian Agamemnon so far that he gets the myth spectacularly wrong:

> Et puis il y a dix ans que les Grecs sont devant Troie. Il n'y a pas un chef dans l'armée qui n'ait perdu un père, un fils, un frère, un ami pour venger l'injure faite aux Atrides. Ce sang des Atrides est-il le seul sang précieux de la Grèce? Tout sentiment d'ambition à part, Agamemnon ne doit-il rien aux dieux? ne doit-il rien aux Grecs? Que de circonstances accumulées pour pallier l'erreur d'un moment! (Corr. III, 238)

One must assume that this is a temporary lapse caused by the enthusiasm of his defence of Agamemnon, for not only was Diderot much too well versed in the classics to be unaware that the sacrifice of Iphigénie took place in Aulide to allow the Greeks to get to rather than from Troy, but the future Trojan war is so strong a theme in Racine's play that no one who has seen or read it can be left unaware of when the events are taking place.

Two other aspects of **Iphigénie** which bring it closer to the **drame** and to other eighteenth-century forms than most of Racine's works can be considered briefly.

Weeping became a fashionable feature of eighteenth-century theatre: Nivelle de La Chaussée's sentimental comedy became known as **comédie larmoyante;** for many of his contemporaries, perhaps the most famous words that Voltaire wrote were: 'Zaïre, vous pleurez?'[15] and in Diderot's **drames,** the scene is frequently bathed in tears. **Iphigénie** anticipates this predilection by being one of the most lachrymose of Racine's tragedies. Again, this fact can be confirmed by statistical means: **Iphigénie** contains 50 references to 'larmes' and derivatives of 'pleurer'; the only one of his plays to have more is, paradoxically, **Bérénice** with 57 occurrences. It is not without significance that third in line is another play that was particularly popular with eighteenth-century audiences, **Andromaque,** with 42 such references.

Our other point of comparison concerns the famous hemistich: 'Vous y serez, ma fille' (II.ii, 1.578) and, indeed, the entire scene leading up to it. This particular line was a favourite with Diderot,[16] although modern readers may not all share his enthusiasm. The scene which this line concludes must have struck a particular chord, since it makes use of dramatic irony in a particularly sentimental way which was to become very common in the **drame.** In the scene in question, Agamemnon, tortured by the fact that he has been called upon to sacrifice his daughter, has his first dialogue with her. She, aware that there is to be a sacrifice but unaware that she is the intended victim, tortures her father even further with innocent remarks such as: 'Quel bonheur de me voir la fille d'un tel père!' (1.546) and finally the question:

> Me sera-t-il permis de me joindre à vos vœux?
> Verra-t-on à l'autel votre heureuse famille?   (ll.576-77)

which elicits that agonized reply: 'Vous y serez, ma fille'.

Similarly touching misunderstandings can be produced in many different ways, and closely analogous situations can be found in a wide variety of sentimental plays. Since such complex situations often take longer to recount than they do to perform, a single example from Diderot's own theatre will suffice to make the comparison. The scene in question is the first of the third act of **Le Fils naturel:** Dorval, who has inadvertently fallen in love with Rosalie, the fiancée of his friend Clairville, rescues the latter from certain death in a fight against two opponents. Dorval, who is already tortured by guilt at his feelings, goes through even greater emotional torment when Clairville explains that he was fighting to defend Dorval's honour, the two adversaries having accused him of being in love with Rosalie. The emotional response generated by these two situations can be seen to be extremely similar, and also much more sentimental than tragic.

* *

*

Despite Diderot's at times apparently unreserved enthusiasm for Racine's work, he does not see him as being above criticism. Paradoxically, certain criticisms can, to a certain extent, be recognized as being complimentary. For instance, we find in the **Lettre sur les sourds et muets:**

> Ah! Monsieur, combien notre entendement est modifié par les signes; et que la diction la plus vive est encore une froide copie de ce qui s'y passe:
>
> Les ronces dégouttantes
> Portent de ses cheveux les dépouilles sanglantes.
>
> Voilà une des peintures les plus ressemblantes que nous ayons. Cependant qu'elle est encore loin de ce que j'imagine!   (DPV, IV, 162)

It is not Racine who is being criticized here, but traditional theatre in general; indeed, Diderot has chosen his example from Racine because he regards him as the supreme practitioner of that art form.[17]

But there are genuine criticisms too. For instance, even Diderot finds one of the more **romanesque** events in **Iphigénie** out of place in a tragedy:

> Si une jeune princesse est conduite vers un autel sur lequel on doit l'immoler, on ne voudra pas qu'un aussi grand événement ne soit fondé que sur l'erreur d'un messager qui suit un chemin, tandis que la princesse et sa mère s'avancent par un autre.   (DPV, X, 352; **OE**, p.210)

Even more fantastic coincidences, however, abound in Diderot's own plays: Dorval falls in love with the fiancée of his best friend and she just happens to turn out to be his sister; the girl with whom Saint-Albin falls in love when he sees her by chance happens to be his cousin; the traveller who is robbed by Simon turns out to be the long-lost father of his friends. One could possibly attempt to justify this inconsistency by arguing that the **drame** lends itself rather better to such coincidences than tragedy, for that is certainly true, but Diderot does not himself make that distinction in the passage from the **Discours de la poésie dramatique** which contains the above criticism and in which he is addressing not just the tragic dramatist, but every playwright.

Another criticism, which is perhaps more consistent with Diderot's own dramatic

passage in which the characters could justifiably exclaim: 'Eh! laissez là le domestique du père de Rosalie, et parlez nous de lui'. Diderot is obviously aiming for an effect of touching pathos, and the force of his writing is such that even at a third of its present length the passage might have succeeded, but at its actual length it is undoubtedly dramatically misguided. Diderot admits in the **Entretiens sur 'Le Fils naturel'** that the narration is problematic:

> 'La scène est pathétique, mais longue.'
>
> Elle eût été et plus pathétique et plus longue, si j'en avais voulu croire André. [...] Il voulait la scène comme elle s'est passée. Vous la voulez comme il convient à l'ouvrage; et c'est moi seul qui ai tort, de vous avoir mécontentés tous les deux.
>
> (DPV, X, 107-09; OE, pp.107 and 109)

Despite its somewhat apologetical tone, this passage does seem to suggest that Diderot believed he had struck the correct balance between length and pathos. Unfortunately, it is difficult to agree with him. That an author as accomplished as Diderot should have made such a grave error of judgement would in itself be surprising, but that he should do so having already criticized Racine for having, in his opinion, committed the same crime of irrelevance in a brief section of the narration of one of his play's key events shows a remarkable blindness concerning the limitations of his own dramatic writing.

It also transpired that Diderot had been unwise to criticize the unfortunate Abbé de Bernis in print on the basis of the vague reports he had received, for he wrote in March 1751, the month after the publication of the **Lettre sur les sourds et muets**, in a letter addressed 'à Monsieur B***, Libraire':[23]

> Mais il me revient de tous côtés, dans ma solitude, que Mr. l'abbé de Bernis n'a prétendu blâmer dans ces vers de Racine que le **hors-de-propos**, et non l'image en elle-même. On ajoute que, bien loin de donner sa critique pour nouvelle, il n'a cité les vers dont il s'agit que comme l'exemple le plus connu et par conséquent le plus propre à convaincre de la foiblesse que les grands hommes ont quelquefois de se laisser entraîner au mauvais goût. (Corr. I, 112)

But all of these criticisms of Racine remain fairly minor; what most strikes us is the considerable admiration which Diderot had for his great predecessor. And this admiration took two forms: we might expect that any artist as open-minded as Diderot would respect the sheer genius of one of his most gifted compatriots, and we find examples of this admiration throughout his works, the few reservations merely serving to confirm that his respect was informed and critical rather than a blind following of traditional attitudes. More surprising is the fact that, despite his wish to renew the French theatre by the inauguration of a new genre, Diderot recognized that there were still things to be learned from the great authors of the past; he rejects, not the masterpieces of the classical tradition, but the relevance of that tradition for his own age.

In the second scene of the third act of **Le Père de famille**, Sophie enters with the words: 'Je ne sais où je suis... Je ne sais où je vais...'. Should we see in those words an unconscious reminiscence of **Phèdre** or a conscious hommage to Racine? Either way, they indicate that Racine was too important an influence on Diderot to be lightly cast off or forgotten.

NOTES

1. See **Corr.** I, 209-17. All references to Diderot's correspondence are to the edition by G. Roth and J. Varloot. Other quotations from Diderot's writings are, where possible, from the new Hermann edition of his complete works, but, again where possible, page references are also given for the volumes published by Classiques Garnier, since these remain the editions of Diderot's works which the majority of readers are likely to have most readily to hand. It is also this edition which has been used as a source of reference for those works which have not yet appeared in the Hermann edition. The following system of abbreviations has been used:

    Corr. Correspondance, edited by G. Roth and J. Varloot, 16 vols (Paris, 1955-70).
    DPV **OEuvres complètes,** edited by H. Dieckmann, J. Proust, J. Varloot and others (Paris, 1975-).
    OE **OEuvres esthétiques,** edited by P. Vernière (Paris, 1968).
    OP **OEuvres philosophiques,** edited by P. Vernière (Paris, 1964).
    OR **OEuvres romanesques,** edited by H. Bénac (Paris, 1962).

2. Diderot's attitudes to Molière have been discussed in detail by Adrienne Hytier, 'Diderot and Molière', **Diderot Studies,** 8 (1966), 77-103.

3. **Les Caractères,** I, 54.

4. Racine, **Théâtre complet,** edited by M. Rat (Paris, 1960), pp.299-300.

5. Jacques Chouillet also points out resemblances to another work of Racine, the preface to **Britannicus** (DPV, X, 341, note 27).

6. Daniel Dupêcher, 'Racine à la Comédie Française, 1680-1774', **Revue d'histoire littéraire de la France,** 78 (1978), 190-201 (p.195).

7. Roland Barthes, **Sur Racine** (Paris, 1969), pp.109-10.

8. Russell Pfohl, **Racine's 'Iphigénie': Literary Rehearsal and Tragic Recognition** (Geneva, 1974), p.4.

9. Alain Niderst, **Les Tragedies de Racine: diversité et unité** (Paris, 1975), p.120.

10. This comparison, rather than a comparison between uses of 'fils' or 'fille' in both plays, is more logical, given that in **Iphigénie** it is the daughter who is the potential victim, whilst in **Andromaque** it is the son.

11. Statistics taken from B.C. Freeman and A. Batson, **Concordance du théâtre et**

des poésies de Jean Racine, 2 vols (Ithaca and New York, 1968).

12. Niderst, pp.121-22.

13. **Phèdre**, V.vi, ll.1498-593; **Iphigénie**, V.vi, ll.1731-94.

14. See Jacques Voisine, 'Traduttore, traditore: **L'Extravagance fatale'**, **Diderot Studies**, 10 (1968), 175-86.

15. **Zaïre**, IV.ii.

16. See DPV, X, 394; **OE**, p.312.

17. See also DPV, X, 104 (**Entretiens sur 'Le Fils naturel'**).

18. 'Diderot et le théâtre lyrique: "le nouveau stile" proposé par **Le Neveu de Rameau'**, **Revue de Musicologie**, 64 (1978), 229-52.

19. Igor Stravinsky and Robert Craft, **Dialogues** (London, 1982), p.22.

20. Henry Prunières, **Lully** (Paris, [1909]), p.110.

21. Diderot did once write of **Athalie:** 'C'est le plus beau drame que nous ayons dans notre langue' (**Corr.** XII, 22), but other references to that play are rare.

22. John C. Lapp, **Aspects of Racinian Tragedy** (Toronto, 1955), p.169.

23. Identified by G. Roth as a Monsieur Bauche (**Corr.** I, 111).

ELEVEN

Goldoni in France
L.A. Zaina

The name of Carlo Goldoni, who was born in Venice on 25 February 1707 and there carried out his reform of the Italian theatre (or rather created a new theatre) between 1748 and 1762, is so inextricably linked with his native city that it is easy to forget that the last thirty years of his life were spent in France, at Versailles and in Paris where he died on 6 February 1793. It was in Paris that he began to write his **Mémoires de M. Goldoni, pour servir à l'histoire de sa vie et à celle de son théâtre** which was approved for printing on 20 January 1787. While correcting the proofs, in June or July, Goldoni added the final chapter, and the work was published by Veuve Duchesne in three volumes in mid-August 1787 with a dedication to Louis XVI. The long list of subscribers includes not only the greatest names in France, beginning with the King himself and members of the Royal Family, but also Catherine the Great, the Elector of Saxony and Prince Henry of Prussia, as well as writers and artists and nearly all the most famous actors of the Parisian theatre - an indication of the widespread esteem and affection with which he was regarded.

The **Mémoires**[1] are divided into three parts. The first, which runs from 1707 to 1748, deals with his childhood, youth and early manhood: studies, escapades, journeys, his career as a lawyer, his passion for the theatre manifested from the earliest years, his marriage to a young Genoese lady, Nicoletta Conio, who would be his faithful companion throughout his long life, and the fateful encounter with the actor Medebach which led him to throw up his legal career and dedicate himself entirely to a work he had already initiated with plays such as **La donna di garbo** (1743), namely the creation of a new Italian theatre. The second part, covering the years from 1748 to 1762, gives a detailed account of his plays, much of it taken from the prefaces to the Pasquali edition,[2] of his relationships with actors and impresarios and the public, and also of the battle, waged against him by critics whom he does not deign to name, which led him to accept the invitation to go to Paris to work for the Comédie Italienne. The final part covers his life in France from 1762.

The **Mémoires** are the work of an old man looking back over a very long and complicated career, so it is not surprising that critics have been able to point out a great many inaccuracies and errors of chronology.   Furthermore, it is clear that Goldoni was setting out to present to posterity an ideal portrait of himself as he wished to be remembered.   He relates, from the first page to the last, the vicissitudes of a vocation for the theatre, consistently put before the reader **as** theatre, to the extent sometimes of even using the form of a scene in a play.   This, however, in no way invalidates the general truth of the work, whether in the portrait of the man or in the events which he relates.   He is not writing a diary but composing a narrative:

> I protagonisti dei **Mémoires** [writes Siro Ferroni] sono persone e cose normali, anche se ingrandite, e non idee superiori.   [...] Goldoni rifiuta ogni meccanica riproduzione della vita.   Tutti gli episodi che popolano i **Mémoires** testimoniano un continuo rispetto delle proporzioni naturali nei rapporti fra persone e cose, tra azioni ed effetti; solo che ovunque c'è poi l'ingrandimento di un dettaglio caratteristico.[3]

The third part presents a convincing and informative picture of Goldoni's relationship with the theatre in Paris and of life in both capital and court as seen by a kindly, detached observer who never tired of the spectacle of other people's lives and activities.   Together with Goldoni's correspondence, it provides the basic text for the matter of the present essay.

The invitation to Paris, offered by the chief actor and manager (**capo-comico**) of the French Comédie Italienne, was probably prompted by the success obtained by a Goldoni scenario, **Il figlio d'Arlecchino perduto e ritrovato,** when it was performed in Paris in July 1761.   Its topical appeal, mingling the comic with the pathetic, in the new climate of **sensibilité** made its author a likely candidate to bring back audiences at a time when that theatre was having difficulties.   Why Goldoni should have accepted is a more complex question.   Although he had established a European reputation for his comedies, which had gone a long way towards converting the old **commedia dell'arte** tradition to a new, more realistic and moralistic theatre, he had obtained neither financial ease nor the universal respect of his fellow Venetians.   The latter case was particularly acute, his last year in Venice poisoned by the 'esprit mordant et belliqueux'[4] of Carlo Gozzi who first pilloried him in a satirical almanach, **La tartana degli influssi per l'anno bisestile 1756** (1757), followed it up with further missiles directed against the bad taste and inferior style of would-be reformers and finally attacked him on his own ground by rivalling him as a playwright:

> io m'impegnava di cagionare maggior concorso delle sue orditure colla fiaba dell'**Amore alle** [sic] **tre melaranze,** racconto delle nonne a'lor nipotini, ridotta a scenica rappresentazione.[5]

The attendant circumstances, the novelty and sheer verve of the play ensured that Gozzi was amply vindicated.   Throughout the 1761-62 season, while some of Goldoni's best plays were appearing, such as the **Villegiatura** trilogy and **Le baruffe chiozzote,** Gozzi produced further **fiabe** with considerable success, bringing back the **commedia dell'arte** masks which Goldoni had succeeded in banishing.

Unlike Gozzi, Goldoni was a peace-loving man with no stomach for direct attack on his enemies and he was seeing the reform for which he had laboured unremittingly over the years apparently slipping away.   On the other hand, he had a contract to provide plays exclusively for the San Luca theatre until the 1766-67 season and he had obligations towards his patron, the Duke of Parma.   The financial situation seems to have tipped the balance: 'si on vouloit m'assurer un état à Venise, soit à titre d'emploi, soit à titre de pension, je préférerois ma Patrie à tout l'Univers'.[6]   The terms of the invitation (which reached him in August 1761) were rather vague: he was not called upon to direct the company, but simply to collaborate with it; the contract was for two years, with travelling expenses to and from Venice, and an annual salary of six thousand **livres.**   He might have compared this sum with the fifteen thousand which a leading actor could expect, but his immediate reaction, expressed on 5 September in a letter to his friend Albergati,[7] was enthusiastic: 'Oh che bella novità le recchera questa lettera!   Goldoni va a Parigi, e partirà, a Dio piacendo, nella ventura quaresima'.[8]   On 2 March 1762, he signed an agreement with the San Luca, undertaking to complete his contract on returning to Venice and meanwhile to send each year, from time to time, a new comedy.   He bade farewell to the Venetian public in the last play of the season, **Una delle ultime sere di Carnovale,** on Shrove Tuesday 1762, moved to tears by their enthusiasm and good wishes for his safe journey and return.   After that, he was able to concentrate on making all the necessary family and business arrangements for his departure.   He finally left Venice, probably on 22 April 1762 (not 1761 as he writes in the **Mémoires**), with his wife and young nephew Antonio, aged fifteen.

The journey was a leisurely one; he had to call on friends and patrons in Bologna, where he fell ill, Modena, Parma, Cortemaggiore (summer residence of the dowager duchess of Parma), and Piacenza, and on his wife's relations in Genoa.   The journey from Genoa to Nice by boat was delayed by storms so that it was not until the end of July that he finally set foot on French soil, invoking the shade of Molière.   From Nice the party had travelled overland; the first night in France was spent at Vidauban and then they went on to Marseilles to visit the Venetian consul who was brother to Goldoni's friends Gabriele and Giovanni Cornet.   They stayed there six days before leaving for Avignon and Lyons.   At Lyons, not surprisingly, there was a reproachful letter from Francesco Zanuzzi, the **capo comico** in Paris;   only then, it seems, did Goldoni begin to have misgivings.   He had not bothered to hurry because payment was not to begin until he reached Paris, but now he heard for the first time of the fusion of the Comédiens Italiens with the Opéra Comique which had taken place in February 1762, with the result that 'le nouveau genre l'emportoit sur l'ancien, et les Italiens, qui faisoient la base de ce Théâtre, n'étoient plus que les accessoires du Spectacle' (**M.**, II, i, 13).   His native optimism prevented him from envisaging too clearly the disadvantages of such a situation, so he continued his journey with unabated enjoyment.   At Villejuif, Zanuzzi and the **première actrice** met the Goldonis to escort them to Paris to an apartment in the Faubourg Saint-Denis where they also lived.   It was 26 August 1762.   They were treated that very evening to a brilliant supper party with members of the company which they enjoyed in spite of their fatigue.

Although he had arrived late, Goldoni was in no hurry to begin his assignment with the Comédie Italienne.   First of all he wished to visit the most brilliant city in Europe and this he insisted on doing on foot in spite of the extreme heat of that summer.   Walking was to remain his favourite way of moving about for thus, as in Venice, he could observe the life going on around him.   On that first day he was quite overcome by the beauty of the Tuileries gardens, by the majesty of the Seine with its great bridges, by the streets crowded with carriages, and by the clamour.   There are many pages in the **Mémoires** where he brings before us not only the outward aspects of the city, for example the Boulevards which were his favourite walk, or the Palais-Royal, but also many trivial details which make up the small coin of daily life, for example the various means of transport, the postal service and the fire brigade. Vittorio Alfieri, who arrived in Paris for the first time in 1767, comments on the filth and malodorousness of the streets and the meanness of the buildings among other aspects of Paris which repelled him, but Goldoni was a more tolerant observer with wider human sympathies and more varied interests - as well, of course, as having no desire to offend his French hosts.   To the end of his days, he continued to enjoy the varied spectacle which the city provided, and to those who criticized Paris he replied: 'vous serez bien ici ou vous serez mal partout' (**M.**, II, xix, 91).

However, Goldoni had not come as a sight-seer but on business, so that first hot walk ended with a visit to the Duc d'Aumont who had been responsible for the invitation to Paris in his capacity as Premier Gentilhomme de la Chambre du Roi in charge of spectacles for that year.   But before Goldoni could begin to work for the company, he needed to get to know his actors, their qualities and defects, and also to get them to understand his ideas.   There were nine of them in all.   The traditional masks were: Charles Bertinazzi, known as Carlin, an Arlequin famous for his **lazzi** and brilliant improvisation but now getting on in years; Camille Veronese, the **soubrette**, a brilliant young actress who had revealed her quality in the 1761 production of Goldoni's

Il figlio d'Arlecchino perduto e ritrovato (she died in 1768 at the age of thirty-three); Collalto, the Pantalon, whom Goldoni had known since 1750 when he took the place of Darbes in Medebach's company in Venice; Alessandro Luigi Chiavarelli, a Neapolitan who played Brighella-Scapin for thirty years from 1739; Frederico Rubini, the Doctor, who would leave in 1764.   The serious characters were: Zanuzzi, the **premier amoureux;** Antonio Balletti, the **second amoureux;** Elena Savi, the **première actrice,** who had acted at the San Samuel and the San Giovanni Grisostomo theatres in Venice (she too died young, in April 1766); Anna Maria Piccinelli, known as La Francesina, the **seconde actrice.**   Goldoni went at once to see the **opéra comique,** 'ce mélange singulier de prose et d'ariettes', and although his first reaction was to consider this genre a monstrosity, he came round to the view that 'puisqu'on doit dans l'Opéra Comique se passer de règles et de vraisemblance, il vaut mieux entendre un dialogue bien récité, que souffrir la monotonie d'un récitatif enuyeux' (**M.,** II, ii, 16).   He also attended the performances of the Italiens and could not but be aware that, whereas the theatre was crowded for the Opéra Comique, it was almost deserted for the Italiens. He attributed this to the fact that they were still tied to the **commedia dell'arte** routine which he hoped to reform as he had done in Italy.   He moved to an apartment in the Rue Comtesse d'Artois near the Hôtel de Bourgogne so as to be near his actors.

The response of the company to Goldoni's ideas for renewal was less than enthusiastic.   The serious actors were prepared to consider them, but the **maschere,** 'habitués à ne rien apprendre par cœur, avoient l'ambition de briller sans se donner la peine d'étudier' (**M.,** II, iii, 19) and were unwilling to exchange their long experience of improvisation on the basis of a scenario for dependance on an author's written text. Goldoni asked for four months in which to get to know the taste of the Parisian public; he tells us that 'je ne fis pendant ce tems-là que voir, que courir, que me promener, que jouir' (**M.,** II, iii, 19).   When the court moved to Fontainebleau, the Italiens had to go too to provide entertainment and Goldoni followed them.   He was able to see the Royal Family and the Court every day at Mass, at the hunt and elsewhere, and found Fontainebleau very restful after Paris.   The troupe presented **L'Enfant d'Arlequin perdu et retrouvé** which had been such a success in 1761 in Paris, but it fell absolutely flat because, as it was a **pièce à sujet,** the actors had introduced some ribaldries from Molière's **Le Cocu imaginaire** which displeased the Court.   This experience made Goldoni all the more determined to press his reform: 'Voilà l'inconvénient des Comédies à sujet.   L'Acteur qui joue de sa tête, parle quelquefois à tort et à travers, gâte une scene et fait tomber une Piece' (**M.,** II, iii, 20-21).   He had reckoned, however, without the actors and the situation in which he found himself: 'je n'avois pas affaire à mes Comédiens d'Italie, je n'étois pas le maître ici comme je l'étois chez moi' (**M.**, II, iii, 21).

On his return to Paris from Fontainebleau, Goldoni moved again to an apartment which looked out on the Palais-Royal, adopting a regular routine of work in the morning (interrupted by the endless interest and distraction provided by the characters and the activities of the Palais-Royal) and socializing during the rest of the day. The actors remained divided in their views, but Goldoni got them to agree that the first play by an author of his reputation must be **dialogué,** though he realized that the subject would have to be very simple. The result was a comedy in three acts, **L'Amour paternel, ou la Suivante reconnaissante.** In a letter to Francesco Albergati of 13 December 1762 (**L.,** II, xc, 54), he complains that the actors are 'des paresseux' because they have still not managed to learn their parts, and speaks of their 'mobilità' and 'negligenza'. He had hoped to put on the play at Christmas, but a letter to Albergati of 24 January 1763 (**L.,** II, xci, 55) tells us that it still had not been shown because the **soubrette** had fallen ill and the **prima donna** had had a baby. In fact we learn from a letter to his editor Giambattista Pasquali of 14 February 1763 (**L.,** II, xcii, 58) that it eventually appeared on 4 February. There was a summary in French for the benefit of those who might find it difficult to follow the Italian dialogue. This letter and others suggest that the play was quite successful, but there were only four performances and in the **Mémoires** Goldoni tells us that he felt like leaving Paris forthwith.[9] However, he was bound by a two-year contract and he very much wanted to stay in Paris, so he decided to make the best of a bad job; the actors wanted only scenarios and the public seemed to expect this. He goes on to say that in the space of two years he produced twenty-four plays of this kind. There are many complaints in his correspondence about the limitations of his actors, and he expresses a bitterness at the situation in which he finds himself which does not appear in the **Mémoires.** Yet, in a sense, this was also a challenge to the ingenuity of the man of the theatre in making use of the means at his disposal in such a way as not to belie his reputation.

In a letter to Albergati of 18 April 1763, he describes a comedy made of 'molte scene, brevi, frizzanti, animati da una perpetua azione, da un movimento continuo, onde i Comici non abbiano a far altro che esseguire più coll'azione, che colle parole' (**L.,** II, xcvii, 64). This was the scenario **L'Eventail,** now lost, which Goldoni later turned into **Il ventaglio,** performed in Venice in February 1765.[10] In this same letter, he described the difficulties he had to face from the point of view of language. Arlequin and Scapin by this time used French but the other characters Italian. So long as all depended on gesture, movement and incident, this did not matter very much. French women, he tells us, had deserted the Italiens because of the language problem so they must be wooed back with novelties, spectacle, a great deal of French and the introduction of French characters. **L'Eventail** was not the success that he had hoped; it proved too demanding for his actors. It was not until September 1763 that Goldoni at last obtained an outstanding success, of the kind that he desired, with **Les Amours d'Arlequin et de Camille.** This time he used a different formula inspired by the **comédie larmoyante** which was all the rage in the new climate of **sensibilité.** The **Mercure de France** in its October number commented:

> On ne sauroit croire combien dans un Sujet si simple il y a de beautés du vrai genre de la Comédie. Rien n'est si riche d'incidents et chacun sort naturellement et presque nécessairement de celui qui le précède. - Dans tout le Drame, le pathétique de la Nature et le Comique le plus plaisant sont tellement assortis et mêlés ensemble, qu'ils ne sont jamais disparates et produisent chacun leur effet sans se détruire.[11]

Goldoni himself writes to Albergati:

> A questa mia [commedia] hanno riso, ed hanno pianto con egual piacere. Il comico li ha divertiti e l'interesse li ha penetrati, e questo nuovo genere li ha incantati. (**L.**, II, viii, 81)

To Voltaire on 13 October, in a letter to accompany two copies of the fifth volume of the Pasquali edition of his works, he expresses his satisfaction:

> Mi è riuscito di colpire finalmente nel gusto universale della nazione. **Les amours d'Arlequin et de Camille** hanno incontrato a Parigi quanto le più fortunate in Italia. (**L.**, II, cix, 83)

In November he followed this up with a sequel, **La Jalousie d'Arlequin,** with the promise of another to complete the trilogy. This was **L'Inquiétude de Camille,** produced on 20 December 1763. The **Mercure de France** of January 1764 says of it:

> Le pathétique en est si naturellement lié au comique, qui naît de la naiveté des deux Personnages intéressants, que le cœur est incessamment partagé entre deux sentiments opposés; mais qui par un art qu'on ne sauroit trop admirer se réunissent pour le plaisir continuel du Spectateur.[12]

Although Goldoni was now able to feel that he had vindicated his reputation, he was still dissatisfied and uncertain of the future. He writes to Albergati on 10 January 1764:

> Non è ch'io non ami Parigi, ma mi pare di essere fuori del mio centro, ed è assai dificile [sic] di continuar a piacere, senza farmi intender col Dialogo ed a forza di situazioni, o ridicole, o patetiche, o interessanti. La cosa è troppo faticosa, e troppo incerta e poi la prosunzione [sic] de'Comici, de'quali non mi posso servire, non lascia di darmi delle inquietudini. (**L.**, II, cxc, 92)

In his introduction to a new edition of **Il ventaglio,** Luigi Lunari suggests that perhaps the actors were right after all and that the only kind of Italian theatre possible in Paris was the traditional **commedia dell'arte** for as long as it could find a public. 'Che senso poteva avere', he asks, 'una commedia di carattere o di costume, psicologica e realistica, ispirata alla realtà contemporanea nata e recitata in italiano a Parigi?'.[13]   As we have seen from his letters, Goldoni was fully aware of these difficulties and used all his ingenuity to circumvent them, to reconcile his desire for realism with what was expected of him. He situates his comedy, for example, amongst Italians resident in Paris, strives to use a language which will be accessible to non-native speakers and puts the emphasis on plot and action rather than speech.   An unfortunate result of Goldoni's success in pleasing the public, from the point of view of his reputation, was that in France he came to be considered as a modernizer of the **commedia dell'arte** rather than as the originator of an important reform of the theatre. Grimm, in his **Correspondance littéraire** of 1 September 1764, sees Goldoni as a master of the **imbroglio,** and Diderot took the same view.   Goldoni quotes him as writing: 'Charles Goldoni a composé une soixantaine de Farces' (**M.**, II, v, 27).   This was in the **Discours sur la poésie dramatique** of 1758.   As Lunari points out, it is no accident that the best play of Goldoni's Parisian period should be **Le Bourru bienfaisant,** written in French and acted by the Comédie Française.

Goldoni lost no time in acquainting himself with the French theatre.   The first play he saw at the Comédie Française was **Le Misanthrope** which he considered Molière's best play:

> Pièce d'une perfection sans égale qui, indépendamment de la régularité de sa marche et de ses beautés de détail, avoit le mérite de l'invention et de la nouveauté des caractères. [...] Molière fut le premier qui osât jouer les mœurs et les ridicules de son siecle et de son pays.
>
> (**M.**, II, v, 25)

He greatly admired actors such as Le Kain, Molé and Préville,   and the acting technique of the Comédie Française.   On emerging from this performance, he was filled with the desire to write a comedy in French which would be performed by these actors.   He next went to see Diderot's **Le Père de famille;**   Diderot's first **drame bourgeois, Le Fils naturel** (1757) had been clearly shown by Fréron to owe a great deal to Goldoni's **Il vero amico** - this was the origin of Diderot's animus against Goldoni. **Le Père de famille** has the same title as a Goldoni play but there the resemblance ends, as Goldoni points out;   Diderot's father is harsh and unforgiving: 'C'est un de ces êtres malheureux qui existent dans la nature, mais je n'aurois jamais osé l'exposer sur la scène' (**M.**, II, v, 27).   This comment is, of course, an indication of the limits of Goldoni's realism.   Goldoni went out of his way to visit Diderot to try to gain his friendship, without success.

It is interesting to see Goldoni's reactions to the performances of the Opéra Français. His first experience was not a happy one; he found the singers difficult to hear and kept on waiting for the arias to liven things up but found that it all seemed like the recitative in an Italian opera. He admired the theatre, the **mise en scène,** the ballets which were interspersed with the action, but when asked how he had liked it replied with undiplomatic candour: 'c'est le paradis des yeux c'est l'enfer des oreilles' (**M.,** II, vi, 31).   Rameau's **Castor et Pollux** pleased him more, but he considered Rameau's greatness to lie rather with his instrumental music. Goldoni, of course, had an expert knowledge of the requirements of opera, having written more than sixty libretti which had been set to music by the foremost composers of his time.   The operatic scene in Paris was changed by the arrival of Glück in 1773; it was the successful production of Niccolo Piccinni's **Orlando** in 1778 (he too had come to Paris at the end of 1776 and stayed until 1789) which precipitated the battle of the Glückistes, Piccinnistes and Ramistes.   There is an allusion to this later in the **Mémoires** (**M.,** II, xxvii, 122-23), but unfortunately Goldoni broke off in mid-sentence because of an attack of the palpitations to which he was subject, and did not take the matter up again.

Another musical experience was that of the **concert spirituel,** concerts which had been instituted in 1762 and which took place at the Tuileries at Eastertide and on feast days when the Opéra was closed.   They were both vocal and instrumental: psalms, hymns, oratorios, motets and symphonies executed by the best that Europe could provide. Goldoni comments on the fact that the vocal items had originally been in Latin:

> mais la prononciation Françoise est si différente de celle des autres nations, que l'Etranger le plus habile et le plus agréable se rendroit ridicule à Paris, s'il s'exposoit à chanter un Motet Latin.   (**M**, II, viii, 33)

- so everyone sang in Italian! Later, French texts were also introduced.

The focal point of Goldoni's social life was the group of friends, nine in all, who called themselves the Dominicaux, because they met on Sundays. Each one in turn received the members for dinner in his home. They were: Pierre-Antoine de La Place, editor of the **Mercure de France,** Philippe Bridard Lagarde, the drama critic for the same, Bernard-Joseph Saurin, dramatist and member of the Académie Française, Antoine Louis, **secrétaire perpétuel** of the Académie Royale de Chirurgie, the Abbé Joseph de La Porte, journalist and writer of compilations, the novelist Crébillon fils, the dramatist Charles-Simon Favart and a certain Monsieur Jouen. Of this last, Goldoni wrote that he 'ne brilloit pas par l'esprit, mais il se distinguoit par la délicatesse de sa table' (**M.,** II, v, 29). This would appear to be his only claim to fame.

La Place and Favart were to remain Goldoni's friends into extreme old age. In a letter of 4 January 1764, to Count Durazzo in Vienna, Favart speaks in glowing terms of 'notre divin Goldoni':

> Nous nous voyons très souvent. Il est d'une petite société de gens de lettres, dont il fait l'ornement; c'est un génie intarissable et qui produit souvent du nouveau. [...] Goldoni [...] est d'une modestie si simple que l'on seroit tenté de croire qu'il ne connoît pas ce qu'il vaut.[14]

Goldoni wrote with similar warmth in dedicating to him **Un curioso accidente** in Volume VII of the Pasquali edition (1764). On 18 April 1768, he writes, thanking Favart for a present of his play **Les Moissonneurs:**[15] 'Votre imagination m'a enchanté, votre morale m'a ravi, vos sentimens m'ont touché' (**L.**, II, cli, 151). He even wishes that he could celebrate his glory in verse, but admits that his attempts to write poetry in French have been a dismal failure. Only one woman succeeded in penetrating this all-male coterie, Sophie Arnould. In the dedication to Favart, Goldoni alludes to 'l'unica Sorella nostra Domenicale'[16] but he does not mention her by name in the **Mémoires.** Other close literary friends of Goldoni were Marmontel and Dorat.

*   *

*

Goldoni's two years with the Théâtre Italien were drawing to a close, to his undisguised relief. From the end of 1763, his letters, particularly to Francesco Albergati, reflect his state of indecision about what should be the next step. He was not only weary of his actors with their quarrels among themselves (Camille the brilliant **soubrette** gave in her notice in March 1764, but she must have withdrawn it as she was still with them when her death in 1768 dealt the Comédie Italienne a heavy blow), but his work for the Court was not satisfying either, as his comedies had to be shortened to fit into a strict time schedule - the King must not be made late for his **souper.** In a letter of 6 April 1764, he refers to his worsening relationship with his actors, but the intervention of the Gentilshommes de la Chambre gave him the whip-hand: 'Devono essi [the actors] dipendere da me in tutto quello che riguarda alle mie Commedie, alla distribuzione delle parti e cose simili' (**L.**, II, cxx, 103). So he no longer felt in the position of having to leave Paris. He would not have been unwilling to return to Venice, but the vituperative attacks against him by the acrimonious Baretti[17] in his **La frusta letteraria**[18] made the prospect less attractive in spite of his nostalgia for his native city. He succeeded in getting released from his obligations even before Easter 1765; in a letter to Albergati of 18 February he writes:

dubito che una stella, levatasi novellamente su quest'orizzonte, voglia
qui fissare il mio soggiorno per più lungo tempo; non pero nella
dipendenza dei Commedianti.   (L., II, cxxx, 116)

Indeed, Goldoni was never again to find himself in that position of dependence which
he had found so irksome.   He expresses his relief in tones of great excitement in a
letter to his friend Gabriele Cornet of 24 February:

> La novità ch'io vi reco con questa lettera è cosi bella, cosi nuova, cosi
> inaspettata [...] la sorte mi vuole ancora a Parigi; la Provvidenza mi ha
> fatto segno de'suoi benefizi, e Dio mi ha liberato dai Comedianti.
>   (L., II, cxxxii, 118)

Both the **Mémoires** and his letters give details of what Goldoni regarded as a
providential solution to his problems.   He had made the acquaintance of Mademoiselle
Sylvestre, Reader to the Dauphine Marie-Josephe de Saxe: 'je lui avois parlé de mon
attachement pour Paris et du regret avec lequel je me voyois forcé de
l'abandonner' (M., II, vii, 35).   Mademoiselle Sylvestre mentioned the matter to the
Dauphine who at once hit on a way of helping him: let him be appointed teacher of
Italian at Court.   Her own children (later to be Louis XVI, Louis XVIII and Charles X)
were as yet too young, but Mesdames de France, Louis XV's unmarried daughters, had
already learnt some Italian and might be happy to continue.   In fact, he became a
teacher of Italian to the eldest, Madame Adélaïde.   These lessons were to take place
for two to three hours in the morning, originally for three days a week and then for
five days as his pupil proved so enthusiastic.   By the beginning of April, Madame
Louise had also decided to take lessons, so Goldoni taught for two hours after lunch as
well.   While he was still living in Paris, a carriage was sent to fetch him and took him
home. Goldoni's letters are full of naïve pleasure at the good fortune that has befallen
him and he is dazzled by the prospect of close contact with members of the Royal
Family:

> E sempre un onore l'essere servitore del Re di Francia, e della Famiglia
> Reale, ma l'esserlo cosi davvicino, che ogni giorno si vedano dappresso le
> persone Reali, e una contentezza, che anima e consola [...].   Chi mai
> poteva sognarsi, ch'io sarei un giorno in un Gabinetto colla Primogenita
> del Re di Francia, e ch'ella mi avrebbe comandato di sedere alla sua
> presenza?   (L., II, cxxxii, 119).

After the years of insecurity, he felt that at last he was in a position to live out the
rest of his life decorously and to make adequate provision for the future of his wife,
his nephew, and even his niece left behind in Venice.   After six months, he was given a
flat in the Château itself, apparently a rare honour for a foreigner.   He wrote to
Albergati on 3 May 1765 that it was 'comodo, bello, in buona veduta e bene
accomodato' (L., II, cxxxv, 125).   To Cornet on 13 May he wrote:

> A Versaglies ho avuto un bello e comodo appartamento in Corte, c'est à
> dire dans le château même, attenant à la Galerie des Princes, con bella
> veduta sopra la grande Rue de la Surintendance, di quattro camere, una
> cucina, ed un bel gabinetto, e tutto bene mobiliato con letti ottimi.
> (**L.**, II, cxxxvi, 128-29)

The address was: 'Versailles, dans le Château, au second escalier, attenant à la galerie des Princes, au fond du Corridor. N.107.' His lodging seems to have been better than that of some of the courtiers who froze in winter and roasted in summer in the attics of the palace.

It is characteristic of Goldoni that he should have made no attempt to discover what his emoluments would be.   In the **Mémoires,** he says:

> Aucun traitement ne me fut proposé, Je n'en demandai aucun;   trop
> glorieux d'un emploi si honorable, et très-sûr des bontés de mes Augustes
> écolieres.   (**M.**, II, vii, 36)

To Cornet he wrote on 24 February 1765:

> Non so ancora quali saranno i miei appuntamenti, perchè io non ho voluto
> dimandare, ma sanno lo stato mio, e il mio bisogno, e la Dolfina ha detto
> a una Dama della sua Corte: **Il ne manquera de rien.** Credo di dovermi
> intieramente fidare ad una si gran Principessa.   (**L.**, II, cxxxii, 119)

Bachaumont reports on 22 March 1765 that he has been given '2000 écus d'appointemens'[19] but Goldoni does not mention this.   On the contrary, he seems to have been in financial straits and he was grateful when he was able to retain the pension paid to him by the Duke of Parma after the latter's death on 17 July 1765. When the Court was plunged into mourning by the death of the Dauphin on 20 December 1765, so that for the moment there was no question of Italian lessons, he writes:

> mes finances alloient mal; j'avois eu une gratification de cent louis sur le
> Trésor Royal mais c'étoit pour une fois;   j'avois besoin de tout, et je
> n'osois rien demander.   (**M.**, II, ix, 46)

He also lost his flat because, as it had been meant for the Dauphine's **accoucheur,** it was no longer at her disposal.   Goldoni did not feel that he could intrude with his problems: 'il n'étoit pas décent que j'allasse porter des plaintes ni demander protection' (**M.**, II, ix, 46).   So he moved out and found a lodging in the town.   The Court was destined to remain in mourning: on 23 February 1766, the Queen's father, Stanislaus, formerly King of Poland, died at Nancy;   on 13 March 1767, the Dauphine followed her husband to the grave and on 24 June 1768, Queen Marie Leszczynska also died.   However, Goldoni had been called back into service on 26 May 1766, and Mesdames made him a present of 'cent louis dans une boîte d'or ciselée' (**M.**, II, ix, 47) and promised that they would try to make his position secure by getting him nominated Instituteur d'Italien des Enfants de France, with appropriate emoluments. They asked for 'six mille livres par an.' In fact, it was not until January 1769 that Goldoni was eventually accorded an annual pension of 4000 **livres** and this was whittled down to 3600 because the treasury withheld 400 **livres** in tax. He comments: 'Si j'avois parlé, j'étois dans le cas, peutêtre, de l'exemption de cet impôt; je ne dis mot; je suis resté là, toujours là' (**M.**, II, ix, 48). He was satisfied with the conditions of his life and with the prospect at some future date of teaching any young princes there might be.

There are a vast number of memoirs and letters which portray the life of the Court under Louis XV and Louis XVI, but the account given by Goldoni is one of peculiar interest because it shows the Royal Family in a much more human light than we find elsewhere. Goldoni was a foreigner and as such stood outside cabals and intrigues (he does not even seem to have been aware of them), he was not a courtier and had no interests to advance. All he ever asked for was a modest livelihood for himself and some kind of employment for his nephew. Madame Adélaïde succeeded in getting Antonio nominated Professeur d'Italien at the Ecole Royale Militaire and, when that post was suppressed, he was attached to the Bureau de la Guerre as an interpreter and remained there until the Revolution. Goldoni's royal pupils had no fear of unseemly ambition or indiscretion on his part and so treated him with unwonted familiarity and extreme kindness. Favart, in a letter to Count Durazzo of 5 March 1765,[20] gives a lively account, which presumably he had from Goldoni himself (it differs slightly from the one in the **Mémoires**), of how, when he was introduced into her apartment, he took the Dauphine for a **femme de chambre** much to her amusement; Madame Adélaïde, when making the arrangements for her lessons, assured him that if he had 'quelque occupation plus sérieuse' all he needed to do was to let her know. Madame Adélaïde is usually represented as a rather dour character with an overweening sense of the respect due to her rank, as, for example, in the **Mémoires** of Madame de Campan.[21] That is not the impression that emerges from Goldoni's **Mémoires**. It has been suggested that Goldoni wished to flatter or at least not to offend his royal patrons (the King took out fifty subscriptions to the **Mémoires**), but the same holds good for the incidents he relates in his private correspondence.

Madame Adélaïde's kindness is shown in the episode which took place towards the beginning of his office when, in the carriage on the way to Versailles, while reading (of all things) Rousseau's **Lettres de la montagne,** he suddenly went almost completely blind. He went up for his lesson in a state of great agitation, hoping that he would be able to teach as usual, but when he opened the book he found that he could not read at all and had to relate what had happened. Madame went into action at once:

elle fait chercher dans sa chambre des eaux salutaires pour la vue; elle permet que je bassine mes yeux;   elle fait arranger les rideaux de manière qu'il ne reste qu'un petit jour pour distinguer les objets, ma vue revient petit à petit, j'y vois peu mais j'y vois assez.   (**M.**, II, vii, 37)

He wanted to go on with the lesson, but Madame insisted on sending him home and getting him treated by her own doctor.   He recovered the use of his right eye but was blind in the left eye for the rest of his days - a great inconvenience when playing cards, a pastime he loved and for which he had ample opportunity at Versailles.   It seems to have been a haemorrhage of the retina.   Another episode which shows the unaffected kindness of Madame Adélaïde took place at Marly.   On her way to dinner, seeing Goldoni, she said: 'A tantôt'.   As in Italian **tantosto** means immediately, Goldoni assumed she wanted her lesson at once after dinner, and just waited, although he had not yet eaten.   He was not summoned eventually until four o'clock.   Madame began by asking, as apparently she usually did, where he had dined that day.   To her astonishment Goldoni replied: 'Aucune part'.   '- Comment, dit-elle, vous n'avez pas dîné? - Non, Madame. - Etes-vous malade? - Non. - Pourquoi donc n'avez-vous pas dîné?' (**M.**, II, viii, 40).   When he had explained, she laughed, closed her book and sent him off to dine.

When the Court moved from Versailles to one of the other royal palaces, the Goldoni family went too, for Mesdames kept up their programme of lessons.   Goldoni delighted in Marly because of the beauty of the gardens and the closer proximity to the Court than in the vast stretches of Versailles.   His wife Nicoletta had already been presented to Madame Adélaïde at Versailles and kept in conversation for half an hour (this must have been in Italian as she never learnt to speak French);   at Marly, they were received by the Dauphin and his wife and the four princesses, to Nicoletta's confusion but, he writes to Gabriel Cornet on 13 May 1765, 'la bontà e la dolcezza di queste Reali persone l'hanno confortata' (**L.**, II, cxxxvii, 129).   Goldoni and Antonio were told that they might go down to the saloon to take part in the gaming (from the **Mémoires** (**M.**, II, viii, 39) we learn that he even played at the King's table) while Nicoletta watched from the balcony above, from which the splendid scene of Court and royalty could be observed.   When they returned two hours later, they found Madame Adélaïde and the Comtesse de Narbonne (her lady-in-waiting, formerly in the service of Madame Elizabeth,   Duchess of Parma) leaning over the balustrade and talking to Nicoletta in Italian.   He exclaims: 'Figuratevi come stava questa povera donnetta, e come le batteva il cuore fra il piacere e la soggezione' (**L.**, II, cxxxvi, 129).   So Nicoletta was not always kept in the background as some biographers have suggested.[22]   The cantata which Goldoni composed and had set to music for the

Dauphine affords another glimpse of royal family life and, incidentally, of the indulgence shown to his ignorance of Court etiquette. The Dauphine invited him to hear it executed after supper, so at ten o'clock he presented himself at the door and was allowed to go through and stand while they were still at supper. When asked if he had his **entrées du soir,** he said that he did not know that there was any difference between the 'entrées du jour' and 'du soir' and explained that the Dauphine herself had asked him to come up after supper, so he had arrived in good time. He was allowed to stay and then later was called in:

> Madame la Dauphine touchoit du clavecin, Madame Adélaïde accompagnoit avec le violon, et c'étoit Mademoiselle Hardy (aujourd'hui Madame de la Brusse) qui chantoit. La musique fit plaisir, et l'on fit à l'Auteur des paroles des complimens que je reçus très modestement. Je voulois sortir, Monsieur le Dauphin eut la bonté de me faire rester; il chanta lui-même, et j'eus le bonheur de l'entendre. (**M.**, II, viii, 41)

What he sang seemed prophetic - a doleful air from an oratorio entitled **Le Pélerin au Sépulcre.**

In a letter to Albergati of 18 March 1765, Goldoni gives an interesting account of his teaching method, an essentially practical one which seems extremely modern. As the time allowed was quite lengthy, it was divided into four: first of all, the reading of an Italian text without translation, paying attention to pronunciation - the first text chosen being Muratori's **Annali,** an excellent example of plain contemporary prose, rather than a Trecento or Renaissance author; there followed a comparison of French and Italian grammatical usage from Goldoni's written notes - Madame having to translate these observations into French for the next day (they even planned to publish them 'cosa che le piace infinitamente'); the third part was taken up with the reading and oral translation of one of his own comedies 'in che ella si diverte moltissimo'; finally, there was practice in speaking and writing Italian. The Duke of Parma sent a present of two hundred volumes of the best Italian authors for the use of his sisters-in-law. Madame Adélaïde went out of her way on a number of occasions to express her satisfaction with her mentor and she seems to have acquired a good knowledge of Italian. Goldoni tells us that the little French he knew was acquired during the three years of lessons with Mesdames:

> elles lisoient les Pöetes et les Prosateurs Italiens: je bégayois une mauvaise traduction en François; elles la répétoient avec grâce, avec élégance, et le Maître apprenoit plus qu'il ne pouvoit enseigner.
> (**M.**, II, viii, 40)

Goldoni derived much innocent pleasure from hob-nobbing with the great, but this was not at any time a source of pride, and he was well aware that the favour he enjoyed might be short-lived.   Certainly, it did not solve his financial problems, as we have seen.   He became genuinely attached to his royal patrons, sharing their griefs as well as their pleasures.   He repeats on two occasions: 'J'étois à la Cour, et je n'étois pas courtisan' (**M.**, II, vii, 36, and ix, 48).   As a foreigner, he felt that he had no cause for complaint and he had made no attempt to profit by his position:

> Pourquoi aurois-je brigué des emplois, des charges, des commissions, qui de droit auroient mieux convenu à un national qu'à un étranger? Je n'ai jamais demandé de grâces pour moi ni pour mon neveu, que dans le cas où un Italien pouvoit être préférable à un François.   (**M.**, II, ix, 48)

He finally achieved the relative security of a regular pension at the moment when Mesdames decided to turn their attention to other studies, but that did not affect the pension and there was the expectation of being called back into service.   He stayed on in Versailles for some time because he enjoyed it and all the pastimes which were easily accessible and he had made many friends (whose names he withholds lest he be accused of vanity).

During the years when he had been free of the yoke of the **comici** he had not ceased to think of the theatre.   He had made the most of opportunities offered by performances at Court;[23] he continued to oversee the Pasquali edition of his works and to correspond with Albergati on theatrical matters;   he wrote him a detailed criticism of his play **L'amor finto,** which he feared might be too harsh (**L.**, II, cxlvi, 142-45).   He was also asked by the Gentilshommes de la Chambre to try to persuade the Arlecchino Sacchi to come to Paris to the Théâtre Italien.   The letter to Albergati on the subject is interesting because of the exact details it gives of the terms and conditions which were offered: the return fare, two to three thousand **lire** for the first year, according to reputation and ability;   if he pleased the public, he was at once accepted for a second year on half or three-quarter pay, and after a suitable interval, 'secondo il merito', on full pay, fourteen thousand **lire** in French money, and a life pension of a thousand **lire** after fifteen years' service (**L.**, II, cxxxvii, 131).   It was the lure of the theatre which took him back to Paris in 1770 for 'les Spectacles qui ne brillent qu'à Paris' (**M.**, II, ix, 49), although for some time he kept a **pied-à-terre** at Versailles.

Once he was back in Paris, the Dominicaux came together again with some of the former members, La Place, Louis and Favart, and some new ones, all connected in some way with the theatre: Coqueley de Chaussepierre,[24] de Veselle,[25] Laujon,[26] Dorat,[27] Colardeau,[28] Doyer de Gastels,[29] Barthe,[30] the painter Claude Vernet,[31] and later the Comte de Coigny.[32]   They met weekly at the Epée de Bois, facing the Louvre; however, these meetings did not continue for long, to Goldoni's regret because he was now fired with the ambition to write a play in French and he wished to perfect his knowledge of the language. He had no stomach for translating his own plays into French and thought little of translations made by others. Even when they were accurate, the effect was not satisfactory: 'point de chaleur, point de **vis comica,** et les plaisanteries Italiennes devenoient des platitudes en François' (**M.**, II, x, 52). The lesson he drew was: 'il faut créer, il faut imaginer, il faut inventer' (**M.**, II, x, 53). The chapters in which he speaks of work for the theatre in this period after his return to Paris are extremely confused in their chronology as the plays he mentions are known to belong to an earlier period, mostly before his employment at Court. He was also invited to go to London and was tempted to accept, but there were royal marriages in the air and he did not wish to miss the fun: 'j'avois assisté à tous les convois de la Cour, je voulois m'y trouver dans les tems des réjouissances' (**M.**, II, xiii, 65).

He was an assiduous playgoer. He enjoyed the **opéras comiques,** such as Sedaine's **Le Roi et le fermier** with the music of Monsigny which he found 'expressive, harmonieuse, agréable' (**M.**, II, xiii, 66), and comments on the **sensibilité** which had invaded the theatre:

Tantôt je vois à ce Spectacle des Drames sérieux, des Drames larmoyans porter le titre de Comédie, et les Acteurs pleurer en chantant et sangloter en mesure. [...]
Tantôt je vois aller aux nues des bagatelles qui ne promettoient rien, tantôt tomber des Pieces bien faites, parce que le sujet n'est pas assez triste pour faire pleurer, ou n'est pas assez gai pour faire rire.

(**M.**, II, xiii, 67)

He defends the Italian tradition of **opéras comiques,** having written six volumes of them, though not, he says, out of choice. The dramatists he praises are Marmontel, Laujon, Favart, and an Englishman who had settled in Paris, Thomas D'Hèle or Hell (Hales), together with the musicians who had worked for them: Philidor, Monsigny, Duny, Grétry, Martini, Dezaides, and of course Piccinni. The actors he names with equal praise are: Clairval, Madame Trial (Maria Giovanna Milon), Mesdemoiselles Colombe and Adeline (Venetian sisters who had begun their career with the Comédie Italienne), Madame du Gazon, and Mesdemoiselles Desbrosses, Renaud and Rinaldi.

* *

*

The marriage of the Dauphin and Marie-Antoinette was celebrated on 16 May 1770; Goldoni gives a brief account of the celebrations at Versailles, commenting on the opening of the new theatre, 'un riche monument dont l'architecture offre plus de majesté que de commodité pour les spectateurs' (**M.**, II, xv, 73).   He goes out of his way to speak well of the young bride, perhaps deliberately, for at the time that he was writing she had become the butt of slander and hatred, and he attributes the prevailing vogue for 'bienfaisance' to her example.   Much poetry was written to mark the event and Goldini, too, tried his hand but did not risk print;   instead, he gave the Dauphin a manuscript copy, for which he was warmly thanked, in good Italian.   This seems to have been the final incentive for the composition of a comedy in French to be offered to the Comédie Française.   **Le Bourru bienfaisant**, 'piece fortunée qui a couronné mes travaux, et mis le sceau à ma réputation' (**M.**, II, xv, 74), was accepted unanimously by the actors in the secret ballot which was their method of dealing with plays presented to them.   He announced this in a letter to Voltaire of 16 March 1771, which continues:

> Oui, Monsieur et cher Ami, je me suis servi de ce même pinceau, que vous m'avez attribué, et que Molière et vous m'avez montré à manier. Vous trouverez même dans une de vos pièces une esquisse de mon caractère principal.[33]   (**L.**, II, clii, 153)

It is the style, he says, which has given him most trouble and he suggests that he might send it to be vetted by 'l'oracle de la France'.   In fact, he did not do this.   Voltaire bought himself a copy of the play;   in a letter to d'Argental of 16 March 1772, he writes: 'Cette comédie m'a paru infiniment agréable.   C'est une époque dans la littérature française qu'une comédie du bon ton faite par un étranger'.   Shortly afterwards, Goldoni sent him a copy for which Voltaire thanked him on 4 April 1772:

> Un vieux malade de soixante et dix-huit ans, presque aveugle, vient de recevoir par Genève le charmant phénomène d'une comédie française très-gaie, très purement écrite, très-morale, composée par un Italien. Cet Italien est fait pour donner dans tout pays des modèles de bon goût. [...] Il rémercie l'auteur avec la plus grande sensibilité.[34]

The comedy must have been given some readings before its performance, as was quite usual, because we have Madame du Deffand's scathing comments in a letter to Horace Walpole of 9 October 1771:

> Il [Caraccioli] m'amena hier Goldoni, pour me lire une comédie qu'on appelle **le Bourru bienfaisant;**   on m'en avait dit tant de bien, que je désirais de l'entendre.   Je fus bien attrapée, c'est la pièce la plus froide, la plus plate qui ait paru de nos jours.[35]

Goldoni considered submitting it to Jean-Jacques Rousseau.   The account of his preliminary visit to Rousseau, which in fact was the only one, contains an amusing piece of dialogue which brings the crabbed philosopher to life.   Rousseau had just told Goldoni that the best thing he could do was to return to his country:

> Monsieur, lui dis-je, en l'interrompant, vous avez raison, j'aurois dû

quitter Paris [...] mais d'autres vues m'y ont arrêté.   Je viens de composer une Piece en François [...] - Vous avez composé une Piece en François, reprend-il, avec un air étonné, que voulez-vous en faire? - La donner au Théâtre. - A quel Théâtre? - A la Comédie Françoise. -Vous m'avez reproché que je perdois mon tems [copying out music]; c'est bien vous qui le perdez sans fruit. - Ma Piece est reçue. - Est-il possible? Je ne m'étonne pas; les Comédiens n'ont pas le sens commun; ils reçoivent et ils refusent à tort et à travers; elle est reçue peut-être, mais elle ne sera pas jouée, et tant pis pour vous si on la joue. - Comment pouvez-vous juger une Piece que vous ne connoissez pas? - Je connois le goût des Italiens et celui des François, il y a trop de distance de l'un à l'autre; et avec votre permission, on ne commence pas à votre âge à écrire et à composer dans une Langue étrangere. - Vos réflexions sont justes, Monsieur, mais on peut surmonter les difficultés.   J'ai confié mon ouvrage à des gens d'esprit, à des connoisseurs, et ils en paroissent contens. - On vous flatte, on vous trompe, vous en serez la dupe. Faites-moi voir votre Piece; je suis franc, je suis vrai, je vous dirai la vérité.

(M., II, xvi, 80-81)

Goldoni wisely thought better of it, realizing that, inevitably, Rousseau would think the **Le Bourru** was based on himself.   It had been suggested that the play was merely a translation of one of his Italian comedies, but Goldoni insists:

Je n'ai pas seulement composé ma Piece en François, mais je pensois à la maniere Françoise quand je l'ai imaginée; elle porte l'empreinte de son origine dans les pensées, dans les images, dans les mœurs, dans le style.

(M., II, xvi, 78)

Indeed, it was as a well-made classical comedy that it appealed to the public.   When Goldoni tried his hand at translating it, he found this just as unsatisfactory as his attempts to translate from Italian into French.   He did eventually make a translation, published in 1789.

The play was performed for the first time in Paris on 4 November 1771, with resounding success.   Goldoni, who had been following it anxiously behind the scenes, found himself pushed on to the stage to receive the applause of the public, something quite foreign to Italian custom which made him feel exceedingly foolish.   Immediately afterwards, he joined his wife and nephew (whose tears of joy turned to laughter as he told them of his experience) in the carriage which was to take them for the night to Fontainebleau, where the play was performed the next day with equal success before the Court.   One had to divine the reactions of the audience: 'Il n'étoit pas alors permis d'applaudir chez le Roi, mais on s'appercevoit, par des mouvemens naturels et permis, de l'effet que la Piece faisoit sur les Spectateurs' (**M.**, II, xvi, 77).   The next day, he was presented to the King in his study, which suggests that Louis XV did not feel with him that paralysing embarrassment which made him seem so cold with courtiers.   His appreciation was marked by a gift of 150 **louis**.   The printed edition of the work, which came out immediately, was dedicated to Madame Marie-Adélaïde de France in gratitude:

> C'est a MADAME, que je dois le bonheur d'habiter encore le séjour des Muses et des Grâces: son goût pour la Langue Italienne m'y a arrêté, ses bontés m'y ont fixé, et c'est pour me mettre en état de l'aider à expliquer les Auteurs Italiens, que j'ai tâché de sçavoir un peu mieux le François. Voici le premier fruit de mon travail et de mes soins.[36]

Goldoni pays tribute to the actors 'qui ont infiniment contribué au succès de mon ouvrage' (**M.**, II, xv, 74).   The title-role was taken by Préville, Dorval by Bellecourt, the comparatively small part of Dalancourt by Molé for a short time (in a later production he took the part of Dorval); the main female roles were played by Madame Préville and Mademoiselle Doligny.   Although the second night was marred by a noisy cabal, there were thirteen performances in all between 4 November and 2 December which drew excellent receipts.   It received favourable notices in the **Mercure de France** and the **Journal encyclopédique** and in the **Année littéraire** where Fréron seized the opportunity to sting Diderot with an allusion to the plagiarism of his first play. Grimm's **Correspondance** for November 1771 includes an article by Mme *** [d'Epinay] which confirms both the success of the play and the excellence of its French. She does make certain criticisms and goes on to suggest how Goldoni might have written it had he had the benefit of her advice.   She also repeats Diderot's view that Goldoni is a writer of scenarios rather than complete plays.   In the **Nota storica** to **Le Bourru** in the Centenary edition, it is suggested that this article may well have been by Diderot himself as there is a passage in **Jacques le fataliste et son maître** in which Diderot rewrites a scene from **Le Bourru.**[37]

It was revived at Versailles before the Court on 20 May 1786, with Préville, appearing on the stage for the last time, in the title-role.   It had not lost its attraction: 'Ma Piece gagna de nouveaux partisans, et moi-même de nouveaux protectuers' (**M.**, II, xxxix, 171).   His relationship with the actors of the Comédie Française remained friendly; he was generously treated by them with an advance of 600 **livres** on future productions, so that in a letter of 22 April 1774, after they had failed to put it on again, he gave his play up to them and even offered to give them back the money he had received if they did not think that the play was worth it:

> je vous prie d'en disposer comme bon vous semblera, de la donner comme et quand vous voudrez, et si quelqu'un n'étoit pas content de son rolle, je vous laisse en liberté de le donner à un autre.   (**L.**, II, clx, 160)

It was performed on four occasions in 1778, six in 1780 and six in each of the years 1781, 1782 and 1783.   In a letter to La Porte of 26 January 1781, he relates that, four or five years before, he had been paid author's rights for eight performances, but now he says: 'je ne sais pas où j'en suis' (**L.**, II, clxxviii, 184); he also enquires about his right to tickets for performances. In October 1788, when Goldoni was in financial straits, the actors of the Comédie lent him 600 **livres** which should have been repaid by 31 January 1789, but in a letter to Molé of 16 January 1789, Goldoni asked to be given a few days grace, and a letter to the same of 21 March 1789 reveals that he was still not in a position to repay:

> Le fait est que je n'ai pas l'argent pour m'acquitter envers vos confrères qui m'ont si noblement obligé, et que je ne puis fixer le jour où je pourrai remplir ce devoir sacré. (**L.**, II, clxxxvii, 192-93)

A further letter, of 21 February 1791, offered to cede his author's rights on **Le Bourru** in exchange for 100 **louis** and the extinction of his debt. A letter of 1 February 1792, addressed to the actors, proves that they accepted his proposal; all he asks more is that his nephew should have the same right to tickets for the theatre as himself (**L.**, II, cxcii, 200-01). The play has remained a part of the repertoire of the Comédie Française ever since.

The story of **L'Avare fastueux**, Goldoni's second French play, from which he hoped for further glory and financial gain, is a very different one. He chose another character study and took his protagonist from 'la classe des gens parvenus, pour éviter le danger de choquer les Grands' (**M.**, II, xx, 92). Goldoni had no desire to trouble the peace of his old age. On this occasion, the play was not well received by the actors, there were unfavourable votes and he was asked to correct it, which wounded his pride, but he was anxious to see it staged so he duly made a number of changes. A letter to the actors of 26 April 1773, tells them: 'J'ai fait les corrections, que j'ai cru nécessaires pour rendre ma pièce digne de vous, et du public' (**L.**, II, clviii, 157) and asks them to arrange for a second reading, while begging them not to require more changes, 'car c'est une chose pour moi insuportable, que de toucher, et retoucher dix fois la même chose' (**L.**, II, clviii, 158). In fact, he was to go on tinkering with it for years. However, it was accepted and eventually included in the repertoire for Fontainebleau during the Court's visit in the autumn of 1776. It should have been one of the first plays performed, but Préville fell ill and took to his bed for two months, so that in effect it was the last play to be put on, on the eve of the King's departure, when a lot of important people had already left, and the actors were weary at the end of the season, on 15 October 1776. The audience was small and the play was received in stony silence. Goldoni at once withdrew it from the repertoire:

> elle étoit née sous une mauvaise étoile, il falloit en craindre les influences, il falloit la condamner à l'oubli, et ma rigueur alla si loin,

que je la refusai à des personnes qui me la demandoient pour la lire.

(**M.**, II, xxii, 106)

The French text was not printed until 1923,[38] but even the extracts which are given in Chapters 20 and 21 of the **Mémoires** suggest that it was just not a good play. Goldoni made an Italian translation in 1776 which was sent to Venice and performed there on a number of occasions, and also in Florence in 1786. This version was printed in the Zatta edition of Goldoni's works.[39] He did not, however, lose hope of seeing the French play performed and went on working at it. A letter to Charles Palissot, undated, but which the editor ascribes to 1788, tells him that as soon as he has finished dealing with work on the Zatta edition of his play, 'je m'appliquerai à rendre traitable le rôle du Marquis dans mon **Avare fastueux,** et j'aurai l'honneur de vous faire part de mes corrections' (**L.**, II, clxxxiii, 189). In the letter to Molé of 21 March 1789, previously quoted, in which he asks to defer payment of his debt, he also says that he is sending the Comédie his **L'Avare fastueux,**

> tel que je l'ai avec le plus grand soin reformé, et si je suis assez malheureux pour ne pas le voir remis sur la scène avant ma mort, on le donnera après, et les Parisiens qui ont eu tant de bontés pour moi, feront honneur, j'espère, à ma mémoire.   (**L.**, II, clxxxvii, 193)

He even proceeds to discuss which actors might be suitable for the various parts. He refers to it again in his letter of 21 February 1791, in which he asks Molé to send him back the copy of **L'Avare,** if the Comédie do not want it, 'qui m'est nécessaire à cause de quelques dernieres corrections que je n'ai pas chez moi' (**L.**, II, cxci, 199-200). This may be the copy on which the modern edition is based. Of these two last works of the dramatist, Siro Ferrone writes:

> ci presentano un Goldoni più letterario e meno 'popolare', abilissimo nel mestiere, ma incapace di conservare i pregi delle opere veneziane [...] doveva sottostare ad altre norme derivate dalla tradizione francese; oltre al carattere unico, la prevalenza di uno stile e di temi sentimentali e nobili, l'attenuazione dei lineamenti sociali dei personaggi, sia nobili che popolari, il privilegio del carattere sull'ambiente.[40]

* *

*

Goldoni was always invited to great occasions at Court. He was at Versailles on 14 May 1771, for the marriage of the Dauphin's brother, the Comte de Provence (later Louis XVIII) to Marie-Louise of Savoy, eldest daughter of the future King Amadeus III. He takes the opportunity to describe the beauty of the gardens at Versailles, and as the **petits spectacles** had been brought over from Paris to amuse the public he gives an account of these: Nicolet's theatre, the Comédiens de Bois, marionettes which made fun of the mannerisms of living actors, later replaced by children; the Variétés Amusantes of the Boulevard Saint-Martin; and the Petits Comédiens, children who mimed the words of adult actors in the wings. On 16 November 1773, it was the turn of the Comte d'Artois (later Charles X) who married Marie-Louise's sister, Marie-Thérèse of Savoy. On this occasion, owing to the season, the entertainment took place indoors. On 10 May 1774, Louis XV died of smallpox, abandoned by everyone except his daughters (who also caught the disease but recovered). Goldoni writes:

> C'étoit le Roi le plus clément, le père le plus tendre, le Maître le plus doux; il avoit les qualités du cœur excellentes, et celles de l'esprit très-heureuses. **(M.,** II, xxxiv, 111)

He spoke in the light of his own experience and also, no doubt, as Louis was seen by his daughters. This is followed by a heartfelt welcome for Louis XVI:

> ses mœurs, sa conduite, son zele pour le bien public, pour la paix, pour la tranquillité de l'Europe; sa religion, sa modération, la probité qu'il exige, l'exemple qu'il en donne. [...] Voilà des vertus rares [...] bien plus utiles à l'Etat que l'esprit de conquête. **(M.,** II, xxiv, 111-12)

When Mesdames went to Choisy to convalesce, Goldoni went to visit them and met there the Prince de Condé who pleased him by speaking well of **Le Bourru bienfaisant** (which in fact he had put on at Chantilly, playing the title-role). When the King's sister, Madame Clotilde, was affianced to thé Prince of Piedmont (the future Charles Emannuel IV), Goldoni was once more pressed into service. He was again given an apartment at Versailles and moved in, probably in February 1775, but he certainly kept his home in Paris and made frequent visits to the capital. He complains that he was only given seven months to prepare the princess. He followed much the same system as he had done with Mesdames, very little formal grammar, some knowledge of Italian authors, and when their daily lessons were interrupted by jewellers, portrait painters, cloth merchants, etc., connected with the approaching wedding, he made use of these occasions to improve her vocabulary. She was a good pupil and his teaching was successful.

The marriage took place by proxy at Versailles on 17 August 1775. As usual, Goldoni had made no arrangements about payment: 'je n'avois rien demandé et je n'avois rien reçu' **(M.,** II, xxiv, 114). In a letter to Stefano Sciugliaga of 18 December 1775, he expresses himself with unwonted bitterness (not about Madame Clotilde who was probably helpless in the matter): 'Ho servito la sorella del Re di Francia, ho impiegato per lei il mio tempo e i miei danari [the sixty **louis** he said it cost him to move to Versailles] e non avro una ricompensa?' (**L.**, II, clxii, 165).   Meanwhile, he kept his apartment at Versailles and waited for another pupil.   The King's younger sister, Madame Elisabeth, aged eleven, was thought old enough to start Italian lessons. She was 'plus dans l'âge de s'amuser que de s'occuper', so he followed more or less the method he had used with her elder sister:

> je ne la tourmentois pas avec des déclinaisons et des conjugaisons qui l'auroit ennuyée [...], je tâchai de rendre mes leçons des conversations agréables.   (**M.**, II, xxiv, 114)

They had dramatic readings of his own comedies in which the Princess and her lady-in-waiting took parts, with another **dame de compagnie** if necessary, and Goldoni taking all the others.   For poetry, they went on to Metastasio.   These lessons, taken in a leisurely fashion, continued for five years or so; 'c'étoit le service le plus doux, le plus agréable du monde', but Goldoni was getting on in years and the climate of Versailles did not suit him, so he passed on his office to his nephew and returned permanently to Paris.

He announces his departure to Vittore Gradenigo, Secretary to the Venetian ambassador, in a letter of 5 May 1780, in which he complains that once more he has had no recompense:

> Sei anni di servizio, sei anni di pigione di casa, di viaggi, di spese, d'incomodi: tutto è contato per nulla.   (**L.**, II, clxxiv, 178)

He even suggests that he might ask to enjoy his pension in Italy, where it would go further, with a special sum as a result of the intercession of Mesdames, to make up for those six years of teaching.   However, he felt that any such special request must be made after he had received his normal pension, due only in September; meanwhile, his need for money was pressing.   He was already in debt to the Venetian ambassador, Marco Zeno, to the tune of fifty **louis,** and Gradenigo also had lent him twenty-five **louis,** which he was in no position to repay.   Now he offers to sell his library of French plays (250 volumes) - including the edition of Corneille given to him by Voltaire - and French novels (135 or 150 volumes), all well bound, for the sum of 600 **louis.** Gradenigo accepted the offer; Goldoni packed up his books and left Versailles on Wednesday 10 May 1780.   His frayed patience was eventually rewarded:

> Je présentai un Mémoire au Roi; il fut protégé par Mesdames, la Reine elle-même eut la bonté de s'intéresser à moi, le Roi eut celle de m'accorder 6000 livres de gratification extraordinaire, et un traitement de 12000 livres annuelles sur la tête de mon neveu.   (**M.**, II, xxiv, 115)

This did not prevent Goldoni from being chronically hard up; he kept two servants, he enjoyed playing cards and gambling, although he did not risk large sums, he went regularly to the theatre and the opera, and had an inordinate passion for chocolate and **diablotins** (a kind of chocolate dragée).

* *

*

In 1777, Goldoni composed a new libretto, **I volponi,** destined for Venice, which expressed his disillusionment with life at Court, but it does not seem to have ever been set to music or produced. In June 1778, some Italian **opera buffa** actors arrived in Paris and played at the Théâtre de l'Académie Royale, at first with some success. It was only when they were in difficulties that they sought out Goldoni, but he declined to pull their chestnuts out of the fire:

> Il faut encore dire que j'étois piqué d'avoir été oublié au moment nécessaire. Je ne me souviens pas d'avoir éprouvé depuis long-tems un chagrin pareil à celui-là.   (**M.,** II, xxvi, 121)

Meanwhile the actors of the Opéra Comique were also in difficulties:

> la Comédie chantante faisoit tout; la Comédie parlante ne faisoit rien. Elle étoit réduite à jouer les mardis et les vendredis, que l'on appelle à ce Spectacle les mauvais jours; et si elle étoit admise à paroître dans les beaux jours, c'étoit pour remplir les vuides entre les deux Pieces qui intéressoient le Public.   (**M.,** II, xxix, 130-31)

The actors appealed to Goldoni who set to work with a will; he produced six plays for them,

> trois grandes et trois petites; ils en étoient contens, ils les avoient payées; ils n'eurent pas le tems apparemment de les étudier, de les jouer; pas une ne parut sur la scène.   (**M.,** II, xxix, 131)

The Italiens were destined to disappoint him to the very end. However, in 1780 the Comédie Italienne was suppressed; the actors were given appropriate pensions or indemnities, with the exception of Carlin who, in recognition of his forty years of service, was kept on to play an Arlequin when required, Coralli[41] who had been brought over specially from Italy to understudy Carlin, and Camerani[42] who succeeded in getting himself accepted by the Opéra Comique and became its senior administrator. Oddly enough, the name Comédie Italienne was retained even when they moved to the Salle Favart on 28 April 1783; it was not changed to Opéra Comique until 1793. Goldoni's last works for the theatre were two libretti, **Il talismano,** performed during the opening season of the new Teatro alla Scala in Milan in 1779, with the music of Salieri and Giacomo Rust, and **Vittorina,** with the music of Piccinni, performed for the first time in London in 1782, according to the Zatta edition.

> beautés qu'il a répandues dans ses **Confessions,** il n'a point aussi son
> insupportable vanité, son impudence cynique, sa folie et sa bile.

He finds the third part most interesting for a French reader and quotes extensively
from it, although he wishes that Goldoni had been more critical.   As usual, he gives
long extracts (including the passage about his own periodical) and takes the
opportunity of the visit to Rousseau to attack the philosopher once more: 'cette
sensibilité de J.J. n'étoit qu'un pur égoïsme, qu'un esprit faux accompagné d'un amour
propre effréné'.   Although he criticizes the over-abundance of detail, the superficiality
of many observations and the style ('souvent incorrect et négligé'), he concludes:

> mais ils amusent, ils intéressent par la vivacité, la gaieté du récit, par un
> ton charmant de candeur, d'honnêteté; et [...] ils font aimer et estimer
> l'Auteur.[46]

On the other hand, there was a vicious review in the **Correspondance littéraire.** The
very goodness and equanimity which shines out of the work seems to have enraged the
critic:

> c'est le radotage d'un bon vieillard qui, [...] ayant pensé mourir de faim
> dans son pays, ne peut se lasser de bénir les bonnes petites pensions et
> les bons dîners qu'il a trouvés en France [...].   Il est aisé de juger
> combien ce sentiment délayé en trois volumes [inexact, as this would
> only apply to the third part] devient plat et fastueux.[47]

Perhaps the choice of 'fastueux' is a deliberate evocation of Goldoni's unsuccessful
French comedy.   A more just reflection of opinion was probably the judgement of
Palissot:

> il a publié sa vie et l'histoire de ses productions dramatiques en trois
> volumes, à l'âge de 80 ans [...].   Il y règne une simplicité naïve, et, si
> nous l'osons dire, une bonhomie qui ajoute à la haute estime que l'on doit
> à ses talens, le sentiment du plus vif intérêt pour sa personne.[48]

Goldoni no doubt survived the barbs of the ill-disposed with equanimity; indeed, he
seems to have foreseen them and had his answer ready in the final paragraph of the
book:

> S'il y avoit cependant quelqu'Ecrivain qui voulût s'occuper de moi, rien
> que pour me donner du chagrin, il perdroit son temps.   Je suis né
> pacifique; j'ai toujours conservé mon sang-froid, à mon âge je lis peu, et
> je ne lis que des livres amusans.   (**M.,** II, xi, 175)

There are not many letters after about 1780 and these are mainly on business
matters.   He maintained the even tenor of his life and activity in spite of the ailments
of old age: he continued to enjoy walking about the city, the company of his friends
(including a succession of Venetian ambassadors), going to the theatre, playing cards,
but life became more and more expensive and uncertain.   In a letter to the Abate

Giammaria Manenti, of 20 May 1791, which prefaces his translation to Madame Riccoboni's novel **Miss Jenny,** published in Venice in 1791 (it was undertaken to help a fellow-Italian, Paolo Bernardi, in distressed circumstances), he mentions, speaking of Paris, 'le turbolenze dalle quali ella è attualmente agitata'.[49] The suppression of his pension by the Convention in July 1792 reduced him and his family to extreme poverty. His last letter, of January 1793, is a supplication to the Convention for the restoration of his sole means of support. It is heartening to think that, even in those dark days, there was still sufficient human feeling left for Marie-Joseph Chénier to support this, so that the restoration was agreed. It seems appropriate that life should reserve one last **coup de théâtre** for the aged dramatist - Goldoni had died serenely the day before, 6 February 1793. Not only did the Convention assign a pension of 1500 **livres** to his widow Nicoletta, but the actors of what was now the Théâtre de la Nation were invited by the minister Clavière, attributing to Goldoni revolutionary sympathies which seem highly unlikely, to put on a performance of **Le Bourru bienfaisant** for the benefit of his widow. This took place on 18 June 1793, and the total takings, 1,859 **livres** and 13 **sous,** were handed over to Nicoletta. So the story of Goldoni in France begins and ends with the theatre, on a note of warm humanity, in contrast with the bloody days which were to follow. Goldoni had timed his exit well.[50]

NOTES

1. All quotations are taken from the **Memorie di Carlo Goldoni, riprodotte dall'edizione originale francese,** volumes XXXVI (1936) and XXXVII (1948) of the centenary edition of the **Opere complete di Carlo Goldoni,** 40 vols (Venice, 1907-60); the two volumes are separately identified as Tomo I and Volume II. All subsequent references to the second volume (containing the **Troisième Partie** and editorial notes) follow the pattern of '**M.,** II, ii, 2', where the small Roman numeral indicates the chapter number.

2. **Delle commedie di C. Goldoni,** 17 vols (Venice, 1761-78).

3. Siro Ferrone, **Carlo Goldoni** (Florence, 1975), p.92.

4. Nicola Mangini, **Goldoni** (Paris, 1969), p.56.

5. Carlo Gozzi, **Memorie inutili,** edited by G. Prezzolini, 2 vols (Bari, 1910), I, 230.

6. **Opere complete,** XXXVI, 438.

7. Marchese Francesco Albergati (1728-1804), senator and Gonfalonier of Justice in Bologna, was a man of letters and patron of the theatre who both acted in and wrote comedies as well as translating a number of plays from the French.

8. **Opere complete,** XXXIX, 26 (Letter lxxiii). Goldoni's correspondence constitutes volumes XXXVIII (1951) and XXXIX (1953) of the **Opere complete**

47.   Friedrich Melchior Grimm, **Correspondance littéraire, philosophique et critique**, edited by M. Tourneux, 16 vols (Paris, 1877-82), XV, 135 (September 1787).

48.   Palissot de Monteney, **Mémoires pour servir à l'histoire de notre littérature**, 2 vols (Paris, 1803), I, 370, quoted in the notes to **M.**, II, xl (pp.569-70).

49.   **Opere complete**, XL, 12.

50.   There is a discussion of Goldoni's use of the French language by G. Folena, 'Il francese di Carlo Goldoni', in **Goldoni en France** (Rome, 1972), pp.47-76.

Index

As well as proper names, this index includes people and plays from the sixteenth to the eighteenth centuries.